Launching the
Imagination

A Comprehensive Guide to Basic Design

fifth edition
Mary **Stewart**

Mc
Graw
Hill
Education

LAUNCHING THE IMAGINATION: A COMPREHENSIVE GUIDE TO BASIC DESIGN, FIFTH EDITION
Published by McGraw-Hill Education, 2 Penn Plaza, New York, NY 10121. Copyright © 2015 by McGraw-Hill Education. All rights reserved. Printed in the United States of America. Previous editions © 2012, 2008, and 2006. No part of this publication may be reproduced or distributed in any form or by any means, or stored in a database or retrieval system, without the prior written consent of McGraw-Hill Education, including, but not limited to, in any network or other electronic storage or transmission, or broadcast for distance learning.

Some ancillaries, including electronic and print components, may not be available to customers outside the United States.

This book is printed on acid-free paper.

1 2 3 4 5 6 7 8 9 0 DOW/DOW 1 0 9 8 7 6 5 4

ISBN 978–0–07–337930–2
MHID 0–07–337930–1

Senior Vice President, Products & Markets: *Kurt L. Strand*
Vice President, General Manager, Products & Markets: *Michael Ryan*
Vice President, Content Production & Technology Services: *Kimberly Meriwether David*
Managing Director: *William R. Glass*
Brand Manager: *Sarah Remington*
Senior Director of Development: *Dawn Groundwater*
Marketing Manager: *Kelly Odom*
Director, Content Production: *Terri Schiesl*
Content Project Manager: *Jennifer Gehl*
Buyer: *Jennifer Pickel*
Designer: *Jana Singer*
Cover Images: *(images top to bottom) #1: Ledelle Moe, Collapse V, 2007. Concrete and Steel, 9 feet tall × 11 feet long × 7 feet wide. © Ledelle Moe; #2: Leo Villareal, Big Bang, 2008. LEDs, aluminum, custom software, and electrical hardware, 59 × 59 × 8 inches. © Leo Villareal, courtesy of Sandra Gering Inc.; #3: Lilian Garcia-Roig, Water and Rock Flows, 2010. Oil on canvas, 48 x 48 inches. Credit lines: © Lilian Garcia-Roig. Private Collection. Courtesy of Valley House Gallery & Sculpture Garden, Dallas; #4: Niklaus Troxler, poster for Willisau Jazz Festival, 1992. © Design by Niklaus Troxler; #5: Colima Rabbit Jar, ca. 200 BC-200 AD. Ceramic, 13 x 9 inches. Photo by Stefan Hagen. Courtesy of Samuel Merrin, The Merrin Gallery, Inc.*
Photo Researcher: *Deborah Anderson*
Senior Content Licensing Specialist: *Lori Hancock*
Compositor: *Lachina Publishing Services*
Typeface: *10.5/14 Palatino Roman*
Printer: *R. R. Donnelley*

All credits appearing on page or at the end of the book are considered to be an extension of the copyright page.

Library of Congress Cataloging-in-Publication Data

Stewart, Mary, 1952– author.
    Launching the imagination: a comprehensive guide to basic design/Mary Stewart, Florida State University.–Fifth Edition.
        pages cm
    Includes index.
        ISBN 978–0–07–337930–2—ISBN 0–07–337930–1 (hard copy: alk. paper)—ISBN 978–0–07–777343–4—ISBN 0–07–777343–8 (hard copy: alk. paper)—ISBN 978–0–07–777344–1—ISBN 0–07–777344–6 (hard copy: alk. paper) 1. Design. I. Title.
        NK1510.S74 2014
        745.4–dc23

                                                                                                2014000501

The Internet addresses listed in the text were accurate at the time of publication. The inclusion of a website does not indicate an endorsement by the authors or McGraw-Hill Education, and McGraw-Hill Education does not guarantee the accuracy of the information presented at these sites.

www.mhhe.com

Launching the Imagination:

A Comprehensive Guide to Basic Design

is dedicated to Scott Betz.

Launching the Imagination treats design as both a verb and a noun—as both a process and a product. By covering the process of creative and critical thinking and presenting the elements and principles used in creating a product, this book offers a unique resource for foundations courses.

The title *Launching the Imagination* suggests the goals of this book and of the foundations year as a whole. Through an immersion in 2D, 3D, and 4D concepts and problems, students learn to develop ways of thinking visually that will serve them throughout their studies and careers. They discover that design is deliberate—a process of exploring a wide range of solutions and choosing the most promising option for development. And they find inspiration in the work of others, analyzing the art of the past and the present for insights.

CREATE what you've only imagined!

Our new self-service website allows you to quickly and easily create custom course materials with McGraw-Hill's comprehensive, cross-disciplinary content and other third-party sources. Add your own content quickly and easily. Tap into other rights-secured third party sources as well. Then, arrange the content in a way that makes the most sense for your course. Even personalize your book with your course name and information and choose the best format for your students—color print, black-and-white print, or eBook. And, when you are done, you'll receive a free PDF review copy in just minutes! To get started, go to **www.mcgrawhillcreate.com** and register today.

> Choose your own content

Need specific chapters? Create a book that contains only the chapters you want, in the order you want. Create will even re-number the pages for you!

Add worksheets

Mary Stewart has developed worksheets for each chapter that are designed to improve student comprehension and increase engagement. Each includes at least one section in which students must apply knowledge gained from the reading to their own artwork.

> Choose your format

Print or eBook? Softcover, spiral-bound, or loose leaf? Black-and-white or color? Perforated, three-hole punched, or regular paper? No matter the format, Create has the best fit for you—and for your students.

> Customize your cover

Pick your own cover image and include your name and course information right on the cover. Students will know they're purchasing the right book—and using everything they purchase!

Introducing McGraw-Hill Create *ExpressBooks*!

ExpressBooks contain a combination of pre-selected chapters, articles, cases, or readings that serve as a starting point to help you quickly and easily build your own text through McGraw-Hill's self-service custom publishing website, Create. These helpful templates are built using content available on Create and organized in ways that match various course outlines across all disciplines. We understand that you have a unique perspective. Use McGraw-Hill Create ExpressBooks to build the book you've only imagined!

HALLMARKS OF OUR NEW EDITION OF *LAUNCHING THE IMAGINATION*

Building on the strengths of the previous four editions, *Launching the Imagination*, fifth edition, is even more

- **Concise**. Content has been refined so that maximum content can be communicated as clearly and concisely as possible.

- **Colorful**. In addition to the full color used throughout the book, the writing is livelier than that in most textbooks. Analogies expand communication, and every visual example has been carefully selected for maximum impact.

- **Comprehensive**. *Launching the Imagination* is the only foundational text with full sections devoted to critical and creative thinking and to time-based design. The photo program is global, represents a myriad of stylistic approaches, and prominently features design and media arts as well as more traditional art forms.

- **Contemporary**. More than half of the visual examples represent artworks completed since 1970, and 120 represent works completed since 2000.

- **Compelling**. Four expanded profiles have been added to this edition. With at least three visual examples per interview, these new profiles follow the process by which leading artists and designers have developed their artworks. In Chapter 5, designer Steve Quinn describes the seven-step sequence he uses in developing websites, logos, and motion graphics. In Chapter 6, Jim Elniski describes *The Greenhouse Chicago*, an adaptive re-use home that is both highly energy efficient and beautiful. In Chapter 7, Kendall Buster describes stages in the completion of a complex sculpture, from preliminary drawing to installation. In Chapter 8, painter Carrie Ann Baade discusses the sources of her images and four major steps in their development. Five profiles have also

been retained from previous editions: illustrator Bob Dacey, painter Suzanne Stryk, metalsmith Marilyn da Silva, ceramicist David MacDonald, and composer Michael Remson.

- Over 100 new images have been added, representing major artists and designers including Janet Echelman, Lilian Garcia-Roig, Michael Mazur, Matthew Ritchie, Sarah Sze, Mark Tansey, Niklaus Troxler, Leo Villareal, Richard Wilson, and Yayoi Kausama.

CHAPTER-BY-CHAPTER CHANGES

Each chapter has been updated and, where needed, reorganized to maximize clarity. Improvements include the following:

Chapter 1: A new section on point has been added, and a previous section on degrees of representation has been moved to Chapter 8, Constructing Meaning.

Chapter 2: Diagrams have been updated and the writing has been further clarified.

Chapter 3: The section on Gestalt better emphasizes six unifying compositional forces, and new compositional diagrams help to illustrate how these forces are used. The section on contrast and emphasis has been substantially revised and updated.

Chapter 4: The writing has been further clarified.

Chapter 5: The writing has been further clarified, and more contemporary examples have been added.

Chapter 6: The "Variations on a Theme" section has been expanded and updated.

Chapter 7: The writing has been further clarified, and more contemporary examples have been added.

Chapter 8: The section entitled "Degrees of Representation" has been moved from Chapter 1 and additional digital examples have been added.

Chapter 9: A new section on point has been added, and sections on line and mass have been updated.

preface

Chapter 10: Sections on contrast and emphasis have been expanded and revised for maximum clarity.

Chapter 11: More contemporary examples have been added.

Chapter 12: More contemporary examples have been added.

Chapter 13: More contemporary examples have been added.

Chapter 14: Narrative analysis of *A League of Their Own* has been added as well as new examples from the world of advertising.

Chapter 15: The writing has been further clarified, and more contemporary examples have been added.

SUPPLEMENTS

Online Learning Center

The Online Learning Center at www.mhhe.com/LTI5e offers student resources for each chapter of the text, including chapter objectives, vocabulary flashcards, activities, studio projects, and short quizzes.

Instructor's Center

Led by Mathew Kelly from Central College, a remarkable team of collaborators has developed an extensive Instructor's Manual that provides advice on course construction, critique skills, and technical resources. It includes over 70 assignments divided into 4 sections: two-dimensional design, concepts and critical thinking, three-dimensional design, and time design. Lecture PowerPoints provide a great resource that instructors can tailor to their individual needs.

MyArtStudio at www.mhhe.com/ArtStudio

Students have access to MyArtStudio, a rich and comprehensive website with interactions that allow students to study and experiment with various elements and principles of art. Students can view videos of art techniques and artists at work. Exercises on the Online Learning Center guide students to MyArtStudio at appropriate points in the text.

ACKNOWLEDGMENTS

This substantially revised edition has been quite a challenge. Senior editor Sarah Remington and content project manager Jennifer Gehl offered consistent and supportive leadership. Developmental editor Thomas Sigel helped strengthen and clarify the writing throughout. Photo researcher Deborah Anderson was remarkably tenacious in pursuing each permission and was wonderfully inventive in suggesting alternatives when necessary. Chris Black and his design team at Lachina worked tirelessly to develop the best possible layouts. Images are at the heart of this book. I would like especially to thank all the artists and designers who granted permission for use of their artworks and the galleries, museums, archives, and private donors who provided the high-resolution images.

This book is dedicated to four master educators. Professor Scott Betz, at Winston-Salem State University has been an exemplar of innovation and dedication throughout his career. During his six years as president, the national organization for foundation education (Foundations in Art: Theory and Education) expanded and evolved into a major force for the greater good. The two-dimensional design version of this book is dedicated to Cynthia Hellyer-Heinz, currently foundations director at Northern Illinois University. A brilliant drawing teacher and gifted administrator, Cindy inspires both her students and her colleagues. The three-dimensional design version is dedicated to Professor Mathew R. Kelly, departmental Chair at Central College, and to Professor Peter Winant, Director, School of Art, George Mason University. Since the beginning, Professor Kelly has been the primary author of the Instructor's Manual for *Launching the Imagination*. As Editor of *FutureForward* (the professional journal of Integrative Teaching International) he has consistently offered great insight and wonderful expertise. In addition to his leadership at George Mason University, Professor Winant has worked on community-building projects in Liberia, Haiti, and in the Washington, DC area. All of these remarkable people are exemplars of the very best in education.

The following reviewers provided valuable insights and suggestions:

For the Fifth Edition:

Debra K. Dow-Iwanusa, *Lansing Community College, Mott Community College*

Lauren Lipinski Eisen, *University of Northern Colorado*

Jason Franz, *University of Cincinnati*

Courtney Grim, *Medaille College*

Carol Hammerman, *Columbia College of Chicago*

Niku Kashef, *California State University, Northridge*

Victoria Reynolds, *California State University, Northridge*

Howard Schneider, *California State University, Northridge*

Tom Stephens, *University of Northern Colorado*

Paul Andrew Wandless, *Harold Washington College*

For the Fourth Edition:

Donald Barrie, *Seattle Central Community College*

Nicholas Bonner, *Northern Kentucky University*

Jeff Boshart, *Eastern Illinois University*

Keith Bryant, *University of North Carolina at Charlotte*

Marie Bukowski, *Louisiana Tech University*

Jessica Calderwood, *University of Wisconsin, Oshkosh*

Ben Cunningham, *Millersville University*

Eileen Doktorski, *Utah State University*

Scott Dooley, *Wittenberg University*

Frankie Flood, *University of Wisconsin, Milwaukee*

Paul Gebhardt, *University of Maine at Fort Kent*

David Griffin, *Eastern Illinois University*

Dan L. Henderson, *Art Institute of Atlanta*

Kevin W. Hughes, *Missouri State University*

Dawn Hunter, *University of South Carolina*

Imi Hwangbo, *University of Georgia*

Rosalie Rosso King, *Western Washington University*

Casey McGuire, *Metropolitan State College*

Erik Miller, *The Community College of Baltimore County*

Alan Moss, *Kent State University*

Gary Nemcosky, *Appalachian State University*

Jane Nodine, *University of South Carolina Upstate*

Laura Prange, *University of Southern Mississippi*

Ann Coddington Rast, *Eastern Illinois University*

Laura Ruby, *University of Hawaii*

For the Third Edition:

Scott Betz, *Winston-Salem State University*

Denise Burge, *University of Cincinnati*

Holly Earhart, *Full Sail Real World Education*

Sarah Gjertson, *University of Denver*

Marth McLeish, *Indiana State University*

Julia Morrisroe, *University of Florida—Gainesville*

John Nettleton, *Ontario College of Art & Design*

Gayle Pendergrass, *Arkansas State University*

Renee Sandell, *George Mason University*

Kyle Trowbridge, *University of Miami*

Jeremy Waltman, *Florida State University*

Peter Winant, *George Mason University*

For the Second Edition:

Kathleen Arkles, *College for Creative Studies*

Donald Barrie, *Seattle Central Community College*

Julie Baugnet, *St. Cloud State University*

Donna Beckis, *Fitchburg State College*

Nancy Blum-Cumming, *University of Wisconsin—Stout*

Debra K. D. Bonnello, *Lansing Community College*

Jeff Boshart, *Eastern Illinois University*

Jacquelin Boulanger, *New College of Florida*

Stephanie Bowman, *Pittsburgh State University*

Peter Brown, *Ringling School of Art*

John Carlander, *Westmont College*

Steven Cost, *Amarillo College*

Michael Croft, *University of Arizona*

Cat Crotchett, *Western Michigan University*

Claire Darley, *Art Academy of Cincinnati*

Anita M. DeAngelis, *East Tennessee State University*

Beverly Dennis, *Jones County Junior College*

Tracy Doreen Dietzel, *Edgewood College*

Jim Doud, *American University*

Clyde L. Edwards, *Valdosta State University*

James Elniski, *School of Art Institute at Chicago*

Jane Fasse, *Edgewood College*

John Ford, *Labette Community College*

Corky Goss, *Cazenovia College*

Arlene Grossman, *Art Institute of Boston at Lesley University*

Danielle Harmon, *West Texas A&M University*

Christopher Hocking, *University of Georgia*

Carol Hodson, *Webster University*

Sara M. Hong, *University of Arizona*

Lorie Jesperson, *Lake Michigan College*

C. Ann Kittredge, *University of Maine—Presque Isle*

Deborah Krupenia, *Endicott College*

Michelle La Perriere, *Maryland Institute College of Art*

In Shile Lee, *Tompkins Cortland Community College*

Richard F. Martin, *New York Institute of Technology*

Christine McCullough, *Youngstown State University*

Julie McWilliams, *Sussex County College*

Nancy Morrow, *Kansas State University*

Byron Myrich, *Jones Junior College*

Kelly Nelson, *Longwood University*

Soon Ee Ngoh, *Mississippi State University*

Lara Nguyen, *California State University, Long Beach*

Grace O'Brien, *Purdue University*

Mark O'Grady, *Pratt Institute*

Sally Packard, *University of North Texas*

William Potter, *Herron School of Art–IUPUI*

Patsy C. Rainey, *University of Mississippi*

Gerson M. Rapaport, *New York Institute of Technology*

Cherri Rittenhouse, *Rock Valley College*

Gil Rocha, *Richland Community College*

William B. Rowe, *Ohio Northern University*

Kim Schrag, *Tompkins Courtland Community College*

Jean Sharer, *Front Range Community College*

Todd Slaughter, *Ohio State University*

Robert Smart, *Lawrence University*

Karen Spears, *Eastern Kentucky University*

Mindy Spritz, *The Art Institute of Atlanta*

Teresa Stoll, *Lake City Community College*

Katherine Stranse, *University of Arkansas—Little Rock*

Rob Tarbell, *Limestone College*

William Travis, *Rowan University*

Linda Vanderkolk, *Purdue University*

Carolynne Whitefeather, *Utica College*

Reid Wood, *Lorain County Community College*

Marilyn H. Wounded Head, *Mesa State College*

Alice Zinnes, *NYC College of Technology, CUNY*

For the First Edition:

Scott Betz, *Weber State University*

Jeff Boshart, *Eastern Illinois University*

Peter Brown, *Ringling School of Art and Design*

Brian Cantley, *California State University, Fullerton*

Laurie Beth Clark, *University of Wisconsin, Madison*

Michael Croft, *University of Arizona*

John Fillwalk, *Ball State University*

David Fobes, *San Diego State University*

Albert Grivetti, *Clarke College*

Imi Hwangbo, *University of Louisville*

Michelle Illuminato, *Bowling Green State University*

Ann Baddeley Keister, *Grand Valley State University*

Margaret Keller, *St. Louis Community College*

Dan Lowery, *Southwestern Illinois College*

Karen Mahaffy, *University of Texas at San Antonio*

Richard Moses, *University of Illinois*

Gary Nemcosky, *Appalachian State University*

Helen Maria Nugent, *Art Institute of Chicago*

Rick Paul, *Purdue University*

Ron Saito, *California State University, Northridge*

Karen Schory, *Johnson County Community College*

Susan Slavick, *Carnegie Mellon University*

Paul Wittenbraker, *Grand Valley State University*

William Zack, *Ball State University*

part one

Concepts and Critical Thinking

Three-Dimensional Design

chapter nine

Three-Dimensional Design Elements 180

chapter ten

Principles of Three-Dimensional Design 217

chapter eleven

Materials and Methods 237

chapter twelve

Physical and Cerebral 260

part three

Author Mary Stewart with **Labyrinth** book.

Author, artist, and educator Mary Stewart is a professor in the Department of Art at Florida State University. Her drawing, prints, and visual books have been shown in over 90 exhibitions nationally and internationally, and she has received two Pennsylvania Arts Council grants for collaborative choreography. A cofounder of Integrative Teaching International, she has given over 50 lectures and workshops on creative inquiry, curriculum design, educational leadership, and storytelling.

As represented here, her *Continuum Series* connects the macroscopic with the microscopic. Fragments of towering trees are juxtaposed with images that suggest activity at a cellular level. In this series, Professor Stewart seeks to explore ways in which we construct and express knowledge, both of ourselves and of the world around us.

Mary Stewart, *Continuum #4*, 2012. Digital collage, 44 × 44 in.

Mary Stewart, *Continuum #8*, 2012. Digital collage, 44 × 44 in.

about the author

What is *Launching the Imagination* about, and how can it be useful to you?

In this book, we will explore

• the components of visual construction,

• ways that these components can be used,

• characteristics of creative and of critical thinking,

• ways to increase your creativity,

• the physical characteristics of various materials,

• ways in which you can use materials to express ideas,

• the components and power of visual storytelling,

• contemporary approaches to visualization.

Because studio courses require hands-on work, we will treat design as a noun *and* as a verb.

As a noun, design may be defined as

• a plan or pattern, such as the blueprint for a house;

• an arrangement of lines, shapes, colors, and textures into an artistic whole, as in the composition of a painting.

As a verb, design can be defined as

• to plan, delineate, or define, as in designing a building or a functional object;

• to create a deliberate sequence of events, as in designing a film storyboard;

• to organize disparate parts into a coherent whole, as in designing a brochure.

Design is deliberate. Rather than simply hoping for the best and accepting the result, artists and designers explore a wide range of

solutions to every problem, and then choose the most promising option for further development. Inspiring examples and informative text can help accelerate your learning process. In this book, over 625 images supply visual examples from many cultures and in all areas of art and design. Nine lively interviews with living artists provide insight into the creative process. Idea generation and critical thinking are thoroughly discussed in Part Two, and key questions (posted at the end of various sections of text) provide a way for you to self-assess your projects as they develop.

How high can you fly? How far can you travel? Will you work traditionally, in a specific discipline such as painting, printmaking, or ceramics? Or will you combine disciplines to create new forms of expression? Having mastered the basics of visual thinking, you will have the versatility and critical judgment needed to pursue a personal path.

Launching the Imagination

A Comprehensive Guide to Basic Design

Lilian Garcia-Roig, *Water and Rock Flows,* **2010,** oil on canvas, 48 × 48 in. (121.9 × 121.9 cm).

Two-Dimensional Design

Creating objects and images is engrossing and exhilarating. Through our studio work, we can heighten our attention, engage our emotions, and build a sense of accomplishment. These personal rewards make art one of the most popular hobbies.

A *career* in art and design demands more from us. As art and design professionals, we must translate our personal insights into public communication. The ideas and emotions a professional wishes to express must engage an audience, whether the encounter occurs in the silence of a museum or in the chaos of a city street.

This ability to communicate visually is developed through years of study plus relentless practice. As professionals, we must develop our visual awareness, create new concepts, and master various techniques. We spend hours in the studio, refining ideas and inventing alternative solutions to each visual problem.

The elements and principles of design are the building blocks from which we create images and express ideas. Chapter One presents point, line, shape, texture, and value. Chapter Two is devoted to the characteristics and compositional impact of color. Chapter Three introduces a wide range of basic organizational strategies, known as the principles of design. Chapter Four expands these basic principles and devotes attention to the illusion of space and the illusion of motion.

Basic Elements

Point, line, shape, texture, value, and color are the building blocks that make up two-dimensional designs. Just as oxygen and hydrogen are powerful both individually and when combined as H_2O, so these visual **elements** operate both independently and in combination. In this chapter, we explore the unique characteristics of the five most basic elements and analyze their uses in art and design. We discuss color, the most complex element, in Chapter Two.

POINT

Defining Point

A **point** is a basic mark, such as a dot, a pixel, or a brushstroke. When we add a point to a blank sheet of paper, we create a dialog between this basic visual element and the surrounding space. This dialog sets a compositional game in motion. In this section, we explore two types of points. A **focal point** is the primary point of interest in a composition. By its size, compositional location, orientation, or color, a focal point activates the design and thus attracts viewer attention. A collection of points creates an **array**. We can create rich textures and entire images using an array.

Using Point

Because points are both simple and powerful, they are often used in logo design. Logos must read clearly in both small and large scale and must be easy to remember. For example, the Think Point Design logo in figure 1.1 is dominated by a circular shape combined with three words. The addition of the small point at the top of the logo adds a splash of darker green and

1.1 Andy Beard and Sharon Sandercock,
Think Point Design logo, 2012. Size variable.

1.2 Pentagram Design, Corella
Publishing logo, 2006. Size variable.

mohawk

1.3 Michael Bierut, lead designer, Pentagram Design, Mohawk Paper logo, 2012. Digital media, size variable.

1.4 Charis Tsevis, *Obama*, 2007. Photo mosaic, size variable.

suggests movement. This quickly communicates a simple message: "Think Point Design is an innovative company and always on the move." By contrast, the point in figure 1.2 transforms a simple black-and-gray shape into a cheerful parrot's head. We immediately want to find out more about Corella Publishing, the business it represents. Our final example is a logo for Mohawk Paper (1.3). Green, orange, violet, blue, and aqua points combined with lines of various colors create an energetic M. This combination of lines and points also refers to the process by which paper is produced and printed as it moves past the inked cylinders. Using a series of colorful points and lines, lead designer Michael Bierut provided a fresh identity for a well-established company.

An array of points can create an entire image while retaining the energy of the individual parts. Magazines often use this approach for their covers or posters. In figure 1.4, Charis Tsevis combined images of hundreds of everyday people to create the image of American President Barack Obama. Many wear blue or hold blue signs further stating their support. The image suggests that Obama is a man of the

people rather than a remote politician. In our final example, Paddy Japaljarri Stewart has created an Australian landscape from hundreds of colorful points. Using a traditional Aboriginal approach, *Bush Cabbage Dreaming at Ngarlu* (1.5) presents an imagined aerial view of the outback. Based on Dreaming, a spiritual practice that is uniquely Aborigine, each mark records the journey of an ancestral presence across the earth.

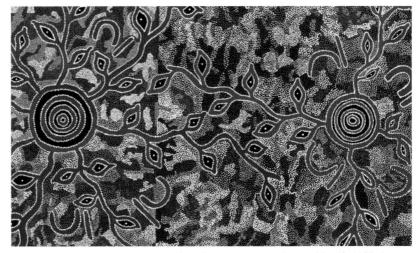

1.5 Paddy Japaljarri Stewart, *Bush Cabbage Dreaming at Ngarlu* (detail), 1986. Acrylic on canvas, 47½ × 93½ in. (120.5 × 237.5 cm).

LINE

Defining Line

Line is one of the simplest and most versatile elements of design. Line may be defined as

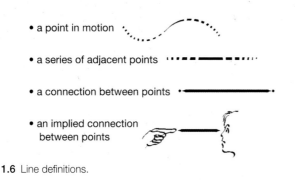

- a point in motion
- a series of adjacent points
- a connection between points
- an implied connection between points

1.6 Line definitions.

The first definition emphasizes the unique dynamism of line. The remaining three definitions emphasize its connective power. Lighter and more fluid than any of the other visual elements, line can add a special energy to a design. Simply by drawing a line, we can activate a space, define a shape, or create a compositional bridge.

Line Quality

Each line has its own distinctive quality. This quality is largely determined by the line's orientation, direction, and degree of continuity, and by the material used.

Orientation refers to the line's horizontal, vertical, or diagonal position. Diagonal lines and curving lines are generally the most dynamic (1.7A, 1.7D). Charged with energy, they suggest action and movement. Horizontal lines are typically the most stable, or static (1.7B). Vertical lines imply *potential* change. When verticals adhere to the edge of the design, they become tethered and thus lose

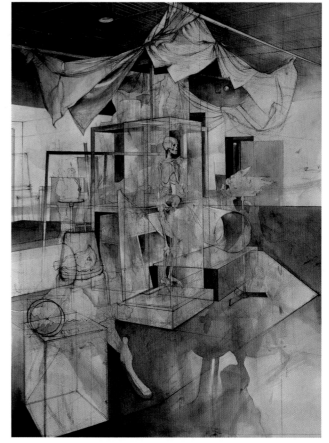

1.8 Kevin Haran, *Still Life with Skeleton*, 2004. Charcoal, ink, and acrylic wash on Arches paper, 30 × 22 in. (76.2 × 55.9 cm).

mobility. Free-floating verticals, on the other hand, seem ready to topple at any moment (1.7C).

Direction refers to the implied movement of a line. We can use line weight to accentuate direction. Generally, a swelling line suggests forward or outward movement, and a shrinking line suggests inward movement. Notice how the top and bottom diagonal lines in figure 1.7A seem to push forward as they become thicker.

Continuity, or linear flow, can enhance direction. Figure 1.7D shows that a continuous line tends to generate a stronger sense of direction than a broken or jagged line.

An artist can use each material to produce a range of distinctive lines. We can use metallic graphite to produce modulating lines of varying thickness. A felt pen produces a crisp, clean, emphatic line. Charcoal and chalk are soft and highly responsive to each change in pressure and direction. Brush and ink offers even wider variation in line width, continuity, and darkness. By experimenting with the range of marks each instrument can produce, we can use each material more expressively.

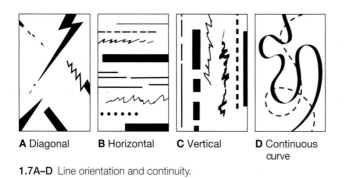

A Diagonal   **B** Horizontal   **C** Vertical   **D** Continuous curve

1.7A–D Line orientation and continuity.

1.9 Frank Thomas and Ollie Johnston, original sketch of Walt Disney Mickey Mouse Cartoon, 1938. © Disney Enterprises, Inc.

1.10 Michael Mazur, *Canto XI (Overview of Hell)*, from the portfolio *Dante's Inferno*, 1999. Etching and aquatint, 25⅛ × 19⅝ in. (63.8 × 49.8 cm).

A strong match between line quality and the expressive intent is essential. In figure 1.8, Kevin Haran used vertical, horizontal, and diagonal lines to map out the positions of various objects in a still life. Spheres, cones, and the detailed skull become focal points in this complex composition. The fluid lines in figure 1.9 express movement and playful energy. Michael Mazur used a variety of lines in his *Overview of Hell* based on Dante's *Inferno* (1.10). As described by poet Dante Alighieri, Hell is divided into nine circular levels, beginning with Limbo at the top and descending through Lust, Gluttony, Greed, Anger, Heresy, Violence, Fraud, and Treachery. Mazur defines these levels (and the tormented souls they contain) using curving black brushstrokes combined with textured passages and open white shapes. This variety of lines helps to distinguish the various levels and activates the entire image.

Actual Lines

Actual lines can describe forms simply and eloquently. In figure 1.11, Eleanor Dickinson presented different views of hands using **contour lines**. Contour lines define the edges of a form and suggest three-dimensionality. In this study, she distilled complex anatomy down to a few

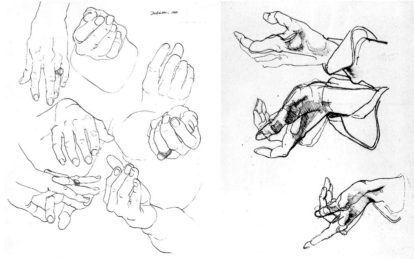

1.11 Eleanor Dickinson, *Study of Hands*, 1964. Pen and ink, 13⅜ × 10⅛ in. (34 × 26 cm). 1.12 Rico Lebrun, *Hand*, 1964. Pen and ink.

1.13 Rembrandt van Rijn, *Two Women Helping a Child to Walk*, c. 1635–37. Red chalk on paper.

simple lines. Similarly, Rico Lebrun's **gesture drawing** of a hand (1.12) captures essential action rather than describing every anatomical detail. We focus on what the hand is *doing* rather than on what the hand *is*. As figure 1.13 shows, Rembrandt often used economical lines to describe the spheres and cylindrical volumes from which figures are made. Because it communicates information using basic volumes, we often call this type of line drawing a **volume summary**.

Calligraphic lines can add even more energy to a drawing or a design. The word *calligraphy* is derived from two Greek words: *kalus*, meaning "beautiful," and *graphein*, meaning "to write." Like handwriting, the calligraphic line is both personal and highly expressive. In figure 1.14, painter Tawaraya Sôtatsu and calligrapher Hon'ami Koetsu used variations in line weight and continuity to suggest the graceful motion of birds. Gu Gan's *No.1 Calligraphy and Painting in Harmony* (1.15) provides a contemporary combination of calligraphic text, delicate drawing, and bold brushstrokes. It seems that we are simultaneously viewing a landscape close up and in the distance.

Artists often use **organizational lines** to create the loose linear "skeleton" on which an artist can build a composition. The artist can develop ideas quickly through line, and easily make compositional changes. The Haran drawing in figure 1.8 shows that these skeletal drawings have great energy and can be presented as artworks in themselves. In other cases, organizational lines provide the framework for elaborate compositions. When we analyze Alfred Leslie's *The Killing Cycle* (1.16), we can see an underlying framework. A dead man on a diagonal board connects a single woman in the lower left corner to the four figures in the upper right. A horizontal line supports these four figures, while their bent arms and legs create even more diagonal lines. The diagonal lines add energy to the composition while the horizontal line adds stability.

1.14 Attributed to Tawaraya Sôtatsu, calligraphy by Hon'ami Koetsu, *Flying Cranes and Poetry*, Edo period (1615–1868). Ink on gray-blue paper, gold flecked, 7⅜ × 6⅜ in. (19 × 16 cm).

1.15 Gu Gan, *No.1 Calligraphy and Painting in Harmony*, 2005. Ink on self-made Chinese paper, 26 × 26 in. (66 × 66 cm).

1.16 Alfred Leslie, *The Killing Cycle #5: Loading Pier*, 1975. Oil on canvas, 9 × 7 ft. (2.7 × 1.8 m).

contours require an elegant form of closure. In a "lost and found" composition, the edges of some shapes are clearly defined, and other shapes appear to merge with the background. When presented with such an image, the viewer must create a mental bridge between the resulting islands of information.

Caravaggio's *The Deposition* (1.19A) uses closure extensively. A contour drawing of this image has many gaps, as details are lost in the shadows (1.19B). Used skillfully, this loss of definition becomes a strength rather than a weakness. Connections made through closure can stimulate the viewer's imagination and encourage a more personal interpretation.

Linear Networks

Multiple lines can add detail to a design and create a convincing illusion of space. **Hatching** produces a range of grays through straight parallel

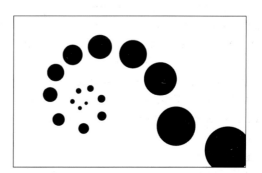

1.17 A series of dots can create an implied line.

Implied Lines

Lines can play a major role in a design even when they are implied rather than actually being drawn. Because **implied lines** simply *suggest* connections, the viewer becomes actively involved in compositions that use this type of line.

Fortunately, we have a natural inclination to seek visual unity. Given enough clues, we will connect separate visual parts by filling in the missing pieces. The visual clues may be quite obvious. For example, we can easily link the circles in figure 1.17 to create a linear spiral. In other cases, the clues are subtle. In Minor White's *Sandblaster* (1.18), the white arrow implies a connection between the numbers in the foreground and the worker's helmet.

This inclination to connect fragmentary information is called **closure**. "Lost and found"

1.18 Minor White, *Sandblaster*, San Francisco, 1949. Gelatin silver print, 10⁷⁄₁₆ × 11⁷⁄₁₆ in. (26.51 × 29.05 cm).

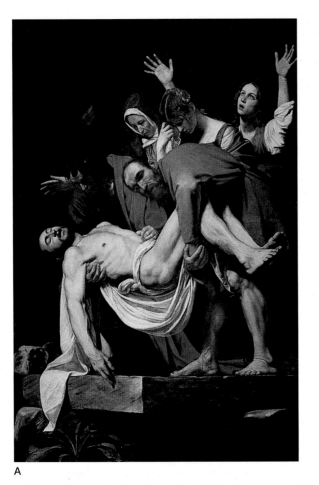

A

B

1.19A–B Caravaggio, *The Deposition*, 1604. Oil on canvas, 9 ft 10⅛ in. × 6 ft 7⅞ in. (3 × 2.03 m).

lines. We can produce an even wider range of grays through **cross-hatching**. Many layers of lines at various angles are used in cross-hatching. Jacques Villon used both hatching and cross-hatching in his portrait of poet Charles Baudelaire (1.20). The head is divided into a series of faceted planes. Hatching defines each shift in the surface of the head, and cross-hatching creates the shadows.

Cross-contours can create an even more powerful illusion of three-dimensionality. Often created using curving parallel lines, cross-contours "map" surface variations across shapes or objects. In figure 1.21, David Mach created a cross-contour sculpture by bending coat hangers into the shape of a human head. In two-dimensional design, we can use drawn lines to produce a similar effect.

Hatching, cross-hatching, and cross-contour are often combined. In *Head of a Satyr* (1.22),

1.20 Jacques Villon, *Baudelaire*, c. 1918. Etching, printed in black, plate 16⅚ × 11 in. (41.4 × 28 cm).

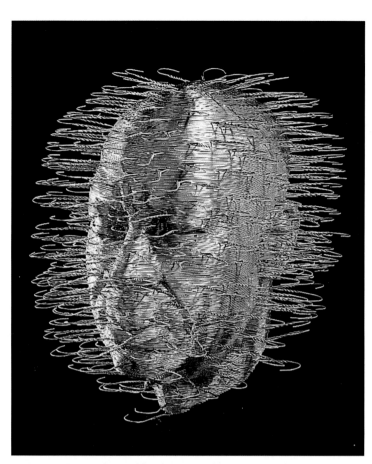

1.21 David Mach, *Eckow*, 1997. Coathangers, 2 ft 2¼ in. × 1 ft 11½ in. × 2 ft 5½ in. (67 × 60 × 75 cm).

1.22 Michelangelo, *Head of a Satyr*, c. 1620–30. Pen and ink over chalk, 10⅝ × 7⅞ in. (27 × 20 cm).

Michelangelo used all these techniques to visually carve out the curves and planes of the head.

Linear networks play an equally important role in more abstract or conceptual art. Sara Mast is fascinated by humanity's connection to the cosmos. She has noted that our bodies and the stars are ultimately made from the same materials. Orion is one of the most visible of the constellations. In *Orion's Gift* (1.23), Mast connects the branching growth of biological forms to the atomic particles in this mysterious constellation. Black and gray lines of varying width reach out from clusters of points, creating pathways reminiscent of neurons in the brain.

Using Line

We can use line to define, enclose, connect, or dissect. Line serves all of these purposes in a New York City subway map (1.24). A curved line has been combined with an angular line to define the wheelchair logo. Another line encloses this logo within a square, emphasizing its importance. Diagonal lines connect the subway entrance to the elevators, and vertical lines dissect the drawing to highlight the location of the elevators. Using this map, a person in a wheelchair can navigate through a busy station and catch the right train.

In a sense, the first line we draw is actually the *fifth* line in a rectangular composition. In his *Self-Portrait* (1.25), Joel Peter Johnson used drawn lines to echo the four pre-existing edges of the composition. His head breaks out of this linear boundary. As a result, the portrait appears to extend beyond the painting's edge and into the world of the viewer.

Lines can serve many purposes at once. In an advertisement for the American Institute of Graphic Arts (1.26), vertical dotted lines at the upper left and lower right highlight the speakers' schedule. A horizontal line creates a connection

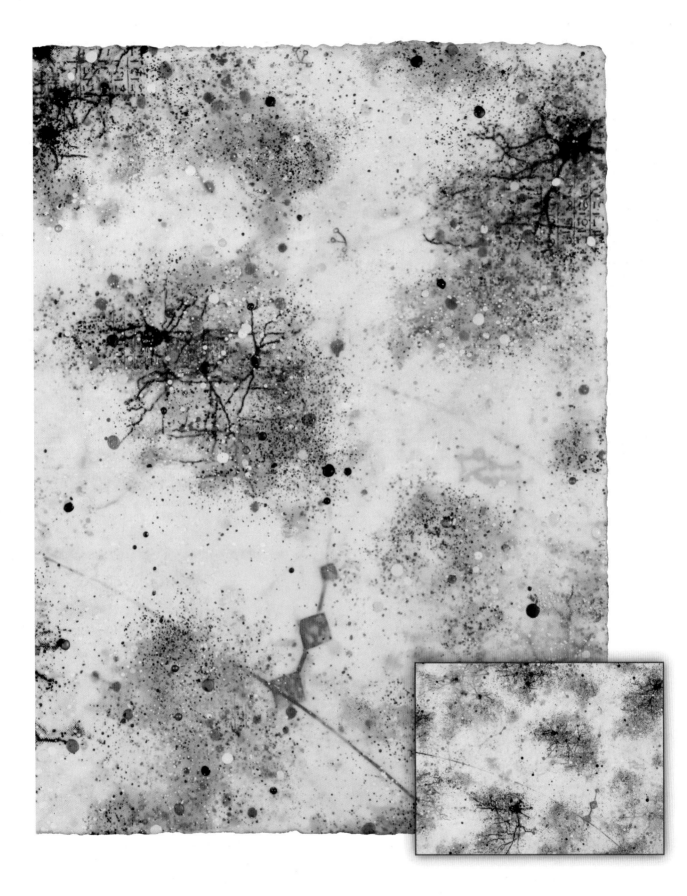

1.23 Sara Mast, *Orion's Gift,* 2010. Detail plus full-sized painting. Encaustic on paper mounted on panel, 22 × 30 in. (50.8 × 76.2 cm).

between the *D* and *B* in the "design to business" logo and separates the top and bottom of the overall layout. We can even read the columns of text as vertical and horizontal lines.

When orientation, direction, continuity, and medium are effectively employed, line can be used to create compositions that are both sophisticated and thoughtful.

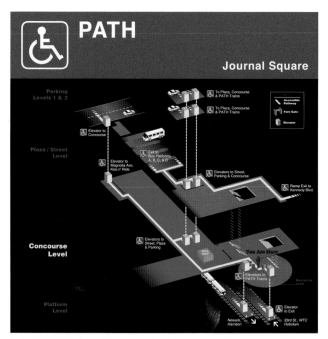

1.24 PATH Station Maps, Louis Nelson Associates, Inc., NY.
Graphic designer: Jennifer Stoller.

1.25 Joel Peter Johnson, *Self-Portrait,* **1999.** Oil on board, 9 × 8 in. (22.86 × 20.32 cm).

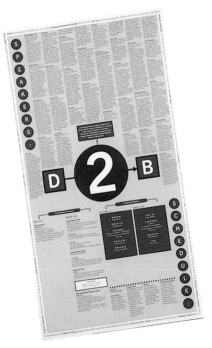

1.26 Brochure from an American Institute of Graphic Arts Conference "Design 2 Business, October 5–6 '96 NYC."
Design Firm: Pentagram, NY.

key questions

LINE

- What is the dominant orientation of the lines in your design—diagonal, vertical, or horizontal? What is the expressive effect?

- What happens when you repeat lines or when lines intersect?

- How would the composition change if you removed one or more lines?

- Consider using line to direct attention to areas of compositional importance.

SHAPE

Defining Shape

A **shape** is a flat, enclosed area (1.27A–D). You can create shapes by:

- Enclosing an area within a continuous line
- Surrounding an area with other shapes
- Filling an area with solid color or texture
- Filling an area with broken color or texture

A three-dimensional enclosure is called a **volume**. Thus, a square is a shape, while a cube is a volume. We can use **gradation** or **shading** to make a two-dimensional shape appear three-dimensional, or volumetric. For example, in figure 1.28, a flat, circular shape becomes a faceted polyhedron when we add a series of gray tones.

Both flat and gradated shapes can be used to create an arresting image. In Aaron Douglas's *Aspects of Negro Life: From Slavery Through Reconstruction* (1.29), flat silhouettes combined with transparent targets create an energetic panorama. We can almost hear the speaker in the center and feel the movement of the crowd. In Rivera's *Detroit Industry* (1.30), a combination of size variation and shading suggests volume and increases the illusion of space.

Graphic designers are equally aware of the expressive power of flat and gradated shapes. In a cover design for *Fearless Beauty* (1.31), Cecilla Sorochin combined a model's volumetric head with a headdress composed from swirling flat shapes. While rooted in reality, the woman seems empowered by her lively imagination.

Gustav Klimt combined flat and volumetric shapes to create *Salomé* (1.32). In this horrific tale from the biblical New Testament, John the

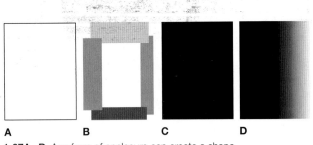

1.27A–D Any form of enclosure can create a shape.

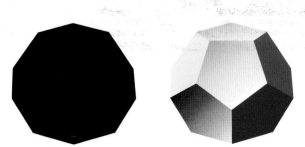

1.28 Variations in shading can transform a shape into an illusory volume.

1.29 Aaron Douglas, *Aspects of Negro Life: From Slavery Through Reconstruction*, **1934.** Oil on canvas, 5 ft × 11 ft 7 in. (1.52 × 3.5 m).

1.30 Diego M. Rivera, detail from *Detroit Industry, North Wall*, 1932–33. Fresco, 17 ft 8½ in. × 45 ft (5.4 × 13.7 m).

Baptist has been imprisoned for his criticism of the royal family. Salomé, the king's niece, performs a stunning dance and the delighted king grants her a single wish. In revenge, Salomé asks for John's head. The tall, vertical shape of the painting is similar to the size and shape of a standing viewer. Flat patterns and color surround the volumetric figures, while two curving lines add a sinuous energy to the center of the design.

Types of Shape

The size and shape of a soccer field are very different from the size and shape of a tennis court. In each case, the playing area defines the game to be played. It is impossible to play soccer on a tennis court or to play tennis on a soccer field.

Similarly, the outer edge of a two-dimensional design provides the playing field for our compositional games. The long, horizontal rectangles used by Douglas and Rivera create an expansive pan-

1.31 Cecilia Sorochin, Sorodesign, cover design for *Fearless Beauty*, 2008, 5.5 × 8.5 in. (14 × 21.6 cm).

1.32 Gustav Klimt, *Salomé*, 1909. Oil on canvas, 70⅛ × 18⅛ in. (178 × 46 cm).

orama, while Klimt's vertical rectangle compresses a sordid drama into a claustrophobic column. Thus, creating a dialog between compositional shapes and the surrounding format is our first concern.

Figure and Ground, Positive and Negative

As shown in figure 1.33A, a shape that is distinguished from the background is called a **positive shape**, or **figure**. The surrounding is called the **negative shape**, or **ground**. Depending on its location relative to the ground, the figure can become dynamic or static, leaden or buoyant (1.33B–D).

In traditional paintings such as Caravaggio's *The Deposition* (page 10), the artist treats the entire composition like a window into an imaginary world. To increase this illusion, Caravaggio lightly sanded the canvas texture before he applied the paint, and he kept heavy brushstrokes at a minimum. We are invited to see *into* the painting, rather than focusing on its surface.

When an artist uses a shaped format we become more aware of the artwork's physicality. The 9-foot-tall teacup in Elizabeth Murray's *Just in Time* (1.34) is monumental in size and loaded with implication. The painted shapes connect directly to the shaped edge, emphasizing the crack running

1.33A–D Various figure/ground relationships. When centered, the figure tends to be static. As it moves to the bottom left, it becomes more dynamic, and becomes even more so when it is diagonally positioned near the top or bottom edge.

down the center of the composition. This is no ordinary teacup. For Murray, this crack in everyday reality invites us to enter an alternative world that extends beyond a simple cup of tea.

When the figure and ground are equally well designed, every square inch of the composition becomes supercharged. In figure 1.35, David McNutt used a single white shape on a black ground to create the head of a master and a servant within the outline of Africa. Used to advertise a South African play, the poster immediately communicates a dramatic human relationship within a specific cultural context.

Figure/ground reversal pushes this effect even further. **Figure/ground reversal** occurs when first the positive and then the negative shapes command our attention. A fragment from *Metamorphosis II* (1.36) shows that M. C. Escher was a master of figure/ground reversal. The organic shapes on the left become an interlocking mass of black and white lizards. The lizards then evolve into a network of hexagons. Combined with the figure/ground reversal, this type of metamorphosis animates the entire 13-foot-long composition.

Figure/ground reversal requires a carefully balanced dialogue between opposing forces. Escher generally achieved this balance by using light and dark shapes of similar size. In figure 1.37, Sam Francis achieved a similar balance between a very small white square and a much larger red rectangle. The crisp boundary and central location strengthen the square. Despite its small size, it holds its own against the larger mass of swirling red paint.

1.34 Elizabeth Murray, *Just in Time*, 1981. Oil on canvas in two sections, 106 × 97 in. (269.24 × 246.38 cm).

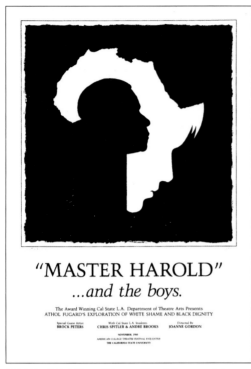

1.36 M. C. Escher, part of *Metamorphosis II*, 1939–40. Woodcut in black, green, and brown, printed from 20 blocks on three combined sheets, 7½ × 153⅜ in. (19 × 390 cm).

1.35 David McNutt, *"Master Harold" . . . and the Boys*, 1985. Poster.

Rectilinear and Curvilinear Shapes

Rectilinear shapes are composed from straight lines and angular corners. **Curvilinear shapes** are dominated by curves and flowing edges. Simple rectilinear shapes, such as squares and rectangles, are generally cooperative. When placed within a rectangular format, they easily connect to other shapes and can run parallel to the compositional edge (1.38A). Curvilinear shapes, especially circles, are generally less cooperative. They retain their individuality even when other shapes partially conceal them (1.38B). As a result, we can use curvilinear shapes as targets that emphasize areas of special importance in a design.

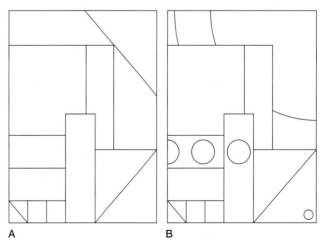

A   B

1.38A–B Rectilinear and curvilinear shapes. Rectilinear shapes can easily be fit together to create a unified design. Curvilinear shapes tend to be more individualistic.

1.37 Sam Francis, *Flash Point,* 1975. Acrylic on paper, 32¼ × 22⅞ in. (82 × 59 cm).

Aubrey Beardsley (1.39) combined rectilinear and curvilinear shapes to create another interpretation of the Salomé story described on page 15. Using an internal boundary line, he emphasized the composition's rectangular shape. Within this boundary, curving black and white shapes create a series of complex visual relationships. A bubble pattern dominates the upper-left corner. In the upper-right corner, Salomé clutches Saint John's head. Extending from the head down to the flower, a white line follows the transformation of the dead saint's blood into a living plant. This line creates a conceptual and compositional connection between the top and bottom edges.

1.39 Aubrey Beardsley, *Salomé with the Head of John the Baptist*, 1894. Line block print, 11 × 6 in. (27.9 × 15.2 cm).

A very different combination of rectilinear and curvilinear shapes activates Robert Rauschenberg's *Brace* (1.40). The central image of three baseball players is surrounded by layered rectangles to the right, left, and bottom. A solid line extends from the catcher to the top edge. Vigorous brushstrokes add power to the painting. Occupying only a small fraction of the composition and surrounded by vigorously painted shapes, the circle *still* dominates the design: we *have* to keep our eyes on the ball!

Geometric and Organic Shapes

Geometric shapes are distinguished by their crisp, precise edges and mathematically consistent curves. They dominate the technological world of architecture and industry, and they appear in nature as crystalline structures and growth patterns. **Organic shapes** are more commonly found in the natural world of plants and animals, sea and sky. As Helen Frankenthaler's *Interior Landscape* shows (1.41), organic shapes can add unpredictable energy to a rectangular composition.

Using Shape

Artists and designers often use simple shapes when they seek clear, direct communication. Gene Anderson and Mary Stewart used just two shapes in figure 1.42 to visualize Hamlet's most famous soliloquy from Shakespeare's play. Commanded by the ghost of his murdered father to kill his uncle, Hamlet is distraught and indecisive. Should he become a murderer himself, based on an encounter with a ghost? What does it mean to be alive—or dead? "To be," on the left edge requires us to live each moment of our lives. "Not to be," on the right, may be an infinite journey into darkness.

More complex shapes are often used when the message is subtle or contradictory. **Collage** is one method for creating such complex shapes. Constructed from visual fragments initially designed for another purpose, a collage combines two kinds of shapes: the shape of each piece of cut paper and the shapes created by the information printed *on* the paper.

1.40 Robert Rauschenberg, *Brace,* 1962. Oil and silkscreen on canvas, 60 × 60 in. (152.4 × 152.4 cm).

1.41 Helen Frankenthaler, *Interior Landscape,* 1964. Acrylic on canvas, 8 ft 8⅞ in. × 7 ft 8⅝ in. (266 × 235 cm).

To	Not
Be	To
Or	Be

1.42 Mary Stewart and Gene Anderson, *Hamlet's Dilemma,* 2013. Digital collaboration.

1.43A Romare Bearden, *The Dove,* 1964. Cut-and-pasted paper, gouache, pencil, and colored pencil on cardboard. 13⅜ × 18¾ in. (34 × 47.5 cm).

1.43B Romare Bearden (compositional diagram). Printed and cut shapes work together to create a complex composition.

In Romare Bearden's *The Dove* (1.43A), the outer edges of each cut fragment create a lively pattern of curvilinear and rectilinear shapes. The lines and textures printed on these photographic fragments create a second set of shapes. A linear diagram of this artwork demonstrates the complexity of the resulting composition (1.43B). Combining his perceptions of contemporary Harlem with childhood memories, Bearden used this interplay of the cut edges and printed textures to create a rich composition from the shifting shapes.

In *Target with Plaster Casts* (1.44), Jasper Johns combined simple shapes with sculptural objects to create an equally complex composition. A series of concentric circles creates a clearly defined target at the center of the painting. Nine sculptural fragments of a human figure line the upper edge—an ear, a hand, a mouth, and so forth. To add further complexity, Johns embedded scraps of newspaper in the colored wax from which he constructed the painting. Equally attracted to the representational body parts above and the symbolic target below, we must reconcile two very different forms of visual information.

▶ key questions

SHAPE

- Experiment with rectilinear, curvilinear, geometric, and organic shapes. Which shape type will best express your idea?

- What happens when you combine flat, solid shapes with gradated shapes? Or fuse negative and positive?

- Contrast adds interest. What happens when you use two or more shape types in a composition?

1.44 Jasper Johns, *Target with Plaster Casts*, 1955. Encaustic and collage on canvas with objects, 51 × 44 × 2½ in. (129.5 × 111.8 × 6.4 cm).

TEXTURE

The surface quality of a two-dimensional shape or a three-dimensional volume is called **texture**. Texture engages our sense of touch as well as our vision, and can enhance the visual surface and conceptual meaning of a design.

Types of Texture

Physical texture creates variations in a surface. The woven texture of canvas, the bumpy texture of thickly applied paint, and the rough texture of wood grain are common examples. **Visual texture** is an illusion. We can create it by using multiple marks that simulate physical texture.

Albrecht Dürer's *The Knight, Death and the Devil* (1.45) employs both visual and physical texture. Dürer created the knight's armor, the horse's glossy hide, the dog's furry coat, and other details using cross-contours, cross-hatching, and patterns of

1.46 Bruce Conner, *Psychedelicatessen Owner*, March 31, 1990. Paper collage, 8 × 6 in. (20.32 × 15.24 cm).

1.45 Albrecht Dürer, *The Knight, Death and the Devil*, 1513. Engraving, 11 × 14 in. (28 × 36 cm).

dots called **stippling**. All are examples of visual texture. Furthermore, this print is an **engraving**. Each dot and line was carefully carved into a thin sheet of copper. Dürer then pressed ink into the grooves and wiped the surface metal clean. He then positioned the plate face up on a printing press and laid damp paper over it. He cranked both through the press, transferring the ink and creating a subtle embossment. As a result, physical texture accentuates the visual texture in this image.

Invented texture is one form of visual texture. Using invented texture, the artist or designer can activate a surface using shapes that have no direct reference to perceptual reality. Bruce Conner used invented textures from many sources to construct his paper collage *Psychedelicatessen Owner* (1.46). He combined floral patterns, visual gemstones, and cross-contours to create a witty and improbable portrait. By contrast, Brad Holland drew all of the textures in figure 1.47, using pen and ink. As the density of the marks increases, the face dissolves into dark masses of pure energy.

1.47 Brad Holland, Illustration for *Confessions of a Short-Order Artist, Persönlich*, 1997. Drawing: *Literary Beast*, 1997. Pen and ink.

Creating Texture

When creating any type of texture, we must take two basic factors into account.

First, every material has its own inherent textural quality. Charcoal is characteristically soft and rich, while a linocut, such as Beardsley's *Salomé* (see figure 1.39), creates crisp, distinct edges. It is very difficult to create soft, atmospheric textures using linocut or to create crisp textures using charcoal.

Second, the support surface contributes its own texture. This surface may be smooth, like most photographs, or quite bumpy, like the canvas and embedded collage that Jasper Johns used for his *Target* (see figure 1.44, page 21). Thus, work with texture requires a heightened sensitivity to both the support surface and the medium that the artist uses to create the design.

Texture and Space

Artists and designers create visual texture whenever they repeat lines, dots, or other shapes. Variations in the size, density, and orientation of these marks can produce different spatial effects.

Larger and darker marks tend to advance outward (1.48A). Finer marks, tightly packed, tend to pull us inward (1.48B). In figure 1.48C, the marks have been organized into a loose spiral. The overall impact is strongest when size, density, and orientation are combined, as in figure 1.48D.

In figure 1.49, Douglas Smith combined texture and linear perspective to produce a dramatic illusion of space. The lines of mortar between the bricks all point toward the truck in the center, while the bricks themselves diminish in size as the distance increases. The truck at the bottom of the wall of bricks seems to be trapped in a claustrophobic space.

By contrast, Robert Indiana's *The Great American Dream: New York* (1.50) is spatially shallow. Indiana constructed a three-dimensional model of a coin or medallion from layers of cardboard. He then laid his drawing paper on top of the construction and made a rubbing, using colored pencils. We can interpret this seemingly simple composition in at least three ways. First, creating a design through rubbing can remind us of the coin rubbings we may have made as children. Second, in many cultures, rubbing coins evokes wealth or good luck. Finally, the rubbing itself creates the *illusion* of the coin or medallion, not the reality. Perhaps the Great American Dream is just an illusion, ready to dissolve into economic chaos.

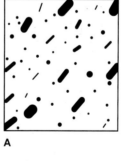

A

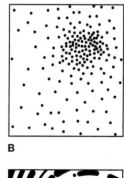

B

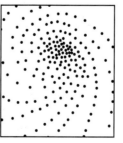

C

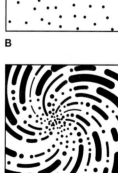

D

1.48A–D Examples of textural size, density, and orientation.

1.49 **Douglas Smith**, *No Turning*, **1986.** Scratchboard and watercolor, 11¼ × 15 in. (29.2 × 38.1 cm).

painting that actually appears to expand architectural space.

Combining Physical and Visual Texture

Each material has a distinctive physical texture, and each drawing method creates a distinctive visual texture. By combining physical and visual textures, we can unify a composition and add another layer of conceptual and compositional energy.

Blended graphite, pastel, or charcoal creates the smooth surface often favored for highly representational images. Claudio Bravo developed the visual textures in *Package* (1.53) using pastel and charcoal. By carefully drawing every fold, he created a convincing simulation of a three-dimensional object.

1.50 **Robert Indiana**, *The Great American Dream: New York (The Glory-Star Version)*, **1966.** Wax crayon on paper, Sheet: 39¹³⁄₁₆ × 26⅛ in. (101.1 × 66.4 cm).

Both spatial and flat textures can be created using letters, numbers, or words. Variations in size, density, and orientation can strongly affect the meaning of these verbal textures. In figure 1.51, African-American painter Glenn Ligon repeatedly wrote, "I feel most colored when I am thrown against a sharp white background" on a gallery wall. As the density of the words increases, the words begin to fuse together, creating variations in the visual texture while reducing verbal clarity.

Trompe L'Oeil

Taken to an extreme, visual texture can so resemble reality that a deception occurs. We call this effect **trompe l'oeil**, from a French term meaning "to fool the eye." Trompe l'oeil can become a simple exercise in technical virtuosity or can significantly alter our perception of reality. By simulating architectural details, Richard Haas created an amazing dialogue between illusion and reality in figure 1.52. Using the textures of stones, stairs, and smoke, he created a wall-sized trompe l'oeil

1.51 Glenn Ligon, Untitled *(I feel most colored when I am thrown against a sharp white background),* **1990.** Oilstick and gesso on wood, 6 ft 6 in. × 30 in. (2 m × 76.2 cm).

1.52 Richard Haas, trompe l'oeil mural on Brotherhood Building, Cincinnati, Ohio, 1989.

1.53 Claudio Bravo, Detail of *Package,* **1969.** Charcoal, pastel, and sanguine chalk, 30⅞ × 22½ in. (78.42 × 57.15 cm).

Cross-hatching creates a more active visual texture. Dugald Stermer constructed his portrait of mathematician Bertrand Russell (1.54) from a network of vigorous lines. The bumpy texture of the paper adds more energy to this lively drawing.

Anselm Kiefer combined physical and visual textures in *Wayland's Song (with Wing)* (1.55). In this myth, a metalsmith named Wayland is captured by the King of Sweden, then crippled and forced to create treasures on demand. In revenge, he murders the king's sons and makes drinking cups from their skulls. He then flees, using wings fashioned from metal sheets. By adding straw and a lead wing to the photographic base image, Kiefer was able to combine the illusionistic qualities of painting with the physical immediacy of sculpture.

Marks and Meanings

Every textural mark that we make can add to or subtract from the composition as a whole. When the texture is random or inappropriate, the composition becomes cluttered and confused. On the other hand, deliberate use of texture can enhance the illusion of space and increase compositional unity.

For example, each brushstroke in Benjamin Marra's *Self-Portrait* (1.56) describes a different facet of the face. Just as a sculptor carves out a portrait

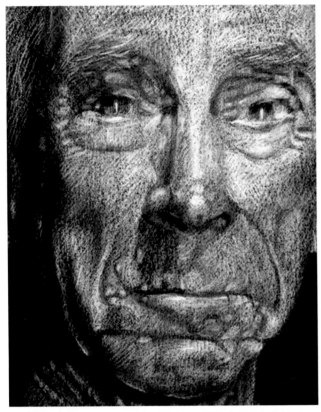

1.54 Dugald Stermer, portrait of Bertrand Russell (detail) for the New York Times Book Review, 2002. Colored pencil.

1.55 Anselm Kiefer, *Wayland's Song (with Wing),* 1982. Oil, emulsion, straw, and photograph with lead wing, 110¼ × 149⅝ in. (280 × 380 cm).

1.56 Benjamin Marra, *Self-Portrait*, 1998. Oil, 8½ × 11 in. (21.6 × 28 cm).

1.57 Chuck Close, *Self-Portrait*, 1997. Oil on canvas, 8 ft 6 in. × 7 ft (2.59 × 2.13 m).

in plaster, so Marra used bold brushstrokes to carve out this portrait in paint. There are no random marks. Using both visual and physical texture, Marra increased the painting's immediacy and dimensionality.

Chuck Close's *Self-Portrait* (1.57) offers a very different interpretation of the head. Working from a photograph, Close methodically reduced the face to a series of squares within a grid. He then painted circles, diamonds, and other simple shapes inside each square. The grid provides structure, while the loosely painted interior shapes create an unexpected invented texture.

In Lilian Garcia-Roig's *Water and Rock Flows* (1.58), the texture of oil paint serves three distinct purposes. First,

1.58 Lilian Garcia-Roig, *Water and Rock Flows*, 2010. Oil on canvas, 48 × 48 in. (121.9 × 121.9 cm).

it creates a physical texture, suggesting the ripples and eddies in the moving water. Second, it brings great energy to every painted shape: we feel the movement; we become mesmerized by the shifting and colorful patterns. Finally, we become connected to the artist herself. Often squeezing paint directly from the tube and onto the canvas, Garcia-Roig builds up vigorous layers of glistening color. As with the natural world, her paintings are both dazzling and highly tactile.

 ## key questions

TEXTURE

- What physical textures can you create with the materials you've chosen?

- What visual textures can you create with the materials you've chosen?

- Can the marks you make enhance the spatial illusion or increase compositional unity?

- How large can the marks become, and how loosely can you draw them?

- What happens to your design when you combine solid shapes and textured shapes?

VALUE

Value refers to the relative lightness or darkness of a surface. The word *relative* is significant. The lightness or darkness of a shape is largely determined by its surroundings. For example, on a white surface, a gray square seems stable and imposing (1.59A). The same gray square has less visual weight and seems luminous when it is surrounded by a black ground (1.59B). A **value scale** further demonstrates the importance of context (1.60). The solid gray line appears luminous when it is placed on a black background. As it crosses over the middle grays and into the white area, it seems to darken.

Contrast

Both communication and expression are affected by **value contrast**, or the amount of difference in values. High contrast tends to increase clarity and improve readability (1.61). Artists and designers often use low contrast for shapes of secondary importance or when the message is subtle. The same text can be dramatic or incoherent depending on the amount of contrast.

Photographers are especially aware of the importance of contrast. By using a filter, changing the print paper, or adjusting the image digitally, they can quickly modify contrast. High contrast give Lewis Hine's *Powerhouse Mechanic* (1.62) a gritty immediacy. Each muscle and piece of machinery is clearly defined. By contrast, the city in Alfred Stieglitz's *The Terminal* (1.63) is quiet and atmospheric. This low-contrast photograph invites the viewer into a preindustrial world of horses and carriages.

Finally, value gradation can suggest a light source, create a sense of three-dimensionality, and enhance the illusion of space. Ray Burggraf's *Eternal Now* (1.64) demonstrates each of these effects.

A   B

1.59A–B Relative value.

1.60 Value scale.

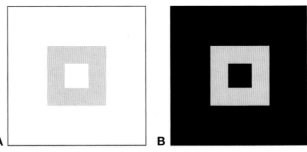

1.61 Contrast affects readability.

1.62 Lewis Hine, *Powerhouse Mechanic*, 1920. Photograph.

1.64 Ray Burggraf, *Eternal Now,* 1975. Brushed acrylic on canvas, 40 × 40 in. (101.6 × 101.6 cm).

1.63 Alfred Stieglitz, *The Terminal*, c. 1892. Chloride print, 3½ × 4½ in. (8.8 × 11.3 cm).

Value Distribution

Value distribution refers to the proportion and arrangement of lights and darks in a composition. Careful use of value distribution can increase emotional impact. A composition that is 80 percent black simply has a different "feel" than a composition that is 80 percent white.

Artists and designers often use values to create a sense of mystery or increase dramatic tension. For example, *Ejecutado* (1.65), by Alice Leora Briggs, combines split images of a seated man in the foreground and a crime scene in the background. The man in the foreground creates a visual and conceptual frame for the tragic scene at the center of the composition. Who is the man drinking coffee? Why was the other man killed? The combination of visual clues and the dark values creates a dramatic mystery.

Lighter values tend to suggest openness, optimism, and clarity. The layout of Kevin Fletcher's *Leaving Wittenberg by Afternoon Train* (1.66) is similar to that of *Ejecutado*. The composition is divided down the center by an architectural beam, and other architectural details frame up the left and right sides. Train tracks lead us into the background. However, in this image, we move from a dark foreground to a brightly lit background. Rather than being trapped in a tragedy, we are liberated by the journey ahead of us.

Value and Volume

When we use a full range of values, a two-dimensional shape can appear three-dimensional, or **volumetric**. Figure 1.67 shows the transformation of a circle into a sphere. We begin with a simple outline, then add the **attached shadows** or values

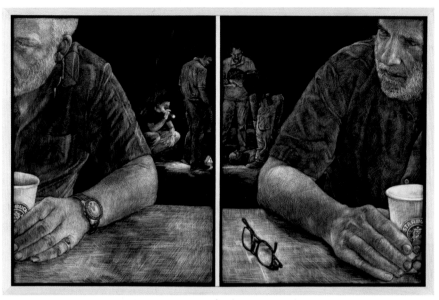

1.65 Alice Leora Briggs, *Ejecutado*, 2009. Sgraffito drawing on panel, 15 × 24 in. (38.1 × 61 cm).

1.66 Kevin G. Fletcher, *Leaving Wittenberg by Afternoon Train*, 2009. Monotype, 9¼ × 11¾ in. (23.5 × 29.8 cm).

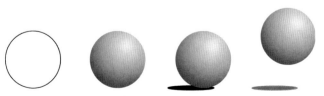

1.67 From shape to volume through use of value.

that directly define the basic form. Addition of a **cast shadow** in the third image grounds the sphere. In the fourth drawing, the separation between the shadow and the sphere creates a floating effect.

This transformation of shapes through value is so convincing that objects can appear to extend out from a two-dimensional surface. The earliest oil painters often used **grisaille**, or a gray underpainting, to create the illusion of three-dimensionality. They then added color, using transparent glazes or layers of paint. A detail from Jan van Eyck's *Ghent Altarpiece* (1.68) shows both the grisaille painting and the full-color painting. Van Eyck painted the two statues in the center using a range of grays and then added color to the kneeling figures on the right and left. Variations in value give all the figures a remarkable dimensionality.

1.68 Jan van Eyck, *Ghent Altarpiece* (closed), completed 1432. Oil on panel, approx. 11 ft 6 in. × 7 ft 7 in. (3.5 × 2.33 m).

Value and Space

When combined in a composition, very dark, crisp shapes tend to advance spatially, and gray, blurry shapes tend to recede. For example, in Thomas Moran's *Noon-Day Rest in Marble Canyon* (1.69), the dark values in the foreground gradually fade until the cliffs in the background become gray and indistinct. This effect, called **atmospheric perspective**, is one of the simplest ways to create the illusion of space.

Chiaroscuro (literally, "light-dark") is another way to create the illusion of space. A primary light source is used to create six or more values. A dark background is added to increase contrast. In *Judith and Her Maidservant with the Head of Holofernes* by Artemesia Gentileschi (1.70), the highlighted areas are clearly delineated, whereas darker areas seem to dissolve into the background. The resulting image is as dramatic as a theatrical stage.

1.69 Thomas Moran, *Noon-Day Rest in Marble Canyon,* from *Exploration of the Colorado River of the West,* by J. W. Powell, 1875. Wood engraving after an original sketch by Thomas Moran, 6½ × 4⅜ in. (16.5 × 11 cm).

1.70 Artemesia Gentileschi, *Judith and Her Maidservant with the Head of Holofernes*, c. 1625. Oil on canvas, 72½ × 54¾ in. (1.84 × 1.42 m).

Value and Lighting

Filmmakers and set designers are especially aware of the expressive uses of value. Working with a wide range of lights, including sharply defined spotlights and more diffused floodlights, they can increase or decrease the illusion of space, emphasize an object or an action, and influence our emotional response to a character.

Figure 1.71 shows four common forms of lighting. As described by Herbert Zettl in *Sight, Sound, Motion: Applied Media Aesthetics,* a key light is the primary source of illumination. Placing this light at a 45-degree angle can enhance the illusion of space. Addition of a backlight separates the actor from the background and adds definition. When a fill light is added, the contrast between light and dark becomes less harsh, and the actor may appear less formidable. In theatrical performances, lighting designers often use powerful side lighting to increase drama while enhancing dimensionality.

Director Michael Curtiz uses all of these aspects of lighting expressively in the 1942 American classic film, *Casablanca*. The lighting is fairly dark when we first enter Rick's Café Américain, the saloon where most of the action occurs. In this dark and mysterious place, a man will be shot, a seduction will be thwarted, and a romance will be rekindled.

The piano player, Sam, and the audience members closest to the stage are brightly lit as he sings an optimistic song (1.72A). The two villains in the film, Major Strasser and Captain Renault, are often strongly side-lit (1.72B), which makes them appear

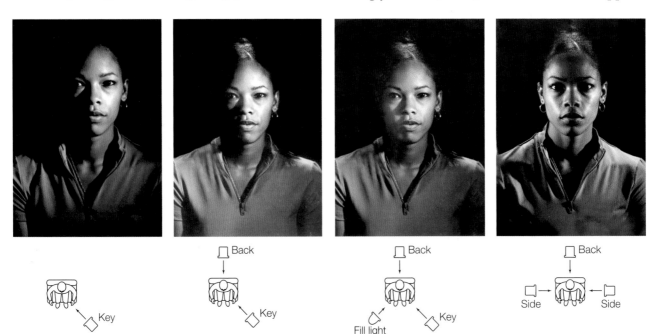

1.71 John Veltri, Lighting Techniques from *Sight, Sound, Motion: Applied Media Aesthetics*, 3rd ed., by Herbert Zettl, 1999.

1.72A *Casablanca* still. Sam and Rick in the bar.

1.72B *Casablanca* still. Major Strasser and Captain Renault hatch a plot.

1.72C *Casablanca* still. Ilsa tries to explain to Rick why she abandoned him in Paris.

1.72D *Casablanca* still. Rick persuades Ilsa to escape with her husband.

more formidable and enhances the texture in their faces. By contrast, Curtiz uses much softer light for the face of the heroine, Ilsa, who is emotionally and politically fragile.

Curtiz also used value and lighting to accentuate Ilsa's emotions throughout the film. When she tries to explain to Rick the reason she left him in Paris two years earlier, Ilsa wears a pure white dress and enters the darkened saloon like a virginal beam of light (1.72C). Later, when she visits Rick in his apartment, shadows cover her face, accentuating her conflicted emotions as she tries to decide whether to remain with her husband, Victor, whom she idealizes, or return to Rick, whom she loves. In the final scene at the airport, diffused lighting again emphasizes Ilsa's vulnerability (1.72D). She and Victor disappear into the foggy night, escaping from Casablanca, while Rick and a reformed Captain Renault stroll away together to join the Foreign Legion.

▶ key questions

VALUE

- What is the advantage of a wide value range? What is the advantage of a narrow value range? Which works better in your design?

- What happens when you invert the values—that is, the black areas become white and the white areas become black?

- Would your design benefit from a stronger illusion of space? If so, how can you use value to accomplish this?

summary

- The elements of two-dimensional design are point, line, shape, texture, value, and color.

- A point is a basic mark, such as a dot, a pixel, or a brushstroke. A focal point is the primary point of interest in a composition, while an array is a collection of points.

- Lines can contain, define, dissect, and connect. You can create line networks using hatching, cross-hatching, and cross-contours.

- A shape is created whenever an area is enclosed. The figure is the primary shape, while the ground, or negative shape, provides the surrounding context.

- When figure and ground shapes are equally strong, figure/ground reversal can occur.

- There are many types of shapes, including rectilinear, curvilinear, geometric, organic, representational, nonrepresentational, and abstract. When gradated, shapes can appear three-dimensional.

- The surface quality of a two-dimensional shape or a three-dimensional volume is called *texture*. We can create visual texture through multiple marks and use variations in the surface to create physical texture.

- Relative lightness or darkness in an artwork is called value. We can use value to create the illusion of space, suggest volume, shift compositional balance, and heighten emotion.

key terms

actual line
array
atmospheric
  perspective
attached shadow
calligraphic line
cast shadow
chiaroscuro
closure
collage
continuity
contour line
cross-contour

cross-hatching
curvilinear shape
direction
elements
engraving
figure/ground
  reversal
focal point
geometric shape
gesture drawing
gradation (shading)
grisaille
hatching

implied line
invented texture
line
negative shape
  (ground)
organic shape
organizational line
orientation
physical texture
point
positive shape
  (figure)
rectilinear shape

shape
stippling
texture
trompe l'oeil
value
value contrast
value distribution
value scale
visual texture
volume
volume summary
volumetric

studio projects

To apply the concepts from this chapter in the studio, check out the Projects page in the Online Learning Center at www.mhhe.com/LTI5e. The following is a sample of the chapter-related assignments in step-by-step detail.

POINT

Point Placement. A photographic series dealing with the use of a focal point.

LINE

Line Inventory. An introduction to the vocabulary and power of line.

Four Lines, Four Times. Sixteen linear compositions.

Line Dynamics. Combining line and balance.

SHAPE

Shape Inventory. Sixteen compositions using shape.

Concealing/Revealing #1. Figure/ground relationships.

Essence/Totality. Exploring abstraction.

TEXTURE

Texture Inventory. Sixteen texture studies.

VALUE

Concealing/Revealing #2. The impact of value on composition and communication.

The World Is a Stage. Light and its emotional impact.

Profile:
Bob Dacey, Illustrator
Tell Me a Story: Illustrating
Miriam's Cup

Bob Dacey is an internationally renowned artist whose drawings and paintings have been published as limited- and multiple-edition prints, as well as in a wide range of books and periodicals, including *McCall's*, Ballantine Books, Book-of-the-Month Club, *Playboy*, and Scholastic Publications. His commercial clients include The White House, ABC, CBS, NBC, PBS, Mobil Oil, Sony, the U.S. Post Office, Air Japan, and many others. Dacey received a Silver Medal from the Society of Illustrators in New York for one of the 16 paintings he produced for Scholastic Publications illustrating *Miriam's Cup*, which is themed on the Exodus of the Israelites from Egypt. Dacey collected an extensive library of books on Egypt and spent almost a year on research. From costumes to musical instruments, Dacey insisted on getting all the details just right.

MS: Give me a bit of background on *Miriam's Cup*. What was the significance of this project, and what aspects of the story did you want to emphasize in the illustrations?

BD: *Miriam's Cup* gave me a chance to expand on my single-image work. I've always approached each illustration as a moment in time, as if it had a "before" and an "after." This book gave me a chance to push that much further. I started every painting by focusing on the emotion in the moment being depicted. I always ask myself: "What is the essence of this moment?" The composition follows. Shapes and values serve the emotional content, while movement is used to unify the composition.

MS: You have said that 75 percent of your work on this project was devoted to research. Can you describe your research and tell me why it was so important?

BD: For *Miriam's Cup*, I had to understand the culture of Egypt and the Jewish culture of the time. Fortunately, I've always had an extensive interest in both. My personal library contains more books on Egypt than the local library system. Research helped open new ideas, leading in some unexpected directions. Those bulrushes are one example. I looked up the word in three

dictionaries and two encyclopedias. One of these sources mentioned that the bulrushes of ancient Egypt are papyrus, those beautiful fan-shaped reeds that can be fashioned into a kind of paper. Without that knowledge, the image I arrived at would have been impossible.

MS: I understand that you have a seven-step process by which you refine and expand your ideas. Can you describe this process as it applies to the cover image for *Miriam's Cup*?

BD: I first consider the intent of each painting: what must this piece communicate? In this painting, I focused on Miriam's exuberance as she celebrates her escape from Egypt. Second, the composition must support my intent. The circular movement of the tambourine and flowers dominates this painting. The movement from the raised hand holding the tambourine, to Miriam's hair, to her face, and on to her cupped hand provides a secondary pattern. And that cupped hand repeats the curve of the flowers. Third, the shapes depend on both the intent and the composition. If I am painting a very stoic character, I use a lot of verticals. Diagonals are used when the character or event is very dynamic. Value is fourth on my checklist. I assign value according to the mood of the painting. Lighter values are used for celebratory images, like this one; darker values dominate when the mood is somber. A mix of light and dark value is best. I base my compositions on the Golden Section [a classic use of proportion], and I often use a 60/40 proportion between light and dark values. Texture, step five, often results from the placement of shape and value—but it really deserves a place of its own, due to its importance as a constructive or destructive factor. When everything else works but the image still suffers, textural discord is usually the culprit! Color comes next. I really have to have the other questions resolved first. Color without composition, value, or intent just doesn't cut it. This painting is dominated by rich pastel colors, which help convey the exuberant emotion.

All of this contributes to the overall image, the final step. If all of the preceding factors serve my intent, the image can emerge naturally and effectively.

MS: In addition to the extensive research you did for *Miriam's Cup,* it seems that you have a very wide range of interests in general.

BD: Well, everything feeds into my work—and I've always been interested in everything! My undergraduate majors included theater and anthropology before I settled on ad design as the field in which I finally got my degree. Now, my readings range from archaeology to philosophy to psychology to paleontology, and more. I'm also developing my interest in writing and plan to pursue a master's in writing in order to increase my understanding of narrative.

MS: One of the questions my students often have is this: how do I get from where I am as a student to where you are as a professional?

BD: Focus on your goals and research the field. Talk to professionals you admire. Set high standards for yourself and be realistic about the level of professionalism and quality required.

MS: Any final bits of advice?

BD: Don't limit yourself. We all have great potential that serves the higher purpose of society. Pursue your goals with the knowledge that you can succeed. And remain flexible and open-minded, so that you can redirect your efforts as opportunities present themselves. Read everything! Draw everything!

Bob Dacey, Cover of *Miriam's Cup,* by Fran Manushkin, 1988. Scholastic Press.

The Element of Color

Color immediately attracts attention. When presented with a collection of bottles filled with liquid in various colors, very young children group the objects by color rather than by size or shape. Color has great emotional power, and designers carefully choose a color palette that supports the mood of each project. An interior designer may use rose-red walls in a restaurant to increase emotional warmth, while using light blue walls in a day-care center to encourage calm.

Selecting the right colors can make or break a design. To assist their clients in project planning, the Neenah Paper Company produced a witty and informative brochure describing the effects of color (2.1). The company gave each color a personality as distinctive as an astrological sign. It then organized the colors in a booklet, creating an easy-to-use index of possibilities.

Although systems of this kind provide a shortcut to basic decision making, in this chapter we will see that color is a complex element. It defies easy formulas. We consider relationships between color and light, describe three major characteristics of color, explore harmony and disharmony, and analyze uses of color in various compositional contexts.

2.1 Brochure for Neenah. Courtesy of Neenah and Partners Design. Color Attributes courtesy of Dewey Color System®, deweycolorsystem.com.

COLOR PHYSICS

To use color fully, we must understand the major types of color, how they are created, and how they interact. **Color theory** is the art and science of color interaction and effects. In *The Art of Color*,[1] Johannes Itten lists the following approaches to color theory:

- The *physicist* studies electromagnetic wavelengths in order to measure and classify color.

- Working with the molecular structure of dyes and pigments, the *chemist* seeks to produce highly permanent colors and excellent paint consistency.

- The *physiologist* investigates the effects of color and light on our eyes and brain.

- The *psychologist* studies the expressive effects of color on our mind and spirit.

As artists and designers, we combine all of these areas of knowledge. Like a physicist, we use color wavelengths to create visual effects. Like a chemist, we must be aware of the safety and permanence of dyes and pigments. We put into practice theories developed by physiologists, and our communication and expression are strongly affected by the psychological impact of color.

Additive and Subtractive Color

Two major color systems are used in art and design. Beams of light create **additive color** (2.2A). Red, green, and blue, the familiar RGB on a computer screen, are the primary colors in this system. We can mix millions of colors from these primaries. **Subtractive color** is created when white light is reflected off a pigmented or dyed surface (2.2B). We commonly identify blue, red, and yellow as the subtractive primaries.

2.2A Light primaries and their additive mixtures.

2.2B Pigment primaries and their subtractive mixtures.

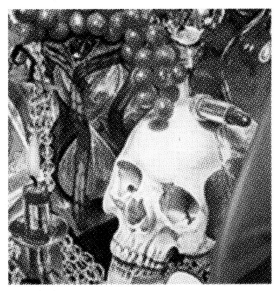

2.3 Color printing detail of *Wheel of Fortune*, showing dot pattern used in CMYK printing.

A Yellow   B Magenta   C Yellow and magenta   D Cyan   E Yellow, magenta, and cyan   F Black   G Full color printing

2.4A–G Color separation in CMYK printing. Dots of yellow, magenta, cyan, and black are layered to create a full-color image.

This book was printed using cyan blue, magenta red, and yellow, the transparent primaries (or **process colors**) commonly used in mass production. Figure 2.3 provides an example of process printing. As viewers, we optically combine thousands of cyan, magenta, and yellow dots to create a coherent image. Black (abbreviated as K in the CMYK printing system) was then added to enhance detail and increase contrast (2.4A–G).

Color and Light

These two systems exist because of the inseparable connection between color and light. When white light passes through a prism, it is refracted, or bent. This creates a wide spectrum of hues, which is dominated by red, orange, yellow, green, blue, blue-violet, and violet (2.5). We define each hue, or separate color, by a specific electromagnetic wavelength. Red is the longest and violet the shortest. When white light hits a colored surface, some wavelengths are reflected, while other wavelengths are absorbed. As figure 2.6A shows, a red surface reflects the red wavelengths while absorbing the blue and green wavelengths. Similarly, a green surface reflects the green wavelengths while absorbing the red and blue (2.6B). All wavelengths are reflected off a white surface (2.6C); all wavelengths are absorbed by a black surface (2.6D). Color reflection and absorption are rarely total. As a result, we can often see hints of various colors within a dominant color.

Using Additive Color

Lighting designers, videographers, and website artists use additive color extensively. They use beams of red, green, and blue light to create a full-color video projection. The mixture of adjacent beams creates cyan, magenta, and yellow, which are the *secondary* colors in the additive system. When all three beams are combined, white light results.

We can quickly and easily create variations in additive color on a computer. In figure 2.7, the current color choice is shown in the center. Variations appear in the eight surrounding squares. Even a 10 percent increase in a given color produces a very different result.

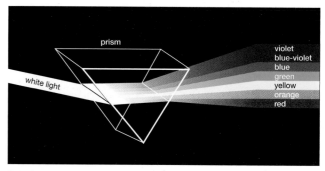

2.5 When white light passes through a prism, the spectrum becomes visible.

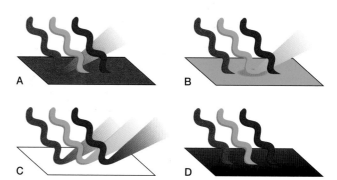

2.6A–D We see color when the primaries of light are reflected off a colored surface. A red surface absorbs the green and blue wavelengths, while reflecting the red. All wavelengths are reflected by a white surface. All wavelengths are absorbed by a black surface.

Our perception of additive color is influenced by the following:

- The intensity (or wattage) of the projected light.

- The light source. Incandescent light tends to be warmer than bluish fluorescent light. Daylight provides the richest color balance.

- The surface quality of the illuminated object. Projected light behaves very differently on transparent, translucent, and textured surfaces.

- The overall amount of light in the environment. Even a dimly lit object will appear to glow if you place it in a very dark room.

Using Subtractive Color

Painters, printmakers, and illustrators use subtractive color in various forms, including acrylics, oils, pastels, and inks. Each pigment or dye used in the manufacture of such materials is chemically

2.7 Color variations using a computer.

unique. Quinacridone red and pthalocyanide blue are transparent and intense. The cadmiums and earth colors are generally opaque. **Color overtones** complicate matters further. Color theorist David Hornung defines an overtone as "a secondary hue bias in a primary color." For example, alizarin crimson is a red with violet overtones, and scarlet is a red with orange overtones. To create a wider range of mixtures, artists and designers often use a six-hue palette, including two reds, two yellows, and two blues, plus black and white. Black and white have no hue and are defined as **achromatic**.

Color Interaction

Color interaction refers to the way colors influence one another. We never see colors in isolation. The blue sheets of paper that we examine in an art supply store may remind us of the blue of the sky, the ocean, or the fabrics in a clothing store. Lighting also affects our perceptions. Incandescent light creates a warm orange glow, and standard fluorescent lights produce a bluish ambiance.

When we add our blue paper to a design, it is profoundly affected by the surrounding colors. **Simultaneous contrast** refers to this apparent change in a color when it is paired with another color. Figure 2.8A–C shows three principles of

simultaneous contrast. The first pair of images shows a light/dark contrast. A blue-green square appears much lighter when it is placed on a black background. The second pair shows a complementary reaction. The same blue-green square appears to glow when it is surrounded by red rather than a neutral gray. In the third pair, the same blue-green square appears almost green when it is surrounded by solid blue, yet it appears almost blue when surrounded by green.

Color interaction becomes especially dramatic when we use complementary colors, such as red-orange and blue-green, in a composition. In the human eye, two types of cells, known as rods and cones, are arranged in layers on the retina. These

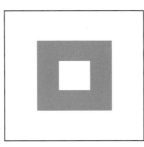 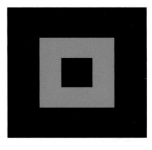

A

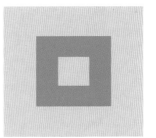 

B

C

2.8A–C Examples of simultaneous contrast. Light/dark contrast is shown in A, a complementary reaction is shown in B, and subtle variations are shown in C. The blue-green square is the same color in all examples but appears different due to the surrounding colors.

cells serve as photoreceptors. The rods record lightness and darkness, while the cones distinguish the hues, such as red and blue. According to **opponent theory**, the cones can register only one color in a complementary pair at a time. Constant shifting between the opposing colors creates a visual overload at the edges of the shapes, resulting in an electric glow. In *Inner Lhamo Waterfall* (2.9), Pat Steir used this effect to suggest the majesty and mystery of the falling water.

We can use a similar characteristic of human vision to create an **afterimage**. If we stare at a red square for 20 seconds (2.10) and then stare at a white sheet of paper, a blue or green shape will seem to appear. This is due to fatigue in the cones, the color sensors in our eyes. Overloaded by the intense red, our eyes revert to the blue and green cones, creating the afterimage.

DEFINING COLOR

Hue

The **hue**, or name of a color, is determined by its wavelength. For example, red, blue, green, and yellow are all hues.

Physicists, painters, and philosophers have devised numerous systems to organize hues. Johannes Itten's 12-step color wheel (2.11) is a clear and simple example. Red, blue, and yellow **primary colors** are in the center. We can mix these colors to produce many other colors. The **secondary colors** of green, orange, and violet follow. These colors are mixed from adjacent primaries. A circular spectrum of **tertiary colors** completes the wheel. The mixture of a secondary

2.9 **Pat Steir, *Inner Lhamo Waterfall*, 1992.** Oil on canvas, 114 × 90¼ in. (289.6 × 229.2 cm).

color and the adjacent primary color creates a tertiary color.

The 10-step Munsell color wheel (2.12) provides a more nuanced organizational structure, and the three-dimensional Munsell color tree (2.13) provides examples of changes in color value and intensity as well as hue.

Artists often use a wide range of hues to capture the richness of reality. In *Wheel of Fortune*

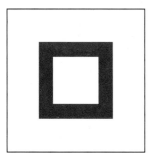

2.10 Afterimage exercise.

2.11 The 12-step Itten color wheel.

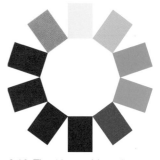

2.12 The 10-step Munsell color wheel.

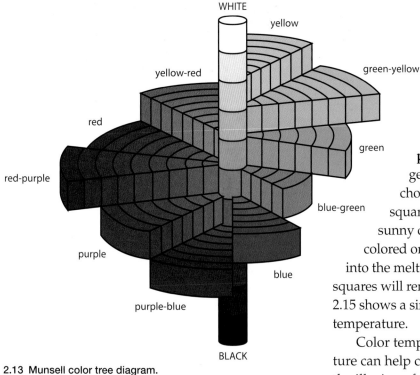

2.13 Munsell color tree diagram.

As demonstrated by Pat Steir's *Waterfall* (2.9), a limited range of hues can be equally effective. In this painting, interaction between just two hues creates an electric visual impact.

Temperature is an especially important aspect of hue. **Temperature** refers to the heat a color generates, both physically and psychologically. Try laying six colored squares of equal value on fresh snow on a sunny day. By the end of the day, the warm-colored oranges, reds, and violets will sink into the melting snow, while the blue and green squares will remain closer to the surface. Figure 2.15 shows a simple division of the color wheel by temperature.

Color temperature can help create the illusion of space. Under most circumstances, warm colors advance, and cool colors recede. Kenneth Noland's *A Warm Sound in a Gray Field* (2.16) clearly

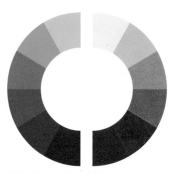

2.15 Separation of the color wheel by temperature.

(2.14), Audrey Flack used a full spectrum of hues to define a collection of symbolic objects in meticulous detail. The makeup and mirrors symbolize vanity; the candles, hourglass, and skull suggest the passage of time; the grapes suggest passion. Reds, blues, and yellows dominate the painting. Hints of orange, violet, and green complete the spectrum.

2.14 Audrey Flack, *Wheel of Fortune*, 1977–78. Oil over acrylic on canvas, 8 × 8 ft. (2.44 × 2.44 m).

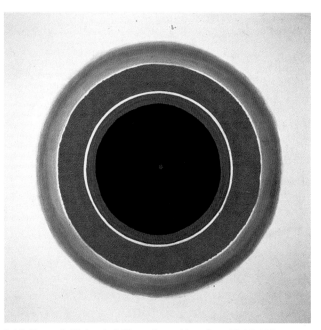

2.16 Kenneth Noland, *A Warm Sound in a Gray Field*, 1961. 6 ft 10½ in. × 6 ft 9 in. (2.1 × 2.06 m). Oil on canvas.

demonstrates this effect. The red ring with its light yellow halo pushes toward us, while the blue-black circle pulls us inward. The small red dot in the center of the composition further activates the void by creating another advancing shape. Temperature can also be used to create a strong emotional effect. In figure 2.17, the glowing oranges and reds create a radiant representation of the Christian gospel of St. Luke.

Value

Value refers to the relative lightness or darkness of a color. By removing hue from the equation, we can create a simple value scale (2.18A) that shifts from white to black through a series of grays. Figure 2.18B shows that hues such as violet, blue, and green are inherently darker in value than are pure yellow or orange. Figure 2.18C shows a translation of color into value. Despite the variety of hues, all the colors shown have nearly the same value.

Figure 2.19 shows three basic variations in value. When we add white to a hue, the resulting **tint** will be lighter in value. The addition of gray produces a **tone**. The addition of black creates a darker **shade**. One of the simplest ways to unify a design is to limit the colors that we use to the tints, tones, and shades of a single hue.

A full range of values can create a very convincing representation of reality. Using value, Georges de la Tour made *Mary Magdalene with the Smoking Flame* (2.20) photographically realistic and emotionally powerful. The contemplative woman, a close companion to the Christian Jesus, looks at a burning candle and holds a skull, both symbols of death. Gradation in value makes all of the forms seem rounded and three-dimensional.

The limited value range in David Hockney's *Mist* (2.21) is equally effective. The gray-green palm trees dissolve into the peach-colored fog as quietly as a whisper.

By making a black-and-white photocopy, we can easily check the range of values in a design. The photocopied image will be quite readable when the value range is broad. When we use a very narrow range of values, the photocopy will produce a solid gray image.

2.17 Page from the *Book of Kells*, late 8th century. Illuminated manuscript, 13 × 8¾ in (330 × 250 mm).

Value is the dominant force in some paintings while hue is a dominant force in others. Each approach has a distinctive emotional effect. Romaine Brooks's *Self-Portrait* (2.22) is essentially a value painting. Blacks, whites, and grays dominate the image. The woman's eyes are concealed by the brim of her hat and the shadow it casts. Patches of red on her lips and coat add just a touch of color. She is wary and reserved. Value, rather than hue, is the appropriate choice for this image.

In contrast, hue dominates Henri Matisse's *Green Stripe* (2.23). Surrounded by large blocks of red, green, and violet, the woman seems bold and self-confident. The avocado-green dividing line separates blocks of pink on the right and lime-green on the left half of her face, suggesting warmer and cooler aspects of her personality. Even her eyes and hair are painted in blue-black, adding yet more color to this expressive portrait.

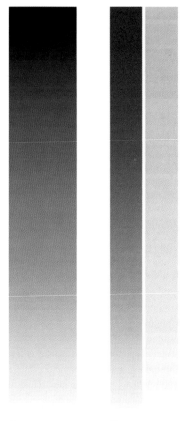

A

B

C

2.18A–C Value scales.

2.20 Georges de la Tour, *Mary Magdalene with the Smoking Flame,* **1630-35.** Oil on canvas. 46¹/₁₆ × 36⅛ in. (117 × 91.76 cm).

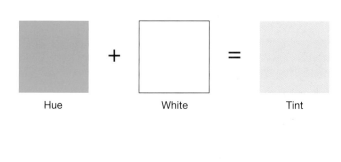

Hue   +   White   =   Tint

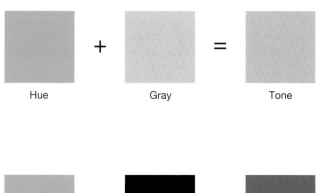

Hue   +   Gray   =   Tone

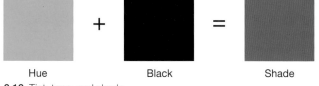

Hue   +   Black   =   Shade

2.19 Tint, tone, and shade.

2.21 David Hockney, *Mist,* **from The Weather Series, 1973.** Lithograph in 5 colors, edition 98, 37 × 32 in. (93.9 × 81.2 cm).

2.22 Romaine Brooks, *Self-Portrait*, 1923. Oil on canvas,
46¼ × 26⅞ in. (117.5 × 68.3 cm).

2.23 Henri Matisse, *Green Stripe (Madame Matisse)*, 1905.
Oil on canvas, 16 × 12¾ in. (40.6 × 32.4 cm).

Intensity

Intensity, **saturation**, and **chroma** all refer to the
purity of a color. The primary colors are the most
intense. This intensity generally diminishes when
colors are mixed.

Figure 2.24A–C presents three intensity scales.
Column A shows the most intense primary, secondary, and tertiary colors. Column B demonstrates the loss of intensity when we add black to
a single color. In column C, two complementary
colors are mixed, producing a range of elegant,
low-intensity colors.

Artists and designers often use high-intensity
colors to maximize impact. In *Daphne II* (2.25),
Cat Crotchett juxtaposed rich violet with glowing yellows and oranges to capture a moment

A   B   C

2.24A–C Intensity scales. The most intense primaries, secondaries,
and tertiaries are shown in A. The addition of black reduces the
intensity of the color red in B. Mixing the complements yellow and
violet creates low-intensity colors in C.

2.25 Cat Crotchett, *Daphne II* (after *Apollo and Daphne* by Gianlorenzo Bernini), 2004. Encaustic on canvas, 32 × 23⅞ in. (81.3 × 60.6 cm).

of dramatic transformation. In a Greek myth, Daphne begs to escape capture by the god Apollo, and is turned into a bay laurel tree. Crotchett used encaustic, a paint made of colored wax, to make the hues even more brilliant.

Low-intensity colors can be equally effective. In figure 2.26, Samantha Fields combined grays, tans, and subdued violets to create a glowing representation of car headlights at night.

▶ key questions

DEFINING COLOR

- Which will work better in your design, a limited or a wide range of hues?

- What proportion of warm and cool colors best communicates your idea?

- What happens when you combine low-intensity colors with high-intensity colors?

2.26 Samantha Fields, *Nocturne #2: Overpass*, 2012. Acrylic on canvas on panel, 48 × 48 in. (121.9 × 121.9 cm).

HARMONY AND DISHARMONY

Relationships among colors are critical to the success or failure of a design, and many theories of **color harmony** help artists, architects, and designers make good choices. A basic color wheel can help illustrate five common approaches.

Monochromatic Color Schemes

Variations on a single hue are used in a **monochromatic** color scheme (2.27). The advantage of this system is a high level of unity: all the colors are strongly related. Boredom, due to the lack of variety,

is a potential disadvantage. Mark Tansey's *Discarding the Frame* (2.28) is almost entirely composed of variations on blue. The mysterious activity depicted, combined with the monochromatic color, raises questions rather than provides answers. Who are these men, and why are they hurling a large picture frame into the abyss? As we will see in Chapter Eight, highly realistic images often evoke metaphors, creating new and complex ideas.

Analogous Color Schemes

Adjacent colors on the color wheel are used in an **analogous** color scheme (2.29). As with monochromatic harmony, a high degree of unity is ensured, but the wider range of hues offers greater variety

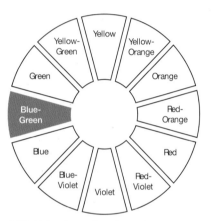

2.27 Monochromatic color system.

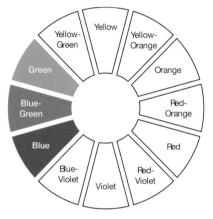

2.29 Analogous color system.

2.28 Mark Tansey, *Discarding the Frame,* **1993.** Oil on canvas, 84 × 74½ in. (213.4 × 189.2 cm).

2.30 *Chromatics Place Settings,* **1970.** Gerald Gulotta, shape designer; Jack Prince, pattern designer. Porcelain, linen, and stainless steel.

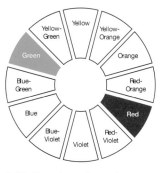

2.31 Complementary color system.

and can increase interest. *Chromatics Place Settings,* shown in figure 2.30, is activated by a surprising variety of blues and greens.

Complementary Color Schemes

The palette dramatically expands in a **complementary** color scheme (2.31). Complementary colors are opposites on the traditional color wheel. When mixed together, they can lower intensity and produce a wide range of browns. When paired in a composition, complementary colors can become powerful partners. Each increases the impact of the other.

Francis Bacon's *Four Studies for a Self-Portrait* (2.32) is dominated by the complements red and green. The design is unified by browns, including the reddish brown filling the background. Vigorous slashes of pure green and red add visual energy and create the illusion of movement.

Chris Kienke used orange and pink to complement blue and green in *From the Hip* (2.33).

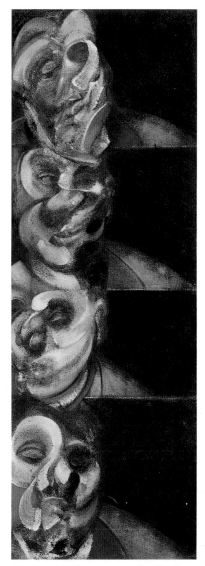

2.32 Francis Bacon, *Four Studies for a Self-Portrait,* **1967.** Oil on canvas, 36 × 13 in. (91.5 × 33 cm).

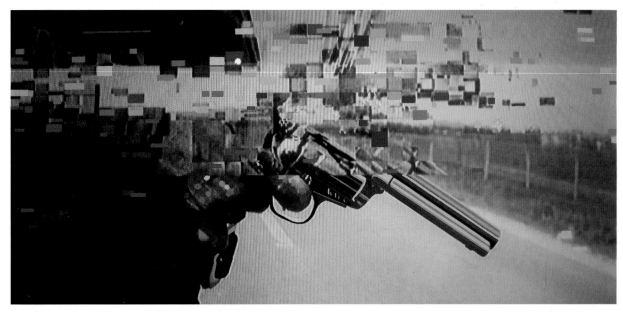

2.33 Chris Kienke, *From the Hip,* **2013.** Oil and digital pigment on canvas, 82 × 38 in. (208 × 97 cm).

Combining digital information with traditional painting, he created this image from subtle vertical lines, photographically realistic shapes, and fragmentary squares and rectangles. The blues and greens that dominate the composition heighten the power of the oranges and pinks we see in the hand.

Each complementary pair has its own distinctive strengths. Violet and yellow provide the widest value range, and orange and blue provide the widest range of variation in temperature. Red and green are closest in value and create extreme agitation when placed side by side. By mixing two complements plus black and white, we can create a range of colors that begins to suggest the power of a full spectrum.

Split Complementary Color Schemes

An even wider range of possibilities is offered by the **split complementary** color scheme (2.34). Rather than pair colors that are in opposite positions on the color wheel, the artist completes the scheme using the two colors on either side of one of the complements. Georgia O'Keeffe's *Jack in the Pulpit No. V* (2.35) is dominated by rich greens and violets, with accents of yellow at the top of the composition and a vertical line of red just to the left of the center.

Triadic Color Schemes

The **triadic** color scheme pushes the choices even farther apart, so that they are now located in a triangular position, equally spaced around the wheel (2.36). Artists and designers often use this scheme when variety and a strong impact are needed. In a brochure for the UCLA extension open house (2.37), variations on yellow-green, red-orange, and blue-violet bring energy to the design, while the white areas provide openness.

Chromatic Grays and Earth Colors

Although the basic color wheel can help us identify many kinds of relationships, two important types of colors are not included: chromatic grays and earth colors. A **chromatic gray** is made from a mixture of various hues, rather than a simple blend

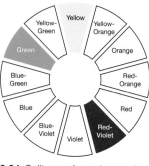

2.34 Split complementary system.

2.35 Georgia O'Keeffe, *Jack in the Pulpit No. V,* 1930. Oil on canvas, 48 × 30 in. (122 × 76 cm).

of black and white. The result is both subtle and vibrant. In *The Magpie* (2.38), the grays vary widely, from the purples and blue-grays in the shadows to the golden-gray light in the foreground and the silvery grays for the snow-covered trees. This is not a dark, sullen winter day. Through the use of chromatic grays, Claude Monet made the warm light and transparent shadows sparkle in the crisp air.

Earth colors, including raw and burnt sienna, raw and burnt umber, and yellow ochre, are made

2.36 Triadic system.

2.37 Tin Yen Studios, *UCLA Extension Open House.*

2.38 Claude Monet, *The Magpie,* 1869. Oil on canvas, 35 × 51 in. (89 × 130 cm).

generally from pigments found in soil. Often warm in temperature, when used together they create a type of analogous harmony. For example, browns, oranges, and tans accentuate the gestural energy and organic shapes in *Bush Cabbage Dreaming at Ngarlu* (2.39), by Australian artist Paddy Japaljarri Stewart. This acrylic painting was inspired by traditional aboriginal artworks, which are literally made from earth colors. When used alone, earth colors can unify even the most agitated composition. When used in combination with high-intensity colors, they can provide an elegant balance between subdued and louder, more overt colors.

Using Disharmony

Selecting the right colors can make the difference between a visual disaster and a visual delight. As a result, color harmony is the subject of endless books offering advice to artists, architects, and surface pattern designers. Monochromatic, analogous, complementary, split complementary, and triadic systems are traditional forms of color harmony.

However, cultural definitions of harmony are as changeable as popular music. In a search for eye-catching images, designers in all fields invent new color combinations each year. For example, the pink, gray, and black prized by designers in one year may seem passé in the next. Consequently, definitions and uses of color harmony are quite fluid.

Furthermore, when skillfully used, color **disharmony** can be as effective as color harmony. Artists and designers often use disharmony when the subject matter is disturbing or when they require an unusual visual approach. In figure 2.40, Francis Bacon used tans, grays, pinks, orange, and blacks to produce a painting that is as disturbing as it is beautiful. The colors in the body suggest disease, while the areas of black, yellow, and gray create a room that is agitated and disorienting. Using

2.39 Paddy Japaljarri Stewart, *Bush Cabbage Dreaming at Ngarlu;* Yuendumn, Central Australia, 1986. Acrylic on canvas, 47½ × 93½ in. (120.5 × 237.5 cm).

similar pinks, gray, black, and yellow-orange, Steve Quinn created a gentle evocation of memory in his Christmas poster (2.41). Here, the words and images shift back and forth in space, as fluid as a dream.

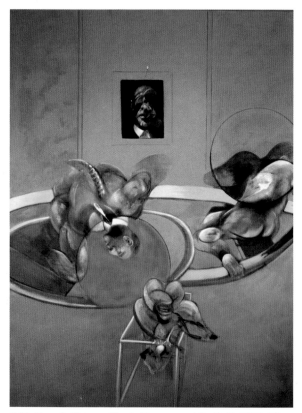

2.40 Francis Bacon, *Three Figures and Portrait,* 1975. Oil and pastel on canvas, 78 × 58 in. (198 × 147.5 cm).

2.41 Steve Quinn, *A Christmas Memory,* 1991. Photoshop, 11 × 17 in. (27.94 × 43.18 cm).

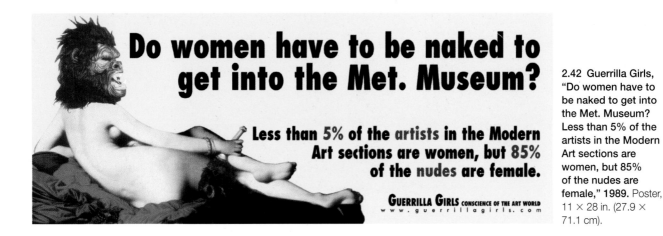

Do women have to be naked to get into the Met. Museum?

Less than 5% of the artists in the Modern Art sections are women, but 85% of the nudes are female.

GUERRILLA GIRLS CONSCIENCE OF THE ART WORLD
www.guerrillagirls.com

2.42 Guerrilla Girls, "Do women have to be naked to get into the Met. Museum? Less than 5% of the artists in the Modern Art sections are women, but 85% of the nudes are female," 1989. Poster, 11 × 28 in. (27.9 × 71.1 cm).

Figure 2.42 shows a third example. Bright yellow and hot pink add pizzazz to an eye-catching poster. Designed to call attention to a disparity in the number of exhibitions granted to male and female artists, this poster had to compete with other information displayed on walls around New York City. A witty image combined with jarring colors was just right in this case.

As these examples demonstrate, the degree and type of harmony that the artist uses must depend on the ideas behind the image and on the visual context in which an image will appear.

▶ key questions

HARMONY AND DISHARMONY

- What are the advantages of each of the traditional color schemes?

- When we use a limited palette, how can a few colors produce the greatest impact? When we use a full palette, how can the colors become harmonized?

- What happens when your composition is dominated by earth colors or chromatic grays? How does it change when you add an intense color?

- Which is more suitable for the idea you want to express: traditional color harmony or some form of disharmony?

COMPOSING WITH COLOR

Composition may be defined as the combination of multiple parts into a harmonious whole. The effect of color on composition is profound. Color can shift visual balance, create a focal point, influence our emotions, and expand communication. In this section, we will consider four major compositional uses of color.

Creating the Illusion of Space

Pictorial space is like a balloon. When we "push" on one side, the other side appears to bulge outward. Through our color choices, we can cause various areas in a composition to expand or contract visually. In most cases, cool, low-intensity colors tend to recede while warm, high-intensity colors tend to advance. In Wolf Kahn's *The Yellow Square* (2.43), the greens and violets defining the exterior of the barn gently pull the viewer into the painting, while the blazing yellow window inside the barn pushes out as forcefully as the beacon in a lighthouse.

This effect can play an even more important role in nonobjective paintings. As described by painter Hans Hofmann, the "push and pull" of color can be a major source of energy in a nonobjective composition. For example, a large block of intense red dominates Hofmann's *Magnum Opus* (2.44). The blue rectangle at the left side pulls us inward, while the crisp yellow shape on the right pushes outward.

Weight and Balance

The effect of color on visual weight and balance is equally dramatic. In *Icarus* (2.45), Henri Matisse

2.43 **Wolf Kahn,** *The Yellow Square,* **1981.** Oil on canvas, 44 × 72 in. (112 × 183 cm).

2.44 **Hans Hofmann,** *Magnum Opus,* **1962.** Oil on canvas, 84⅛ × 78⅛ in. (213 × 198 cm).

2.45 **Henri Matisse,** *Icarus,* from *Jazz* series, **1947.** Stencil print, 17⅛ × 13⅜ in. (43.6 × 34 cm).

2.46 Nancy Crow, *Double Mexican Wedding Rings 1*, 1990. Hand quilted by Marie Moore. 72 × 72 in. (183 × 183 cm).

visually tells the story of the boy who flew too close to the sun, melting his wax wings and plunging into the ocean. The heavy black body "falls" into the blue background, while a vibrant red heart seems to pull the figure upward, away from death. Six bursts of yellow surround the figure. Equally suggestive of the stars above the boy and of light shimmering on the water below, these simple shapes add energy to the composition and meaning to the myth.

Distribution and Proportion

Through careful distribution, even the most disharmonious colors can work together beautifully. Four rectilinear gray shapes dominate Nancy Crow's *Double Mexican Wedding Rings 1* (2.46). Gradated values extend outward, creating a subtle glow. Four small multi-colored squares accentuate the edges of the four large squares, and eight colorful rectangles frame up the composition as a whole. In most compositions, the earth colors, chromatic grays, and high-intensity reds, blues, and yellows would clash. In this composition, an even distribution of colors creates a unified composition.

Color as Emphasis

Graphic designers often use color to emphasize critical information in a composition. The subway map in figure 2.47 provides a good example. Cooler areas of gray, green, and blue, placed on a black background, provide basic structural information. The bright yellow lines show the path through the subway. Red, which is used at only one point in the diagram, clearly locates the viewer on the map. A single color can make an equally powerful statement. In figure 2.48, a large block of yellow combined with the word *not* attracts our attention to the message in the lower-left corner.

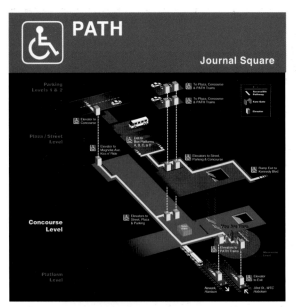

2.47 **PATH Station Maps, Louis Nelson Associates, Inc., NY.** Graphic designer: Jennifer Stoller.

We can also use color to create a focal point. A small red astronomical observatory dominates Vernon Fisher's *Objects in a Field* (2.49). Located just above the center of the painting, it commands our attention while echoing the curved shape of the white parachute in the foreground.

2.48 **Mark Schwartz, Greg Oznowich, and Teresa Snow, Nesnadny and Schwartz Design, Annual Report for Eaton Corporation, "This is NOT business as usual," 2002.**

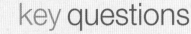

key questions

COMPOSING WITH COLOR

- How much space do you need in your composition, and how can color increase the illusion of space?

- How "heavy" is each of your colors? How does weight affect balance?

- Can color proportion or distribution shift, enhance, or unify your overall composition?

- Can color add emphasis to your design?

2.49 **Vernon Fisher, *Objects in a Field*, 1986.** Acrylic on canvas, 8 × 8 ft (2.4 × 2.4 m).

2.50 Andrew Wyeth, *Wind from the Sea*, 1947. Tempera on hardboard, 18½ × 27½ in. (47 × 69.9 cm).

EMOTION AND EXPRESSION

Colors are never emotionally neutral. In Andrew Wyeth's *Wind from the Sea* (2.50), subtle browns and greens suggest the faded color of a nineteenth-century photograph. They evoke the slow pace and serenity of a countryside at rest. Richard Diebenkorn's *Interior with Book* (2.51), painted just 12 years later, provides a very different interpretation of a similar interior scene. The intense yellows and oranges in the background push toward us, while the solid blocks of blue pull inward, flattening the image. The tension and power thus generated create a California landscape that is a world apart from Wyeth's New England. The color in Sandy Skoglund's *Radioactive Cats* (2.52) creates yet another interpretation of an interior space. The gray walls, furniture, and clothing suggest a world that is lifeless and coated in ash. In contrast, the lime-green cats glow with an inquisitive energy that may be toxic!

2.51 Richard Diebenkorn, *Interior with Book*, 1959. Oil on canvas, 70 × 64 in. (178 × 163 cm).

Color Keys

A dominant color, or **color key**, can heighten psychological as well as compositional impact. The blues that dominate Joseph Spadaford's *Illustrated Man* (2.53) suggest both magic and melancholy. Based on a book by Ray Bradbury, Spadaford had to suggest the torment of a man whose tattoos come to life at night. At the other extreme, in Egon Schiele's *Portrait of Paris von Gütersloh* (2.54), the flaming orange around and within the figure places the anxious man in an emotional electric chair. Designers also use color keys. Blood red dominates Chaz Maviyane-Davis's *Our Fear Is Their Best Weapon* (2.55). The soldier's face is tightly cropped, highlighting his fierce red

2.52 Sandy Skoglund, *Radioactive Cats,* **1980.** Cibachrome print, 30 × 40 in. (76.2 × 101.6 cm). © 1980 Sandy Skoglund.

eyes. The powerful slogan, presented in faded black letters, is almost consumed by the red background.

2.53 Joseph Spadaford, *Illustrated Man,* **1998.** Acrylic, 10 × 8 in. (25.4 × 20.3 cm).

2.54 Egon Schiele, *Portrait of Paris von Gütersloh,* **1918.** Oil on canvas, 55¼ × 43¼ in. (140.3 × 109.8 cm).

2.55 Chaz Maviyane-Davis, *Our Fear Is Their Best Weapon*, 2002. Offset poster.

As the text says, the voice of the people will be lost if fear is allowed to prevail. Likewise, when color surrounds the viewer, as in Hiroshi Senju's installations (2.56), the emotional impact can be profound. When immersed in color, we enter an alternative world. In each case, the artists used color to heighten emotion rather than represent reality.

Symbolic Color

Colors are often assigned symbolic meaning. These meanings may vary widely from culture to culture. In *The Primary Colors*, Alexander Theroux writes:

> [Blue] is the symbol of baby boys in America, mourning in Borneo, tribulation to the American Indian and the direction South in Tibet. Blue indicates mercy in the Kabbalah and carbon monoxide in gas canisters. Chinese emperors wore blue to worship the sky. To Egyptians it represented virtue, faith, and truth. The color was worn by slaves in Gaul. It was the color of the sixth level of the Temple of Nebuchadnezzar II, devoted to the planet Mercury. In Jerusalem a blue hand painted on a door gives protection . . . and in East Africa, blue beads represent fertility.[2]

2.56 Hiroshi Senju, *New Light from Afar*, exhibition at Sundaram Tagore Gallery, 2008. Fluorescent pigment on rice paper on board.

2.57 **Butterfly Maiden, Hopi Kachina.** Carved cottonwood, 13½ in. (35 cm).

2.58 Rogier van der Weyden, *Deposition*, from an altarpiece commissioned by the Crossbowman's Guild Louvain, Brabant, Belgium, c. 1435. Oil on panel, 7 ft 2⅝ in. × 8 ft 7⅛ in. (2.2 × 2.6 m).

In Hopi culture, colors symbolize spatial location and geographic direction. The Kachina doll in figure 2.57 represents Butterfly Maiden, a benevolent spirit. Red represents a southerly direction; white, the east or northeast; blue or green, the west.

Similarly, in the Christian tradition, the Virgin Mary is typically shown wearing a blue cloak, as a symbol of both purity and grief. In this detail from Rogier van der Weyden's *Deposition* (2.58), Mary collapses as her dead son is lowered from the cross.

The Power of Color

Color and value each have unique strengths. The black-and-white self-portrait by Kathe Kollwitz in figure 2.59 has a simple eloguence. Her profile is clearly defined, whereas the back of her head seems to dissolve into the surrounding space. In the second image, (2.60) Kollwitz juxtaposed a full-color portrait with a blue-gray background. There seems to be a hint of vulnerability in the first portrait and a solidity and strength in the second.

Color can increase the power of a given shape, shift compositional weight, and create a focal point. It can enhance the illusion of space, suggest volume, and heighten emotion. Well used, color is one of the most expressive elements of art and design.

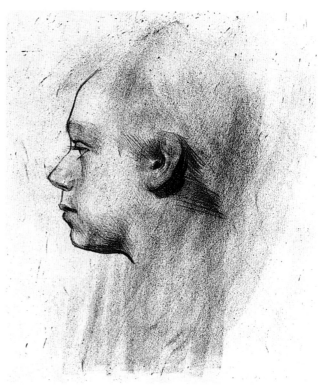

2.59 Käthe Kollwitz, *Self-Portrait in Profile, Facing Left, I* (detail), **1889.** Lithograph, 5⅞ × 5⅞ in. (15 × 15 cm).

2.60 Käthe Kollwitz, *Selbstbildnis im Profil Nach Rechts,* **c. 1900.** Pastel on laid paper, 19 × 14⅜ in. (46.8 × 36.5 cm).

▶ key questions

EMOTION AND EXPRESSION

- Sepia browns tend to evoke the past, while bright, high-contrast colors tend to suggest the present. What range of colors is appropriate for your design?

- Will a dominant color key increase the emotional impact of your design?

- Have you chosen colors with strong symbolic meaning? If so, how can such symbolic meaning enrich your composition?

- How much or how little color is needed for the ideas you wish to express?

summary

- Color immediately attracts attention. Its emotional and physiological impact strengthens communication and heightens expression.

- Red, green, and blue are the additive color primaries. Blue, red, and yellow are the subtractive color primaries.

- The three basic qualities of color are hue (the name of the color), value (its lightness or darkness), and intensity (its purity).

- Using a monochromatic, analogous, complementary, split complementary, or triadic color scheme can increase harmony in your design.

- The level of color harmony must match the expressive intent. In the right context, disharmony can be more expressive than harmony.

- In a composition, color can enhance the illusion of space, shift visual weight and balance, and help emphasize compositional details.

- Distribution and proportion can help unify disharmonious colors.

- Colors are never emotionally neutral. A dominant color key can heighten psychological impact, while a symbolic color provides a cultural reference.

key terms

achromatic	color theory	process colors	tertiary colors
additive color	complementary	saturation	tint
afterimage	composition	secondary colors	tone
analogous	disharmony	shade	triadic
chroma	earth colors	simultaneous contrast	value
chromatic gray	hue	split complementary	
color harmony	intensity	subtractive color	
color interaction	monochromatic	temperature	
color key	opponent theory		
color overtones	primary colors		

studio projects

To apply the concepts from this chapter in the studio, check out the Projects page in the Online Learning Center at www.mhhe.com /LTI5e. The following is a sample of the chapter-related assignments in step-by-step detail.

Concealing/Revealing #3. Color and communication.

Expressive Color. Exploring meaning through color.

Sun and Substance. Exploring shape and color as metaphors.

Profile:
Suzanne Stryk, Painter
An Art of Observation

Suzanne Stryk's artwork has appeared in over 60 group shows, and in solo exhibitions at the National Academy of Sciences, the Morris Museum of Art, the Eleanor B. Wilson Museum, and the William King Museum (an affiliate of the Virginia Museum of Fine Arts). Among the collections that own her work are the Tennessee State Museum, Bank of America's Southeastern Collection, the Taubman Museum of Art, and the Smithsonian Institution.

MS: You initially studied fine art and biology and then shifted to major in art history. Why?

SS: When I began my studies, I didn't really fit into the abstract expressionist and pop art approaches that were prevalent at the time. I was fascinated—and still am—with the depiction of nature in the art of different cultures. My papers explored topics such as animals in Egyptian tomb painting and nature marginalia drawn into medieval manuscripts. This "detour" into art history turned out to be invaluable to me as an artist.

MS: You then developed a career as a scientific illustrator. What kinds of jobs did you do, and what did you learn from these jobs?

SS: Seeking to merge my interest in nature and art, I studied scientific illustration in the early eighties. I then worked in a university biology department, drawing graphs and charts, along with the fun stuff—plant specimens and animals. The job required discipline and patience, which remains with me to this day, along with the arrows, labels, measurements, and grids that fill my images.

MS: When and why did you shift toward more self-directed studio work?

SS: Scientific illustration stimulated more and more questions. I wondered, "What does my precise drawing really say about an animal? Doesn't it say more about us as a species of observers?" In the mid-eighties, I discovered Russian icons, which often use a grid format to depict events in a saint's life. I decided to put a cicada's life cycle in a similar grid. This inspired a whole series

called *Life Cycles*. Then, a couple of these paintings were selected for my first major exhibition in Chicago. You know, if you're doing work that makes you think, "Either this is the stupidest thing in the world or really profound," then you might be onto something! It was the turning point in my discovery of personal voice.

MS: What are the greatest challenges in your work?

SS: Well, it's always a great challenge to make the concept and the visual idea seamless. Right now, I'm constructing life-sized birds from printouts of their genomic sequences. The finished birds will perch or hang around my paintings. I've done very little three-dimensional work and must therefore become fluent in a new "language."

MS: Your sketchbooks are numbered and lined up on a shelf in your studio, 30 in a row. Why are they so well organized, and what do they contribute to your studio practice?

SS: My sketchbooks are the primary source for my finished images. They include drawings of creatures surrounded by my notes, dates, measurements, and names, like a field naturalist's journal. But you'll also find interpretive notes about my personal response to the animal. As an illustrator, I focus on observation. As an artist, I must turn my observations into meaning.

MS: You look up the specific species of beetle or other subject. Why is specificity important?

SS: Knowing the species leads me to learn more about the animal, about its special features or behaviors. For example, I may discover a plump green caterpillar with tiny bristles and reddish dots. When I identify it as a Luna moth larva, I learn to feed it walnut leaves. I can then witness it pupate and, if lucky, watch it emerge as a huge milky-green adult. This is no small thing for me, for my whole worldview—as reflected in my art—centers on the awareness of other lives.

MS: You emphasize the importance of intuition. Please describe intuition and give us an example.

SS: It may sound like a contradiction, but a lot of intuition is learned. For instance, in my *Genomes and Daily Observations* series, I invent microorganisms or insect parts from the accidental stains and drips on the paper. I recognize that it just "feels right." These examples of intuition may take years of painting and familiarity with biological forms to do convincingly. Louis Pasteur got it right when he said, "Chance favors the prepared mind."

I can also be very analytical. While working on a drawing, I may use a high-powered magnifier to help me meticulously paint tiny bristles on a beetle's leg. But isn't the analytical—knowing where and when to use it—informed by the intuitive? For me, the analytical and the intuitive are partners.

MS: Do you purposely seek subjects for your work?

SS: Not with the *Daily Observations* series. When my path crosses with, say, a salamander, then it's a salamander painting that day. This series is simultaneous with the other art projects I do—it keeps me grounded with actual living things.

MS: You show your work in a wide variety of settings, from galleries and museums to science centers. What do you most want to communicate?

SS: Art humanizes science. It suggests nature is not just something "out there" or in the realm of laboratories, but part of our own story. I'm humbled when my work hangs next to the armature of a dinosaur or a display of beetles in a natural history museum. Evolution is, in the end, the greatest artist of all.

Recently I painted a blue finch on what looks like a torn piece of paper floating in a suggestive landscape. I'd like viewers to ask questions, such as, "Is this image about our partial understanding of the natural world? About the fragmentation of nature? Our own fragmentation? Is it a memory? A personal dream?" But a viewer said, "Oh, I love the blue of that bird against the white!" So you see, the first communication begins as a purely visual experience. The conceptual sneaks in there after the eye is seduced.

MS: Do you have any advice for my students?

SS: Find your own voice. Ask yourself, "What sight makes me want to make an image? Soldiers on a battlefield? Graffiti? The patterned wing of a moth?" The answer should help point you in a personal direction. Probe what it is that attracts you, visually and conceptually. As artists, we must embrace a life that is fully engaged, connected to the experience of being alive. I think of a life in art as analogous to evolution: it winds around, mutates, some creations live, others fail, and along the way surprising and even marvelous things are made.

Suzanne Stryk, *Genomes and Daily Observations Series*, 2005. Mixed media on paper, 10 × 14 in. (25.4 × 35.6 cm).

Principles of Two-Dimensional Design

Imagine yourself practicing jump shots on a deserted basketball court. By focusing all of your attention on the basket, you can master the sequence of moves needed to score. Now imagine yourself playing in a high-paced game. You are surrounded by skillful and cooperative teammates. The skills you practiced alone become heightened as you take passes and make shots. The complexities increase and the stakes rise when 10 players fill the court.

Developing a rich, complex composition can be equally exhilarating. We can define **composition** as the combination of multiple parts into a unified whole. In a well-composed design, point, line, shape, texture, value, and color work together, as a team. As one element becomes dominant, the other elements must adjust. This creates a dialogue between positive and negative shapes, and multiple visual forces increase vitality rather than create confusion.

We begin this chapter with a discussion of unity and variety, the basis on which all design is built. We then define and discuss balance, scale, proportion, rhythm, and emphasis. Connections between concept and composition will be emphasized throughout.

UNITY AND VARIETY

Unity can be defined as similarity, oneness, togetherness, or cohesion. **Variety** can be defined as difference. Unity and variety are the cornerstones of composition. In the right combination, unity and variety can create compositions that are both cohesive and lively.

Mark Riedy used three major strategies to unify figure 3.1A. These strategies are diagrammed in figure 3.1B. First, all the major shapes are organized diagonally, from the lower left to the upper right. A series of parallel lines in the sand and sea emphasizes this diagonal structure. The cast shadows add another diagonal pattern, running from the upper left to the lower right. Second, the top third of the painting is filled with the blue water, while the beach fills the bottom two-thirds. This proportional relationship has been used since antiquity to create a dynamic form of balance. Third, one shape repeats 19 times, creating the graceful collection of umbrellas. Repetition in any form tends to increase unity.

A sailboat, nine groups of bathers, and especially the single red umbrella add variety. The red umbrella breaks the pattern set by the 18 white umbrellas. The resulting focal point attracts our attention to a particular spot on the beach. As we begin to notice the number of people clustered around this

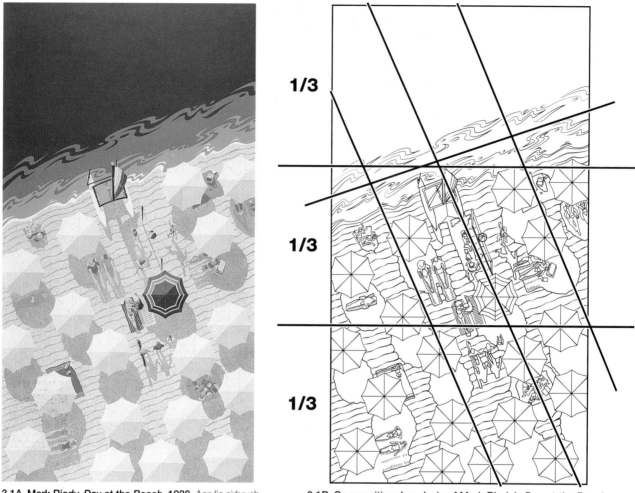

3.1A Mark Riedy, *Day at the Beach*, 1988. Acrylic airbrush.

3.1B Compositional analysis of Mark Riedy's *Day at the Beach*.

umbrella, we are pulled into the painting and the miniature world it represents. One small red circle dramatically changes our visual and emotional response to the entire painting.

We face a new compositional challenge with each design we make. There are no simple formulas: each idea has its own expressive requirements. For example, in figure 3.2, Vija Celmins used a highly unified drawing to create a quiet, contemplative image. The size and shape of the waves are the only variations. At the other extreme, Hannah Höch's *Cut with a Kitchen Knife* (3.3) is crowded with conflicting images and fragmentary words. Political figures (from the deposed Emperor Wilhelm II to philosopher Karl Marx) appear along with physicist Albert Einstein and artist Käthe Kollwitz. There are repeated references to Dada, an art movement that rejected reason and conventional rules. Created shortly after the end of World War I, this collage reflects the tumultuous economic and

3.2 Vija Celmins, *Untitled (Ocean)*, 1969. Graphite on acrylic ground on paper, 14 × 18 in. (35.6 × 45.7 cm).

3.3 **Hannah Höch,** *Cut with a Kitchen Knife,* **1919.** Collage, 44⅞ × 35½ in. (114 × 90 cm).

political conditions in postwar Germany. Celmins used a repetitive pattern of waves to suggest the ocean's hypnotic power, while Höch used a collection of conflicting images to suggest chaos. Using very different approaches, each artist created an appropriate composition for the concept she wished to convey.

Excessive unity can be monotonous, and excessive variety can be chaotic. In the following section, we explore ways to create an effective partnership between the two.

Unifying Forces

Artists and designers use many strategies to create unified compositions. **Gestalt psychology** offers a fascinating analysis of these strategies. According to this theory, we understand visual information holistically before we examine it separately. We first scan the entire puzzle, then analyze the specific parts. An image composed of units that are unrelated in size, style, orientation, and color appears chaotic and unresolved. The implications of Gestalt are complex, and there are many books on this subject. In this brief introduction, we focus on six essential aspects.

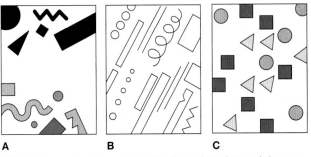

A   **B**   **C**

3.4A–C Examples of grouping by location, orientation, and shape.

Grouping

When presented with a collection of separate visual units, we immediately try to create order and make connections. **Grouping** is one of the first steps in this process. We generally group visual units by location, orientation, shape, and color. For example, the units in figure 3.4A form two distinct groups despite their dissimilarity in shape. Orientation creates group cohesion in figure 3.4B. The diagonal placement of the various elements creates unity despite the variations in shape. Figure 3.4C shows grouping by shape. We mentally organize this set of units as circles, squares, and triangles in spite of their similarity in size and value.

Rama and Lakshmana Bound by Arrow-Snakes (3.5) demonstrates the compositional and conceptual power of grouping. Multiple groups of humans and animals fill the long, horizontal rectangle. Next, we may notice that the composition is divided into three sections, each dominated by a distinctive background color. Blue and gray dominate the section on the left; red and orange dominate the section on the right. A yellow background fills the center. Within these major groups, we can discern further subdivisions, including the two clusters of monkeys on the left, the four compositional boxes on the right, and the throng of horsemen in the center.

Like a graphic novel, this painting tells a complex story of prophecy, magical transformation, imprisonment, and escape. It begins in the rose-colored box on the right, as Indrajit devises a defense against Rama and Lakshmana, who are about to attack the palace. On the left, Indrajit's arrows turn into writhing snakes, binding the attackers. Indrajit's triumphal march dominates

3.5 Sahibdin and workshop, *Rama and Lakshmana Bound by Arrow-Snakes,* from the *Ramayana,* Mewar, c. 1650–52. Opaque watercolor on paper, 9 × 15⅛ in. (22.86 × 38.42 cm).

the center of the composition. By grouping the various events, the artist was able to present complex visual information effectively.

Containment

As we can see from figure 3.5, groups are most easily created when visual units are placed inside a container. **Containment** is a unifying force created by the outer edge of a composition or by a boundary within a composition. A container encourages us to seek connections among visual units and adds definition to the negative space around each positive shape. The random collection of shapes in figure 3.6A becomes more unified when we add a simple boundary (3.6B). Any shift in the location of this boundary creates a new set of relationships. A vertical rectangle tends to create a rising or sinking effect, while a horizontal format can create an expansive effect (3.6C). The circular container in figure 3.6D draws our attention both to the center and to the outer edges of the composition.

Larry Moore's illustration in figure 3.7 uses containment in an especially inventive way. He

uses three containers in this composition. The edge of the drawing provides the first container, the curtains provide the second, and the face itself provides the third. A variety of corporate

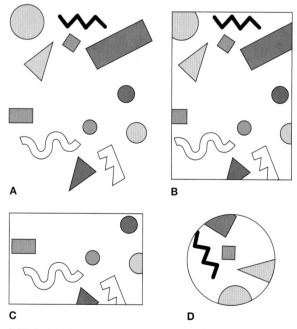

3.6A–D A container of any kind helps unify disparate visual units.

3.7 Larry Moore, *Tattoo Face Man*. Pastel on paper, 10 × 15 in. (25.4 × 38.1 cm).

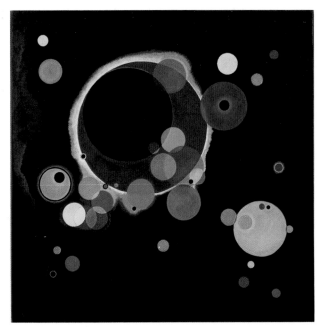

3.8 Wassily Kandinsky, *Several Circles*, 1926. Oil on canvas, 55¼ × 55 ⅜ in. (140.3 × 140.7 cm).

3.9 Aaron Macsai, *Panels of Movement*, 2002. Bracelet, 18K gold, sterling, copper, ⅞ × 7 in. (2 × 18 cm).

logos cover the face. Logos must attract the viewer's attention, regardless of the context in which they are placed, and each of these logos was originally designed as a distinct visual unit. In this composition, however, the individualistic logos become a cooperative team. The connections created by the three levels of containment are stronger than the separations created by the individualistic logos.

Repetition

Repetition occurs when we use the same visual element or effect over and over. Wassily Kandinsky's *Several Circles* (3.8) is unified by shape. The repeated circles create a cohesive design despite the wide range of colors. Repeated textures unify

many works, including the Villon portrait on page 10, the Dürer engraving on page 22, and the Moran landscape on page 31.

In his work *Panels of Movement* (3.9), Aaron Macsai uses similar lines, shapes, textures, and colors in each of the 10 bracelet panels. A spiral shape, an undulating line, a sphere, and at least one triangular shape appear in each of the panels. Despite their variations in size, texture, and location, these repeated shapes create a strong connection from panel to panel.

Proximity

In design, the distance between visual elements is called **proximity**. Figure 3.10A shows how close proximity helps increase unity. More distant shapes read as separate events (3.10B). **Fusion** occurs when shapes or volumes are placed so close together that they share common edges. When shapes of similar color and texture fuse, they can create new negative shapes as the surrounding area becomes more clearly defined (3.10C).

Careful use of proximity can create visual tension, adding energy to the design. A detail from Michelangelo's *Creation of Adam* (3.11) demonstrates the expressive power of visual tension. Jehovah's hand, on the right, nearly touches Adam's hand, on the left. As we gaze at the ceiling of the Sistine Chapel, less than 6 inches of space separates the two. In this cosmology, all of human history begins when the spark of life jumps this gap. If the hands had been placed too far apart or too close together, the spark that animates both the man and the painting would have been lost.

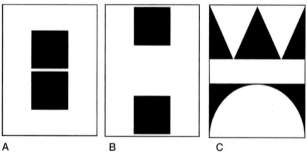

A   B   C

3.10A–C Variations in proximity.

3.11 Michelangelo, *Creation of Adam* (detail), c. 1510. Fresco. Sistine Chapel, Rome.

3.12 Frank Stella, *Lac Laronge IV*, 1969. Acrylic polymer on canvas, 9 ft ⅛ in. × 13 ft 6 in. (2.75 × 3.11 m).

Continuity

Continuity may be defined as a fluid connection among compositional parts. This connection can be actual or implied. With actual continuity, each shape touches an adjoining shape. With implied continuity, we mentally make the connections.

Skillful use of continuity can add visual movement to a design. **Movement** creates deliberate visual pathways and helps direct the viewer's attention to areas of particular interest. In Frank Stella's *Lac Laronge IV* (3.12), curving lines and shapes flow from one circle to the next, creating actual continuity. Color distribution creates implied continuity, which enhances this visual flow. The upward curve of blue in the upper-left corner is echoed by a quarter turn of blue in the lower-right corner. The violet curve on the left side is echoed by a quarter turn of scarlet in the upper-right corner. The hints of olive and brown add a further spin to the wheel.

Movement can play an equally important role in a representational design. In *Raft of the Medusa* (3.13A), Théodore Géricault used a pattern of diagonal lines (3.13B) to direct our attention to a single **focal point**. The arms and legs of the sailors, the floorboards of the raft, and even the angle of the sail all lead us toward the rescue ship in the upper-right corner. This dramatic use of movement greatly increases the emotional power of this historical painting. One hundred forty-nine survivors from a sinking ship began a desperate journey on the raft. When rescued two weeks later, only 15 had survived. The pattern of bodies and extended arms pulls us irresistibly toward the sailor at the front of the raft, whose very life depends on the attention he can attract.

3.13A Théodore Géricault, *Raft of the Medusa*, 1818–19. Oil on canvas, 16 ft 1 in. × 23 ft 6 in. (4.9 × 7.2 m).

3.13B Diagram of *Raft of the Medusa*, showing eye movement toward focal point.

Closure

Closure refers to the mind's inclination to connect fragmentary information to produce a completed form. In figure 3.14, Devorah Sperber has connected thousands of spools of thread to form blocks of color. Using closure, we then read these blocks of color as the face of painter Jan Van Eyck.

Closure makes it possible to communicate using implication. Freed of the necessity to provide every detail, the artist or designer can convey an idea through suggestion, rather than description. When the viewer completes the image in his or her mind, it is often more memorable than an image that leaves no room for participation.

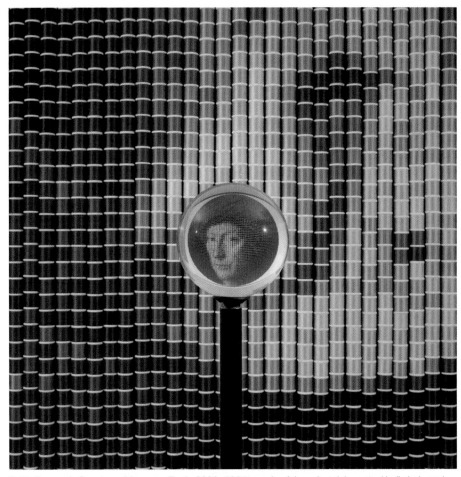

3.14 Devorah Sperber, *After van Eyck*, 2006. 5024 spools of thread, stainless steel ball chain and hanging apparatus, clear acrylic sphere on metal stand, 120 ×100 in. (305 × 254 cm).

Combining Gestalt Principles

Artists and designers often combine all the principles of Gestalt in a single composition. In figure 3.15, closure makes it possible for us to turn hundreds of dots into a face and 15 letters in different fonts into words. The repeated dots in the face and the larger yellow and pink dots in the bottom section help unify the design. Both the pink face at the top and the black-and-white face in the lower left corner lean to the left, increasing unity through orientation. Tightly contained within the rectangular format, the variety of visual components creates an exuberant yet cohesive composition.

3.15 Morla Design, Mexican Museum Twentieth Anniversary poster, 1997.

3.17 Illustrated page from *The Canterbury Tales*, 1896. William Morris, designer; Edward Burne-Jones, illustrator.

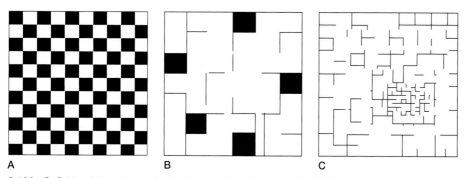

A   B   C

3.16A–C Grid variations. A simple checkerboard is a highly unified grid. Any variation on the basic structure increases variety, adding interest.

Patterns and Grids

A **pattern** is created when any visual element is systematically repeated over an extended area. Many patterns are based on a module, or basic visual unit. A **grid** is created through a series of intersecting lines. We can fill in a simple grid with black and white squares, creating a checkerboard (3.16A). Gaps in this simple grid create a more complex composition (3.16B–C), and variations in grid density can add even more variety. Both patterns and grids increase compositional unity by creating containment, suggesting continuity, strengthening proximity, and encouraging closure.

Artists and designers often use patterns to decorate walls, books, or fabrics. In his page from *The Canterbury Tales* (3.17), designer William Morris used complex floral patterns to create multiple borders and backgrounds. The borders are filled with curving floral patterns. The flowing text at the top of the page echoes these curving shapes and creates an additional pattern.

3.18 Dorothy LeBoeuf, Anna Williams inspired quilt, 2011. Cotton fabric and batting, 40 × 40 in. (101.6 × 101.6 cm).

Multiple fragments of visual information can also be unified through pattern. Dorothy LeBeouf constructed the quilt in figure 3.18 from hundreds of fragments of cloth. She used solids, plaids, and patterns in a wide range of colors. The results could have been chaotic. However, by organizing all of the pieces into square, modular units, she was able to unify this seemingly random collection of fabric scraps into a vibrant composition.

Compositional grids are most commonly created using vertical and horizontal lines. Their unifying power is so great that even the most disparate information gains cohesion when a grid is used.

key questions

UNITY AND VARIETY

- What strategies have you used to unify your composition?

- What gives your composition variety?

- Is the balance between unity and variety appropriate for the ideas you want to express?

- What would happen if you constructed your composition using a pattern or a grid?

- What happens when some areas in a pattern are disrupted?

- What happens when some areas in a grid compress while others expand?

BALANCE

In design, **balance** refers to the distribution of weight or force within a composition. Negative and positive shapes can work together to create an equilibrium among compositional units, regardless of variations in their size, weight, or shape.

Weight and Gravity

We can define **visual weight** in two ways. First, *weight* refers to the inclination of shapes to float or sink. Second, *weight* can refer to the relative importance of a visual element within a design.

The compositional forces that most influence visual weight are the size and type of shape, its texture or value, its location within the compositional frame, and its orientation.

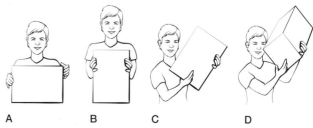

3.19A–D Which box is the most static? Which is the most dynamic?

As noted in figure 1.33A–D (on page 16), a shape tends to gain stability when it is placed in the center of a composition, while it tends to become more dynamic when it goes off the edge.

The orientation of the composition as a whole also affects weight and balance. Try this simple experiment. Which is the most dynamic and which is the most stable position of the box in figure 3.19A–D? Most viewers find positions A and B the

3.20 Berenice Abbott, *Exchange Place, New York,* **1934.** Photograph.

3.21 Kathryn Frund, *Radical Acts,* **2008.** Mixed mediums with found objects and paper mounted on aluminum, 48 × 48 in. (121.9 × 121.9 cm).

most stable. The box is at rest, with its vertical and horizontal edges reconfirming the stability we experience in daily life. By contrast, positions C and D place the box in an unstable, or dynamic position. It is halfway between standing and falling. Likewise, a composition that is dominated by diagonals tends to be visually dynamic, while a composition that is dominated by horizontals tends to be stable.

The overall compositional format also affects balance. Using dramatic vertical shapes within a tall vertical format, Berenice Abbott captures the soaring energy of Wall Street in figure 3.20. The compositional dynamics change dramatically when a square format is used. In *Radical Acts* (3.21), Kathryn Frund combined the stability of a square with the dynamism of the diagonal lines that dissect the painting from upper left to lower right. Integrating flat painting and actual objects, she presents us with a puzzle. Why construct an image using actual journal pages, a plumb-bob weight, a tiny ladder, and large, dramatic blocks of color? Frund challenges viewers to reconcile these seemingly contradictory visual forces to create a wide range of possible meanings.

Visual weight can also refer to the relative importance of a visual element within a design. In *Moonrise, Hernandez, New Mexico* (3.22), Ansel Adams combined balance, gravity, and movement to create an image that is both tranquil and dramatic. A squarish format dominated by horizontal lines provides stability. The quiet village sinks to the bottom of the design. The tiny moon, positioned just to the left of the compositional center, pulls us into the velvety black sky at the top half of the image. As the focal point for the image, the tiny moon has the most visual weight in this photograph.

Symmetrical Balance

Symmetrical balance occurs when shapes are mirrored on either side of an axis, as in a composition that is vertically divided down the center (3.23A).

3.22 Ansel Adams, *Moonrise, Hernandez, New Mexico*, **1941.** Silver print, 18½ × 23 in. (47 × 58.4 cm).

A shift in this axis (3.23B) creates symmetry between the top and bottom of the design.

A symmetrically balanced design can appeal to our desire for equilibrium and communicate calm

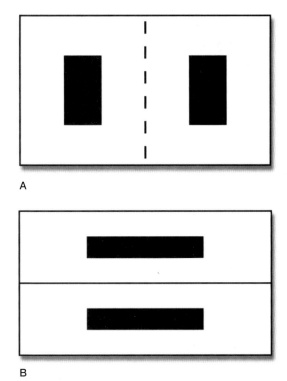

A

B

3.23A–B Examples of symmetrical balance.

3.24 Taj Mahal, Agra, India, 1630–48.

and stability. The Taj Mahal (3.24) was built by a seventeenth-century Indian emperor as a tomb for his beloved wife. The three white marble domes and the four flanking towers create architectural symmetry. In the reflecting pool, a mirror image appears, making it even more symmetrical. The building is both graceful and serene.

Approximate symmetry is created when similar imagery appears on either side of a central axis. For example, in Richard Estes's *Miami Rug Company* (3.25), actual and reflected light poles divide the space as decisively as a gate. Radiating from the center of the composition, a network of diagonal lines pulls us into the painting. At the same time, the large pane of glass on the left side pushes toward us, shimmering with darkened reflections of the buildings on the right side. The overall effect is unnerving. The seemingly symmetrical shapes are actually quite different, and the resulting image is disorienting rather than serene.

3.25 Richard Estes, *Miami Rug Company,* 1974. Oil on canvas, 40 × 54 in. (101.6 × 137.16 cm).

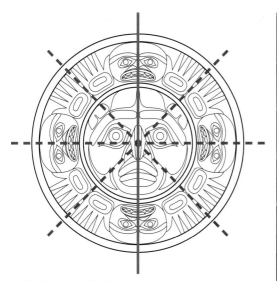

3.26 Diagram of Bella Coola mask. The central face is symmetrically balanced. The outer ring is an example of radial symmetry.

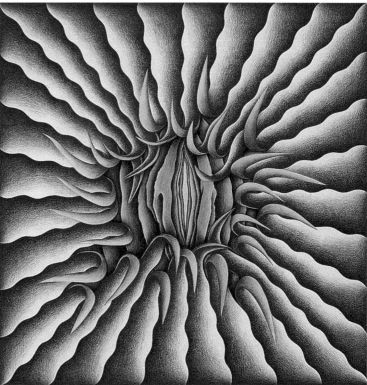

3.27 Judy Chicago, *Rejection Quintet: Female Rejection Drawing*, **1974.** Prismacolor and graphite on rag board, 39⅝ × 29⅝ in. (101 × 75 cm).

3.28 Workshop of Peter Paul Rubens, *Tiger Hunt*, **c. 1616.** Oil on canvas, 38⅞ × 49¼ in. (98.8 × 125 cm).

Radial Symmetry

With **radial symmetry**, lines and shapes are mirrored both vertically and horizontally, with the center of the composition acting as a focal point. For example, the center of the Bella Coola mask in figure 3.26 is symmetrically balanced. By contrast, the surrounding ring of faces and hands creates radial balance. Judy Chicago's *Rejection Quintet: Female Rejection Drawing* (3.27) is even more radial. Because the format is divided diagonally as well as vertically and horizontally, the entire design radiates from the center. Glowing and gradated colors accentuate the effect.

An alternative to radial balance is a spiral. A spiral can increase energy within a circular format or add movement to a rectangular composition. In Peter Paul Rubens's *Tiger Hunt* (3.28), a spiral pulls the tiger and the hunters together in the center of the painting. It then spins outward, breaking apart near the edges. The resulting composition harnesses the compressive power of centripetal force and the expansive power of centrifugal force.

Asymmetrical Balance

Asymmetrical balance creates equilibrium among visual elements that do *not* mirror each other on either side of an axis. Depending on the degree of asymmetry, the resulting design may be quite stable, very dynamic, or nearly chaotic.

We can use many strategies to create asymmetrical balance:

- We can place a large shape close to the fulcrum, while placing a small shape farther away. Just as a child at the end of a seesaw can balance an adult near the center, so large and small shapes can be balanced in a design (3.29A).

- We can use several small shapes to balance a larger shape (3.29B).

- A small, solid square can balance a large, open circle. The solidity and stability of the square give it additional weight (3.29C).

- We can balance a textured shape near the fulcrum with a lighter open shape that we place farther away (3.29D).

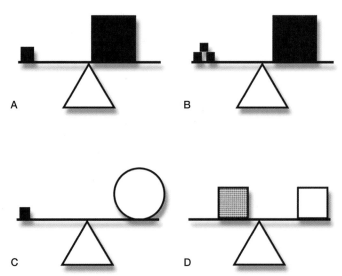

3.29A–D Creating asymmetrical balance.

Asymmetrical balance becomes even more interesting when we add a boundary. Because the negative space is as important as each positive shape, we can now create more complex compositions:

- A small shape placed near the bottom of the format balances a large shape placed along the top. Especially within a tall rectangle, shapes placed near the top tend to rise, and shapes placed near the bottom tend to sink (3.30A).

- When the small square intersects the bottom edge and the large square moves away from the edge, the differences in weight become even more pronounced (3.30B).

- The top shape now gains energy through its diagonal orientation. We need three bottom shapes to create balance (3.30C).

- Finally, a small, aggressive triangle can balance a large, passive rectangle (3.30D).

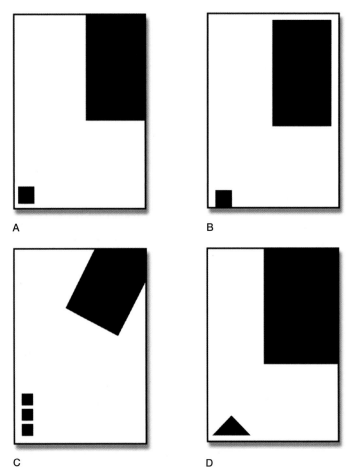

3.30A–D Examples of asymmetrical balance.

Balance in a composition shifts each time we add or subtract a visual element. Richard Diebenkorn's *Ocean Park 54* (3.31) is primarily constructed from vertical and diagonal lines and shapes. A bright yellow band accentuates the top edge, and vertical lines accentuate the left and right edges. Subtle diagonal lines appear in the upper-right

3.31 Richard Diebenkorn, *Ocean Park 54*, 1972. Oil on canvas, 100 × 81 in. (254 × 205.74 cm).

3.32 Interaction/Motion: A poster for the 2006 "Exposed" lecture series sponsored by the Graphic Design Department, The University of the Arts, Philadelphia. Concept and Design: Hans-Ulrich Allemann, Principal. Allemann Almquist & Jones, Design/Strategic Communications, Philadelphia. Digital image.

corner, and a blue square pulls our eyes to the upper-right corner.

In figure 3.32, designer Hans-Ulrich Allemann balanced multiple layers of text within a vertical rectangle. Returning to our earlier discussion of Gestalt, let's deconstruct this image step by step. A light-blue shape fills the top half of the image, then dissolves into the white shape at the bottom. A horizontal block of text is positioned slightly below the center, while along the right edge a vertical block of text pulls our eyes upward. The word *action* is enclosed by a fine line. Five lines of red text connect the horizontal and vertical axes, with three near the bottom and two running parallel to the right edge. The tiny red logo positioned nearby creates a visual exclamation point.

3.33 Frida Kahlo, *Las Dos Fridas*, 1939. Oil on canvas, 69⅛ × 69⅛ in. (176 × 176 cm).

3.34 Eric Fischl, *Barbeque,* **1982.** Oil on canvas. 5 ft 5 in. × 8 ft 4 in. (165 × 254 cm).

Expressive Uses of Balance

Each type of balance has its advantages. The approximate symmetry that Frida Kahlo used for her double self-portrait (3.33) is symbolically appropriate and compositionally effective. Painted in response to her divorce from painter Diego Rivera, it presents the beloved Frida in a native costume on the right and the rejected Frida in European dress on the left. A linear vein connects the women's hearts. In figure 3.27 (page 77), Judy Chicago used radial symmetry to pull the viewer into the composition. And in figure 3.1A (see page 66), Mark Riedy used asymmetrical balance to animate his beach scene and accentuate the red umbrella.

And, in some cases a degree of **imbalance** is necessary. Eric Fischl used distortion to create imbalance in *Barbeque* (3.34). The table in the foreground is tilted, and the bowl of fish seems impossibly large. Pulled by the diagonal lines leading to the house, the pool also seems skewed, while the tiny women are more like dolls than people. Manning the grill, the father looks on approvingly as his son engages in a little recreational fire-breathing. Spatial distortion combined with a bizarre collection of objects and events turns a family picnic into a suburban nightmare.

▶ **key questions**

BALANCE

- Which is the "heaviest" shape in your design? Does its weight match its importance?

- How does the outer shape of your design affect its compositional balance?

- In your composition, how does negative space affect overall balance?

- We described various forms of balance in this section. Which is most effective for the ideas and emotions you want to express?

PROPORTION AND SCALE

Proportion and scale create two types of size relationships. Both strongly affect compositional balance and emotional impact. **Proportion** refers to the relative size of visual elements *within* an image or within a figure. When we compare the width of the head with its height or divide a composition into thirds, we are establishing a proportional relationship (3.35). Similarly, in *The Hobbit* and *The Lord of the Rings* movies, the warrior elf Legolas is tall and lean, and the warrior dwarf Gimli is short and stout. **Scale** commonly refers to the size of a form when compared with our own human size. Thus, a 50-foot-long painting is a large-scale artwork, while a 10-square-inch square painting is an example of small scale.

Most designs distribute information fairly evenly within the format, with only modest size variation among the parts. Exaggerating these proportions can be eye-catching, because the image immediately stands out from the norm. In *Save Our City*, by Michael Bierut (3.36), a heavy black rectangle at the top presses down on the white shape below, covering the top part of the word *Save*. Meanwhile, the small vertical lines of white text suggest a city skyline and help pull the white section of the poster upward. Finally, a rectangle of tiny red text appears in the lower-left corner. This tension between the upper and lower sections of the design perfectly matches the urgency of the message.

Likewise, expressive possibilities expand when scale is exaggerated. The New Museum in New York City regularly uses the tall, vertical side of the building as a screening area for a site-specific commissioned series of projected

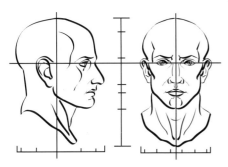

3.35 Proportion is an essential part of figure drawing.

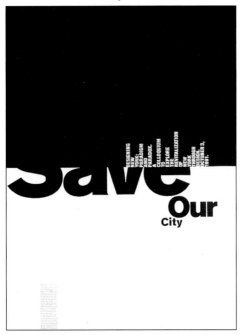

3.36 Michael Bierut, Pentagram Design. *Save Our City* poster, 1991.

3.37 New Museum and Nuit Blanche New York presented a series of site-specific projections for Festival of Ideas, 2011. Photograph of video projection featuring work by Daniel Arsham.

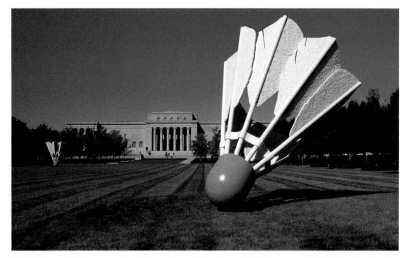

3.38 Claes Oldenburg and Coosje van Bruggen, *Shuttlecocks*, **1994.** South facade of the Nelson-Atkins Museum of Art and the Kansas City Sculpture Park. Aluminum, fiberglass-reinforced plastic, and paint. 230⁹⁄₁₆ × 191⅞ in. (585.63 × 487.36 cm).

3.39 Ken Stout, *Intermission*, **1994.** Oil on canvas, 9 × 50 ft (2.74 × 15.24 m).

artworks. In figure 3.37, an enormous man appears to be climbing up the wall, creating both a humorous and eye-catching display. Claes Oldenburg and Coosje van Bruggen have also used scale extensively in their artwork. Nearly 18 feet long, their four *Shuttlecocks* (3.38) add a whimsical note to the formidable exterior of the Nelson-Atkins Museum of Art.

The scale of the artwork itself also expands the expressive possibilities. Ken Stout's *Intermission* (3.39) is 50 feet long. As a result, we can sequentially view various aspects of the painting as we walk past. We visually enter the theater through the pink doorway at the far left. Cool blue light bathes the restless audience. Two men in the balcony add to the action, as one aims a peashooter and another launches a paper airplane. On the stage, a tiny actor creates a transition between the audience and the stage crew. The painting ends in a final burst of red, at the far right side. Taking advantage of each square inch, Stout created a swirling panorama of figures engaged in a variety of theatrical activities, on and offstage.

▶ **key questions**

PROPORTION AND SCALE

- Which is the largest shape in your design? Which is the smallest? Do their sizes match their significance?

- How can you make a small shape the most powerful compositional component?

- Can extremes in scale or proportion increase visual impact in your design?

RHYTHM

Rhythm is a sense of movement that is created by repetition of multiple units in a deliberate pattern. Visual rhythm is similar to musical rhythm. In music, rhythm is created through the organization of sound in time. We can combine meter (the basic pattern of sound and silence), accents (which emphasize specific notes), and tempo (the speed at which the music is played) to create a dazzling array of compositional possibilities.

As with music, the rhythm in a visual composition can take many forms. In *Drift No. 2* (3.40), Bridget Riley repeated a simple line to create an undulating rhythm similar to the waves on water. Vibrant words create a spatial rhythm in figure 3.41. Warm and cool colors in various values and intensities cause some words to advance while others recede.

Niklaus Troxler used a looser and more layered approach to rhythm in his poster for the Willisau Jazz Festival (3.42). Breaking every rule of good design, he combined multiple fonts in various sizes. Seemingly random punctuation marks complicate matters further. Like a sophisticated jazz piece, the entire composition balances on the verge of chaos. It is held together by an underlying rhythm of dots, circles, and straight lines.

Visual rhythm can be as regular as a waltz or as syncopated as jazz. Multiplication, fragmentation, and superimposition propel the nude descending

3.40 Bridget Riley, *Drift No. 2*, **1966.** Acrylic on canvas, 7 ft 7½ in. × 7 ft 5½ in. (2.32 × 2.27 m).

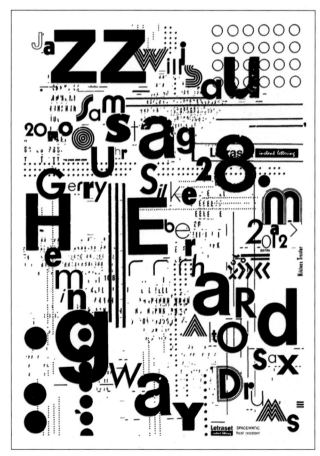

3.42 Niklaus Troxler, Willisau Jazz Festival poster, 1992.

3.41 A repeated word becomes a rhythmic design through color choices.

Marcel Duchamp's staircase (3.43). The jerking rhythm demonstrates the alternating stability and instability of human locomotion, rather than physical grace. When walking, we continually fall forward, then catch ourselves as we take the next step.

3.43 Marcel Duchamp, *Nude Descending a Staircase, No. 2,* **1912.** Oil on canvas, 58 × 35 in. (147.3 × 88.9 cm).

> ## key questions
>
> ### RHYTHM
>
> - What visual elements repeat in your design?
>
> - Through deliberate use of repetition, can they create a more powerful and unified design?
>
> - Is a consistent rhythm best for your idea, or do you need more variety?

EMPHASIS

Each player in a basketball game has a particular role to play. The guards primarily focus on defense, the forwards on offense. The point guard plays a dominant role, calling plays and controlling the action. Likewise, the various visual elements in a composition must work together as a team. In most cases, a few carefully selected visual elements dominate, or stand out, while others play a supporting role.

Emphasis gives prominence to part of a design. As noted in Chapter One, a focal point can be used to create emphasis. Both emphasis and focal point attract attention and increase visual and conceptual impact.

Emphasis by Isolation

Any **anomaly**, or break from the norm, tends to stand out. Because we seek to connect the verbal and visual information that we are given, a mismatched word or an isolated shape immediately attracts our attention. In figure 3.44, Pentagram emphasized the word *design* through its separation from the word *magazine.* By placing this anomaly at the bottom edge of the composition, they made it even more eye-catching.

Just as a pattern tends to increase connection among visual elements, so any break in the pattern emphasizes isolation. In figure 3.1A (page 66), 18 white umbrellas establish the pattern that is so beautifully broken by the single red umbrella. Do Ho Suh's *Fallen Star* (3.45) is a three-quarter sized cottage based on an actual house in Providence,

3.44 Pentagram Design, Magazine. Publisher: Art Center College of Design, Pasadena, CA.

3.45 Do Ho Suh, *Fallen Star***, 2012.** House construction materials and furniture; roughly 15 × 18 ft (4.6 × 5.5 m). Stuart Collection, University of California at San Diego.

Rhode Island. When Suh traveled to the United States to study at the Rhode Island School of Design, he felt like he had dropped from the sky into another world. If *Fallen Star* was placed on the ground in a suburban setting, it would simply read as a very small house. Tilted and precariously perched on the side of a campus building seven stories up, it creates a powerful anomaly.

Emphasis by Placement

Every square inch of a composition has a distinctive power. As a result, placement alone can increase the importance of a selected shape.

The compositional center is especially potent. In *The Power of the Center,* psychologist Rudolph Arnheim discusses **centricity** (compressive compositional force) and **eccentricity** (expansive compositional force). Both centricity and eccentricity activate *Flash Point* (3.46). The central white square pulls us into the middle of the painting, while the explosive red rectangle pushes toward the outer edge.

This effect is even more pronounced in figure 3.47. Any representation of another human attracts our attention, and faces are of particular interest. Four major lines and a series of concentric circles direct us inward, toward the man's left eye. Fragments of text extend outward, beyond the edge of the composition. Continually compressing and expanding, the seemingly simple

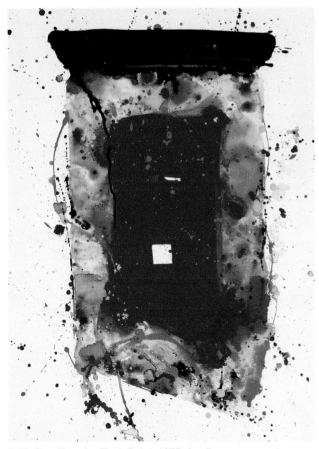

3.46 Sam Francis, *Flash Point***, 1975.** Acrylic on paper, 32¼ × 22⅞ in. (82 × 59 cm).

3.47 Jacey, *Untitled***, 1995.** Digital design.

image pulls the viewer inward while simultaneously appearing to extend outward, beyond the boundary.

Emphasis Through Contrast

Contrast is created when two or more forces operate in opposition. By reviewing the elements and principles of design discussed in this section, we can quickly create a long list of potential adversaries, including static/dynamic (3.48A), small/large (3.48B), solid/textured (3.48C), and curvilinear/rectilinear (3.48D).

When the balance is just right, we can create powerful compositions from any of these combinations. Devoting about 80 percent of the compositional space to one force and about 20 percent to the other is especially effective. The larger force sets the standard, while the smaller force creates the exception. Just as a single basketball player wearing a blue uniform will stand out if the other four players wear yellow, so a smaller force can dominate a design. Consider these examples:

- *Contrast in scale.* In figure 3.49, the small airplane and the moon become charged with meaning when combined with the image of the sleeping child. Dreams take flight.

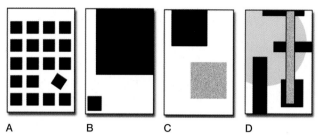

A   B   C   D

3.48A–D Examples of contrast: static/dynamic, small/large, solid/textured, curvilinear/rectilinear.

- *Contrast in shape.* Zurbarán's *Saint Serapion* (3.50) provides a brilliant example of contrast by shape as well as emphasis by separation. The small note pinned at the right edge of the canvas gains so much power that it easily balances the large figure filling the rest of the frame.

- *Contrast in color.* One of the most compelling uses of emphasis by color occurs in *Schindler's List*, a film directed by Steven Spielberg (3.51). Midway through the black-and-white film, a small girl in a red coat is shown walking toward her death. She breaks away from the line and runs back to hide under a bed in a nearby house. This is the only use of color in the main body of the film. When her red coat appears again, her body is being transported to a bonfire. This simple use of color creates one of the most emotional moments in a remarkable film.

3.49 Robert Crawford, *Jamie Sleeping,* **1988.** Acrylic on canvas, 20 × 14 in. (50.8 × 35.5 cm).

3.50 Francisco de Zurbarán, *Saint Serapion,* **1628.** Oil on canvas, 47½ × 41 in. (120.7 × 103.5 cm).

3.51 Still from *Schindler's List,* 1993, by Steven Spielberg.

> **key questions**
>
> **EMPHASIS**
>
> - What would happen conceptually if you dramatically changed the scale, shape, or color of a crucial visual unit?
>
> - Is there a dominant shape in your composition? If so, is it the shape you most *want* to emphasize?
>
> - Is there a focal point in your composition? If not, should there be?
>
> - Contrast tends to add interest. Can a shift in contrast strengthen your composition?

summary

- Using composition, we can organize multiple parts into a harmonious whole. In a well-composed design, visual elements work together as a team.

- Gestalt psychology describes six unifying strategies: grouping, containment, repetition, proximity, continuity, and closure.

- Effective design requires a dialogue between unity and variety. Too much unity can lead to boredom, while too much variety can lead to chaos.

- Any similarity between visual elements tends to increase unity; any difference between visual elements tends to increase variety.

- Symmetry, radial symmetry, and asymmetry are three common forms of balance. Visual balance creates equilibrium among compositional units, regardless of variations in their size, weight, or shape.

- Scale and proportion are two types of size relationships. Proportion refers to the size relationships within an image, while scale involves a size comparison to our physical reality.

- Emphasis is most commonly created through isolation, placement, or contrast. A focal point can strengthen emphasis.

key terms

anomaly	containment	grid	rhythm
approximate symmetry	continuity	grouping	scale
	contrast	imbalance	symmetrical balance
asymmetrical balance	eccentricity	movement	
	emphasis	pattern	unity
balance	focal point	proportion	variety
centricity	fusion	proximity	visual weight
closure	Gestalt psychology	radial symmetry	
composition		repetition	

studio projects

To apply the concepts from this chapter in the studio, check out the Projects page in the Online Learning Center at www.mhhe.com /LTI5e. The following is a sample of the chapter-related assignments in step-by-step detail.

The Parts and the Puzzle. Exploring unity and variety through line and shape.

Dualities. Integrating line, shape, texture, and color in a special kind of self-portrait.

Pushing Proportion. How proportion affects meaning.

Illusion of Space,
Illusion of Motion

The Battle of Issus, fought by Alexander the Great of Macedonia and Darius III of Persia in 333 BCE., changed human history. Control of all of Asia Minor (present-day Turkey and the Middle East) was at stake. At age 47, Darius III ruled the greatest empire of its time. At age 23, Alexander was king of the small mountainous empire north of modern-day Greece. Alexander began the battle on a rocky hillside and seemed doomed to fail. When Darius moved in for the kill, additional Macedonian troops swept in from the side, split the Persian army, and won the battle. This triumph launched Alexander's 10-year campaign to extend his empire from Greece to India, setting the stage for the subsequent Roman empire.

In his *Battle of Issus* (4.1), Albrecht Altdorfer created an apocalyptic vision, combining the dramatic landscape and swirling armies with a crescent moon (representing Darius) and a blazing sun (representing Alexander). Commissioned by the Duke of Bavaria in anticipation of his own battle against Turkish forces, the painting was a clarion call to his countrymen. The illusion of space provided the setting for the desperate battle, and the illusion of motion captured both the movement of men and the shimmering sky.

In Chapter Three, we found that each image and idea presents unique challenges. Jasper Johns' *Target with Plaster Casts* (figure 1.44, page 21) demanded a confrontational approach. Johns chose to reaffirm the flatness of the canvas surface. Altdorfer, on the other hand, needed deep space for his epic battle. How can you best meet the challenges presented by your own ideas? In this chapter, we explore ways to create the illusion of space and of motion and consider the conceptual implications of each.

4.1 Albrecht Altdorfer, *Battle of Issus*, 1529. Limewood, 47¼ × 62¼ in. (120 × 158 cm).

CREATING THE ILLUSION OF SPACE

Linear Perspective

Linear perspective is a mathematical system for projecting the apparent dimensions of a three-dimensional object onto a flat surface. This surface, called the **picture plane**, is comparable to a window overlooking a city street. By tracing the outlines of the buildings on the pane of glass, you can make a simple perspective drawing.

Developed during the Renaissance, perspective offered a methodical approach to depicting the rational reality perceived by artists in the fifteenth century. It soon gained wide acceptance as a means of systematically diminishing the size of objects as they recede in space. Raphael's *School of Athens* (figure 4.2) is an example. A broad arch in the foreground frames the compositional stage. Three additional arches diminish in size, pulling us into the painting. The diagonal lines in the buildings and floor converge at a point in the center. The viewer is invited to enter into an illusory world.

Even though many recent philosophical and aesthetic theories challenge this conception of reality, perspective remains the most pervasive Western system for suggesting three-dimensionality on the two-dimensional surface. Linear perspective is based on five basic concepts, shown in figures 4.3 and 4.4.

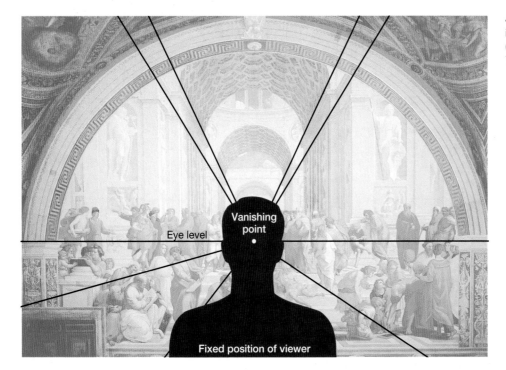

4.2 Diagram of perspective used in Raphael's *School of Athens* (for the full painting, see figure 7.4 on page 143).

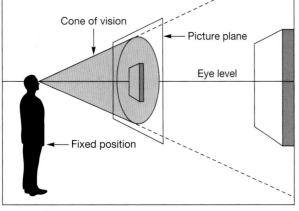

4.3 Fundamentals of linear perspective.

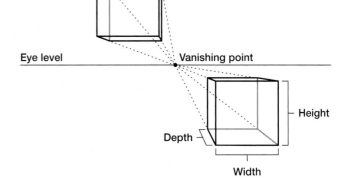

4.4 Example of one-point perspective.

1. Objects appear to diminish in size as they recede into the distance. Perspective is possible because the rate at which objects appear to diminish is regular and consistent.

2. The point at which objects disappear entirely is called a **vanishing point**. Sets of parallel lines (such as train tracks) converge at a vanishing point as they go into the distance, creating an illusion of space.

3. In basic one- and two-point perspective, all vanishing points are positioned on the **eye level**, or **horizon line**, which is level with the artist's eyes.

4. Because all proportional relationships shift with each change in position, a fixed viewing position is an essential characteristic of linear perspective.

5. Only a limited area is clearly visible from a fixed position. To accommodate a larger viewing area, you must move farther away from the object you are drawing. This expands the **cone of vision** and increases the viewing area.

We use **one-point perspective** to represent a straight frontal view of a scene (4.4). The lines representing depth are angled to converge on a single point at eye level, and the lines representing height are perpendicular to the horizon line. One-point perspective is relatively simple to master and can pull the viewer into the image with a single dramatic focal point (4.5).

Two-point perspective is effective for representing an object that is angled in space. A cube drawn in two-point perspective will not have any lines positioned parallel to the horizon line. Instead, the lines representing depth and width are angled to converge on two vanishing points (4.6). Because two-point perspective is effective in showing both the front and sides of a structure, it is often used for diagrams and architectural drawings (4.7).

4.5 Jan Vredeman de Vries, *Perspective Study*, from *Perspective*, Leiden, 1604.

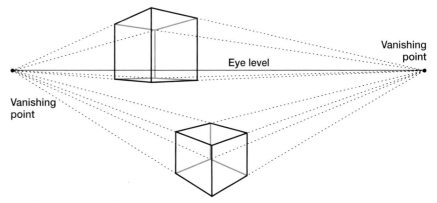

4.6 Example of two-point perspective.

4.7 Frank Lloyd Wright, Detail from Drawing for *Fallingwater*, Kaufmann House, Bear Run, Pennsylvania, 1936. 15⅝ × 27¼ in. (39 × 69 cm).

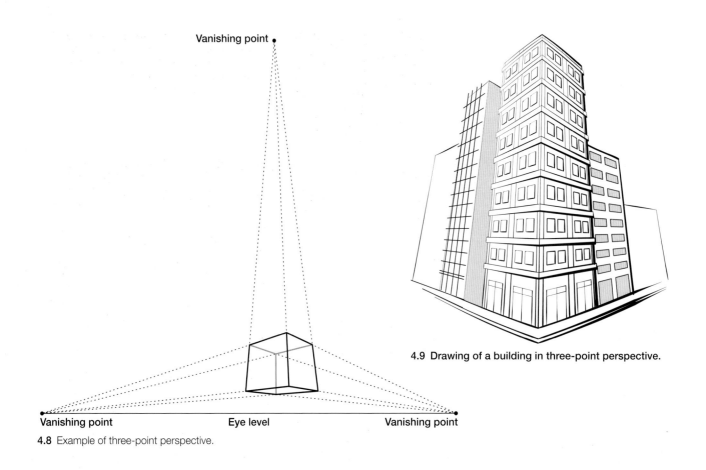

Vanishing point

Vanishing point   Eye level   Vanishing point

4.8 Example of three-point perspective.

4.9 Drawing of a building in three-point perspective.

In one- and two-point perspective, the lines representing height are perpendicular to the horizon line. In **three-point perspective** (4.8), these lines are tilted so that they converge on a third vanishing point, high *above* or *below* eye level. The lines representing depth and width converge on two points at eye level, as in two-point perspective. We can use three-point perspective to exaggerate the sense of space and to present a unique "bird's-eye" or "worm's-eye" view, as illustrated in figure 4.9.

Other Ways to Create the Illusion of Space

- *Overlap.* Overlap is the simplest way to suggest space. It is especially effective when combined with size variation. In *Deposition* (4.10), Rogier van der Weyden used overlap combined with value to create a convincing drama within a crowded compositional space.

- *Size variation.* Because the diminishing size of distant objects is a basic characteristic of

human vision, any systematic variation in size can enhance the illusion of space. This effect is demonstrated most clearly when the distance is great, as in figure 4.1.

- *Definition.* Sharply focused shapes also tend to advance, while blurred shapes tend to recede. When we look at a landscape, dust and water droplets in the air blur outlines and add a blue-gray color to distant shapes. This effect is known as **atmospheric perspective**. In *The Rocky Mountains, Lander's Peak* (4.11), Albert Bierstadt combined dramatic lighting with atmospheric perspective to increase the illusion of space.

- *Location.* Visual elements placed near the top of the page tend to recede, and shapes placed at the bottom tend to advance. In *Landscape in the Style of Dong Yuan* (4.12), the mountains at the top of the scroll appear more distant, despite their large size.

- *Color.* Dramatic contrast in hue, value, or color temperature can enhance the illusion of space.

4.11 Albert Bierstadt, *The Rocky Mountains, Lander's Peak*, 1863. Oil on canvas, 6 ft 1¼ in. × 10 ft ¾ in. (186.7 × 306.7 cm).

4.12 Wen Jia, _Landscape in the Style of Dong Yuan_, 1577. China, Ming dynasty (1368–1644). Hanging scroll; ink and light colors on paper. 65½ × 20½ in. (167.0 × 52.0 cm).

4.13 Salvador Dalí, _Christ of St. John of the Cross_, 1951. Oil on canvas, 80⅝ × 45⅝ in. (204.8 × 115.9 cm).

Using the Illusion of Space

Through the illusion of space, artists invite viewers to enter into an imaginary world. Expression can be heightened when this world is particularly intriguing or when the illusion is especially dramatic.

We call the exaggerated use of perspective **amplified perspective**. We can create amplified perspective by using an unusual viewing position, such as a bird's-eye view, exaggerated spatial convergence, or distortion.

4.14 David Hockney, *Henry Moore Much Hadham 23rd July 1982*. Composite Polaroid, 21 × 14 in. (53 × 36 cm).

In Salvador Dalí's *Christ of St. John of the Cross* (4.13), amplified perspective changes our interpretation of the crucifixion of Jesus. Dramatic three-point perspective emphasizes the importance of the note pinned at the top of the cross. As we look down, the vulnerability of Jesus emphasizes his humanity, while the hovering position of the figure suggests his divinity.

By combining multiple viewpoints, we can also create **fractured space**. In his portrait of sculptor Henry Moore (4.14), David Hockney used multiple photographs to manipulate space and suggest the passage of time. The repeated hands gesture to us as we visually converse with the old master.

Layered space can be created when the foreground, middle ground, and background are clearly defined. Director Orson Welles used layered space many times in *Citizen Kane*, a film classic. In figure 4.15, young Charlie Kane plays in the background, while his mother in the foreground signs over his care to a lawyer. His father, who opposes this action, occupies the middle ground, caught between the mother and the child. The tensions in the family, the determination of the mother, and the innocence of the child are heightened when Charlie shouts, "The Union forever!" as part of his game. When the lawyer takes charge of Charlie, the family will be split apart forever. These three compositional layers communicate complex emotions while telling a story.

4.15 Scene from *Citizen Kane*. Three layers of space divide this shot from *Citizen Kane*: the mother in the foreground, the father in the middle ground, and the child in the background.

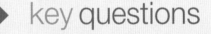

▶ key questions

CREATING THE ILLUSION OF SPACE

- Which is more appropriate for your idea: a flat design or a spatial design?
- How can you increase or decrease spatial depth in your composition?
- If you use a spatial illusion, where will you place the viewer relative to the setting you create?

SPATIAL DYNAMICS
A Compositional Setting

Like a theatrical stage, the illusion of space creates a setting for compositional action. Objects can move within this illusory world, or the setting itself can begin to shift. Both create **dynamic space**, space that embodies movement. In *Inside Running Animals/Reindeer Way*, Robert Stackhouse combined diagonal lines with definition and size variation to pull us into a mysterious tunnel (4.16). Ann Strassman's *Humphrey I* (4.17) comes charging out of the picture plane, ready to lick us or attack us. Cropping (the cutting away of part of

the image) combined with vigorous brushstrokes helps push the dog forward. Finally, Mark Messersmith activated *Vapid Visionaires* (4.18) using layer upon layer of visual information. A vertical pole compositionally dissects the painting and six scarlet flowers seem to hover over the image. We then encounter a collection of windows and framed paintings in the foreground followed by two figures clutching an alligator and a collection of tropical birds. A mysterious factory belching smoke fills the background.

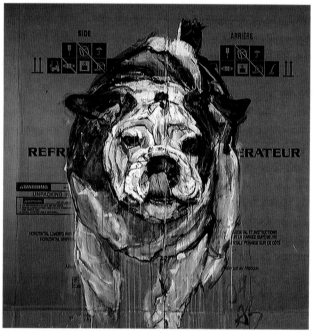

4.17 Ann Strassman, *Humphrey I*, 2004. Acrylic on cardboard, 70 × 65 in. (177.8 × 165.1 cm).

4.16 Robert Stackhouse, *Inside Running Animals/Reindeer Way*, 1977. Mixed mediums, 64 × 43¾ × 2 in. (162.6 × 111 × 5.1 cm).

▶ key questions

SPATIAL DYNAMICS

- What can the setting itself contribute to your design?

- When is a realistic setting most appropriate? When is an imaginary setting most appropriate?

4.18 Mark Messersmith, *Vapid Visionaires*, **2010.** Oil on canvas with carved wooden flowers and top pediment wood pole plus mixed media predella box across bottom, 65 × 82 in. (165.1 × 208.3 cm).

THE ILLUSION OF MOTION

Animated films are constructed from thousands of tiny frames. When run through a film projector, they create fluid movement. Animation is possible because we have the perceptual ability to integrate the sequential images into a continuous flow.

Substantial audience involvement is also required to create the illusion of motion within a static drawing or sculpture. When presented with multiple images on a single surface, we must feel the movement, complete the action, or anticipate the next event. Based on our day-to-day experience in an ever-changing world, we use our imagination to connect static images to create the illusion of motion.

The Kinesthetic Response

Kinesthetics is the science of movement. Through the very process of walking, we consistently engage in a complex balancing act as we fall forward, then catch ourselves with the next step. When we are confronted by a life-sized figure, such as the man from Robert Longo's *Men in Cities* series (4.19), the lurching movement of the model resonates on a physical level: we feel as well as see the gesture. Capturing the gesture at the right moment is critical. In Myron's *Discus Thrower* (4.20), the athlete is caught at the moment *before* the whirling vortex of energy explodes, releasing the disc. By capturing this moment rather than the moment of release, the sculptor has trapped within the marble the implied energy of the throw.

The Decisive Moment

Photographer Henri Cartier-Bresson used his understanding of impending change to formulate a theory of photography he called "the decisive moment." A pioneer in the use of the 35-mm camera, he specialized in capturing the most telling moment in time. In *Gare Saint Lazare* (4.21), Cartier-Bresson caught a man in mid-leap as he attempted to jump across a large puddle. The man is suspended just above the water, perfectly mirrored. Clearly, in the next instant, he will break the smooth surface, destroying the magical image and drenching his clothes. By capturing a particular moment in time, Cartier-Bresson created a classic photograph.

4.20 Myron, *Discus Thrower (Diskobolos)*. Roman copy after the original bronze of c. 450 BCE. Marble, height 5 ft 1 in. (1.54 m).

Before and After

The kinesthetic response and the perception of a decisive moment are based on our past experience and our ability to relate this experience to the images we see. Based on our physical experience, we can feel the awkward and unbalanced position of the Longo figure. Likewise, through our emotional experience, when we look at the Cartier-Bresson photograph, we realize that we are seeing a single moment in a more extensive story.

To create a story through a single image, many illustrators deliberately plan the moment that takes place *before* and the moment that takes place *after* an actual event. An example of this is illustrated in Chris Van Allsburg's book *The Mysteries of Harris Burdick* (4.22). Each drawing in the book is accompanied by a title and a short piece of text. Based on the clues in the title, text, and image, we can invent all sorts of stories.

4.19 Robert Longo, *Untitled*, 1980. From the *Men in Cities* series. Crayon and graphite on paper, 40½ × 28 in. (102.9 × 71.1 cm).

Fragmentation

As an object moves, it sequentially occupies various positions in space. We can use visual fragmentation to simulate this effect in art. For example, the superimposed figures in Thomas Eakins' *Double Jump* (4.23) record the multiple positions the man occupies during an athletic event. Even when figures are simply repeated, as in Edgar Degas' *Frieze of Dancers* (4.24), movement is strongly suggested.

For Eakins, Degas, Longo, and Van Allsburg, the illusion of motion expanded both the conceptual and the emotional possibilities in an image. Always searching for more effective means of visual expression, any artist or designer can gain from the use of this powerful tool.

4.22 Chris Van Allsburg, "Under the Rug" from *The Mysteries of Harris Burdick*, Houghton-Mifflin, 1984.

4.23 Thomas Eakins, *Double Jump*, **1885.** Modern print from a dry-plate negative, 4 × 5 in. (10.2 × 12.7 cm).

4.24 Edgar Degas, *Frieze of Dancers*, **c. 1895.** Oil on canvas, 27.6 × 79 in. (70 × 200.5 cm).

Multiplication

Multiplication can also play a role in visual story-telling. In this page from *Inhumans* (4.25), by Paul Jenkins and Jae Lee, a dialogue between an alien child and a human politician unfolds over five panels. Notice how "time" moves faster in the four smaller panels, and how Jenkins used a close-up when the child delivers his ultimatum. Multiplication creates a very different effect in George Tooker's *Government Bureau* (4.26). Repeated images of the central male figure combined with endless bureaucratic faces create a scene from a nightmare. No matter where the man goes in this hall of mirrors, he always returns to the beginning.

4.25 Paul Jenkins and Jae Lee, from *Inhumans:* "First Contact." Volume 2, Issue 5, March 1999. Comic book.
© 2010 Marvel Characters, Inc.

4.26 George Tooker, *Government Bureau*, 1956. Egg tempera on gesso panel, 19⅝ × 29⅝ in. (50 × 75 cm).

key questions

ILLUSION OF MOTION

- Will the illusion of motion enhance the idea you want to express? If so, how can you create this illusion?

- To what extent is the illusion of motion affected by the illusion of space?

- What happens when you use static (unmoving) and dynamic (moving) shapes together in a design?

summary

- You can create the illusion of space using linear perspective, overlap, size variation, location, definition, atmospheric perspective, and use of color.
- Linear perspective is based on five fundamental concepts, listed on page 90.
- Three common types of linear perspective are one-point, two-point, and three-point perspective.

- Overlap, size variation, definition, location, and color can also create the illusion of space.
- You can create the illusion of motion by selecting the most decisive moment in an event, through fragmentation, or through various types of multiplication.

key terms

amplified
  perspective
atmospheric
  perspective
cone of vision

dynamic space
eye level
  (horizon line)
fractured space
kinesthetics

layered space
linear perspective
one-point
  perspective
picture plane

three-point
  perspective
two-point
  perspective
vanishing point

studio projects

To apply the concepts from this chapter in the studio, check out the Projects page in the Online Learning Center at www.mhhe.com /LTI5e. The following is a sample of the chapter-related assignments in step-by-step detail.

Architectural Abstraction. An introduction to perspective.

Homage to Hockney. An exploration of space and movement.

Strata. Increasing complexity through layers of space.

Roger Shimomura, *Stereotypes and Admonitions* **Series, 2003.** Acrylic on canvas, 20 × 24 in. (50.8 × 61 cm).

Concepts and Critical Thinking

In *A Kick in the Seat of the Pants*, Roger Von Oech identifies four distinct roles in the creative process.

First, the *explorer* learns as much as possible about the problem. Research is crucial. Ignorance may result in a compositional or conceptual cliché.

Second, the *artist* experiments with a variety of solutions, using all sorts of combinations, proportions, and materials. By creating 10 answers to each question, the artist can select the best solution rather than accepting the only solution.

Third, the *judge* assesses the work in progress and determines what revisions are required. Innovative ideas are never fully developed when first presented; most need extensive revision and expansion. Rather than discard an underdeveloped idea, the judge identifies its potential and determines ways to increase its strength.

Finally, the *warrior* implements the idea. When obstacles appear, the warrior assesses the situation, determines the best course of action, and then moves ahead decisively.

We explore each of these roles in the next four chapters. Chapter Five deals with concept development and visual problem solving. Strategies for cultivating creativity and improving time management are discussed in Chapter Six. Chapter Seven is devoted to critical thinking and provides specific ways to improve any design. In Chapter Eight, we expand our discussion of visual communication and consider ways to create more meaningful artworks.

Problem Seeking and Problem Solving

You can increase the visual power of your work by mastering the basic elements and principles of design described in Parts One and Three. Composition, however, is only part of the puzzle. With the increasing emphasis on visual communication, ideas have become increasingly complex. In contemporary art and design, conceptual invention is just as important as compositional strength.

So, to help expand your creativity, we will now explore ways to better define and solve a variety of problems.

PROBLEM SEEKING

The Design Process

In its most basic form, we can distill the design process to four basic steps. When beginning a project, the designer asks:

1. What do we want?
2. What existing designs are similar to the design we want?
3. What are the differences between the existing designs and our new design?
4. How can we combine the best ideas from past inventions with our new ideas?

By studying the classic Eames chair, we can see this process clearly. Charles and Ray Eames were two of the most innovative and influential postwar era designers. Trained as an architect, Charles was a master of engineering. He continually combined "big picture" thinking with attention to detail. Trained as a painter, Ray contributed a love of visual structure, a sense of adventure, and an understanding of marketing. Combining their strengths, this husband-and-wife team designed furniture, toys, exhibitions, and architecture and directed more than 80 experimental films.

Their first breakthrough in furniture design came in 1940, when they entered a chair competition that the Museum of Modern Art in New York City sponsored. Many architects had designed furniture, and the Eameses were eager to explore this field.

Many similar products existed. The most common was the overstuffed chair, which continues to dominate American living rooms. Extensive padding on a boxy framework supported the sitter. Another popular design was the Adirondack chair, constructed from a series of flat wooden planes. Of greatest interest, however, were designs by architects such as Marcel Breuer (5.1) and Alvar Aalto (5.2). Using modern materials such as plywood and steel, Breuer and Aalto had begun to re-define chair design.

By comparing existing chairs with the chair that they wanted, Charles and Ray could identify qualities to retain, discard, or change. The familiar overstuffed chair (5.3) was bulky and awkward, but it was comfortable. The Adirondack chair (5.4) was easy to mass-produce, but too large for interior use. The modern chairs were elegant and inventive, but they were expensive to produce and often uncomfortable. The Eameses wanted to create a modern chair that was comfortable, elegant, and inexpensive.

During World War II, the Eames team had designed and manufactured molded plywood splints, which doctors in the U.S. Navy used. After extensive research and experimentation, they had mastered the process of steaming and reshaping the plywood sheets into complex curves. The resulting splints supported sailors' broken legs without using the precious aluminum and steel needed in the war effort.

So, to develop their competition entry, they combined their knowledge of splints, love of modern chairs, understanding of anatomy, and mastery of architecture. After their plywood chair won the

first prize, they created a more refined model (5.5) that combined plywood with aluminum.

A series of Eames designs followed, including numerous cast plastic versions. Variations on these stackable chairs are still being used in many schools. To create the plastic chairs, the Eames team invented a new manufacturing process. This led to a breakthrough in the field of furniture design.

By addressing a need, researching existing designs, making comparisons, and combining the best characteristics of existing chairs, the Eames team produced a new kind of chair and thus firmly established themselves as leaders in the design field.

The Fine Art Process

As this example demonstrates, the design process begins when a client requests help or the designer identifies a societal need. With the Eames chair, the museum competition provided the impetus for an experiment that reshaped an industry.

By contrast, contemporary sculptors, filmmakers, painters, and other fine artists generally invent their own aesthetic problems. Ideas often arise from personal experience. Combining self-awareness with empathy for others, many artists have transformed a specific event into a universal statement. For example, Pablo Picasso's *Guernica*,

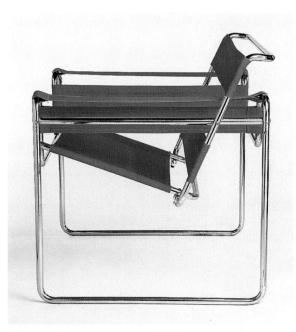

5.1 Marcel Breuer, *Armchair*, 1925. Tubular steel, canvas, 28¹¹⁄₁₆ × 30⁵⁄₁₆ × 26¾ in. (72.8 × 77 × 68 cm).

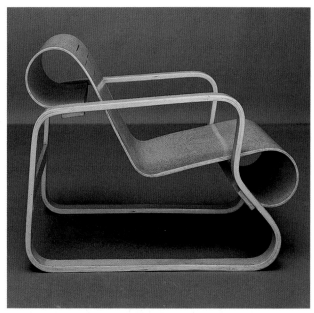

5.2 Alvar Aalto, *Paimio Lounge Chair*, 1931–33. Laminated birch, molded plywood, lacquered, 26 × 23¾ × 34⅞ in. (66 × 60.5 × 88.5 cm).

5.3 Overstuffed chair.

5.4 Adirondack chair.

painted in response to the 1937 bombing of a Spanish village, is now seen as a universal statement about the horrors of war. Working more independently than designers and with fewer deadlines, artists can more easily explore ideas and issues of personal interest.

Sources of Ideas

Regardless of the initial motivation for their work, both artists and designers constantly scan their surroundings in a relentless search for images and ideas. As the interviews that appear throughout this book demonstrate, the most improbable object or idea may provide inspiration. Biological systems and architecture inspire sculptor Kendall Buster. Images from art history inspire painter Carrie Ann Baade. Jim Elniski and Frances Whitehead combined a commitment to their urban community with a fascination with solar and geothermal energy to create their "greenhouse." If you are at a loss for an idea, take a fresh look at your surroundings. Here are three strategies.

Transform a Common Object

Architect Frank Gehry based the exuberant armchair in figure 5.6 on the wood-strip bushel basket that farmers use (5.7). If you consider all the ideas that you can generate from a set of car keys, a pair of scissors, or a compass, you will have more than enough to start a project.

5.5 Charles and Ray Eames, *Side Chair, Model DCM***, 1946.**
Molded ash plywood, steel rod, and rubber shockmounts, 28¾ × 19½ × 20 in. (73 × 49.5 × 50.8 cm).

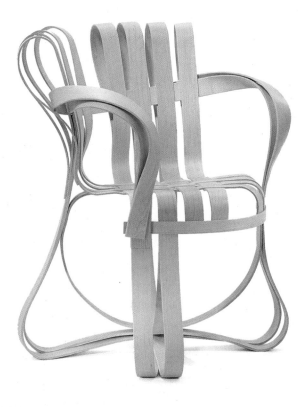

5.6 Frank Gehry, *Cross Check Armchair***, 1992.** Maple, 33⅝ × 28½ × 28½ in. (85.3 × 72.4 × 72.4 cm).

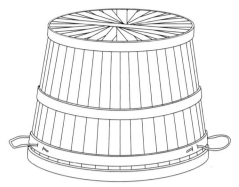

5.7 Wood-strip bushel basket.

5.8 Ray Rogers, *Vessel*, New Zealand, 1984. Large, pit-fired (porous and nonfunctional) with "fungoid" decorative treatment in relief. Diameter approximately 21⅔ in. (55 cm).

Study Nature

Many natural forms, including mushrooms, stones, and aquatic life, have inspired ceramicist Ray Rogers. His spherical pots (5.8) often suggest the colors, textures, and economy of nature. In figure 5.9, Vera Lisková used the fluidity and transparency of glass to create a humorous version of a prosaic porcupine. Through an inventive use of materials, both artists have reinterpreted nature.

Visit a Museum

Artists and designers frequently visit all kinds of museums. Carefully observed, any culture's history and physical objects can be both instructive and inspirational. Looking at non-Western artwork is especially valuable. Unfamiliar concepts and compositions can stimulate creativity. Richard Hunt's Sisiutl mask (5.10) in one example. In Native American mythology, *Sisiutl* is a giant three-headed sea serpent whose glance can turn an adversary into stone. A benevolent and powerful presence, his image is often carved into the cross beams of clan houses. When he transforms himself into an invincible war canoe, or into a magic belt, Sisiutl becomes a powerful ally. By understanding the story and studying this mask, you can more readily design a mask based on your own experiences.

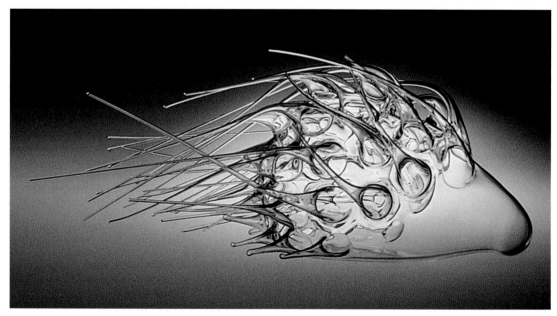

5.9 Vera Lisková, *Porcupine*, 1972–80. Flame-worked glass, 4¼ × 11 in. (10.8 × 28.2 cm).

5.10 Dr. Richard Hunt, *Raven and Sisiutl Transformation Mask,* 1988. Red cedar wood, cloth and string, paint black, red, green, approximately 16 in. wide × 14 in. tall × 20 in. long.

Historical examples such as Albrecht Dürer's *The Knight, Death and the Devil* (5.11) can be equally inspiring. Two hundred years before this print was made, the Black Plague killed nearly half the population of Europe. This horrific disease remained a threat in Dürer's time. As a result, Renaissance conceptions of life and death were very different from our contemporary viewpoint. This difference can spark a new way of thinking and lead you to a fresh idea.

Characteristics of a Good Problem

Regardless of its source, the problem at hand must fully engage either the artist or the designer. Whether somebody commissions it or you invent it, a good problem generally includes the following characteristics.

5.11 Albrecht Dürer, Detail of *The Knight, Death and the Devil,* 1513. Engraving, 11 × 14 in. (28 × 36 cm).

Significant

Identifying and prioritizing your major goals can help you determine a task's significance. Is it truly essential, or just a distant dream?

Socially Responsible

With the human population exceeding 7 billion, it is unwise to pursue a project that squanders natural resources. What materials will you need, and how will you dispose of resulting waste? Today, artists and designers often consider each project's environmental and economic implications.

Comprehensible

It is impossible to solve a problem that you don't fully understand. Ask questions if the assignment specifications and objectives are unclear to you.

Open to Experimentation

It is important to distinguish between clear definition and restrictive limitations. Consider the following two assignment descriptions:

1. Organize at least 20 photocopies in such a way that they convey an idea or emotion.
2. Organize 20 photographs by American Civil War photographer Mathew Brady to tell a story about the life of Abraham Lincoln.

In the first case, the project requirements are clearly stated, but the solution remains open. The second case describes the *solution* as well as the *problem*.

For the professional artist or designer, there are no "bad" problems, only bad solutions. However, when limited to a narrow range of possible solutions, even the most inventive person will become frustrated. If you find yourself in a straitjacket, rethink the problem and try a new approach.

Authentic

Regardless of the source, every person approaches each problem on his or her own terms. Each of us has a unique perspective, and the connections we make will vary. As a student, you will learn more when you really embrace each assignment and make it your own. Ask questions so that you can understand each project's conceptual implications. When you reframe the *question* in your own terms, the creative possibilities will expand and your imagination will soar.

CONVERGENT AND DIVERGENT THINKING

Now, let's work our way through an actual assignment, using two problem-solving strategies.

> *Problem:* Organize up to 20 photocopies from historical sources so that they tell a story. Use any size and type of format. You can enlarge, reduce, crop, or repeat any image.

Using Convergent Thinking

Convergent thinking involves the pursuit of a predetermined goal, usually in a linear progression and through a highly focused problem-solving technique. The word *prose* can help you remember the basic steps:

1. Define the *problem*.
2. Do *research*.
3. Determine your *objective*.
4. Devise a *strategy*.
5. *Execute* the strategy.
6. *Evaluate* the results.

In convergent thinking, the end determines the means. You know what you are seeking before you begin. For this reason, clear definition of the problem is essential: the most brilliant idea is useless if it doesn't solve the problem.

Convergent thinking is familiar to most of us in the scientific method, which follows the same basic procedure. It is orderly, logical, and empirical. There are clear boundaries and specific guidelines. Clearly focused on the final result, convergent thinking is a good way to achieve a goal and meet a deadline. Let's analyze each step.

Define the Problem

Determine all of the assignment's physical and technical requirements and ask whether there are any stylistic limitations. Be sure that you understand the preliminary steps as well as the final due date.

Next, assess your strengths and weaknesses relative to the assigned problem, and determine your best work strategy. Let's consider the approaches of two hypothetical students, Jeremy (as a convergent thinker) and Angela (as a divergent thinker).

Using a dictionary, Jeremy begins by analyzing the words *story* and *images*. He finds that a *story* is shorter than a novel, that it may be true or fictitious, that it requires a series of connected events, and that it may take many forms, including a memoir, a play, or a newspaper article. Next, he determines that an *image* is a representation of a person or thing, a visual impression that a reflection in a mirror produces, or a mental picture. This means that photographs from books, magazines, and the Internet are all fair game. Jeremy realizes that he can even include a mirror in the project, to reflect the viewer's own image.

He spends the first hour of class on brainstorming, and then decides to develop a story about Irish immigration to America in the 1890s.

Do Research

Creativity is highly dependent on seeking connections and making new combinations. The more information that you have, the more connections you can make. For this assignment, Jeremy reads extensively, then develops a plausible story based on immigrant diaries. He begins to collect images of ships, cities, and people.

Determine Your Objective

Jeremy now has the necessary raw material to solve the problem. However, many questions remain unanswered, including the following:

- What happens in this story? Is it fiction or nonfiction?

- Who is the storyteller? A 12-year-old boy will tell a very different story than will a 20-year-old woman.

- What is the best format to use? A dozen letters that fictitious brothers in Dublin and Boston sent to one another? A Website describing actual families? A photo album?

At this point, Jeremy pauses to rethink his strategy. What does he really want to communicate? He considers:

- *Does it solve the problem?* He reviews the assignment parameters.

- *Is the solution conceptually inventive?* Is it really intriguing, or is it something that we have all seen before, a cliché?

- *Is the planned solution visually compelling?*

- *Can he complete this solution by the due date?* To meet the due date, it may be necessary to distill a complex problem down to an essential statement. In this case, Jeremy decides to simplify his project by focusing on one main character.

Devise a Strategy

Although Jeremy can complete some assignments in an afternoon, three-dimensional projects and multiple-image works tend to take longer. Jeremy determines the supplies that he needs and considers the best time and place to work on the project.

Execute the Strategy

Now, Jeremy just digs in and works. He works best with great concentration and determination at this point, rather than second-guessing himself.

Evaluate the Results

At the end of each work session, Jeremy considers the strengths and weaknesses of the work in progress. What areas in each composition seem cluttered or confusing? How can he strengthen those areas? He finally presents the project for a class critique.

Convergent Thinking Applications

Convergent thinking is most effective when

- You can clearly define the problem.
- You can solve the problem rationally.
- You must solve the problem sequentially.
- You must meet firm deadlines.

Because many problems in science and industry fit these criteria, scientists, businesspeople, and graphic designers favor convergent thinking.

Using Divergent Thinking

The advantages of convergent thinking are clarity, control, focus, and a strong sense of direction. For many tasks, convergent thinking is ideal. In some cases, however, convergent thinking can offer *too* much clarity and not enough chaos. Inspiration is elusive. Over-the-edge creativity is often messy and rarely occurs in an orderly progression. If you want to find something completely new, you will have to leave the beaten path.

In **divergent thinking**, the means determines the end. The process is more open-ended. Specific results are hard to predict. Divergent thinking is a great way to generate completely new ideas.

Two major differences exist between convergent and divergent thinking. First, in divergent thinking, we define the problem much more broadly. Research is more expansive and less tightly focused. Second, because the convergent thinker discards weak ideas in the thumbnail stage, the final image is more preplanned and predictable. The divergent thinker, on the other hand, generates many variables, is less methodical, and may have to produce multiple drafts of a composition to obtain a polished result.

Whereas convergent thinking is usually more efficient, divergent thinking is often more inventive. It opens up unfamiliar lines of inquiry and can lead to a creative breakthrough. Divergent thinking is a high-risk/high-gain approach. By breaking traditional rules, the artist can explore unexpected connections and create new possibilities.

Let's try the same assignment again, now using Angela's divergent thinking.

> *Problem:* Organize up to 20 photocopies from historical sources so that they tell a story. Use any size and type of format. You can enlarge, reduce, crop, or repeat any image.

Realizing that the strength of the source images is critical, Angela immediately heads for the library section devoted to photography. By leafing through a dozen books, she finds 40 great photographs, ranging from images of train stations to trapeze artists. She scans the photographs, and then enlarges or reduces pictures to provide more options. Laying them out on a table or on a large computer screen, she begins to move the images around, considering various stories that they might generate. Angela soon discards twenty of the images. They are unrelated to the circus story that she decides to develop. She then finds ten more images to flesh out her idea.

At this point, her process becomes similar to the final steps that we described in the preceding section. Like Jeremy, she must clarify her objective, develop characters, decide on a format, and construct the final piece. However, because she started with such a disparate collection of images, her final story is more likely to be nonlinear. Like a dream, her images may *evoke* feelings rather than *describe* specific events.

Divergent Thinking Applications

Divergent thinking is most effective when

- The problem definition is elusive or evolving.
- A rational solution is not required.
- A methodical approach is unnecessary.
- Deadlines are flexible.

Which is better—convergent or divergent thinking? A good problem-solving strategy is one that works. If five people are working on a Website design, a clear sense of direction, agreement on style, an understanding of individual responsibilities, and adherence to deadlines are essential. On the other hand, when an artist is working independently, the open-ended divergent approach can lead to a major breakthrough. Combining convergent and divergent thinking is ideal. When you need to expand an idea through open-ended exploration, use divergent thinking. When you need focus or distillation, shift to convergent thinking.

BRAINSTORMING

Brainstorming plays an important role in both convergent and divergent thinking. It is a great way to expand ideas, see connections, and explore implications. Following are four common strategies.

Make a List

Suppose that the assignment involves visualizing an emotion. Start by listing every emotion that you can, regardless of your interest in any specific area. Getting into the practice of opening up and actively exploring possibilities is crucial—just pour out ideas!

> **joy   sorrow   anger   passion   jealousy   sympathy   horror   exaltation**

From the list of emotions, circle one that looks promising. To move from the intangible name of the emotion to a visual solution, develop a list of the *kinds*, *causes*, and *effects* of the emotion. Following is one example, using *anger* as a starting point.

KINDS	CAUSES	EFFECTS
annoyance	wrong number phone call at 5 A.M.	slammed down phone
smoldering rage	friend gets award you want	argument with friend
desperate anger	fired from job	shouted at your child
anger at self	poor performance on test	major studying

By investigating specific kinds of anger and determining the causes and the effects, you now have many specific images that you can develop.

Use a Thesaurus

Another way to explore an idea's potential is to use a thesaurus. Be sure to access a thesaurus that lists words conceptually rather than alphabetically. Use the index in the back to look up the specific word that you need. For example, *The Concise*

Roget's International Thesaurus has a section titled "Feelings," including everything from *acrimony* to *zeal*. Here is a listing of synonyms from the section on resentment and anger: *anger, wrath, ire, indignation, heat, more heat than light, dudgeon, fit of anger, tantrum, outburst, explosion, storm, scene, passion, fury, burn, vehemence, violence, vent one's anger, seethe, simmer,* and *sizzle!* Thinking about a wide range of implications and connections to other emotions can give you a new approach to a familiar word.

Explore Connections

By drawing a conceptual diagram, you can create your own thesaurus. Start with a central word. Then, branch out in all directions, pursuing connections and word associations as widely as possible. In a sense, this approach lets you visualize your thinking, as the branches show the patterns and connections that occurred as you explored the idea (5.12).

In *Structure of the Visual Book,* Keith Smith demonstrates the value of verbal connections. Smith seeks immersion in his subject. He wants to know it so well that he can pursue his images intuitively, with all the power and grace of a

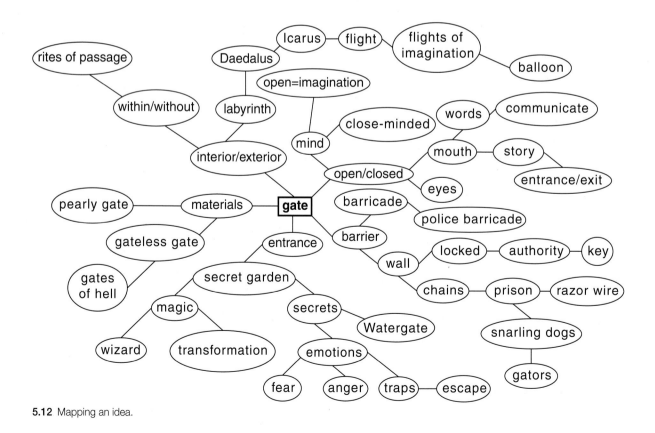

5.12 Mapping an idea.

skilled cyclist. Try to follow the steps in figure 5.13, as he explores the word *bicycle.* Using a single object, he explores movement, friendship, and geometry.

Keep a Journal

Keeping a journal or a sketchbook is an ideal way to record your ideas and create connections. In it, you can

- Classify, arrange, and record information

- Develop new ideas

- Examine your current beliefs and analyze the beliefs of others

- Record your responses to critiques

- Make connections among your various classes

Recording your ideas at the end of each class and reviewing them at the beginning of the next can help you construct your own learning process.

Anything that expands your thinking is fair game, including

- Plans for projects, such as thumbnail sketches and rough drafts

- Comments on how you can improve your work

- Notes from textbook readings and clippings from magazines

- Notes on visiting artists or gallery visits

- Technical notes or information on class materials

- Questions that you want to pose in the next class meeting

Your record keeping can take many forms, including

- Drawings and diagrams

- Written ideas, descriptions, and lists

- Poetry and song lyrics

If I am going to make drawings or photographs which include a bicycle, I might go for a bike ride, but more importantly I would fantasize about a bike. I would picture a bike in my mind. The most obvious depiction is the side view because this is the significant profile. I would then imagine a standing bicycle with no rider, looking from above, directly down on the bike, or from behind or in front of the standing bike with my eye-level midway between the ground and the handlebars. In these three positions the bicycle is seen from the least significant profile. It is a thin vertical line with horizontal protrusions of the pedals, seat and handlebars. The area viewed is so minimal that the bicycle almost disappears.

Before long in examining a bike I would become involved with circles. Looking at the tires, I think about the suspension of the rim and the tire, indeed, the entire vehicle and rider, by the thin spokes. It amazes me that everything is floating in space, connected only by thin lines. I imagine riding the bike through puddles and the trace of the linear journey from the congruent and diverging water marks left by the tread on the pavement. I might think about two friends together and separated. Symbolism.

I think about cycles of being with friends and apart. And again I would think literally of cycles, circles and tires.

I would think of the full moon as a circle and how in its cycle it turns into a line. I would see the tires from the significant profile and in my mind I would turn it in space and it would become an ellipse.

If I turned it further, until it was on an axis 90 degrees from the significant profile, it would no longer be a circle or an ellipse, but it would be a line. So again, line comes into my thoughts.

A circle is a line.

A circle is a straight line.[1]

5.13 Keith Smith. Brainstorming.

Periodically ask yourself the following questions:

- What was the most compelling image that I saw today? What made it compelling?
- What similarities and differences were there among my studio classes this week?
- What connections were there between my lecture classes and my studio classes?
- What do I need to know to push my ideas further?

Viewing the journal as a record of your creative process is liberating. A random idea today can help you solve a specific problem tomorrow. It is wise to review the journal as you move into upper-level classes. Many ideas that were too ambitious for a first-year class are perfectly suited to further development later on.

Collaborative Creativity

Designers generally use group brainstorming. This helps them explore a wider range of possibilities and better meet client needs. In *The Art of Innovation*, IDEO general manager Tom Kelley lists seven characteristics of effective group brainstorming. The following list is based on a chapter titled "The Perfect Brainstorm."

1. Sharpen your focus. A good brainstormer will generate a lot of ideas. When these ideas all address the same problem, many viable solutions result. On the other hand, when participants don't understand the problem, chaos can result.

2. Use playful rules, such as "write it down" and "think bigger." A visual and verbal record of your ideas is helpful. Premature criticism is not.

3. Number your ideas. Numbers ("Let's aim for 50 ideas in the next hour") can create quantitative targets and provide a record of the order in which ideas occurred.

4. Build and jump. As the momentum builds, more and more ideas burst forth. A thoughtful question can then help the group leap to the next level, rather than getting stuck on a plateau.

5. The space remembers. Fill your brainstorming space with 22 × 30-inch Post-it notes covered with ideas that the group has developed. By *seeing* the information, you can more easily spot bridges and build connections.

6. Warm up. If you are working with a completely new group, it may be necessary to provide an icebreaker to build trust. This is especially true if the participants are unfamiliar with brainstorming. I often ask each participant to present one succinct question or to draw a quick cartoon of the problem as they see it. It may be an enraged elephant, a tangle of thorns, or a whirling chain saw. Both the questions and the cartoons can reveal participant insights without demanding too much too soon.

7. Get physical. A wide range of simple materials opens up possibilities, especially if you are brainstorming a three-dimensional design problem. Cardboard, plasticine, and canvas all behave very differently. Playing with various materials can lead to a wider range of possibilities.

VISUAL RESEARCH

Thumbnail Sketches

Now let's practice turning ideas into images.

Return to the original list of emotions that you developed in the brainstorming exercise. Circle the most promising words or phrases and look for connections between them. Start working on thumbnail sketches, about 1.5 × 2 inches in size (5.14). Be sure to draw a clear boundary for the sketches. The edge of the frame is like an electric fence. By using the edge wisely, you can generate considerable power!

5.14 Examples of thumbnail sketches.

As with the verbal brainstorming, move fast and stay loose at this point. It is better to generate 10 to 20 possibilities than to refine any single idea. You may find yourself producing very different solutions, or you may make a series of multiple solutions to the same idea. Either approach is fine—just keep moving!

Model Making

When working two-dimensionally, it is often necessary to make one or more full-sized rough drafts to see how the design looks when enlarged. Refinements that you make at this stage can mean the difference between an adequate solution and an inspired solution.

Prototypes, models, and maquettes serve a similar purpose when you are working three-dimensionally. A **maquette** is a well-developed three-dimensional sketch. Figure 5.15A shows Peter Forbes's maquette for *Shelter/Surveillance*

Sculpture. In this chipboard "sketch," Forbes determined the sculpture's size relative to the viewer and developed a construction strategy. As a result, when he constructed the final, 11-foot-tall sculpture (5.15B), Forbes was able to proceed with confidence. A **model** is a technical experiment. A **prototype** can be quite refined, such as the fully functional test cars that automobile companies develop. In addition to the aesthetic benefit of these preliminary studies, we often need them to help solve technical problems. Is the cardboard that you are using heavy enough to stand vertically, or does it bow? Is your adhesive strong enough? If there are moving parts, is the action fluid and easy, or does the mechanism constantly get stuck?

By completing these preliminary studies, you can refine the idea, strengthen the composition, and improve the final piece. As with a well-rehearsed performance, the work that you bring to the critique now is ready for discussion.

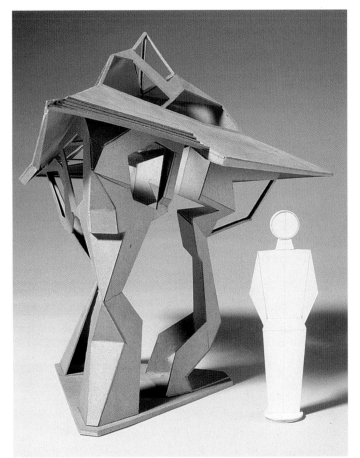

5.15A Peter Forbes, *Model for Shelter/Surveillance Sculpture*, 1994.
Mixed mediums, 10½ × 9½ × 9 in. (27 × 24 × 23 cm).

5.15B Peter Forbes, *Shelter/Surveillance Sculpture*, 1994.
Mixed mediums, 11 ft 2 in. × 10 ft 4 in. × 10 ft (3.4 × 3.2 × 3 m).

AN OPEN MIND

The very best artists and designers are often accomplished in more than one field. For example, Michelangelo was acclaimed as a painter, sculptor, and poet, and Leonardo da Vinci was a master of art, biology, and engineering. The study of philosophy has had a major impact on videographer Bill Viola and on installation artist Robert Irwin. Jim Elniski and Frances Whitehead researched energy systems, roof gardens, and architecture to create a unique artwork—which is also their home (5.16). Whenever the base of knowledge expands, the range of potential connections increases. When the islands of knowledge are widely scattered, as with inter-disciplinary work, we can create transformative connections.

The message is clear: the more you know, the more you can say. Read a book. Attend a lecture. Take a course in astronomy, archaeology, psychology, or poetry. Use ideas from academic courses to expand your studio work. Art and design require conceptual development as well as perceptual and technical skill. By engaging your heart, your eye, your hand, and your mind, you can fully use your emotional, perceptual, technical, and conceptual resources to create your very best work.

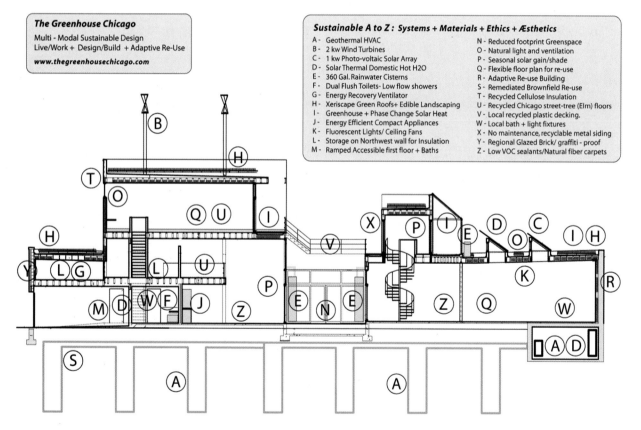

The Greenhouse Chicago
Multi - Modal Sustainable Design
Live/Work + Design/Build + Adaptive Re-Use
www.thegreenhousechicago.com

Sustainable A to Z : Systems + Materials + Ethics + Æsthetics

A - Geothermal HVAC
B - 2 kw Wind Turbines
C - 1 kw Photo-voltaic Solar Array
D - Solar Thermal Domestic Hot H2O
E - 360 Gal. Rainwater Cisterns
F - Dual Flush Toilets- Low flow showers
G - Energy Recovery Ventilator
H - Xeriscape Green Roofs+ Edible Landscaping
I - Greenhouse + Phase Change Solar Heat
J - Energy Efficient Compact Appliances
K - Fluorescent Lights/ Ceiling Fans
L - Storage on Northwest wall for Insulation
M - Ramped Accessible first floor + Baths

N - Reduced footprint Greenspace
O - Natural light and ventilation
P - Seasonal solar gain/shade
Q - Flexible floor plan for re-use
R - Adaptive Re-use Building
S - Remediated Brownfield Re-use
T - Recycled Cellulose Insulation
U - Recycled Chicago street-tree (Elm) floors
V - Local recycled plastic decking.
W - Local bath + light fixtures
X - No maintenance, recyclable metal siding
Y - Regional Glazed Brick/ graffiti - proof
Z - Low VOC sealants/Natural fiber carpets

5.16 Frances Whitehead, *The A to Z*, 2007. Diagram of multimodal sustainable features.

summary

- Concept and composition are equally important aspects of art and design.

- Designers usually solve problems that their clients present. Artists usually invent aesthetic problems for themselves.

- Ideas come from many sources, including common objects, nature, mythology, and history.

- Good problems are significant, socially responsible, comprehensible, and authentic. They provide basic parameters without inhibiting exploration.

- Convergent thinking is highly linear. The word *prose* can help you remember the steps.

- Divergent thinking is nonlinear and more open-ended than convergent thinking. It is less predictable and may lead to a creative breakthrough.

- You can expand or enrich any idea using brainstorming. Making lists, using a thesaurus, making a conceptual diagram, and creating connections are all common strategies.

- Visual and verbal research can provide the background information that you need to create a truly inventive solution.

- The best artists and designers have a wide range of interests and approach new challenges with an open mind.

key terms

brainstorming
convergent thinking

divergent thinking
maquette

model
prototype

studio projects

To apply the concepts from this chapter in the studio, check out the Projects page in the Online Learning Center at www.mhhe.com /LTI5e. The following is a sample of the chapter-related assignments in step-by-step detail.

Poster Design. Discovering the importance of research to creating an effective ad.

Limited/Unlimited. Using the limitations of a design problem as a springboard to solutions.

Superhero Mask/Headgear Design. Exploring a variety of strategies for developing a three-dimensional design.

Profile:
Steve Quinn, Designer
Problem-Solving Through Design

Steve Quinn is a highly versatile designer. His business, Quinn Design, develops Websites, branding, and advertising for a wide range of public organizations and private companies, such as Kimberly Clark, Milwaukee Ballet, and the City of Chicago. As a professor at Northern Illinois University, he developed a clear description of a seven-step problem-solving process that can be applied to all types of design. We will first explore this process. We will then see how it applies to an actual Website design.

MS: Let's start with your seven-step process.

SQ: Sure. This process can be used for large and small projects and can frame up our entire discussion.

Step One: Develop a Problem Statement. Clients arrive with problems they want designers to solve. However, they may underestimate or misread the real problem and thus completely miss the mark. For example, simply redesigning a logo will not improve sales if a poor product is the real problem. So, I begin my work by asking a lot of questions and listening carefully. As an advocate for the customer as well as the client, I must view the problem from multiple perspectives.

Step Two: Define Objectives. It is impossible to hit a target I can't see. By defining our objectives, both the client and I can agree on the targets we must hit. This stage further clarifies our overall intention and creates a strong bridge between the problem statement and problem solution.

Step Three: Set Parameters. Every design problem is developed within various restrictions, or parameters. What is the budget? If I am designing a brochure, how large can it be and how many colors can I use? When working on a video advertisement, what is the maximum duration? What is the deadline? Without clear parameters, we could waste a lot of time and money on infeasible proposals. I continue to advocate for both the client and the user at this stage. We want the best possible solution, delivered on time, within defined parameters.

Step Four: Research. Research provides us with deeper understanding of potential solutions and of potential obstacles we must overcome. Reviewing existing solutions to similar problems is especially valuable. By looking at solutions offered by other designers, we can get a sense of the range of possibilities. Of course, the client and I both seek a distinctive approach. When we know what already exists, we can deliberately push our solution a bit further. On large, complex projects, research may also include customer surveys, reading up on specific subjects related to the project, and simply tracking customer response to a Website or use of a product.

Step Five: Solution Development. We can focus on the solution once we have defined the problem, clarified the objectives, and conducted the research. Based on knowledge I gain in the first four steps of this process, I think through or sketch out many ideas before I begin to finalize anything.

Step Six: Evaluation and Feedback. When we have a range of potential solutions sketched out, we can evaluate each one. Does each solution meet the objectives—and solve the problem—while still working within the set parameters? Which ones meet the criteria most fully and provide the most distinctive visual solutions? When working on a Website, I often test-drive it with actual clients to identify problem areas and increase ease of navigation.

Step Seven: Execution. The project is finalized at this point. Just as a weak design can ruin a great idea, poor craftsmanship or substandard materials can ruin a great design. By seeing the project through to the end, I can ensure the best quality possible—which always pays off in the long run.

MS: This is a very clear and comprehensive sequence. Can you talk us through an actual project, based on this problem-solving sequence?

SQ: In 2012, a kitchen design firm called Past Basket Design hired me to develop new signage, a Website, and a brochure. Developed in 1988, this company was most known for offering high-quality and custom kitchens within a very user-friendly sales environment. They wanted to establish themselves as a forward-looking firm— yet had "past" built right into their name!

Rather than starting on a simple redesign of their existing Website, I therefore started with Step One: Problem Statement. I asked lots of questions about their mission and what they really wanted to accomplish as a company.

Moving on to Step Two, I interviewed three customers at some length regarding what they wanted to see in a new design. What attracted them to Past Basket in the first place? What information did they need when considering the investment in a custom-made kitchen design? I learned that knowledgeable and friendly marketing staff was a major attraction, that seeing many beautiful design examples was essential,

and that women between the ages of 40 and 70 made most of the purchase decisions.

These initial steps set the stage for all the remaining steps. Based on what I had learned, I concluded that the Website had to be clean, clear, user friendly, and focused on particular content the users wanted to see. Functionality is always a top priority, and especially so when the customer is seeking information quickly.

I have created complex Websites, with motion graphics and other effects. However, flashy effects or complicated designs would not attract Past Basket customers, so I distilled the design down as much as I possibly could. We featured many beautiful photographs of past projects, each accompanied with a brief description. The friendly sales staff was a major asset, so I featured them in two areas, in a section called "about us" and in a section devoted to the design process itself. A section on testimonials from happy customers and accolades (such as awards won by the firm) provided even more information and increased confidence in the company. Customers may spend $75,000 or more on a custom kitchen and must feel assured that a good design and build process will yield a great result.

MS: How many designs does the client need to see?

SQ: Paul Rand, one of the masters of graphic design, presented only one solution to his clients, because he had such an ingrained sense of process and was able to hit the nail on the head just about every time. I generally follow this

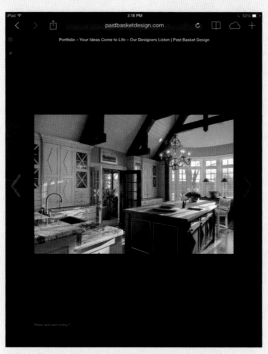

Steve Quinn, *Past Basket Website page*, 2013.

model. Using the problem-solving sequence I've described, I can generally create an effective design that will be accepted, with only minor changes.

MS: Let's "think outside the box" has become a cliché—but it describes an important idea. When we "think outside the box" we go beyond the ordinary, seeking something challenging and new. To what extent does your design process invite such invention?

SQ: Actually, I start by thinking *inside* the box created by the problem statement, client objectives, and design parameters. Without understanding these essentials, I could create a wonderful design that totally misses the mark. I can become really

inventive once I understand the limitations: it is like playing a game within various rules.

MS: You've talked and written considerably about the social responsibility of design. Do you have any advice for my students?

SQ: Designers are responsible for making much of what we see in the public environment. We have an important responsibility to ensure that what we put in that space is enhancing it, not adding to the already polluted visual environment. Designers should have the goal to provide a meaningful service to their clients, be an advocate for the user, be proactive in being problem solvers, and provide engaging, effective solutions—no matter who the client is.

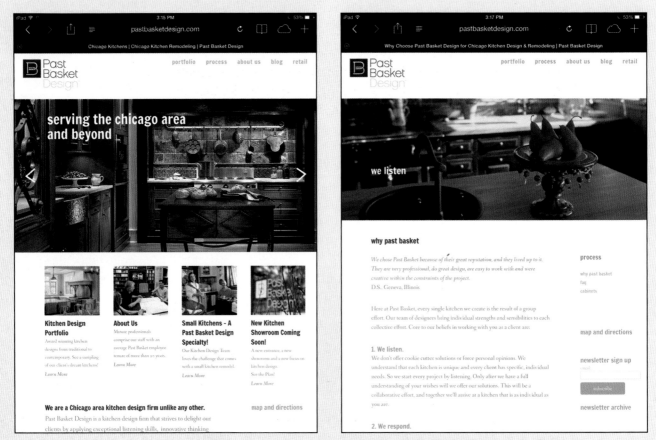

Steve Quinn, *Past Basket Website page*, 2013.

Steve Quinn, *Past Basket Website page*, 2013.

Cultivating Creativity

"The heart of all new ideas lies in the borrowing, adding, combining or modifying of old ones. Do it by accident and people call you lucky. Do it by design and they'll call you creative."

Michael LeBoeuf, in *Imagineering*

The convergent problem-solving process described in Chapter Five seems methodical and predictable. Even the more open-ended divergent thinking process is based on an alternating pattern between idea expansion and idea selection. Why, then, do we need to know anything more about creativity?

The answer is simple. We confront much messier creative challenges whenever we begin our work. Artists and designers often encounter creative blocks or problems that stubbornly resist solution. So, this chapter is designed to help bridge the gap between the ideal situation that we explored in Chapter Five and your actual experience in the studio. In it we consider characteristics of creative people, discuss goal setting, list time-management strategies, and explore habits of mind and habits of work that you can use to increase success.

SEVEN CHARACTERISTICS OF CREATIVE THINKING

"Conditions for creativity are to be puzzled, to concentrate, to accept conflict and tension, to be born every day, to feel a sense of self."

Erich Fromm, in *Creativity and Its Cultivation*

Creativity is inherently unpredictable. Through creative thinking, we break old habits and transform familiar patterns of thought. Anything can happen. Predicting the future based on past experience becomes inadequate when a creative breakthrough occurs. Like a shimmering drop of mercury, creativity eludes capture.

We can actively cultivate creative thinking, however. Rather than waiting for inspiration, we can set up the conditions that favor inspiration. First, let's look at the characteristics of highly creative people, based on the work of many researchers.

chapter six

Receptivity

Creative people are open to new ideas and welcome new experiences. Never complacent, they question the status quo and embrace alternative solutions to existing problems. Listening more and talking less is helpful. As journalist Larry King says, "I never learn anything new when I'm the one talking!"

Curiosity

Researching unfamiliar topics and exploring unusual systems is a source of delight for most creative people. "How does it work?" and "How can it work better?" are questions that creative people frequently ask.

Wide Range of Interests

With a broad knowledge base, a creative person can make a wider range of connections. Consider the number of words that you can create from the letters in the word *image:*

age, game, gem, am, aim, a, I, me

Try the same game with the word *imagination:*

gin, nation, gnat, ton, tan, not, man, again, gain, oat, got, tag, am, aim, ant, no, on, tin, gamin, inn, ingot, main, a, I

With more components, the number of combinations increases. Likewise, an artist who has a background in literature, geology, archery, music, and other subjects can make more connections than can a strict specialist.

Attentiveness

Realizing that every experience is valuable, creative people pay attention to seemingly minor details. Scientists often develop major theories by observing small events, which they then organize into complex patterns. Artists can often see past superficial visual chaos to see an underlying order. Playwrights develop dramatic stories by looking past the surface of human behavior to explore the comedy (and tragedy) of human existence. By looking carefully, creative people see possibilities that others miss.

Connection Seeking

A creative breakthrough often occurs when we see connections between seemingly random fragments. For example, Egyptian hieroglyphs became readable when a young French scholar realized that they carried the same message as an adjacent Greek inscription on a slab of stone, now called the Rosetta Stone (6.1). By comparing the two and cracking the code, Jean-François Champollion opened the door for all subsequent students of ancient Egyptian culture.

Conviction

Because we often derive new ideas from old ideas, it is foolish to ignore or dismiss the past. However, creative people embrace change and actively pursue an alternative path. Never satisfied with routine answers to familiar questions, they invent new possibilities and often challenge the status quo.

Complexity

In lectures, our instructors encourage us to think rationally and write clearly. In studio classes, they encourage us to explore, experiment, and use our

6.1 Rosetta Stone, Egypt, Ptolemaic Period, 196 BCE. 5.7 × 28.5 × 11 in. (14.4 × 72.3 × 27.9 cm).

intuition. Synthesis, visualization, spatial perception, and nonlinear thinking are highly valued in art and design.

To be fully effective, a creative person needs to combine the rational and the intuitive. Although we may use intuition to generate a new idea, we often need logic and analysis for its realization. As a result, the actions of creative people are often complex or even contradictory. As psychologist Mihaly Csikszentmihalyi[1] noted, creative people often combine

- *Physical energy with a respect for rest.* They work long hours with great concentration, then rest and relax, fully recharging their batteries.

- *Savvy with innocence.* Creative people tend to view the world and themselves with a sense of wonder, rather than clinging to preconceptions or stereotypes. They use common sense as well as intellect in completing their work.

- *Responsibility with playfulness.* When the situation requires serious attention, creative people are remarkably diligent and determined. They realize that there is no substitute for hard work and drive themselves tirelessly when nearing completion of a major project. On the other hand, when the situation permits, they may adopt a playful, devil-may-care attitude. This provides a release from the previous work period.

- *Risk-taking with safekeeping.* Creativity expert George Prince has noted two behavioral extremes in people.[2] Safekeepers look before they leap, avoid surprises, punish mistakes, follow the rules, and watch the clock. A safekeeper is most comfortable when there is only one right answer to memorize or one solution to consider. Risk-takers are just the opposite. They break the rules, leap before they look, like surprises, are impetuous, and may lose track of time. A risk-taker loves inventing multiple answers to every question.

  Creative thinking requires a mix of risk-taking and safekeeping. When brainstorming new ideas, risk-takers use open-ended exploration. However, when implementing new ideas, deadlines, budgets, and feasibility become

major concerns. It often seems that the risk-taker jump-starts the job and the safekeeper completes it.

- *Extroversion with introversion.* When starting a new project, creative people are often talkative and gregarious, eager to share insights and explore ideas. When a clear sense of direction develops, however, they often withdraw, seeking solitude and quiet work time. This capacity for solitude is crucial. Several studies have shown that talented teenagers who cannot stand solitude will rarely develop their creative skills.

- *Passion with objectivity.* Mature artists tend to plunge into new projects, convinced of the importance of the work and confident of their skills. Any attempt to distract or dissuade them is futile. However, when they complete a model or preliminary study, most pause to assess their progress. At that point, a dispassionate objectivity replaces the emotional attachment required while creating. The artist reworks or discards the work that does not pass this review, regardless of the hours that he or she has spent. In major projects, this alternating process of creation and analysis may be repeated many times.

- *Disregard for time with attention to deadlines.* Time often dissolves when studio work begins. An artist or a designer can become engrossed in a project: when the work is going well, 6 hours can feel like 20 minutes. On the other hand, attention to deadlines is necessary when preparing an exhibition or working for a client.

- *Modesty with pride.* As they mature, creative people often become increasingly aware of how teachers, family, and colleagues have contributed to their success. Rather than brag about past accomplishments, they tend to focus on current projects. On the other hand, as creative people become aware of their significance within a field, they gain a powerful sense of purpose. They delete distractions from the schedule, and set increasingly ambitious goals.

When the balance is right, all these complex characteristics fuel even greater achievement.

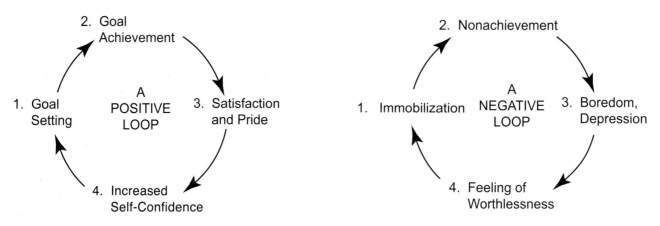

6.2 Michael LeBoeuf, *Imagineering*, 1980. Achievement feeds self-confidence, while nonachievement induces inertia.

GOAL SETTING

As humans, our behavior is strongly goal directed. Every action occurs for a reason. When we focus our attention on a specific task, we can channel our energy and better manage our time. When we reach our goals, our self-esteem increases. Michael LeBoeuf has diagrammed this effect clearly (6.2). Goal achievement creates a positive loop; procrastination or failure creates a negative loop. Because they are so important, let us now consider ways to develop good personal goals.

Characteristics of Good Goals

Ambitious yet Achievable

Too modest a goal will provide no sense of accomplishment. Too ambitious a goal will reduce, rather than increase, motivation. No one wants to fight a losing battle! Analyzing your strengths and weaknesses can help you set realistic goals.

Compatible

To train for the Boston Marathon while simultaneously trying to gain 20 pounds is unwise, because you will burn off every calorie that you consume. Trying to save a thousand dollars while touring Europe is unrealistic, because travel always costs more than you expect. On the other hand, by taking a dance class or joining a hiking club, you may be able to combine a fitness goal with a social goal.

Self-Directed

It is best to avoid goals that are primarily dependent on someone else's actions or opinions. "I

want to earn an A in drawing" is a common example. Because the instructor determines your grade, your control in this area is limited. Instead, focus on improving your drawing as much as possible. This will increase your receptivity to learning and will focus your attention on actions that you *can* control. When you do your best work, good grades generally follow.

Temporary

Set clear target dates, get the job done, and move on to the next project. As figure 6.2 shows, each completed task increases your self-confidence and adds momentum. By contrast, unfinished work can drain energy and decrease momentum. If you are overloaded, delete secondary goals so that you can complete primary goals.

TIME MANAGEMENT

Time management can help you achieve your goals. Working smarter is usually more effective than simply working harder. In a world bursting with opportunity, using your work time well can increase the time available for travel, volunteer work, or socializing. Many artists and designers have used the following time-management strategies.

Set the Stage

Choosing when and where to work can significantly increase your output. If you are a lark, bursting with energy and enthusiasm early in the morning, tackle major projects before noon. If you are a fierce and nocturnal owl, work on major projects after dinner. If you are distracted by clutter, clean your desk before beginning your workday, and tidy up your desk before you leave. These seemingly minor actions can really increase your productivity.

Prioritize

Note which tasks are most *urgent* and which tasks are most *important*. Timing can be crucial. When you pay your phone bill on time, you easily complete an urgent but unimportant task. When your phone bill is overdue and the service is cut off, this unimportant task becomes a major headache. Dispense with urgent tasks quickly so that you can focus on more important issues.

See the Big Picture

Use a monthly calendar to record your major projects and obligations. Organizing your calendar by months can help you see which weeks will be packed with deadlines and which weeks will be relatively quiet. To avoid all-nighters, distribute large, important tasks over several weeks. To avoid missing a pivotal lecture or critique, schedule out-of-town trips during "slow" weeks.

Work Sequentially

Often, it is most effective to tackle activities in a specific sequence. If you are writing a 20-page paper, you should start with research, craft an outline, complete a rough draft, make revisions, and *then* write the final draft. If you are designing a poster, begin with research, make thumbnail sketches, assess the results, create a full-size rough draft, consult the client, and *then* complete the poster. To eliminate the intermediate steps and move directly to the final draft rarely works. With most large projects, you learn more, save time, and do better work by tackling the problem one step at a time.

Use Parts to Create the Whole

When you look at a major project as a whole, it can become overwhelming. In an extreme case, creative paralysis sets in, resulting in a condition similar to writer's block. Breaking down big jobs into smaller parts helps enormously. In *Bird by*

Bird, Anne Lamott provides a wonderful description of this process:

> Thirty years ago my other brother, who was ten years old at the time, was trying to get a report on birds written that he'd had three months to write. [It] was due the next day. . . . He was at the kitchen table close to tears, surrounded by binder paper and pencils and unopened books on birds, immobilized by the hugeness of the task ahead. Then my father sat down beside him, put his arm around my brother's shoulder, and said, "Bird by bird, buddy. Just take it bird by bird."[3]

By breaking the job down into manageable parts, you are likely to learn more and procrastinate less.

Make the Most of Class Time

Psychologists tell us that beginnings and endings of events are especially memorable. An experienced teacher knows that the first 10 minutes of class set the tone for the rest of the session and that a summary at the end can help students remember the lesson. Similarly, the wise student arrives 5 minutes early for class and maintains attention to the end of class.

Be an active learner. You can use that 5 minutes before class to review your notes from the previous session or set up your materials. Try to end the class on a high note, either by completing a project or by clearly determining the strengths and weaknesses of the work in progress. By analyzing your progress, you can organize your thinking and provide a solid beginning point for the next work session.

When in Doubt, Crank It Out

Fear is one of the greatest obstacles to creative thinking. When we are afraid, we tend to avoid action. Consequently, we may miss opportunities.

Both habit and perfectionism feed fear. If you consistently repeat the same activities and limit yourself to familiar friendships, you may become even more anxious about new experiences. Perfectionism is especially destructive during brainstorming, which requires a loose, open approach.

Creativity takes courage. As IBM founder Thomas Watson noted, "If you are not satisfied

6.3 M. C. Escher, Part of *Metamorphosis II*, 1939–40. Woodcut in black, green, and brown, printed from 20 blocks on three combined sheets, 7½ × 153⅜ in. (19 × 390 cm).

with your rate of success, try failing more." Base-ball player Reggie Jackson is renowned for his 563 home runs—but he also struck out 2,597 times. Thomas Edison's research team tried more than 6,000 materials before finding the carbon-fiber filament used in light bulbs. "When in doubt, don't!" is the safekeeper's motto. "When in doubt, do!" is the risk-taker's motto. By starting each project with a sense of adventure, you increase your level of both learning and creativity.

Work Together

Many areas of art and design, including digital media, industrial design, and advertising design, often occur collaboratively. Working together, artists and designers can complete projects that are too complex or time-consuming to be done solo. Collaborative thinking helps us break familiar patterns and teaches us to listen to alternative or opposing ideas.

Here is an example from one of my own classes. We began with *Metamorphosis II*, an 8 × 160-inch banner by M. C. Escher (6.3). I provided each student with a 1-inch strip of the banner to provide a beginning point and another 1-inch strip of the banner to provide the ending point for a design (6.4A). Each person then invented an 8½ × 11-inch connection between the two strips. They used buildings, plants, chess pieces, and other images to bridge the gap (6.4B). We then connected all images end to end, like cars in a train. This produced a collaborative 20-foot banner. Each collaborator had to negotiate with the person in front and with the person in back to make a continuous banner with graceful transitions. In effect, all 20 participants became

members of a creative team. Finally, we photocopied and traded each 8½ × 11-inch section, providing each person with the completed artwork. In such collaboration, everyone gains, both in the learning process and in sharing the final product.

Lexicon (6.5A–C), a year-long project by Lynda Lowe in Washington and Georgiana Nehl in Oregon, beautifully demonstrates the value of collaboration. The artists took turns initiating and responding to each other's images as they sent small groups of paintings back and forth through the mail. Despite distinct stylistic differences, the artists share a mutual fascination with the unconscious, commitment to the power of symbols, and mastery of composition. By working together, Lowe and Nehl were able to complete a remarkable series of 100 paintings that have been shown nationally.

VARIATIONS ON A THEME

The *Lexicon* project clearly demonstrates the power of creative evolution. As a project evolves, we can reveal new possibilities that extend beyond our initial intentions. By pursuing these implications, we can exceed our original expectations. Just as the landscape appears to expand when we climb a mountain, so an image can expand when our conceptual understanding increases.

One way to get more mileage out of an idea is through variations on a theme. Professional artists rarely complete just one painting or sculpture from a given idea—most do many variations before moving to a new subject.

6.4A Examples of Escher Starter Images.

6.4B Mary Stewart and Jesse Wummer, Expanded Escher Collaboration, 2000. Student work.

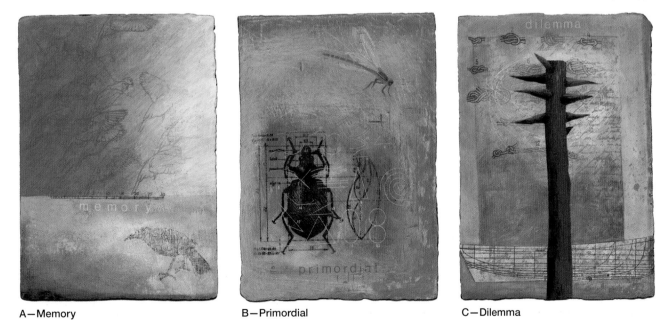

A—Memory

B—Primordial

C—Dilemma

6.5A–C Lynda Lowe and Georgiana Nehl, *Lexicon*, 2000. Mixed mediums on paper, 5 × 7 in. (13 × 18 cm).

6.6A Katsushika Hokusai, *Thirty-Six Views of Mount Fuji: Under the Mannen Bridge at Fukagawa*, Edo Period, c. 1830. Color woodblock print, 10¹/₁₆ × 14¹¹/₁₆ in. (25.7 × 37.5 cm).

6.6B Katsushika Hokusai, *Thirty-Six Views of Mount Fuji: The Great Wave off Kanagawa*, Edo Period, c. 1830. Color woodblock print, 10⁹/₁₆ × 14¹⁵/₁₆ in. (25.9 × 37.5 cm).

Thirty-Six Views of Mount Fuji is one example. Printmaker Katsushika Hokusai was 70 years old when he began this series. The revered and beautiful Mount Fuji appeared in each of the designs in some way. Variations in the time of year and the size of the mountain helped Hokusai produce dramatically different variations on the same theme (6.6A–C).

The next two figures show variations on the standard chess set. Completed by industrial design students in response to a design competition, each set offers a unique approach to an ancient game. Eddie Chui's *Let's Dance* (6.7) retains the familiar forms of the various pieces but adds a curved bottom. Rather than sitting stoically in place, the knights, pawns, and other pieces tend to dance back and forth, while magnets connect them to the board. By contrast, Sergio Silva provided a carrying case along with his cubic

6.6C Katsushika Hokusai, *Thirty-Six Views of Mount Fuji: Near Umezawa in Sagami Province*, Edo Period, c. 1830. Color woodblock print, 10¹/₁₆ × 14⁷/₈ in. (25.6 × 37.8 cm).

chessmen (6.8). Based on squares and rectangles, his set is crisp and highly unified.

Contemporary artists often ignore boundaries between two- and three-dimensional work.

6.7 Eddie Chui, *Let's Dance*, 2005. Maple, magnets, and silicon.

6.8 Sergio Silva, *Chess Set*, 2005. Anodized aluminum and wood.

6.9 Matthew Ritchie, *No Sign of the World*, 2004. Oil and marker on canvas, 99 × 154 in. (251 × 391 cm).

As a result, their thematic variations may include drawings, sculpture, animation, and other media. In figures 6.9 and 6.10, Matthew Ritchie uses lines, shapes, and patterns to create paintings, animations, and sculptural objects that express his conceptions of knowledge.

6.10 Matthew Ritchie and Aranda Lasch in collaboration with Arup AGU, *The Evening Line,* 2008. Laser-cut aluminum, aggregated paint, video. Fabrication Sheetfabs Nottingham Ltd. Commissioned by Thyssen-Bornemisza Art Contemporary.

6.11 Cubes from above, study models from Auburn University School of Architecture.

Finally, figure 6.11 shows many variations on a cube. Submitted by beginning architecture students at Auburn University, they demonstrate one advantage of studying art and design in a classroom setting: you are able to see variations on a theme every time an assignment is due!

ACTIVELY SEEK SUCCESS

Personal initiative is powerful. Indeed, a highly motived person with average ability can surpass an unmotivated genius. Consider these final success strategies.

Habits of Mind

Dr. Arthur L. Costa and Dr. Bena Kallick have identified 16 "habits of mind" essential to success. Four attributes that are especially important in art and design follow.

Flexibility

Convergent, divergent, and collaborative problem-solving strategies present distinct advantages and disadvantages. Limiting yourself to just one approach reduces your ability to solve a wide range of problems. Flexibility, on the other hand, gives you the ability to question existing assumptions, adopt new ideas, and shift strategies as needed.

Analytical Thinking

In general, designers are hired to solve a client's problem. Complications arise when time is limited and expenses increase. An analytical mind-set helps the designer continue to focus on the real problem rather than wasting time on an imagined problem.

Capacity for Synthesis

We can define *synthesis* as the capacity to combine separate parts to create a coherent whole. Two aspects of synthesis are particularly important for artists and designers. First, they must be able to combine visual elements to create unified designs. Second, they must be able to apply past knowledge to new situations. You can accumulate a vast storehouse of knowledge by simply remembering past solutions to similar problems.

Responsible Risk Taking

Risk-takers are willing to risk failure to achieve success. They view setbacks as opportunities for growth rather than occasions for despair. Irresponsible risk-takers leap before they look. Responsible risk-takers weigh benefits and hazards, gather their energy, and then leap.

Habits of Work

To provide beginners with a realistic checklist, Professor Rusty Smith and his colleagues in the School of Architecture at Auburn University have developed the following "habits of work."

Self-Reliance

Essentially, self-reliance creates an active approach to work. Rather than waiting for directions or blaming others for delays, each person actively generates possibilities, weighs options, and makes choices. To a substantial degree, self-reliant students drive their own learning process.

Organized Persistence

Beating your head against a brick wall is an example of mindless persistence. It is impressive but ineffective. Chiseling away at the mortar between the bricks until the wall falls apart is an example of organized persistence. Organized persistence gives us the ability to prevail, even when we are faced with the most daunting task.

Daily Practice

Momentum is extremely powerful when you are working on a difficult problem. Daily practice helps maintain momentum. Working an hour a day on a project is sometimes better than working for eight hours on a single day.

Appropriate Speed

Some tasks are best completed quickly, with brisk decision making and decisive action. Slowing down to reframe a question and weigh alternative solutions is necessary in other cases.

Incremental Excellence

Most art and design problems are best developed in a series of stages. Ideas evolve, skills improve, and compositions are distilled. Rather than trying for the "perfect solution" on the first day of work, it is better to start with a "funky junky" draft.

Direct Engagement

Talk is cheap. Work is hard. The only way to solve most art and design problems is to get involved. You will never win a race when you are standing on the sidelines!

summary

- Creative people are receptive to new ideas, are curious, have a wide range of interests, are attentive, seek connections, and work with great conviction.
- A combination of rational and intuitive thinking feeds creativity. Although we can use intuition to generate a new idea, we may need logic and objective analysis for its completion.
- Good goals are ambitious yet achievable, compatible, self-directed, and temporary. Intermediate deadlines can help us meet our goals.
- Completing tasks in an appropriate sequence, making the most of each work period, main-

taining momentum, and reducing stress are major aspects of time management.
- Collaborative work can help us expand ideas, explore new fields, and pursue projects that are too complex to do alone.
- We can explore ideas more fully using variations on a theme.
- Flexibility, analytical ability, the capacity for syntheses, and responsible risk-taking are crucial habits of mind.
- Self-reliance, organized persistence, daily practice, appropriate speed, and direct engagement are crucial habits of work.

studio projects

To apply the concepts from this chapter in the studio, check out the Projects page in the Online Learning Center at www.mmhe .com/LTI5e. The following is a sample of the chapter-related assignments that we describe in detail.

Collaborative Compositions. Digitally creating a collaborative collage.

Expanding Escher. Working within the boundaries of a partner's design.

Audio Assemblage. Building a musical instrument.

Profile:
Jim Elniski, Artist
Exploring Sustainable Architecture

From 2003 to 2007, Jim Elniski and partner Frances Whitehead envisioned and constructed *The Greenhouse Chicago*, a home plus studio demonstration project for sustainable urban living. This remarkable undertaking combines cutting-edge energy technology with locally sourced materials that becomes both architecture and an artwork.

Jim Elniski is a social practice artist, educator, and clinical social worker. His work with groups and communities employs a hybrid approach, linking individual and collective expressions to create socially engaged artworks. Jim's partner, Frances Whitehead, a self-proclaimed "designist," explores the juncture of art, science, and design. Trained as a studio artist, she went on to establish a collaborative design studio for hybrid public projects that are driven by her commitment to place-based research and biologic communities.

My conversation with Jim Elniski focuses on *The Greenhouse Chicago* and how it reflects his art practice.

MS: Please introduce us to *The Greenhouse*.

JE: *The Greenhouse* is a 4,000-square-foot residence with studios in Chicago's Westown neighborhood. Reclaimed from an underutilized brick warehouse, this live/work space combines sustainable technology, adaptive reuse, and affordable green design. Fifty percent of the energy we use is produced by a geothermal heating and cooling system, two wind turbines, solar photovoltaic roof panels, and solar thermal roof panels. Radiant heating in the floor, dual-flush toilets, energy-star appliances, rainwater cisterns, and a green roof further reduce our carbon footprint. On the rooftop we also grow vegetables and maintain beehives.

MS: This project was extraordinarily labor intensive, taking over 4 years to plan and complete. What inspired you to start?

JE: We had been living and working in a very large and energy-inefficient loft building. Since both of us are strongly committed to sustainability and systems thinking, we decided to design a smaller and smarter place to live.

MS: What is adaptive reuse, and why is it important?

JE: Adaptive reuse is the process of transforming an outmoded, existing building for a new purpose. This approach required us to work creatively with what we found rather than building a new structure from scratch. It challenged us to clearly assess the strengths and weaknesses of the site and then make choices that would produce the desired results. As artist/designers, this critical thinking process is very familiar—we analyze, assess, discard, and rethink every project as it evolves through multiple iterations.

MS: You've described this as a "design/build" project. What does that mean?

JE: The design/build approach helped us to embrace new ideas and make adjustments as the building

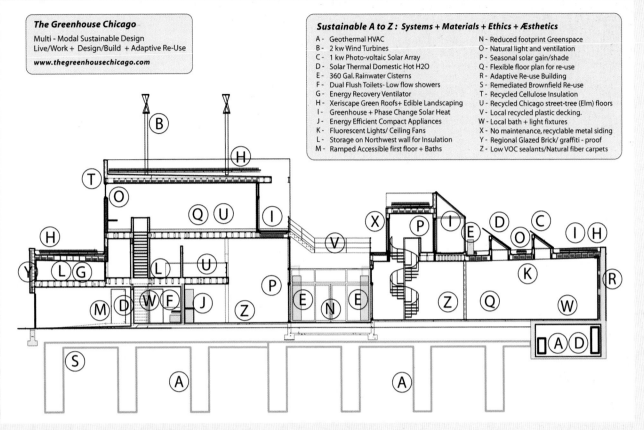

The Greenhouse Chicago
Multi - Modal Sustainable Design
Live/Work + Design/Build + Adaptive Re-Use
www.thegreenhousechicago.com

Sustainable A to Z : Systems + Materials + Ethics + Æsthetics

A - Geothermal HVAC
B - 2 kw Wind Turbines
C - 1 kw Photo-voltaic Solar Array
D - Solar Thermal Domestic Hot H2O
E - 360 Gal. Rainwater Cisterns
F - Dual Flush Toilets- Low flow showers
G - Energy Recovery Ventilator
H - Xeriscape Green Roofs+ Edible Landscaping
I - Greenhouse + Phase Change Solar Heat
J - Energy Efficient Compact Appliances
K - Fluorescent Lights/ Ceiling Fans
L - Storage on Northwest wall for Insulation
M - Ramped Accessible first floor + Baths

N - Reduced footprint Greenspace
O - Natural light and ventilation
P - Seasonal solar gain/shade
Q - Flexible floor plan for re-use
R - Adaptive Re-use Building
S - Remediated Brownfield Re-use
T - Recycled Cellulose Insulation
U - Recycled Chicago street-tree (Elm) floors
V - Local recycled plastic decking.
W - Local bath + light fixtures
X - No maintenance, recyclable metal siding
Y - Regional Glazed Brick/ graffiti - proof
Z - Low VOC sealants/Natural fiber carpets

Frances Whitehead, *The A to Z*, 2007. Diagram of multimodal sustainable features.

was being constructed. For example, once construction began, we could see more clearly the dialog between the interior and the exterior spaces, and thus understand the interrelated systems that the structure could incorporate.

MS: Can you take us through the major steps in the process?

JE: We began with this question. How could we create a smaller, smarter, and sustainable live/work space? Next, we conducted extensive research. What technologies were being used in sustainable architecture, and how could they be applied to our project? Working with architect William James and his associate Mhari McVicar, we then developed a layout of how the various spaces would relate to each other. An open-air courtyard was at the heart of our vision. We integrated many ethical design ideas with classical modernist architectural beauty to show that the "alternative" technologies lifestyle could go mainstream effectively.

Beyond that point, the process became more fluid. As with any of our art projects, we

planned, built, evaluated, reconsidered, and revised our plans.

Because the architect also was our general contractor, he was able to respond to unexpected changes we had to make along the way. For example, while we were trying to decide whether to have either solar photovoltaic panels (for electricity) or solar thermal panels (for hot water), the possibility of our home incorporating a complete set of sustainable building elements emerged. That's when we realized that *The Greenhouse* was becoming an art project.

MS: I love the graphic Frances created linking the systems you incorporated. Can you explain how the building systems relate to each other?

JE: Let's consider ways the solar panels and geothermal systems work together. In the winter months, the fluid pumping through our geothermal heating system collects the heat of the earth (about 55 degrees), is augmented by the heat from our solar thermal panels (about 120 degrees), and then passes through the heat pump, which uses electricity (generated in part from our solar

Jim Elniski/Frances Whitehead, *The Greenhouse*, Chicago, **2006–present.** Photograph of architectural site.

Jim Elniski/Frances Whitehead, *The Greenhouse*, Chicago, **2006–present.** Photograph of one of the green roof gardens.

photovoltaic panels and wind turbines) to extract the heat from the fluid into our radiant floor. Since everything connects to everything else, it got pretty complex. We saw this multi-systemic interconnectedness not as a problem to be solved but rather as a condition to be explored.

MS: *The Greenhouse* has been featured on the Discovery Channel and in various architecture magazines. Professionals from the American Institute of Architects and classes of architecture students tour the site regularly. What is its significance? Why are people drawn to this project?

JE: The house is very deliberate, in every sense of the word. Every choice has been made to maximize the ecology of the house as a whole and to position it elegantly within an urban setting, as kind of a machine for urban living.

In many ways *The Greenhouse* is experienced as kind of a Rubik's cube puzzle. This live/work space is a series of interlinked systems; heat, ventilation, light, water, ADA accessible, and so on. Each discrete space visually frames an adjacent space. The open-air central courtyard animates the entire building.

As a machine for urban living, *The Greenhouse* continues to evolve. Recently, I installed two beehives on the roof over my studio space. I continue to be in awe of how these bee colonies so gracefully contribute to the nested layers of their ecology and the ways they respond and sustainably use their living space. In many ways, *The Greenhouse* reflects how essential it is for us, as artists, to situate our work in that space between art and life.

MS: How did *The Greenhouse* connect to your existing art practice, and how did it expand your existing art practice?

JE: As *The Greenhouse* evolved from inception to completion, I appreciated anew my artistic intention to focus on the literal ways we are linked and to make visible aspects of the communal common ground that all too often are invisible.

The Greenhouse continues to challenge me as an artist to address the complexity of the relational interchange that is inherent in many of my community-centered art projects, and to explore the many ways we are all interdependently connected.

Developing Critical Thinking

Critical thinking challenges us to

- Analyze visual relationships
- Evaluate our conceptual and compositional choices
- Invent alternative solutions

Using critical thinking, we can determine what to keep and what to change in a composition. By enhancing the best aspects of a design and deleting the weak areas, we can dramatically increase both communication and expression.

ESTABLISHING CRITERIA

Let's begin by establishing the criteria on which we will make judgments. For example, craftsmanship is highly valued when we take a technical workshop, while brainstorming is highly valued in a concepts course. More specifically, if we are given a complementary color problem, a black-and-white painting will not meet the criteria, no matter how well it is composed. By determining the major questions in an assignment, we can understand the basis on which judgments will be reached.

So, when starting an assignment, consider the following questions:

- What is the assignment's purpose? What new knowledge can we gain?
- What are the assignment parameters? Are there limitations in the size, style, content, or materials?
- When is the assignment due, and in what form must it be presented?

It is important to distinguish between determining assignment criteria and seeking the "right answer." In the first case, by understanding assignment criteria, we can effectively direct our energy as we begin to work. Just as we can use a magnifying glass to focus sunlight into a powerful beam, so assignment parameters can help to focus creative energy. On the other hand, students who try to determine the "right answer" to a problem may just want to know the instructor's solution. Such knowledge is rarely helpful. The assignment simply sets a learning process in motion: we learn through the work that we do.

chapter seven

FORM, SUBJECT, CONTENT

We may define **form** as the physical manifestation of an idea or emotion. We can construct two-dimensional forms using point, line, shape, texture, value, and color. The building blocks of three-dimensional forms are point, line, plane, volume, mass, space, texture, and color. We can combine duration, tempo, intensity, scope, setting, and chronology to create time-based art forms. For example, *Star Wars,* a classic science fiction movie, appears in the art form that we call film.

The **subject,** or topic, of an artwork is most apparent when it clearly represents a person, an object, an event, or a setting. For example, the war between the rebels and the Empire provides the subject for *Star Wars.*

An artwork's emotional or intellectual message provides its **content,** or underlying theme. The *Star Wars'* theme is the journey into the self. Luke Skywalker's gradual understanding of himself and his acceptance of the villainous Darth Vader as his father provide an essential emotional undercurrent to the entire series.

Each artwork also occurs within a geographical and temporal **context.** This context can substantially affect the artwork's meaning. For example, Mary Lucier's video showing a fragile monarch butterfly's death is astonishing and poignant when we see it at Times Square, the bustling theater district in the heart of New York City (7.1). If we viewed the same event while hiking, we would consider it a normal occurrence rather than a statement about the fragility of life.

STOP, LOOK, LISTEN, LEARN

We typically discuss artworks using a critique process. During a **critique,** our peers and professors analyze our work and offer advice. They identify compositional strengths and weaknesses, and reveal areas that need revision. We can use these insights to improve the current design or to generate possibilities for the next assignment.

Depending on the amount and type of student involvement, critiques can be extremely helpful, extremely destructive, or really boring. Specific recommendations are most helpful. Be sure to substantiate each recommendation you offer so that the rationale is clear.

Whether we are giving or receiving advice, it is important to arrive with our minds open, rather than with our fists closed. A critique is not a combat zone! We must listen carefully to explanations and generously offer our insights to others. Likewise, we can receive suggestions gracefully rather than defensively. Each of us will make the final decision on revisions: thus, if someone gives us bad advice, we can quietly discard it. Because a substantial and supportive critique is the best way to determine the effect that our design has on an audience, it is best to speak thoughtfully and weigh every suggestion seriously.

7.1 Mary Lucier, *Migration* in Times Square.

OBJECTIVE AND SUBJECTIVE CRITIQUES

When beginning a critique, it is useful to distinguish between objective and subjective criticism. We use **objective criticism** to assess how well a work of art or design uses the elements and principles of design. Discussion generally focuses on basic compositional concerns, such as the following:

- The type of balance that the artist used in the composition and its effect
- The spatial depth of a design and its compositional effect
- The degree of unity in a design and how the artist achieved it

We base objective criticism on direct observation and a shared understanding of assignment parameters. Discussion is usually clear and straightforward. We may discuss alternative compositional solutions in depth.

We use **subjective criticism** to describe an image's personal impact, an idea's narrative implications, or an action's cultural ramifications. Discussion generally focuses on the design's subject and content, including the following:

- The artwork's meaning
- The feelings it evokes
- Its relationship to other cultural events
- The artist's intent

Because we do not base subjective criticism on simple observation, it is more difficult for most groups to remain focused on the artwork itself or to reach clear conclusions on possible improvements. The discussion may range widely, as we analyze political or social questions that the works of art and design raise.

CRITIQUE STRATEGIES

Description

The first step is to look carefully and report clearly. Without evaluating, telling stories, drawing conclusions, or making recommendations, we can simply describe the work's visual organization. A **descriptive critique** can help us see details and heighten our understanding of the design. We can identify which design aspects are most eye-catching and which areas are muddled and require work.

This is a particularly useful exercise when analyzing a complex piece, such as figure 7.2A. In an art history class, we might write:

> French impressionist painter Gustave Caillebotte's *Place de l'Europe on a Rainy Day* is a rectangular painting depicting a street in Paris. A vertical lamppost and its shadow extend from the top edge to the bottom edge, neatly dividing the painting in half. A horizon line, extending from the left side and three-quarters of the way to the right, further divides the painting, creating four major quadrants. Because this horizon line is positioned just above center, the composition's bottom half is slightly larger than the top half. A dozen pedestrians with umbrellas occupy the painting's bottom half. At the right edge, a man strides into the painting, while next to him a couple moves out of the painting, toward the viewer. To the left of the lamppost, most of the movement is horizontal, as people cross the cobblestone streets.

When using description in a spoken studio class critique, it is useful to note these essential compositional characteristics:

- What is the shape of the overall composition? A circle or sphere presents a different compositional playing field than does a square or a cube.
- What range of colors has the artist used? A black-and-white design is different from a full-color design.
- What is the size of the project? Extremes are especially notable. A sculpture that is 10 feet tall or a painting that is 1-inch square will immediately attract attention.
- Is the visual information tightly packed, creating a very dense design, or is the design more open and spacious?

The Key Questions that appear throughout this book can provide a springboard for a descriptive critique.

7.2A Gustave Caillebotte, *Place de l'Europe on a Rainy Day*, 1877. Oil on canvas, 83½ × 108¾ in. (212.2 × 276.2 cm).

Major division #1

| ½ | ½ |

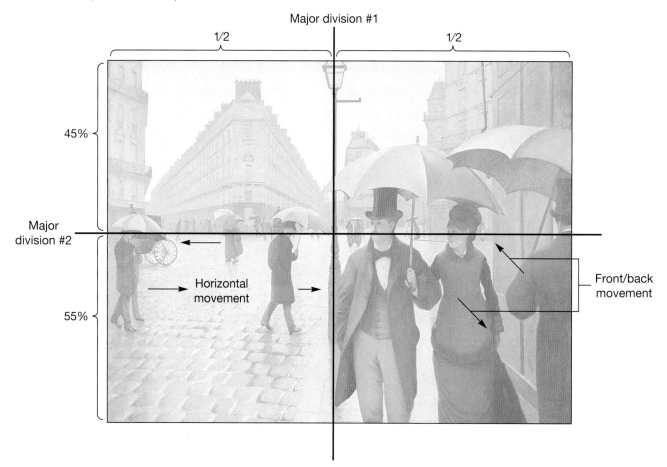

45%

Major division #2

Horizontal movement

Front/back movement

55%

7.2B Gustave Caillebotte, *Place de l'Europe on a Rainy Day*, 1877. Compositional diagram.

Cause and Effect

A descriptive critique helps us analyze an artist's compositional choices. A **cause-and-effect critique** (also known as a **formal analysis**) builds on this description. In a simple description, we might say that diagonal shapes dominate a design. Using cause and effect, we might conclude that *because* of the many diagonals, the design is very dynamic. Essentially, in a cause-and-effect critique, we discuss *consequences* as well as choices. Here is an example:

> *Place de l'Europe on a Rainy Day* depicts a city street in Paris near the end of the nineteenth century.
>
> A lamppost, positioned near the center, vertically bisects the painting. The horizon line creates a second major division, with roughly 45 percent of the space above and 55 percent below this line. When combined, these vertical and horizontal divisions create a focal point near the painting's center.
>
> A dozen pedestrians in dark clothing cross the cobblestone streets from left to right, creating a flowing movement. To the right of the post, the pedestrians move in and out of the painting, from background to foreground. Both types of movement add compositional energy. Two men and one woman are the most prominent figures. The man at the far right edge pulls us into the painting, while the couple to his immediate left moves toward us, pushing out of their world and into our world.

As figure 7.2B shows, a visual diagram can support your written comments.

Although we use a written formal analysis more often in art history classes than in studio classes, artists often mentally assess their own work using the same strategy. American sculptor Rodger Mack described *The Oracle's Tears* (7.3) as follows:

> This sculpture is made from five major parts. The column dominates, structurally and conceptually. Just above it, I have placed a form that has reappeared in my work for 30 years, the Oracle. It is like an image on a tarot card, the hanging man, perhaps. A smaller piece, based on a shape I found in a market in Athens, connects the oracle

and the column. The tears are created using three descending lines. The base is the final element. It provides a stable support and adds a sense of completion.

A description of technical aspects of the project can enhance the viewers' understanding of the artwork. Professor Mack wrote:

> I used a combination of fabrication and casting. The oracle form was made by cutting shapes

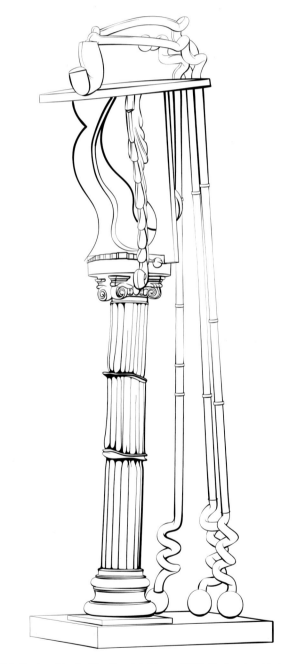

7.3 Rodger Mack, *The Oracle's Tears*, 1999. Cast and welded bronze, 17 × 6 × 4 ft (5.18 × 1.83 × 1.22 m).

from a sheet of ⅛-inch bronze and welding them together. The tears and the column were cast in sections, then welded. A potassium dichloride patina, applied using a blowtorch, gives the piece its golden color.

Professor Mack then concluded his commentary with a subjective discussion of his intentions:

I've always been drawn to ancient cities and architectural forms and have been working with mythological themes for the past six years. I've completed a series of maidens, a minotaur, a Trojan horse, and several oracles so far. When I visit these ancient civilizations, it saddens me that they are gone, destroyed to make way for new civilizations.

Because fellowship applications and grant proposals often require such written descriptions, developing your analytical skills and your writing ability can pay off professionally.

Compare and Contrast

In a compare/contrast critique, we identify similarities and differences between two images. Let's return to the Caillebotte painting one more time, now comparing it to Italian Renaissance painter Raphael's *The School of Athens* (7.4).

The city streets in *The School of Athens* and *Place de l'Europe* demonstrate many differences between the Renaissance and Impressionist perspective.

The one-point perspective that Raphael uses in his painting leads our eyes to Plato and Aristotle, positioned just below the composition's center. The other figures in the painting are massed in a horizontal band from the far right to the far left side and in two lower groups, to the right and left of the central figures. A man sprawled on the steps to the right and the scribes' tables on the left direct our attention back to the philosophers at the center. Like a proscenium arch in a theater, a broad arch in the foreground frames the scene. Overlapping arches add to the painting's depth. This composition combines the stability of one-point perspective with a powerful illusion of space.

Both *The School of Athens* and *Place de l'Europe on a Rainy Day* are carefully divided both vertically and horizontally. However, in the Caillebotte painting a lamppost occupies center stage, rather than a philosopher. The perspective in the cobblestone street and in the building on the right is complicated by the perspective that the artist uses for a triangular building to the left of the lamppost. This unusual illusion of space, combined with the pedestrians' movement, creates a feeling of instability.

Art history classes often use compare-and-contrast essays. This form of analysis helps demonstrate differences in historical periods or artistic styles. However, we can use the same approach in the studio, for either spoken or written critiques. The following, written by Cally Iden and Tricia Tripp, two students in a basic design class, is an example. The assignment was to complete an 18 × 24-inch design, transforming the music building (Crouse College) into a labyrinth.

Looking at Cally's design (7.5), Trish wrote:

Cally's artwork uses strong black-and-white contrast, with both negative and positive space clearly defined. In contrast, my design is brightly colored, representing a kaleidoscope based on the stained glass windows in the building.

We both use the staircase as a major element. Cally's stair leads you in and around the building, creating a way to explore the space. My stair becomes part of a complex overall pattern.

I thought of the labyrinth as an abstract puzzle, a design you could draw your pencil through to find the end. I wanted my design to be playful. Cally's design focuses on the psychological, creating an entry into the human mind. Cally's design is mysterious and somewhat ominous.

We both use lines very deliberately. Where one line ends, another begins. Without lines in a labyrinth, it wouldn't be as puzzling or mysterious. It would just be another design, rather than a puzzle to solve or a fun house to explore.

Looking at Trish's design (7.6), Cally wrote:

My labyrinth uses black and white to form a high-contrast composition; Trish uses color to transform

7.4 Raphael, *The School of Athens*, 1509–11. Fresco, 26 × 18 ft (7.92 × 5.49 m). Stanza della Segnatura, Vatican, Rome.

the building into a complex pattern. My vertical format helps suggest the height of the building, which is dominated by two amazing staircases. Trish's horizontal format contains a design that is as abstract as a computer circuit board.

There are also conceptual differences in our solutions. My drawing is representational, depicting a psychological labyrinth; whereas Trish's turns

7.5 Cally Iden, *Crouse College as a Labyrinth*. Student work, 18 × 24 in. (45.7 × 61 cm).

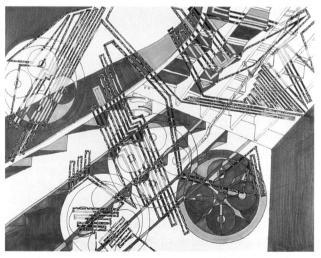

7.6 Tricia Tripp, *Crouse College as a Labyrinth*, 1999. Student work, 24 × 18 in. (61 × 45.7 cm).

the labyrinth into a puzzle. The space is generally flat in her design. Color is used to create a balanced composition rather than being used to create any illusion of space. On the other hand, because my design is representational, I used size variation to create a convincing interior space.

One similarity between our drawings is in the inclusion of the staircase. Trish used the stairs as a background shape that adds dynamism to the composition. I used the stair as a primary motif, a means by which people using the building can explore their own minds.

For me, Trish's design creates a sense of alienation. There is no evidence of human experience here—it is a purely visual world, made up of complex shapes. It is as beautiful as an image in a kaleidoscope.

On the other hand, there are hints of "the human" in my composition, but it is lost within the maze of repetitive stairs: only traces remain. I want to convey the feeling of being caught in a labyrinth, solving a mystery, and finding one's self.

The critiques are honest, but not abusive and offer a discussion of both concept and composition. Although the critiques are very different, each student clearly respects the other's approach.

Greatest Strength/Unrealized Potential

Many projects have several notable strengths and one glaring weakness. To create a positive atmosphere, we can begin by pointing out the strengths using the following list:

- What is the level of unity in the design, and how did the artist achieve it?

- How much variety is there, and does it generate visual energy?

- What type of balance did the artist use? What is its emotional effect?

- Is the artwork brash and bold, or more subtle and quiet? This could include a discussion of craftsmanship, conceptual nuance, or compositional economy.

- Is there an unexpected conceptual spark? We all love to see an unexpected solution that redefines a project's imaginative potential.

Weaknesses tend to undermine compositional strengths. Thus, by removing a weakness, we can enhance compositional strengths. Using figure 7.7A as an example, we could say:

The primary strength of this project is unity. The use of black marker throughout gives the design a simple, clean, and consistent look. The repetition of the arches helps tie it all together. Vertical and horizontal lines dominate, creating a type of grid.

Next, we might consider ways to improve the project. Mentally we can arm ourselves with a magic wand. If we could instantly transform the design, what single aspect would we change? How can we more fully realize the project's potential? Here are some basic questions:

- Is it big enough? Is it small enough?

- Is it bold enough? Is it subtle enough?

- How rich is the concept? Can it be expanded?

- Can the concept be more clearly communicated?

- Can the concept be communicated more fully?

The assignment was to create a labyrinth. Figure 7.7A is spatially shallow. To strengthen the composition, we might suggest:

When I think about a labyrinth, I think of a mysterious place that I can enter and explore. Right now, this design is spatially flat: it gives me no place to go. Greater size variation in the arches, with larger ones in the front and smaller ones in the back would increase the illusion of space. Overlapping some of the arches could increase the space even more and add visual rhythm. Have you considered using gray marker for the background shapes? This would reduce the contrast and push those shapes back in space. By increasing the illusion of space, you could provide an entry into your labyrinth.

The resulting design (7.7B) is now more spatially complex.

DEVELOPING A LONG-TERM PROJECT

Critiquing is useful at many points in a project, not just at the end. When working on a project for 10 hours or more, it is useful to assess progress at

7.7A Initial design. **7.7B** Design variation.

the beginning or the end of each work period. We can facilitate this in a large-group critique, in small teams, in discussion with the instructor, or on our own. Several effective strategies follow.

Week One Assessment

Determine Essential Concept

As a project begins to evolve from brainstorming thumbnails to rough drafts, the concept may also evolve. Our initial idea may expand or shift as we translate it from the mind to the hand to the page. Stopping to reconsider the central concept and refine our image can bring great clarity and purpose to the work. What is the design *really* about? We can speak more forcefully when we know what we want to say.

Explore Polarities

Sometimes, the best way to strengthen an idea is to present the exact opposite. For example, if we want to show a political prisoner's *joy* upon release from jail, we may need to show the *despair* that she felt before her release. To increase the *dynamism* in a design, we can add some emphatically *static* elements. The contrast that polarities create can heighten communication.

Move from General to Specific

"Be specific!" demands the writing instructor. Vague generalities weaken our writing, and vague generalities can weaken our designs. Details are important. "A bird watched people walk down the street" is far less compelling than "Two vultures hovered over University Avenue, hungrily watching the two hapless students stagger from bar to bar." Specifying the kind of bird, type of people, and exact location makes the image come alive.

Move from Personal to Universal

Autobiography is a rich source of images and ideas. The authenticity of personal experience is extremely powerful. However, if we cling too tightly to our own families, friends, and experiences, the viewer can feel like a bystander rather than a participant. Using a personal story to express a universal experience can help. We can expand a story about a pivotal experience in our first year away from home to say something about *all* rites of passage from childhood to adulthood.

Week Two Assessment

A well-developed rough draft or a full-scale model may be presented at this stage. The purpose of this critique is to help the artist or designer determine ways to increase the visual and conceptual impact of an existing idea. Three major strategies follow.

Develop Alternatives

By helping a friend solve a problem, we can often solve our own problem. Organize a team of four or five classmates. Working individually, design 5 to 10 possible solutions to a visual problem using 2×3-inch thumbnail sketches. Then have one person present his or her ideas verbally and visually. Each team member must then propose an alternative way to solve the problem. We can do this verbally; however, once we get going, it is more effective and stimulating if everyone (including the artist) draws alternative solutions. This process helps the artist see the unrealized potential in his or her idea. Because of the number of alternatives, the artist rarely adopts any single suggestion. Instead, the exercise simply becomes a means of demonstrating ways to clarify, expand, and strengthen already formed intentions.

Edit Out Nonessentials

Have you ever found it difficult to determine the real point of a lengthy lecture and thus lost interest? Seeking to communicate fully, teachers sometimes provide so many examples and references that students get lost. Likewise, if our designs are overloaded with nonessential detail, or if we give a secondary visual element the starring role, the result will be cluttered. Clutter reduces impact. Look carefully at your design, focusing on visual relationships. Are there any elements that you can delete?

Amplify Essentials

Just as it is necessary to delete extraneous information, so it is equally important to strengthen the most important information. We can review the section on emphasis in Chapter Three and then consider ways to heighten compositional impact. By "going too far" and wildly exaggerating the size, color, or texture of a visual element, we can transform the composition. By making extraordinary compositional choices, we can create extraordinary images.

TURN UP THE HEAT: PUSHING YOUR PROJECT'S POTENTIAL

Some compositions are so bold that they seem to explode off the page. Other compositions have all the right ingredients but never really take off. By asking the following questions, we can more fully realize the potential of any assignment.

Basic Arithmetic

1. Should we *add* anything to the design? If our composition lacks energy, we might add another layer of information or increase the illusion of space. Notice how texture changes the composition in figures 7.8A and 7.8B.

2. Should we *subtract* anything? If the composition is cluttered, we might discard 25 percent of the visual information. We can then use the remaining shapes more deliberately (7.9A and B). Let's get as much as possible from every visual element. Economy is a virtue.

3. What happens when we *multiply* any component? On page 145, figures 7.7A and 7.7B show that repetition can unify a design, add rhythm, and increase the illusion of space.

4. Can we *divide* the design into two or more separate compositions? When a design is too complicated, it may become impossible to resolve. Packing 20 ideas into a single composition can diminish rather than improve communication. In figures 7.10A and 7.10B, the artist has separated a complicated source image into several designs, creating a group of stronger images.

Transformation

Works of art and design present ideas in physical form. The materials that we use, the relationships that we create, and the viewing context that we select strongly influences each composition. Let's consider the following alternatives:

1. What happens when the artist changes the material? Even when the shapes stay the same, a silver teapot is very different from a glass, steel, or ceramic teapot. Sculptors Claes Oldenburg and Coosje van Bruggen have extensively used transformations in material, often changing hard, reflective materials into soft vinyl. This form of transformation is especially effective when the new material brings structural qualities and conceptual connotations that challenge our expectations.

2. What is the size relationship between the artwork and the viewer? What happens when an artist reduces a chair to the size of a salt shaker, or when there is a 19-foot-tall badminton shuttlecock installation in front of a museum (7.11)?

3. When working three-dimensionally, are we creating compositions that are interesting from all viewpoints?

4. Will a change in viewing context increase meaning? The badminton shuttlecocks immediately added whimsical energy with their placement in front of the very serious-looking art museum.

7.8A Linear design.

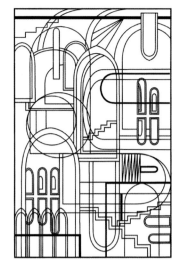

7.9A Visual clutter.

7.10A Completed labyrinth design.

7.8B Adding invented texture.

7.9B Visual clarity.

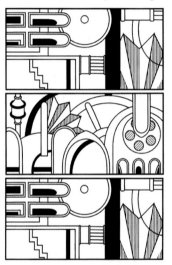

7.10B Divided labyrinth design.

7.11 Claes Oldenburg and Coosje van Bruggen, *Shuttlecocks*, 1994. South facade of the Nelson-Atkins Museum of Art and the Kansas City Sculpture Park. Aluminum, fiberglass-reinforced plastic, and paint. 230⁹⁄₁₆ × 191⅞ in. (585.63 × 487.36 cm).

Reorganization

We generally construct time-based work, such as visual books, comic books, film, and video, from multiple images. Changing the organization of the puzzle pieces can completely alter meaning. For example, let's say Angela contemplates entering a mysterious building in the sequence in figure 7.12. By reorganizing the same three images, in figure 7.13, we can show that Angela now wonders what will happen when she opens the door at the top of the stairs. By repeating Angela's image, we can present a dilemma: she is now in a labyrinth—which route should she take (7.14)?

Although this strategy is most dramatic when we are working with film or video, we can apply the idea of reorganizing existing information to all kinds of objects and images. Such reorganization often occurs in website and video game design, such as the Genomics Digital Lab (7.15). The home page typically provides an overview of the entire site. By scanning a collection of thumbnail images, viewers can understand the range and type of information or adventure available. Each specific page within the site then provides information or an activity in greater depth. As the site unfolds, general information reorganizes and represents itself in increasing detail.

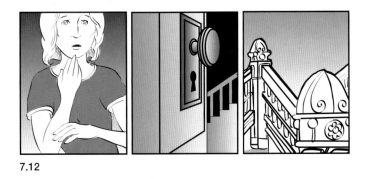

7.12

7.13

7.14

Developing a Self-Assignment

Independent thinking is the ultimate goal. As we end this chapter, Jason Chin describes the development of a month-long self-assignment that he completed at the end of his freshman year. The original project proposal is at the top of the first page. The rest of the text is devoted to Jason's analysis of his actual work process. This type of personal assessment can bring an extended project to a memorable conclusion. The more self-directed you are, the more independent you become.

TAKING RESPONSIBILITY

Regardless of the critique strategy used, two facts are inescapable. First, we will learn only what we want to learn. If we reject all advice or if we avoid responsibility for our conceptual and compositional choices, we will gain nothing from the experience. Second, there are no free rides. Everyone in the class is responsible for the success of a critique. When we receive a superficial response to a project, insisting on further clarification is not easy. Yet, we are all responsible. We can greatly improve our artwork when others offer substantial advice. Professor Jim Elniski from the School of the Art Institute of Chicago sums it up beautifully:

"Speak with the expectation of being heard, and listen with the possibility of being changed."

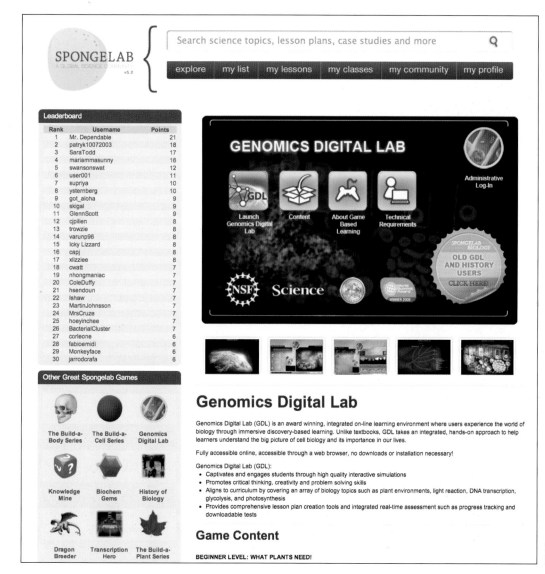

7.15 Genomics Digital Lab.

Self-Assignment:
Jason Chin
The Mythological Alphabet

Original Proposal

Description: I plan to make an illustrated alphabet book with 32 pages and a cover. The theme of the book will be myths and heroes. I am interested in illustrating the essence of each hero's story. Specifically, how can I visually communicate the story of a tragic hero versus a triumphant one? Further concerns with the book will be making it work as a whole. That means keeping it balanced and making it flow: I don't want the images to become disjointed.

Primary Concerns

1. How do I communicate the individual nature of the characters?
2. How do I connect each hero to all the others?
3. How will the book affect the reader? I want to get the reader fully involved in the book.
4. How can I best use the unique characteristics of the book format?

Time Management

Week 1: Research myths and heroes. Identify possible characters for the book.

Week 2: Bring at least 20 thumbnail sketches to the first team meeting.

Week 3: Bring finalized design/layout for book. Each page must have a final design in the form of thumbnails.

Week 4: Complete half of the pages.

Week 5: Finish remaining pages and present at the critique.

Commentary

The independent project was both a blessing and a curse. Given the freedom to do what I chose was liberating, but the burden of what to do with that freedom was great. Ultimately, it became one of the best learning experiences of my freshman year.

I had decided to pursue illustration as my major, because of my interest in storytelling. This interest in stories led me to choose to make a book for my project. The next step was to find a story to tell. To limit my workload, I looked for a story that had already been told, one that I could reinterpret, as opposed to writing my own story. At this point, I came across two books, one of Greek myths, and an alphabet

book illustrated by Norman Rockwell, and my initial concept was born.

Once the idea was initiated, I set to work researching Greek myths. The idea was to find one character for each letter of the alphabet. It proved more difficult than I had first thought. I found about 20 names with no problem, but I soon realized that several letters in our alphabet did not exist in the Greek alphabet. To overcome this hurdle, I took some liberties on the original problem and did not limit myself strictly to characters from myths (for example, I included the White Island for the letter W). Once the subject of each illustration was chosen, I set about the task of doing the images and designing the format of the book.

Doing the illustrations and designing the format of the book all came together at about the same time. As I was working out the drawings I made several key decisions that heavily influenced the outcome of the project. First, I decided that each picture would have to be black-and-white if I was going to pull this whole thing off. Second, I knew that they would have to be relatively small. Through my art history class, I gained a strong interest in Japanese woodblock prints and was especially attracted to their strong compositional sensibility. This became the focus of my attention while working out the illustrations. Finally, the decision to make the illustrations small helped determine the way I used text in the book, because it all but eliminated the possibility of overlaying text on image.

I designed each image in my sketchbook, doing thumbnails and comp sketches of all sizes and shapes, until I found the image that I felt best represented the character. For example, Zeus has the biggest and busiest frame in the book because he is the king of the gods, while the image of the White Island is quite serene because it is a burial ground.

When I had each individual image worked out, I redrew them in order in the pages of my sketch book as if they were in the real book. I could now see how each image would work as a double-page spread, as well as how well the book could flow visually. With this mockup of the book in front of me it was very easy to see obvious mistakes and correct them before going to final art.

I did the final illustrations in pen and ink, on illustration board, and when they were finished, it was time to drop in the text. My first concept for the text was to be very minimal; each page would read,

"A is for," "B is for," and so on. However, I soon realized that making each page rhyme would drastically increase the reader's interest in the book. So I wrote a more extensive text and put the rhyming parts on opposite pages in order to give the reader one more incentive to turn the page.

The final touch for the book was putting the colored paper down. The decision to do this came when I went to place the type. The only means I had to get good type was to print it out on the computer, but I had no way to print it on the illustration board. So I had to put it on printer paper and cut and paste it. No matter how carefully I cut the paper and pasted it on, it just didn't look right. I came up with two solutions: one, print the words on colored paper and paste it on, or two, cut frames of colored paper to cover over the entire page except for the image and the text. I chose the latter and was pleased to discover that the local art store had a vast selection of handmade and colored papers.

Today I look back on this project as a pivotal experience in my art education, because I had free range to pursue storytelling, something that has since become an essential aspect of my art. In the professional world, bookmaking is rarely an individual process. It is a collaborative process, involving editors, artists, and writers, so for me to be able to pursue it on my own was in fact a blessing. I got to make a book the way that I thought it should be done, and pursue my own personal vision of what a Mythological Alphabet should be. By making this book, I discovered something that I love to do, and want to make a career of doing, and to me the vision that I have gained from this experience is invaluable.

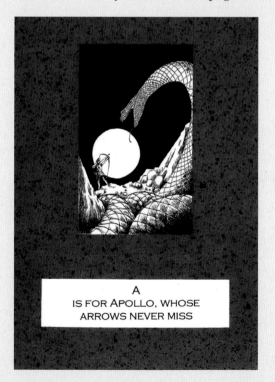

Jason Chin, *A Is for Apollo* (left) and *U Is for Urania* (right), **2000.** Student work.

A
IS FOR APOLLO, WHOSE
ARROWS NEVER MISS

U
IS FOR URANIA THE MUSE OF
CELESTIAL FORCES IS SHE

summary

- Critical thinking helps us identify strengths and weaknesses in a project and determine the improvements that we need to make.

- Understanding the criteria on which one will judge a project helps focus critical thinking.

- We can analyze many artworks in terms of four basic aspects: form, subject, content and context.

- Objective critiques focus on observable facts. Subjective critiques focus on feelings, intentions, and implications.

- Four common critique methods are description, cause and effect, compare and contrast, and greatest strength/unrealized potential.

- When working on long-term projects, in-progress critiques can help us to explore alternatives, delete non-essentials, and strengthen essentials.

- Basic arithmetic, transformation, and reorganization can increase compositional impact.

- An open mind combined with a willingness to share ideas can strengthen any critique.

key terms

cause-and-effect critique
content
context
critique

descriptive critique
form
formal analysis
objective criticism

subject
subjective criticism

studio projects

To apply the concepts from this chapter in the studio, check out the Projects page in the Online Learning Center at www.mhhe.com/LTI5e. The following is a sample of the chapter-related assignments in step-by-step detail.

Capstone Project. Expanding creativity through in-depth exploration.

Profile:
Kendall Buster, Sculptor
Biological Architecture

Kendall Buster's large-scale sculptural projects have been exhibited at Artist's Space and the American Academy of Arts and Letters in New York City; the Hirshhorn Museum and the Kreeger Museum in Washington, DC; the Kemper Museum in Kansas City; Suyama Space in Seattle; the Nevada Museum of Art in Reno; and the KZNSA Gallery in South Africa. Buster has created commissioned sculptures for the Washington, DC, Convention Center, Massey Cancer Center in Richmond, VA, and the Agave Library in Phoenix. Recent projects include commissions for Princeton University, Johns Hopkins University, and the Indianapolis Museum of Art.

MS: Microbiology was your initial academic passion, and you worked in this field for 12 years. What attracted you to microbiology, and what did you learn from it?

KB: Peering into a microscope gave me access to an intricate and beautiful world that was beyond ordinary perception. As I learned more, I became increasingly interested in the architecture of natural forms—the way cells are constructed to maximize efficiency or the permeability of a particular cell wall. The sculptures I now create begin with an internal skeleton that I wrap in a fabric or plastic skin. And, I am still fascinated by shifts in perception, from very small scale to very large scale. For me, art and science are simply aspects of the same impulse.

MS: How do you translate your ideas into large-scale objects? Most of your recent projects could fill an entire gymnasium!

KB: Ideas often occur just as I am waking up. At this point, they are more intuitive than intentional. I begin to record possibilities through pencil drawings. Drawing is crucial—it is the first step in getting the idea out of my head and into the world. I work with standard small sketchbooks, drawing in pen, sometimes scanning these sketches and then collaging, and redrawing. For me creating the drawing is really not so different from actual building. As the form becomes more and more articulated on the paper I am also imagining how this might be realized materially. I make schematics for how one section or shape might connect to another. So I am visualizing as I draw, not from observation of anything in front of me, but from the forms in my mind's eye.

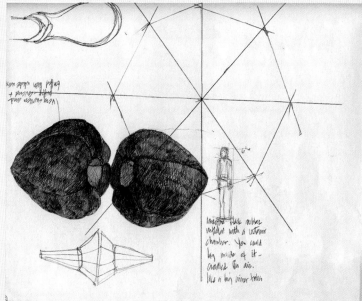

Kendall Buster, Preliminary drawing for *New Growth*.

I then move to what I see as three-dimensional sketching, using carved Styrofoam, wire, or various types of board. I call this three-dimensional sketching. We sometimes see a sketch as something limited to drawing on a flat surface. But a sketch can also be a three-dimensional exploration. To work quickly and intuitively with one's hands and minimal tools in a very direct way is essential to form generation for me.

As I continue, these 3-D models get increasingly more refined. My works are usually quite large, and so this three-dimensional sketching is a way to work out ideas in a manageable scale with a spontaneous process that is realized in a more planned way in the fabrication shop.

For *New Growth* I was especially interested in how a work with multiple sections might operate. I was able to explore how the 'buildings' in *New Growth* would configure into a larger three-dimensional composition.

My models operate for me not only practically but also conceptually. First, I see the model as the site of imagination and possibility, a place where scale is still negotiable. Even my large works I see as models. For example, one might ask, "Is the tower piece a high-rise in miniature, or is it a microscopic thing grown to enormous size?

I then use computer-aided renderings to explore how the forms will behave in the installation space and to analyze their structural requirements. The computer can also create the exacting templates that are like patterns when we begin to build the steel frames.

With my studio team, I also create physical models of the building in which the artwork will be placed in order to study the ways in which the sculpture converses with the site. I have a project coordinator who works with the client on the architectural particulars and a rigger who is an installation specialist.

MS: How are the pieces actually constructed?
KB: My large-scale sculptures are made with many interlocked parts. Creating patterns for the parts is critical. These patterns, both computer generated and hand drawn on the studio floor, are used for shaping and welding the steel frames or cutting planar material. The frames are professionally powder-coated. When the frames are covered in scrim fabric I might work with as many as 10 to 20 helpers in a marathon "screening party."

MS: Please talk us through *New Growth*, installed in the Boise Art Museum.
KB: *New Growth* is an inventory of architectural models that function like biological systems. In this imagined city, old forms generate new forms through processes that suggest germination, budding, merging, hybridization, or absorption. The model city is conceived as a single organism constructed from many interdependent parts. Some structures are connected by passageways that suggest either umbilical cords or parasitic invasions. Contiguous membranes create distinct regions in the city, and the transparency of these

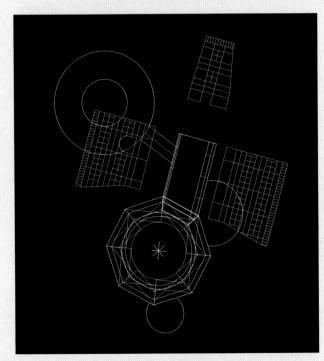

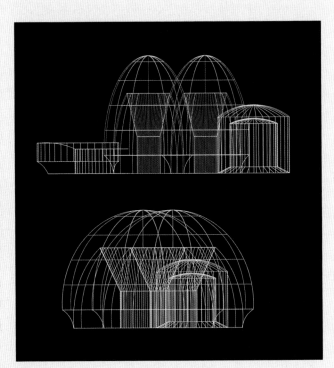

Kendall Buster, Studies for *New Growth*.

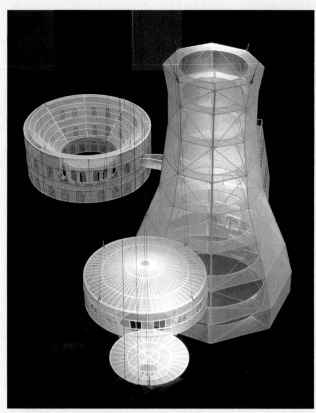

Kendall Buster, *New Growth*, 2007, detail.

place to create shifting sight lines; how narrow entryways or low passages act in direct confrontation with the body; how space is compressed and movement directed; how one is at times hidden, and at times exposed.

New Growth is also a response to the particulars of the Boise Art Museum site. On my first visit I visualized a kind of floating cityscape made up of forms that behaved both as individual structures and as a continuous membrane. The sculpture that I finally built connected to the exhibition site in unexpected ways. Curved rooftops in my architectural models seemed to echo the arched beams in the ceiling, and the ever-changing light penetrating through the floor-to-ceiling windows created subtle shades of white and gray on the transparent layers of fabric.

Scale shifts between the viewer's initial 'panoramic' overview, and the more closely observed details were also important. At one moment, the viewer is dwarfed by the artwork; at another, the artwork reads as a model that the viewer can command. As a result, the viewer is enveloped, embraced, and engaged—all at the same time.

membranes allows inner layers to be visible through the outer shell.

Architectural structures form and re-form the fabric of cities over time. To evoke this process, I wanted to build a structure that seems to be based on a precise blueprint, while at the same time contradict this idea by creating a structure that seems dynamic, continually changing.

I am also interested in exploring the tension between what is revealed and what is concealed; how windows link interior space with exterior

MS: What advice do you have for beginning students?

KB: I have three pieces of advice. First, realize that each of us has our own work process and embrace the process that is right for you. Second, find the right balance between conceptual breadth (lateral thinking) and conceptual depth (vertical thinking). Too much lateral thinking can lead you to a place where you never reach any real depth in your work, while too much vertical thinking can narrow your possibilities. Finally, embrace the idea of an ongoing and preferably daily studio practice. Complex ideas and structures can't be made overnight!

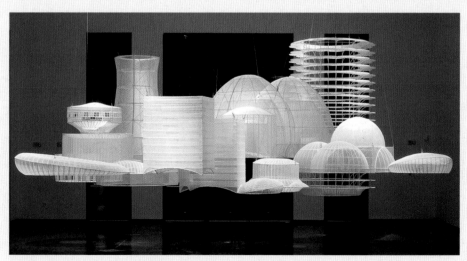

Kendall Buster, *New Growth*, 2007. Dimensions variable. As installed in Boise Art Museum.

Constructing Meaning

Seeking and solving visual problems, cultivating creativity, and developing critical judgment all require hours of hard work. Why do artists, designers, and college teachers so strongly value these skills?

The answer is simple. At a professional level, art and design projects communicate ideas and express emotions. Turning elusive concepts into effective communication is not easy. Clay, ink, metal, paint, and other physical materials must somehow stimulate an audience to see, understand, and respond. In this chapter, we explore the essentials of visual communication and identify some of the strategies that artists and designers use to construct meaning.

BUILDING BRIDGES

Shared Language

A shared language is the basis on which we build all communication. For example, if you are fully fluent in English and I am effective as a writer, the ideas that I want to communicate in this chapter should make sense to you. On the other hand, if English is your second language, some of the vocabulary may be unfamiliar. In that case, you may have to strengthen the bridge between us by looking up some words in a dictionary.

Figure 8.1 demonstrates the importance of shared language. For a reader of Chinese, the graceful brushstrokes form characters that communicate specific ideas. For those of us who don't know Chinese, the calligraphy is visually engaging, but conveys no information. We cannot understand the meaning of the characters.

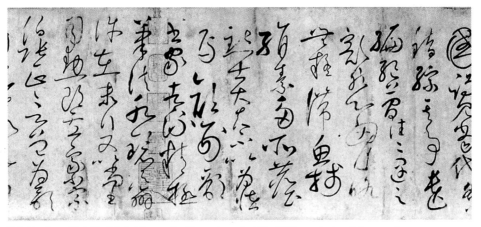

8.1 Huai-su, Detail of *Autobiography*, Tang dynasty, 7th–10th centuries. Ink on paper.

Historical and cultural "literacy" can create another type of bridge. As an American, I live within a framework that is driven by a capitalist economic structure, a two-party political system, and social systems dominated by Judeo-Christian values. South African artist William Kentridge brings a different frame of reference to his artwork. Born in 1951 as the son of white civil rights lawyers, he observed apartheid (state-sponsored racism) firsthand. Kentridge has extensive knowledge of the history of many African genocides. In *Black Box/Chambre Noir* (8.2), he used a miniature theater to tell the story of one such genocide, which nearly wiped out the Herero people. Powered by an ink-jet printer mechanism, six robotic figures enter and exit the stage. Projections of historical documents, combined with fragments of music from Mozart's opera *The Magic Flute* and Namibian songs, tell the tragic story. Although any viewer may be attracted to the fascinating structure and the intriguing projections, we must understand African history if we want to fully understand the meaning of Kentridge's story.

8.2 View of William Kentridge's *Black Box/Chambre Noire*, 2005. Miniature theater with mechanized objects, projections, and sound, dimensions variable.

Iconography

Many artworks depend on cultural and historical references to build meaning. **Iconography** (literally, "describing images") is the study of such symbolic visual systems.

Deborah Haylor-McDowell's *The Serpent Didn't Lie* (8.3) is loaded with references. Leonardo da Vinci's anatomical diagram of a fetus appears in the upper-left corner, and the nude couple near the center is based on *The Kiss,* a sculpture by Auguste Rodin. Einstein's computations for the theory of relativity appear in the upper-right corner, and in the foreground a baby takes his first steps. A detailed snakeskin border surrounds the image. What does it all mean? Haylor-McDowell says:

> Ignorance may spare us the pain of difficult decisions. However, we pay a high price. Can humankind's greatest gifts, emotion and intellect, mature in a world that is free of suffering? In the absence of adversity, will our humanness be lost? *The Serpent Didn't Lie* is based on a biblical text dealing with good and evil in the Garden of Eden. What is the price we pay for knowledge?

8.3 Deborah Haylor-McDowell, *The Serpent Didn't Lie*, 1997. Etching, 15 × 23 in. (38.1 × 58.42 cm).

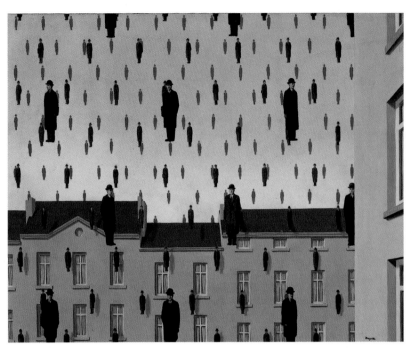

8.4 Milton Glaser, *Art is . . . WHATEVER*, 1996. Poster.

8.5 René Magritte, *Golconde*, 1953. Oil on canvas, 31¾ × 38⅝ in. (80.65 × 98.11 cm).

The images I used in the composition deal with the complexities and responsibilities of our pursuit of knowledge.

Through a sophisticated use of iconography, Haylor-McDowell created a puzzle that is filled with ideas for us to explore. For those who understand the cultural references, this elegant print represents many forms of knowledge. However, for those who do not understand the references, the print is simply a beautifully crafted collection of architectural and figurative fragments.

Graphic designers are especially aware of the importance of iconography. On a purely visual level, Milton Glaser's 1996 poster for the School of Visual Arts (8.4) is intriguing and evocative in itself. The hovering hat, shadowy figure, and curious text raise many questions. When we compare the poster with surrealist René Magritte's *Golconde* (8.5), the ideas expand much further. In this and other paintings by Magritte, the man in the bowler hat represents anyone who is courageously navigating through the chaos of contemporary life. By connecting Glaser's floating bowler hat to Magritte's painting, we begin to understand the complexity of this seemingly simple poster. Like the man in the bowler hat, each art student must pursue a personal path in order to develop a meaningful and distinctive approach to his or her work.

Audience

Just as films are targeted and rated for specific audiences, so many forms of visual communication are designed for specific viewers. George Balanchine was a master choreographer renowned for his love of classical ballet as well as his commitment to endless invention. The poster in figure 8.6 is powerful yet restrained. Traditional text on a blue background carefully balances the dancers in blue.

By contrast, Saul Bass's poster for *West Side Story* (8.7) is gritty and bold. This modern retelling of Shakespeare's *Romeo and Juliet* combines gang warfare, racism, and romance in a tragic love story. The silhouetted figures dance on fire escape ladders between their apartments, not on a traditional stage. In the film itself, male dancers often wear blue jeans, T-shirts, and street shoes. The music is powerful and percussive. Both shows attracted diverse audiences, but the marketing minds behind the publicity targeted the Balanchine poster at those seeking more traditional ballet, while they pitched the *West Side Story* poster to those seeking modern dance.

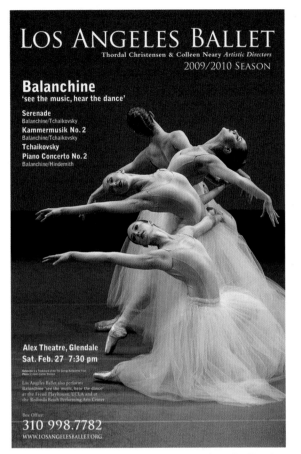

8.6 Poster design by Catherine Kanner, photo by Reed Hutchinson, *Serenade* by George Balanchine, Los Angeles Ballet, 2009.

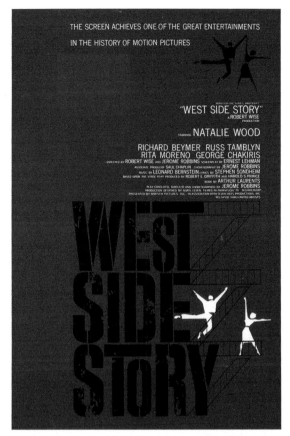

8.7 Saul Bass, *West Side Story* poster, 1961. Written by Ernest Lehman, directed by Jerome Robbins, Robert Wise.

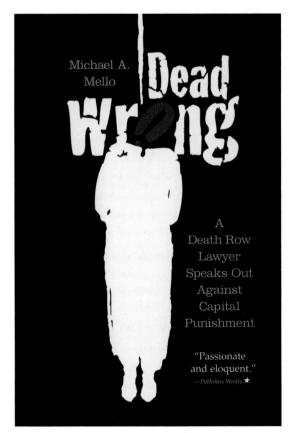

8.8 Mark Maccaulay, *Dead Wrong*, 1997. Book jacket.

Immediacy

When the bridge between the image and the audience is explicit, communication can occur almost instantaneously. When the iconography is elusive or complex, communication takes longer and may vary more. Each approach can be effective in the right time and place. When we are driving a car, our lives depend on the immediate message that we receive when a traffic light turns red. The "Stop!" is clear and emphatic. However, when visiting a museum, we often seek greater complexity and emotional resonance.

Graphic designers generally aim for a combination of immediacy, clarity, and resonance. Their goal is to create effective visual communication that viewers can understand at a glance. Figure 8.8 is an excellent example. The bold shape of a hanged man immediately attracts attention, and the book title itself is simple and direct. The position of the figure's head adds another layer of meaning to this critique of capital punishment.

8.9 Markus Schaller, *Some Words*, 2007. Steel, 157.5 × 354.3 × 0.6 in. (400 × 900 × 1.5 cm).

By contrast, *Some Words* (8.9) by Markus Schaller requires extended viewer involvement. Created from a sequence of stream-of-consciousness texts inscribed onto 70 iron panels, this German artist designed the installation as a meditation on the very process of thinking. Viewers entering a visual labyrinth had to be willing to puzzle over the words and explore their own cognitive responses. The message was neither explicit nor immediate. In fact, forcing the viewer to think was the main objective. As with Haylor-McDowell's work (see figure 8.3), the viewer must piece together a complex set of clues, then reach his or her own conclusions about the nature of knowledge and the development of language.

Stereotypes

A **stereotype** is a fixed generalization based on a preconception. When we use a stereotype, we ignore individual characteristics and emphasize group characteristics. For example, shipping crates often feature a broken wine glass (figure 8.10) to communicate fragility. Glass is actually a versatile material that can be cast as bricks, spun into fiber-optic cables, and polished to create lenses. Nonetheless, we are most familiar with fragile wine glasses and bottles. Relying on this *general* perception, the shipping label designer used a stereotype to communicate fragility.

Racial stereotyping tends to exaggerate negative generalizations. Even when people positively make an assumption (such as "Asian Americans are brainy overachievers"), the overall effect is demeaning. Rather than learning about an individual person, we are making judgments based on our preconceptions.

Confined to a World War II internment camp as a young child, Roger Shimomura and his family have had very direct experience with racism. Following the Japanese attack on Pearl Harbor, the American government removed roughly 110,000 Japanese Americans living along the West Coast from their homes and sent them to remote camps in Idaho, Wyoming, and other states. In his *Stereotypes and Admonitions* series (8.11), Shimomura used this experience and subsequent encounters with stereotypes as a primary theme. A story accompanies each image. In this example, Shimomura recounts an awkward social encounter. No matter how many times he said "Roger," the woman he was meeting was still convinced that he was an exotic foreigner with an unpronounceable first name. In the painting, he exaggerated her perception by portraying himself as a fierce, yellow Japanese warrior. The text that accompanies the image follows:

8.10 "Fragile" pictogram.

8.11 Roger Shimomura, *Florence, South Carolina*, from *Stereotypes and Admonitions*, **2003.** Acrylic on canvas, 20 × 24 in. (51 × 61 cm).

In l969, after graduating from Syracuse University, Roger and his first wife visited their good friend Alvin, in Florence, South Carolina. Alvin's mother threw a dinner party for her friends and relatives, all long-time residents of Florence. The purpose of the party was for everyone to meet Alvin's "friends from Japan" despite Roger and his wife's repeated insistence that they were Americans who happened to be of Japanese descent.

During pre-dinner cocktails, Roger was introduced to Fran, one of Alvin's favorite aunts. Fran was a schoolteacher and college graduate, often referred to as the "intellectual" of the family. As introductory pleasantries were exchanged, Fran asked Roger his name. Roger said his first name and then, in very crisp English, Fran repeated her question to Roger. After Roger repeated his first name, Fran commented very slowly, so as not to be misunderstood, "Well, I guess my name sounds as weird to you as yours does to me."

Yet, despite the potential hazards, designers may deliberately use stereotypes to create the bridge on which communication depends. Because they are based on preconceptions, stereotypes require little thought. The viewer responds automatically. In some situations, an automatic response is ideal. Figure 8.12 shows four airport pictograms. Can you determine the meaning of each? If the designer is successful, even an exhausted traveler will be able to determine at a glance where to find a baggage locker, an elevator, or a toilet. Especially notice the use of the male and female stereotypes for the toilet pictograms. Despite the wide range of clothing that female travelers wear, the designers used a dress to create a stereotypical female.

Clichés

A **cliché** is an overused expression or a predictable treatment of an idea. Phrases such as "Let's level the playing field" and "Think outside the box" are powerful the first time. However, when we hear them repeatedly, they lose their impact and become clichés. Visual clichés are equally predictable. Skulls representing death and seagulls representing tranquility may be effective at first, but tend to become worn out when we use these images repeatedly.

Surprise

A shift in a stereotype or cliché upsets our expectations and challenges our assumptions. The resulting shock can surprise or delight an audience, making the message more memorable. Originally based on the American cowboy stereotype, the "Marlboro Man" was an early advertising icon. Television and print ads showed this rugged individual confidently

8.12 Roger Cook and Don Shanosky, images from a poster introducing the signage symbol system developed for the U.S. Department of Transportation, 1974.

8.13 Asher & Partners for the California Department of Public Health, "I miss my lung, Bob," 2003.

riding across a Western landscape. Of course, the Marlboro was his cigarette of choice. The Adbusters spoof in figure 8.13 suggests that "cowboys are a dying breed" because of the cancer caused by their smoking. By breaking the stereotype, the designers attracted the viewers' attention, challenged the conventional cigarette ad, and strengthened their nonsmoking message.

Na Zha Cradle (8.14) is equally surprising. Cradles are "supposed" to be soft, safe, and comforting. This cradle is metallic, threatening, and dangerous. Metaphorically commenting on the aggressive capitalism that has driven the Chinese economy in recent years, Shi Jinsong suggests that we pay a price when society progresses too quickly.

8.14 Shi Jinsong, *Na Zha Cradle*, 2005. Stainless steel, 24 × 31.9 × 24.3 in. (61.4 × 81.7 × 62.2 cm).

▶ key questions

BUILDING BRIDGES

- Are there any symbolic or cultural meanings embedded in your composition? Are these meanings consistent with the message that you want to convey?

- Have you used a stereotype or a cliché? If so, does that add or subtract from your message?

- What audience do you want to reach? Are the form and content of your design appropriate for that audience?

PURPOSE AND INTENT

Any number of approaches to visual communication can be effective. We simply choose the style, iconography, and composition best suited to our purpose.

Let's consider five different uses of human anatomy. *Arterial Fibrillation* (8.15) was developed for the cover of a medical journal. With equal training in art and science, medical illustrator Kim Martens combined anatomical accuracy with artistic imagination to create this design. To increase sales, the magazine's art director requested an image that was both physically accurate and visually attractive.

Figure 8.16 shows an extensive online training system developed by the National Cancer Institute. Despite the encyclopedic amount of information, this website is visually simple and easy to navigate. Rather than introduce flashy effects, the

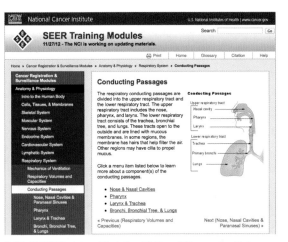

8.16 SEER Training Modules, National Cancer Institute, Conducting Respiratory Passages, 2013. http://training .seer.cancer.gov/

designers used a methodical structure that presents each lesson very clearly. As a result, readers can focus on the course content, from the conducting respiratory passages to the complexities of the cardiovascular system.

Figure 8.17 requires even greater clarity and economy. Designed to demonstrate a life-saving emergency procedure, this graphic relies on simple line drawings. A close-up view of the essential hand position is more important than attractive colors or anatomical detail.

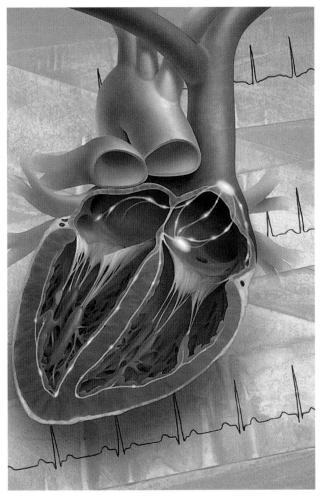

8.15 Kim Martens, *Arterial Fibrillation*, 2000. Photoshop.

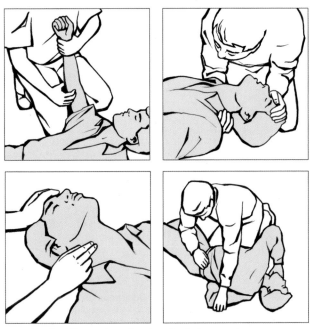

8.17 Medical illustration, directions for first responders.

Shifting our attention to fine art, Robert Rauschenberg's *Booster* (8.18) presents his body as a series of X-rays. This unconventional self-portrait combines the personal X-rays with images of an astronomer's chart, diagrams of hand drills, arrows, graphs, and an empty chair. The title adds further meaning, suggesting a connection to booster shots, booster rockets, and booster seats, which increase the height of an ordinary chair so that young children can sit at a table comfortably. Reduced to an X-ray image and surrounded by fragments of technological information, the artist becomes a cog in the technological machinery. By contrast, the woman in Kiki Smith's *Virgin Mary* (8.19) seems both vulnerable and graceful. She displays her flayed body unapologetically, extending her open hands in a type of blessing.

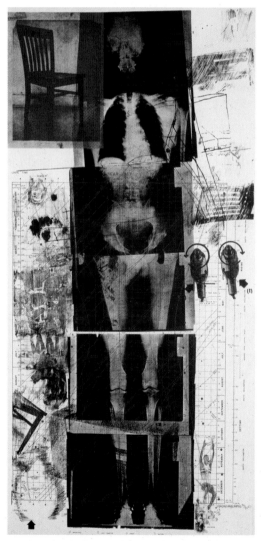

8.18 Robert Rauschenberg, *Booster*, 1967.
Lithograph and serigraph, printed in color, composition, 71⁹⁄₁₆ × 35⅛ in. (181.7 × 89.1 cm).

8.19 Kiki Smith, *Virgin Mary*, 1992. Beeswax, microcrystalline wax, cheesecloth, and wood on steel base, 67½ × 26 × 14½ in. (171.5 × 66 × 36.8 cm).

DEGREES OF REPRESENTATION

Nonobjective or **nonrepresentational shapes,** such as circles, rectangles, and squares, are **pure forms**. Pure forms are shapes that we create without direct reference to reality. Artists often use pure form to embody elusive emotions or express universal meaning. For example, in *Several Circles* (8.20), Wassily Kandinsky sought to express his complex spiritual feelings. For him, the simple circular shapes were as poignant and expressive as music.

We derive **representational shapes** from specific subject matter that is strongly based on direct observation. Most photographs are representational and highly descriptive. For example, in Ansel Adams's *Monolith, The Face of Half Dome, Yosemite Valley* (8.21), each variation in the cliff's surface is clearly defined.

Between these two extremes, **abstract shapes** are derived from visual reality but are distilled and transformed, reducing their resemblance to the original source. In *Seventh Sister* (8.22), Robert

Moskowitz deleted surface details from the rocky mountain. His abstracted cliff is a general representation of a vertical surface rather than a descriptive painting of a specific cliff.

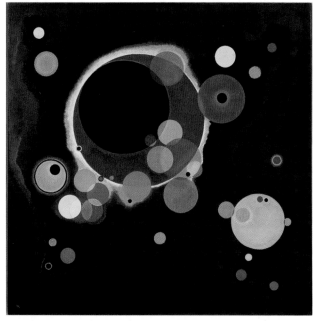

8.20 Wassily Kandinsky, *Several Circles*, 1926. Oil on canvas, 55¼ × 55⅜ in. (140.3 × 140.7 cm).

8.21 Ansel Adams, *Monolith, The Face of Half Dome, Yosemite Valley*. 1927. Photograph.

8.22 Robert Moskowitz, *Seventh Sister*, 1982. Oil on canvas, 108 × 39 in. (274.3 × 99 cm).

Reference to reality is a traditional way to increase meaning in an artwork. Drawing on their experience in the physical world, viewers can connect to the illusion of reality presented in the painting. In a nonobjective image, lines, shapes, textures, and colors must generate all of the meaning. Because there is no explicit subject matter, some viewers find it more difficult to understand nonobjective images.

Abstract images can combine the power of association with the power of pure form. Charles Demuth's *And the Home of the Brave* (8.23) demonstrates the power of abstraction. He has transformed a factory into a series of lines and geometric shapes. Variations on red, white, and blue add a symbolic connection to the American flag. Painted during a period of nationwide unemployment, the factory is dark and forbidding. The ironic title (which is based on the concluding words from the American national anthem) adds a pointed political statement.

DEGREES OF DEFINITION

Definition is the degree to which we distinguish one visual component from another. **High definition** creates strong contrast between shapes and tends to increase clarity and immediacy of communication. For this reason, the diagrams in this book generally feature black figures on a white background. **Low-definition** shapes, including soft-edged shapes, gradations, and transparencies, can increase the complexity of the design and encourage multiple interpretations.

Definition is an inherent aspect of photography. In addition to variations in focus, the photographer can choose finer-grained film and slick paper to create a crisper image, and coarser-grained film and textured paper to create a softer image.

Variations in photographic definition can substantially affect meaning. We normally expect to see high definition in the foreground and low definition in the background. In *Gun 1, New York* (8.24), William Klein reversed this expectation. Pointed directly at the viewer's face, the gun itself is blurred, menacing, and monstrously large. Even more disturbing, however, is the scowling face of the boy holding the gun. Fierce and sharply focused, his face epitomizes both fear and rage.

8.23 Charles Demuth, . . . *And the Home of the Brave*, 1931. Oil on composition board, 29½ × 23⅝ in. (74.8 × 59.7 cm).

8.24 William Klein, *Gun 1, New York*, 1955. Gelatin silver print, 15¾ × 11¾ in. (40 × 29.8 cm).

DEFINITION AND REPRESENTATION

- Which will best express your idea—representation, nonrepresentation, or abstraction?

- Variations in definition can increase the illusion of space. Will your design benefit from greater depth?

- Definition can also direct the viewer's attention to specific areas in the design. How can definition enhance meaning in your design?

8.26 Alfred Eisenstadt, *Winston Churchill*, Liverpool, **1957.** Gelatin silver print.

CONTEXT

As we noted in Chapter Seven, the context in which any image appears profoundly influences meaning. Viewers tend to connect informational fragments. For example, in figure 8.25, the juxtaposition of discouraged flood survivors with a propagandistic billboard makes us rethink the phrase "There's no way like the American way."

8.27 **Minnesota Children's Museum, Pentagram design, New York, NY.** Tracy Cameron and Michael Bierut, Designers.

8.25 Margaret Bourke-White, *At the Time of the Louisville Flood*, **1937.** Gelatin silver print.

The social context in which an image appears is equally important. In figure 8.26, Winston Churchill, the prime minister most responsible for British victory during World War II, extends two fingers to create the famous "V for victory" gesture that he used throughout the war. If we are familiar with Churchill and know about the British people's desperate struggle during the war, we immediately make the correct connection. In figure 8.27, the same gesture communicates a different idea. As part of the signage for the Minnesota Children's Museum, the

8.28 Sean O'Meallie, *Out-Boxed Finger Puppets Perform the Numbers 1 Through 5 in No Particular Order*, 1999. Polychromed wood, 17.5 × 42 × 11 in. (44.5 × 106.7 × 27.9 cm).

8.29 Jimmy Margulies, Editorial Cartoon, 2006.

extended fingers now communicate the number 2. Because children may not be able to read, this icon can help them find their way in the museum. Finally, in Sean O'Meallie's *Out-Boxed Finger Puppets Perform the Numbers 1 Through 5 in No Particular Order* (8.28), the same gesture becomes a playful piece of sculpture, as well as an indication of the number 2. We now see the extended fingers in the context of a series of whimsical forms. In each of these three cases, the meaning of the two fingers depends on the context.

CONNECTIONS

Analogies, similes, and metaphors are figures of speech that link one thing to another. An **analogy** creates a general connection between unrelated objects or ideas, whereas a **simile** creates the connection using the word *as* or *like*, as in "She has a heart as big as Texas." A **metaphor** is more explicit: Speaking metaphorically, we would say "Her heart *is* Texas." As we can see, a substantial shift in meaning occurs when we use a metaphor.

In all cases, we give the original word the qualities of the linked word. For example, when Robert Burns wrote the simile "My love is like a red red rose," he gave the abstract concept of "love" the attributes of a glorious, colorful, fragrant, thorny, and transient rose.

We can use **metaphorical thinking** to connect an image and an idea. Take the phrase "I have butterflies in my stomach." We widely use this phrase to

describe nervousness. Let's substitute other insects for butterflies, such as bees or wasps. How does this change the meaning? To push it even further, start with the phrase "My mind was full of clouds." What happens when you replace "clouds" with mice on treadmills, rats in mazes, shadowy staircases, beating drums, screaming children—or even butterflies? When my mind is full of butterflies, I am happy, but butterflies in my stomach indicate fear. In addition to expanding ideas, metaphors can help provide specific images for elusive emotions.

To strengthen communication, artists and designers have always used metaphorical thinking. Editorial cartoons offer many examples. In figure 8.29, a congressional hand puppet vows independence from the very lobbyist who is controlling his vote.

AESTHETICS

Cultural Values

In *Design in the Visual Arts,* Roy Behrens noted the difference between the words *anesthetic* and *aesthetic*. We use an **anesthetic** to induce insensitivity or unconsciousness. In an anesthetic state, we are numbed and disoriented. We may not be able to determine the size or location of objects or the sequence of events. On the other hand, **aesthetics** is the study of human responses to beauty. An aesthetic experience enhances our feelings and our understanding expands. As a result, an aesthetic experience tends to heighten meaning, whereas an anesthetic experience tends to dull meaning.

Dentists use anesthetics; artists and designers use aesthetics.

Aesthetic theories reflect social values and thus vary greatly from culture to culture. For example, an exalted conception of Christianity dominated civic life during the Middle Ages in Europe. To express their faith, architects developed ingenious building strategies to create the soaring Gothic cathedrals that we associate with that period (8.30).

By contrast, the Unitarian congregation that commissioned Frank Lloyd Wright's Unity Temple (8.31) most valued a sense of community. As a result, their sanctuary is essentially a cube, with rows of seats facing inward from three sides. Congregants face each other while simultaneously maintaining close contact with the minister. Pompidou Center (8.32), by Renzo Piano and Richard Rogers, offers a third approach to public architecture. From the outside, it looks more like a roller coaster than a major art museum. To emphasize the importance of technology in contemporary life, these architects have highlighted the blue ventilation ducts, red elevators, and green water pipes rather than hiding them.

Because cultural values are so variable, before we conclude our discussion of visual communication, we must delve into contemporary aesthetics.

Modern and Postmodern

Postmodernism was the dominant art movement from around 1975–2005 and remains a powerful force in contemporary art. The word itself emphasizes the extent to which artists and designers often seek solutions that challenge or exceed modernism. Thus, to understand contemporary aesthetics, we must first examine the essential characteristics of both of these aesthetic periods.

In the arts, **modernism** is a general term that encompasses a wide range of individual movements. Beginning in Europe in the latter part of the nineteenth century, modernism became the dominant force in art and design from around 1900 to 1975.

In a sense, modernism rose from the ashes of World War I. After this devastating conflict, traditional attitudes and images seemed inadequate and out of date. Architects began to strip away traditional ornamentation to reveal the underlying structures and spaces in their buildings.

8.30 Notre-Dame Cathedral, Paris.

8.31 Frank Lloyd Wright, Unity Temple interior, 1906. Oak Park, Illinois.

Designers such as Marcel Breuer (see figure 5.1), Raymond Lowry, and Charles and Ray Eames (see figure 5.5) used plastic, metals, and glass to mass-produce objects and images for an expanding consumer market. Artists such as Wassily Kandinsky (see figure 8.20), Barnett Newman, and Mark Rothko (8.33) valued abstraction over traditional

8.32 **Renzo Piano and Richard Rogers, Pompidou Center.** Paris, France. 1976.

8.33 **Mark Rothko, *White Center (Yellow, Pink and Lavender on Rose)*, 1950.** Oil on canvas, 81 × 56 in. (205.8 × 141 cm).

representation. The international art world became a hotbed of experimentation.

Many modernists shared four fundamental beliefs. First, they were fascinated by **form**, meaning the physical manifestation of an idea. "Less is more" became a mantra for designers, and "the form is the content" became a catchphrase for many painters. Second, modernists readily embraced new materials and production methods. Concrete, plastic, and glass began to replace traditional materials such as wood, brick, and stone, especially in architecture. Third, the early modernists strongly believed in the social significance

of the arts. They wanted to bring art and design to the general population, rather than working for the elite. Finally, many modernists sought to understand and express universal truths. No longer satisfied with a conventional representation of reality, they began to develop a new visual language based on distillation and abstraction.

These fundamental beliefs stimulated innovation in all areas of art, architecture, and design, thus producing an enormous amount of brilliant work. Over time, however, many modernists became trapped by their own success. Constructed from hard, reflective materials and dominated by right angles, modernist buildings could seem cold and uninviting. Based on an underlying grid and typographical conventions, modernist posters could become stale and predictable. Reduced to essential forms, late modernist painting and sculpture became detached from the chaos and complexity of contemporary life. Artists and designers seemed to have answered all the questions of modernism. Something had to change.

The 1966 publication of *Complexity and Contradiction in Architecture* set the stage for postmodern architecture. In it, architect Robert Venturi extolled the energy and ambiguities of renaissance architecture:

> I like elements which are hybrid rather than "pure," compromising rather than "clean," distorted rather than "articulated," perverse as well as impersonal, boring as well as "interesting," conventional rather than "designed," accommodating rather than excluding, redundant rather than simple, vestigial as well as innovating, inconsistent and equivocal rather than direct and clear. I am for messy vitality over obvious unity.

At the same time, philosophers Jean-François Lyotard, Jacques Derrida, Michel Foucault, and Roland Barthes began to challenge previous aesthetic theories. They argued that both knowledge and communication change constantly: there *are* no universal truths. Because the audience rather than the artist ultimately responds to the artwork, interpretation is inherently open-ended. Furthermore, postmodern theorists tended to see knowledge as cyclical rather than progressive. They argued that we are pursuing a complex path with multiple branches rather than a grand journey leading to human perfection.

Influenced by these theorists and seeking fresh ideas and approaches, many contemporary artists and designers reject the central tenets of modernism. For the postmodernist, context and content are as important as pure form. Postmodern use of materials tends to be open-ended and often irreverent. For example, an artist may construct an artwork from trash, while he or she may manipulate fiberglass to mimic steel.

Interested in all forms of experience, postmodernists tend to question distinctions between "high art" (such as painting and sculpture) and "low art" (such as advertising and crafts). Since various aspects of visual culture are intertwined, the postmodernist may recycle images and ideas, deliberately "appropriating" them for use in a new context. Finally, for the postmodernist there are multiple rather than universal truths—and all truths change continually. As a result, where late modernism tended to be stable and reductive, postmodernism tends to be expansive and dynamic. As Venturi suggested, we can view complexity and contradiction as strengths.

For the past 30 years, the collision between modernism and postmodernism has released an enormous amount of energy. Artists have broken taboos repeatedly, and the criteria for excellence continue to evolve.

Postmodern Strategies

Five common characteristics of postmodern art and design follow.

We often use **appropriation** (the reuse of an existing artwork) to create a connection between past and present cultural values. In *We Don't Need Another Hero* (8.34), Barbara Kruger borrowed a Norman Rockwell illustration in which a young girl admires her male counterpart's muscles. The emphatic text shifts the meaning from the original gender stereotype to a powerful feminist statement.

Recontextualization is another postmodern strategy. Constructed from steel pins and placed in a gallery, Mona Hatoum's *Doormat II* (8.35) forces us to rethink a commonplace object. As part of a series on racism, this artwork suggests that the opportunities offered by civil rights legislation may be as ironic as a welcome mat made of pins.

Artists often use **layering** to create complex or even contradictory meanings. In *The Red Mean:*

8.34 Barbara Kruger, *Untitled (We Don't Need Another Hero),* **1987.** Photographic silkscreen, vinyl lettering on Plexiglas, 109 × 210 in. (276.9 × 533.4 cm).

8.35 Mona Hatoum, *Doormat II,* **2000–01.** Steel and rubber, 1 × 28 × 16 in. (2.5 × 71 × 40.6 cm).

Self-Portrait (8.36), Jaune Quick-to-See Smith reinterprets Leonardo da Vinci's famous drawing of ideal human proportions (8.37). As a Renaissance man, Leonardo was fascinated by both perfection and the grotesque. In this drawing, he mapped out an idealized figure radiating out from the navel in the center. Despite its superficial similarity, the aesthetic basis for Smith's self-portrait is entirely different. Her circular outline simultaneously suggests a target, cancellation, and the four directions emphasized by many Native American spiritual practices. A sign proclaiming "Made in the USA" combined with the artist's tribal identification number covers the figure's chest, and tribal newspapers fill the background. While the da Vinci drawing is simple and elegant, Smith's self-portrait provides a rich commentary on the complexities of her life as a Native American.

These examples demonstrate a fourth postmodern characteristic: we often integrate words and images to expand emotional impact or to create conflict. The postmodernist celebrates contradiction and complexity as facts of life and sources of inspiration.

Finally, we can define **hybridity** as the creation of artworks using disparate media and meanings to create a unified conceptual statement. Jaune Quick-to-See Smith constructed her *Self-Portrait* from newspapers, posters, and identity cards, as well as paint. Kathryn Frund combined government documents and a carpenter's plumb bob with paint on aluminum to create *Radical Acts* (see figure 3.21, page 74). Mark Messersmith combined painting and sculpture in *Vapid Visionaries* (8.38). He even included a series of small boxes at the bottom of the painting, filled with hidden treasures. For the postmodernist, visual impact and conceptual meaning are more important than technical purity.

DRAMA

Regardless of the medium or the message, we can strengthen all communication through dramatic delivery. Even Martin Luther King, Jr.'s "I Have a Dream" speech loses much of its power when one delivers it in a flat, monotonous tone of voice. Just as a playwright sets the stage for the story that he or she seeks to tell, so an artist can set the stage for visual communication.

8.36 Jaune Quick-to-See Smith, *The Red Mean: Self-Portrait*, 1992. Mixed medium.

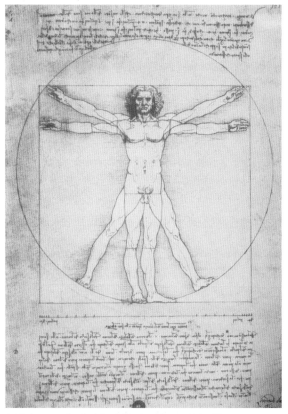

8.37 Leonardo da Vinci, *Proportions of the Human Figure* (after Vitruvius), c. 1485–90. Pen and ink, 13½ × 9¾ in. (34.3 × 24.8 cm).

8.38 Mark Messersmith, *Vapid Visionaries*, 2010. Oil on canvas with carved wooden top parts and mixed media predella box on bottom, 65 × 82 in. (165.1 × 208.3 cm).

We can use all of the design elements and principles that we describe in this book to increase *compositional* drama. To increase *conceptual* drama, we can:

• *Personify the idea.* When we identify with a character in a play, we become more empathetic and involved in the story. Likewise, when we identify with a character in a painting or a poster, we are much more likely to remember the idea or emotion. Figure 8.39 represents one of the most effective campaigns that Mothers Against Drunk Driving use. These posters combined before and after photographs of young drivers to show the devastating results of traffic accidents.

• *Focus on essentials.* Some say that theater is "life with the boring parts left out." To be meaningful to an audience, the characters and events in a play must have a strong relationship to direct experience. However, a playwright rarely shows a character flossing his or her teeth. Too much detail clutters the composition, confuses the audience, and muddles the message. Including the right amount of information in just the right way can add drama to even the simplest idea.

• *Seek significance.* We can use any event, character, or time period to create an effective play.

Likewise, we can use any object, event, or idea in our quest for visual communication. For example, Sean O'Meallie turned a simple sequence of numbers into a witty series of sculptures. A unique approach to a familiar subject or an insightful interpretation of personal and political events can add significance and increase impact.

Not everyone who gets hit by a drunk driver dies.

Jacqueline Saburido was 20 years old when the car she was riding in was hit by a drunk driver. Today, at 24, she is still working to put her life back together.
Learn more at www.helpjacqui.com

DON'T DRINK & DRIVE

Texas Department of Public Safety • Texas Alcoholic Beverage Commission • Texans Standing Tall • Partnership for a Drug-Free Texas • Texas Commission on Alcohol and Drug Abuse

8.39 Mothers Against Drunk Driving ad.

summary

- A shared language is the basis on which we build all communication.

- Iconography (the study of symbolic visual systems) provides us with a way to analyze the meaning of images and objects.

- Just as films target specific audiences, artists and designers use different forms of visual communication for different audiences.

- Graphic designers often seek visual immediacy. By comparison, many paintings require extended viewer involvement and longer viewing time.

- A stereotype is a fixed generalization based on a preconception. Stereotypes can easily create a bridge between the image and the audience.

- A cliché is an overused expression or predictable treatment of an idea. Even the most interesting image will lose its power if we overuse it.

- A shift in a stereotype or cliché challenges our assumptions and can increase impact.

- Artists and designers choose the style, iconography, and composition best suited to their purpose. A mismatch between the type of image and its purpose creates confusion.

- The visual and social context in which an image appears will profoundly affect its meaning.

- Analogies, similes, and metaphors are figures of speech that link one thing to another. Visual communication, especially, widely uses metaphors.

- Appropriation, recontextualization, layering, word/image integration, and hybridity are five common strategies that we use to create postmodern meaning.

- Dramatic delivery of a message enhances meaning.

key terms

abstract shapes	hybridity	postmodernism
aesthetics	iconography	pure form
analogy	layering	recontextualization
anesthetic	low definition	representational shapes
appropriation	metaphor	simile
cliché	metaphorical thinking	stereotype
definition	modernism	
high definition	nonobjective shapes	

studio projects 💿

To apply the concepts from this chapter in the studio, check out the Projects page in the Online Learning Center at www.mhhe.com /LTI5e. The following is a sample of the chapter-related assignments in step-by-step detail.

Benign to Sublime. Transforming a benign still life into a compelling vehicle for the communication of an idea.

Build a Concept Generator. A basic cube turns into a conceptual toy.

Word/Image Synergy. Using Photoshop or photocopies to combine one or more images with a single word to create an unexpected message.

Profile:
Carrie Ann Baade, Painter
From the Autobiographical to the Universal

Inspired by literature and art history, Carrie Ann Baade is an internationally renowned artist whose surreal oil paintings are rich with allegorical meta-narratives. Her art has been exhibited nationally and internationally, and various books and journals prominently feature her works. Originally from Colorado, she has traveled all over the world and currently lives in Tallahassee, Florida.

MS: You first attended the School of the Art Institute of Chicago, one of the most progressive art schools in America. You then completed your MFA at the University of Delaware, gaining a mastery of painting techniques that artists developed roughly 500 years ago.

Both experiences are evident in your work. The paintings have the visual elegance and technical skill of a Renaissance masterpiece—yet express a contemporary sensibility. How and why do you combine sensibilities and processes that seem so utterly different?

CB: I am attracted to symbolism as used in art history, and I have a great respect for the power of both narrative and figurative imagery. Yet in the twentieth century, many leading artists tended to reject both the figure and the narrative, and some theorists argued that painting was dead. I took this very personally.

So, I began to collect photocopies of obscure Renaissance paintings. By cutting up these paintings and using them to create collages, I combined the power of these historical masterworks with my own experience as a contemporary artist. I took historical images that appeared meaningless and breathed new life, my life, into them.

MS: How do you start?

CB: I see the complete image in my mind, and then seek the source material needed to construct the vision. In a sense, it is like reverse engineering—starting with the end result, then finding my way back to the beginning. Even though copyright issues don't apply to artworks that are 500 years old, I was initially very cautious about using historical sources. However, I soon realized that they had been utterly transformed by their compositional and conceptual context.

MS: Cinema and literature seem better suited to complex storytelling. Why use paint?

CB: Some of my professors in grad school suggested that I quit painting because what I was trying to do was impossible. But for me, art is a perpetual motion machine that presents impossible problems for both the artist and the viewer to solve. Reaching for concepts that are beyond my grasp simply makes me more determined! And, I expect a high level of viewer commitment, as well. I don't *want* to make 90-second paintings that can be grasped quickly!

MS: You have suffered profound personal losses that have fueled numerous images of distressed and weeping women. Your current work is much broader, referencing politics and social problems. How did this change occur?

CB: The artist's own thoughts and feelings pour into the image, which necessarily reflects his or her perceptions, experiences, and emotions. Art really can be a place in which we mourn and grieve. However, over time I realized that, "What we think, we become," as Buddha observed. By filling my mind and art with suffering, I attracted more suffering and sufferers. Catharsis is important, but it is better as a place to pass through than a place to live!

Some say, "Art cannot change the world." But, close your eyes; imagine the world without painting, music, architecture, color, or dancing.

Is this the world we want? Art may not be necessary for survival, but it makes survival worthwhile.

MS: It seems that you construct each of your paintings in layers of images, references, ideas, and emotions. Please talk us through *The Bride Stripping the Bachelors Bare*.

CB: I decided to reference Marcel Duchamp's *The Bride Being Stripped Bare by the Bachelors Even*, which deals in part with male and female lust from a man's point of view. The title is remixed to emphasize the female point of view.

First, to form the composition, I completed a prototype collage of layered scraps with cut edges (figure 1). Some of these are photographs of me; others are derived from historical sources. Next, I created an ink under-drawing based on the collage (figure 2). The multiple layers with cut edges are not intended to make a harmonious synthesis—instead, the fragments suggest the complexity of individual psychology. We see the exposed masks and the concealed secrets. Finally, to create the visually rich effects, I build the image on top of the drawing using layer after layer of oil paint (figures 3 and 4).

Figure 2 Ink under-drawing, *The Bride Stripping the Bachelors Bare*, 2008.

Figure 1 Collage, *The Bride Stripping the Bachelors Bare*, 2008.

Figure 3 Oil glazes for painting, *The Bride Stripping the Bachelors Bare*, 2008.

Figure 4 Completed painting, *The Bride Stripping the Bachelors Bare*, 2008.

MS: Can you describe the basic iconography?

CB: The bride holds her wedding ring, which is a symbol of love, faithfulness, and commitment. Once it is worn, the woman is trusted to stay faithful to the one who placed it on her finger and marks her as a possession. However, the bride's hand has been cut off, much as in some cultures a thief would lose a hand. Like Hester Prynne, the heroine of Nathaniel Hawthorne's *The Scarlet Letter*, she wears a scarlet "A" on her chest—but notice that this "A" is pinned there like an award.

Changing from maiden to bride, then from bride to wife, transforms her identity. If an act of infidelity interrupts this process, she is removed from the sacred to the profane and becomes an outcast. I seek to maximize meaning through contradictions and multiple references.

MS: How important is the physical object, the painting you meticulously craft through many hours of work?

CB: For me, art is simply the by-product of the development of consciousness. Through my paintings, I share my understanding with others. If I weren't developing my own consciousness, I would have nothing to say.

MS: Do you have any advice for beginning students?

CB: *Do not become an artist!* If you can do something else, do it. This will never be an easy path. Our eyes, our hands, our minds are committed to service. Every battle you fight, and every sacrifice you make proves your conviction that no one and nothing can tear you from your station.

Eva Hild, *Lamella*, **2008.** Stoneware, 26 × 23 × 22 in. (66 × 58 × 55 cm).

Three-Dimensional Design

At the beginning level, many of us have more experience with two-dimensional design than with three-dimensional design. Working in three dimensions tends to require a wider range of materials, development of many technical skills, and more studio space. Why, then, is understanding of three-dimensional design so important?

The answer is simple. Three-dimensional design offers powerful new ways to express ideas and emotions. When working two-dimensionally, we create flat visual patterns or convincing illusions. The viewer *mentally* creates meaning. In contrast, our experience in the three-dimensional world is physical and direct. As we traverse an architectural space, we alter our perception with each step we take. When we circle a sculpture, we encounter new information on each side. The materials that an artist uses in a three-dimensional object determine its aesthetic appeal as well as its structural strength. As a result, we enter into a unique perceptual realm when we shift from a world of patterns and illusions to a world of physical objects.

This section is devoted to the elements, organization, and implications of three-dimensional design. We will explore the basic elements of three-dimensional design in Chapter Nine. Chapter Ten is devoted to the principles of three-dimensional design. Chapter Eleven focuses on materials and their meanings. In Chapter Twelve, we will more thoroughly explore the unique characteristics of three-dimensional experience.

Three-Dimensional Design Elements

Eddie Chui's chess pieces (figure 6.7, page 130) rock back and forth on their curving bottoms. When the pieces are used in a game, their polished sides and hefty weight delight the players who hold them.

Richard Hunt's *Sisiutl Mask* (figure 5.10, page 110) represents a mythic three-headed sea serpent whose glance can transform an adversary into stone.

Xu Bing's *A Book from the Sky* (9.1) is more conceptually challenging. It consists of printed volumes and scrolls containing thousands of "false" Chinese characters that he invented and then painstakingly hand-cut into wooden printing blocks. Those of us who are not fluent in Chinese may admire the graceful characters and wonder at their meaning. Those who *do* know Chinese find that their familiar cultural references have turned into conceptual chaos.

In each of these three examples, we are engaged physically, mentally, and emotionally. While a painting or video can pull us into an imaginative world, a sculptural object offers a tangible presence that is powerful in itself. In the hands of a skillful artist or designer, this raw power translates into insight and energy.

Point, line, plane, volume, mass, space, texture, light, color, and time are the basic building blocks of three-dimensional design. In this chapter, we consider the unique characteristics of each.

9.1 Xu Bing, *A Book from the Sky*, 1987–91. Hand printed books, ceiling and wall scrolls printed from wood letterpress type using false Chinese characters, dimensions variable.

FORM

In Chapter Seven, we defined **form** as the physical manifestation of an idea. **Content** refers to the idea itself, including the subject matter plus its emotional, intellectual, spiritual, and symbolic implications. In three-dimensional design, *form* can refer also to three-dimensionality itself. For example, a circle, a square, and a triangle are two-dimensional shapes, and a sphere, a cube, and a pyramid are three-dimensional forms.

Types of Form

- We generally define an empty three-dimensional form as a **volume**, while we generally define a solid form as a **mass**.

- An effective three-dimensional composition balances **positive forms** (areas of substance) with **negative space** (areas that are open).

- **Organic forms** (forms that visually suggest nature or natural forces) create a very different effect than **geometric forms** based on cubes, spheres, and other simple volumes. **Mechanical forms**, such as belts and gears, can suggest an industrial source.

- The degree of actual or implied movement in a form can expand our vocabulary even further. **Static forms** appear stable and unmoving. Designed to last forever, the Great Pyramids at Giza exemplify stability and repose. **Dynamic forms** imply movement. Suspended from the ceiling, Richard Wilson's *Slipstream* (9.2) captures the twisting action of a stunt plane

in flight. **Kinetic forms** actually move. Theo Jansen's *Strandbeest Series* (9.3) includes enormous wind-propelled structures that wiggle, walk, or slither down the beach. They seem to have been born of a marriage between an erector set and Jurassic Park.

9.2 **Richard Wilson,** *Slipstream*, **2014.** Aluminum, size variable, installed in Terminal 2, Heathrow Airport.

9.3 **Theo Jansen,** *Strandbeest Series*, **2000–present.** Wind-activated kinetic sculpture, size variable.

Form and Function

A sculptor explores an idea, chooses materials, and develops a composition based on his or her aesthetic intention. Public art projects, such as Eero Saarinen's *Jefferson National Expansion Memorial* (9.4), and ritual objects, such as the Sisiutl mask, commemorate historical events or express social values.

A designer uses the same mastery of concept, composition, and materials to create an object that is *functional* as well as beautiful. Before creating a new line of aquatic gear, designer Bob Evans carefully analyzes the needs of different types of swimmers. The basic *Force Fin* (9.5A) provides the required maneuverability for snorkeling. He designed the *Multi Force Fin* (9.5B) as a strength-training device. The *Excellerating Force Fin* (9.5C) provides the extended power that scuba divers need. For designers such as Evans, the form must fulfill a specific **function**, or purpose.

Visualizing Form

Height, width, and depth are the three dimensions in three-dimensional design. In computer-aided design, we define these three dimensions using the *x*-, *y*-, and *z*-axes from geometry (9.6). Using the cube as a basic building block, we can create many variations on these basic dimensions. In figure 9.7A, the cube is modified through removal and displacement. In figure 9.7B and C, additional planes and unexpected intersections increase complexity.

There are many methods of depicting three-dimensional form on a two-dimensional surface. **Orthographic projection** is one of the most useful. Unlike perspective drawing, which relies on vanishing points to create the illusion of space, orthographic projection uses parallel lines to define structural details.

An orthographic projection represents six views of a three-dimensional form. Imagine that your project is enclosed in a glass box (9.8A). As you look through the top, bottom, front, and back, then through the right and left sides, you can see six distinctive views. In effect, you can create an orthographic drawing when you unfold and flatten this imaginary box (9.8B). Using orthographic projection, we can examine and record various surfaces of a three-dimensional object (9.8C).

9.4 Eero Saarinen and Hannskarl Bandel, *Jefferson National Expansion Memorial* (Gateway Arch), St. Louis, 1963–65. 54 × 630 ft. (16.5 × 192 m).

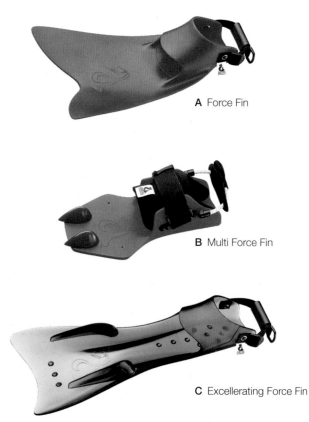

A Force Fin

B Multi Force Fin

C Excellerating Force Fin

9.5A–C Bob Evans, *Force Fin Variations*, 1990–present. Molded polyurethane, size variable.

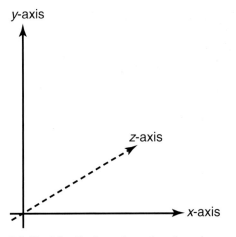

y-axis

z-axis

x-axis

9.6 We define the three dimensions through height, width, and depth.

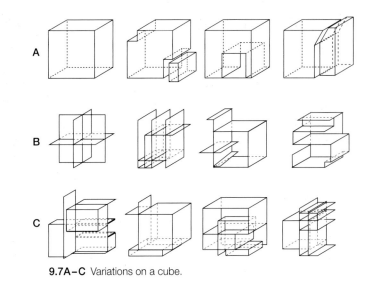

A

B

C

9.7A–C Variations on a cube.

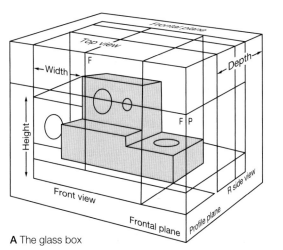

Frontal plane

Top view

Width

F

Depth

Height

F P

Front view

Frontal plane

Profile plane

R side view

A The glass box

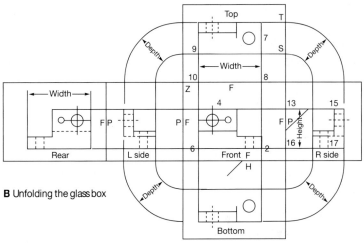

Top   T

Depth

9   S

Width

7

10   8

Z   F

Width

4

P F

13   15

F P

Height

6   2

16   17

Rear   L side   Front F   R side

H

Depth   Depth

Bottom

B Unfolding the glass box

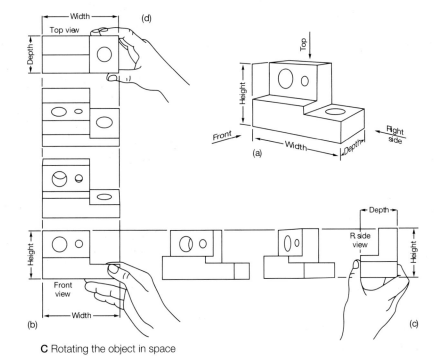

Width   (d)

Top view

Depth

Top

Height

Front   Right side

Width   Depth

(a)

Height

Depth

R side view

Front view   Height

Width

(b)   (c)

C Rotating the object in space

9.8A–C We can use orthographic projection to define structural details.

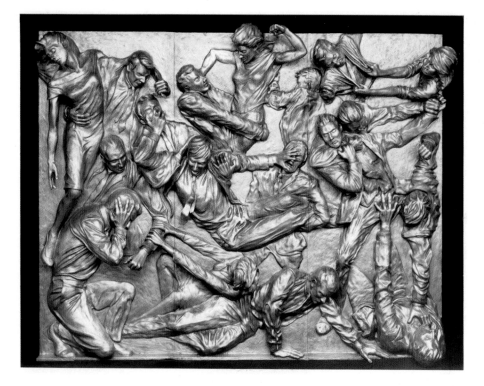

9.9 Robert Longo, *Corporate Wars* (detail), 1982. Cast aluminum, lacquer on wood relief, 7 × 9 × 3 ft (2.1 × 2.7 × 0.9 m).

Degrees of Dimensionality

The degree of dimensionality greatly influences our response to sculptural objects. Relatively flat artworks can combine the strengths of two- and three-dimensional design, while we are invited to view free-standing artworks from many angles.

Relief

When working in **relief**, the artist uses a flat backing as a base for three-dimensional forms. For example, Robert Longo's *Corporate Wars* (9.9), is like a sculptural painting. Using the boundaries created by the supporting wall and the four outer edges, it presents a group of white-collar warriors engaged in hand-to-hand combat. The figures are trapped, bound both to the backing and by their struggle for money.

Three-Quarter Works

A **three-quarter work**, such as Jean-Baptiste Carpeaux's *The Dance* (9.10) is more three-dimensional. We can walk around this piece, examining the front and two sides. As a result, the joyous figures seem to dance right out of the wall.

Freestanding Works

Freestanding works can be viewed from all sides. When we circle Auguste Rodin's *The Kiss* (9.11A

and B), we capture every nuance of figurative movement. Details (such as the man's stroking hand and the woman's raised heel) bring life to the inanimate stone.

9.10 Jean-Baptiste Carpeaux, *The Dance* (after restoration), 1868–69. Marble, 7 ft 6½ in. (2.3 m).

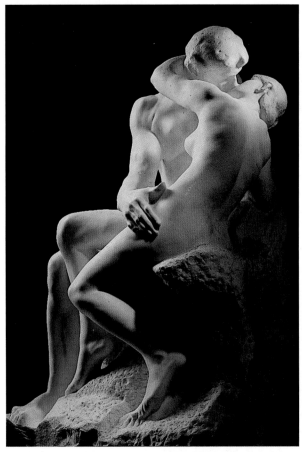

9.11A Auguste Rodin, *The Kiss*, 1886–98. Marble, over life size. Dramatic lighting accentuates form and can heighten emotion.

9.11B Auguste Rodin, *The Kiss*, 1886–98. Marble, over life size. A slight change in the viewer's position substantially changes the apparent orientation of the figures.

Environmental Works

An **environmental work** (or **environment**) presents a space that we can enter physically. Installations (which are usually indoors) and earthworks (which are usually outdoors) are two major types of environments. Such works often require active audience participation and may present a series of images, ideas, and experiences that unfold over time.

Installations

An **installation** is an ensemble of images and objects that are presented within a three-dimensional environment.

9.12 Yayoi Kusama, *Fireflies on the Water*, **2002.** Installed at the Whitney Museum of American Art, 2012. Mirror, plexiglas, 150 lights and water, overall size 111 × 144½ × 144½ in. (281.9 × 367 × 367 cm).

Surrounded by information, we become emotionally and physically involved. Yayoi Kausama's *Fireflies on Water* (9.12) is a spectacular example. Combining mirror plexiglas, 150 suspended lights,

and a pool of water, she created a shimmering and apparently infinite world. Upon entering the space via a small platform, each viewer becomes part of the artwork itself.

Earthworks

An **earthwork** is a large-scale outdoor installation. Often extending over great distances in time and space, earthworks may require substantial physical engagement by the artist, the audience, and inhabitants of the site. Robert Smithson's *Spiral Jetty* (9.13) is a classic example. This 1,500-foot-long coil of rock and earth extends from the shore into the water of the Great Salt Lake in Utah. For Smithson, the spiral created "a dot in the vast infinity of universes, an imperceptible point in a cosmic immensity, a speck in an impenetrable nowhere."[1] Remote and mysterious, this artwork evokes a cosmic connection that extends far beyond the walls of a museum or gallery.

Site-Specific Artwork

A **site-specific** artwork is designed for and installed in a particular place. Commissioned by the port city of Algeciras in Spain, *Mano y Bola* (9.14) rests on a bluff overlooking the Strait of Gibraltar. The 40-foot-long hand may be catching or throwing the 20-foot-tall ball positioned roughly 50 feet away. This artwork metaphorically alludes to the historical exchange of religion, power, and conflict between Europe and Africa. To heighten the metaphor, sculptor Todd Slaughter designed the hand to disappear when the wind blows. He covered it with over one thousand movable panels that create the image of a hand. A brisk wind shifts the panels to a horizontal position, causing the image to dissolve visually into the surrounding sky.

9.13 Robert Smithson, *Spiral Jetty*, 1970. Earthworks sculpture made of 6,650 tons of black basalt, 1,500 ft (457.2 m).

9.14 Todd Slaughter, *Mano y Bola* (details), 1997. Aluminum and steel, hand 27 × 40 × 4 ft (8.2 × 12.2 × 1.2 m), ball 20 ft (6 m) diameter. Overlooking the Strait of Gibraltar.

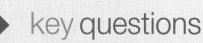

key questions

FORM

- Experiment with organic, geometric, and mechanical forms. Which is best suited to the idea that you wish to express?

- What mix of static and dynamic artwork will best support your idea?

- Will the addition of a kinetic component add to the overall effect?

- When you are creating a freestanding artwork, how much similarity and how much contrast do you require on each side? What does the viewer gain by walking around the artwork?

POINT

A **point** is a basic mark, such as a dot, a pebble, or a brushstroke. Just as the appearance of a single actor on an empty stage can electrify an audience, so the simplest point immediately creates a dialog with the surrounding space. For example, in figure 9.15, Andy Goldsworthy transformed a pile of stones by covering just one of them with bright red leaves.

When multiplied, points produce an **array** of visual information that an artist can use to create rich textures or build entire images. German design firm Art+Com created *Kinetic Rain* (9.16)

9.16 Art+Com Designers, *Kinetic Rain*, 2012. Installation at the Changi Airport, Singapore. Copper-plated aluminum raindrops, wire, computer-controlled motors, 810 × 810 × 24 ft (246.9 × 246.9 × 7.3 m).

from hundreds of metal raindrops controlled by tiny motors. Continually shifting, these points create a wide range of sculptural variations.

key questions

POINT

- When is a single point most effective, and when is an array needed?

- Should your points be evenly distributed in space, or unevenly distributed?

- A focal point draws attention to a specific area or aspect in a composition. How might your composition benefit from use of a focal point?

LINE

Line is one of the most versatile elements. In three-dimensional design, we can create **line** through the following:

- *A series of adjacent points.* The cars that make up Ant Farm's *Cadillac Ranch* (9.17) are distinct objects in themselves as well as the points that create a line of cars. Commissioned by a rancher in Texas, some have described this sculpture as a requiem for the gas-guzzling American automobile.[2]

9.15 Andy Goldsworthy, *Red Rock*, 1989. Leaves and stones.

9.17 Ant Farm (Chip Lord, Hudson Marquez, Doug Michels), *Cadillac Ranch*, 1974. Ten Cadillacs, Amarillo, TX.

9.19 Taos Ski Valley evening torchlight parade.

9.18 Kenneth Snelson, *Free Ride Home*, 1974. Aluminum and stainless steel, 30 × 30 × 60 ft (9.1 × 9.1 × 18.2 m). Storm King Art Center, Mountainville, NY.

- *A connection between points.* Kenneth Snelson constructed *Free Ride Home* (9.18) using two types of line. The aluminum tubes provide a linear skeleton that becomes elevated when the connecting lines are attached. The resulting diagonal lines seem to defy gravity.

- *A point in motion.* In combination with New Year's Eve fireworks, skiers in Taos, New Mexico, zoom down a major slope carrying flashlights. Figure 9.19 shows that they create lines of light from each moving point.

Line Quality

Each line has its own distinctive quality. Orientation, direction, continuity, and material all contribute to this distinctive quality.

Orientation

Orientation refers to the line's horizontal, vertical, or diagonal position. Based on our experience in the natural world, we tend to associate horizontal lines with stability and diagonal lines with movement. Vertical lines tend to accentuate height and can make an object or an interior appear grand and imposing.

Mark di Suvero uses all three types of line in *Are Years What?* (9.20) as does Peter Pierobon in *Ladderback Chair* (9.21). A vertical I-beam combined with one horizontal beam stabilizes di Suvero's large-scale sculpture. Six diagonals suggest movement and increase dynamism. By contrast, it is the tall vertical back that transforms Pierobon's chair into a whimsical sculpture. Its

9.20 Mark di Suvero, *Are Years What?*, 1967. Painted steel, 480 × 480 × 360 in. (1219.2 × 1219.2 × 914.4 cm).

9.21 Peter Pierobon, *Ladderback Chair*. Ebonized mahogany and leather, 66 × 17 × 17 in. (167.6 × 43.2 × 43.2 cm).

exaggerated height pulls our eyes upward and provides support for the nine jagged lines that create the rungs of the ladder.

Curved lines can carve out complex patterns in space and may encompass an object to create a harmonious whole. Rob Ley's *Draper* (9.22), transforms straight vertical lines into a cascade of silvery movement. By distorting the original sheet of aluminum, Ley created a large-scale artwork that is beautiful and light in weight.

9.22 Rob Ley, *Draper*, 2011. Installed at Florida State University. Stainless steel, 75 × 18 × 4 ft (22.3 × 5.5 × 1.2 m).

Direction

Direction refers to the implied movement of a line. A line of consistent width tends to suggest equal movement in both directions. Varying line width can create a more specific sense of direction. For example, in *Jefferson National Expansion Memorial* (see figure 9.4, page 182), the massive lines at the bottom drive downward into the earth, while the tapered arch at the top lifts our eyes skyward.

Continuity

Continuity, or linear flow, can increase movement and accentuate form. In Chris Burden's *Medusa's Head* (9.23), a mad tangle of toy train tracks flows around and through the mass of stone, plywood, and cement. Representing the snakes that crowned the head of a mythical monster, these writhing lines accentuate the spherical mass and give us a fresh interpretation of an ancient Greek myth.

9.23 Chris Burden, *Medusa's Head*, 1989–92. Cement, wood, stone, train tracks, 16 ft (4.8 m) diameter, 5 tons.

Actual Lines

Through their physical presence, **actual lines** can connect, define, or divide a design. *Laocoön and His Two Sons* (9.24) depicts a scene from the Trojan War. When the Greeks offer a large, hollow wooden horse to the Trojans, Laocoön warns against accepting the gift. The Greek goddess Athena then sends two serpents to attack and kill the seer, thereby gaining entry into Troy for the soldiers hiding in the horse. The writhing serpent compositionally connects the terrified men while adding emotional intensity to this depiction of Athena's wrath.

Implied Lines

Implied lines are created through mental rather than physical connections. *The Rape of the Sabine Women,* by Giovanni da Bologna (9.25), relies on a series of implied lines for its impact. Starting at the bottom and exploding upward, the repeated diagonals in the sculpture create a visual vortex as powerful as a tornado. At the bottom is the husband of the captured woman. In the center, a standing Roman soldier is intent on stealing a wife for himself. The agitated movement culminates at the top with the embattled woman's extended arm.

A **sight line** activates Nancy Holt's *Sun Tunnels* (9.26). At first glance, the four 22-ton

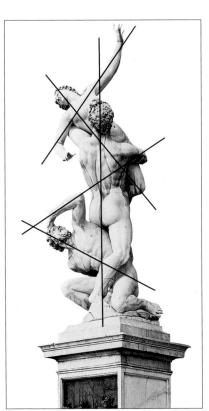

9.25 Giovanni da Bologna, *The Rape of the Sabine Women*, completed 1583. Marble, 13 ft 6 in. (4.1 m).

9.26A–B Nancy Holt, *Sun Tunnels*, 1973–76. Great Basin Desert, UT. Four tunnels, each 18 ft long × 9 ft 4 in. diameter (5.5 × 2.8 m), each axis 86 ft long (26.2 m). Aligned with sunrises and sunsets on the solstices.

9.24 *Laocoön and His Two Sons*. Marble, 7 ft (2.13 m).

concrete tunnels seem static. Upon entering each tunnel, the viewer discovers a series of holes that duplicate the stars' size and position in four major constellations. The light pouring in through these holes shifts as the sun rises and travels across the sky. During the winter and summer solstices, the sculpture further transforms as the circular tunnels' alignment frames light from the rising and setting sun. Like a telescope, the massive cylinders are more important for the visions that they create than as objects in themselves.

Linear Networks

Both artists and designers use linear networks in many different ways. In figure 9.27, interlocking metal lines form the woven mesh on a fencer's mask. Due to its linear construction, it is light in weight and protects the athlete's face without blocking vision. Janet Echleman's *Tsunami 1.26* (figure 9.28) was created using thousands of polyester fiber threads. Suspended above a busy city street, this artwork continually shifts shape, like an undulating jellyfish. Single lines can bring a simple eloquence to a design, while multiple lines can be used to create strong, complex, and versatile forms.

▶ key questions

LINE

- Vertical, horizontal, diagonal, and curving lines all have unique strengths. What can each type contribute to your design?

- What can line continuity or discontinuity contribute to your composition?

- What happens when you dramatically increase or decrease the number of lines?

- Can intersecting lines strengthen your design, both structurally and compositionally?

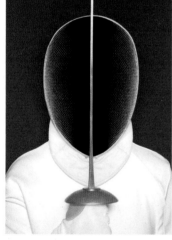

9.27 Steve McAllister, *Fencing Mask*. Photograph.

9.28 Janet Echelman, *Tsunami 1.26*, 2011. Suspended from the Sydney Town Hall over George Street, Sydney, Australia. Spectra® fiber, high-tenacity polyester fiber, and colored lighting; dimensions of net: 230 × 63 × 30 ft (70.1 × 19.2 x 9.1 m).

PLANE

A **plane** is a three-dimensional form that has length and width but minimal thickness. Depending on the material used, planes can be transparent or opaque, rigid or flexible, flat or curved. We can construct enclosures using folded or bent planes.

9.29 Scapes cards. Artist: Darren Waterston. Designer: Ryan Burlinson. Art direction: Kurt Wolken. Client: Bellevue Art Museum. Wolken, Communica, Seattle, WA.

9.30 Maya Lin, *Blue Lake Pass* (detail), 2006. Duraflake particleboard, 20 blocks, approx. 5¾ × 17½ × 22½ ft (1.75 × 5.3 × 6.8 m).

When slotted together, planes can create a variety of sturdy forms (9.29). As Maya Lin's *Blue Lake Pass* (9.30) demonstrates, when modified incrementally and organized sequentially, planes can create forms that are as descriptive as a mountain climber's map.

Planar contructions can be relatively light in weight as well as physically strong. As we noted on page 181, Richard Wilson designed *Slipstream* for Terminal 2 at London's Heathrow Airport. Inspired by the movements of a flying plane, he needed to capture an elusive idea within a suspended form. By combining a wooden interior structure with thin sheets of aluminum, he was able to suggest motion across the 230-foot-long sculpture.

▶ key questions

PLANE

- Consider the limitations of the material you are using. Can you cut, score, and fold it to create curving planes?

- What are the structural and compositional advantages of curved or twisted planes versus flat planes?

- What happens to your design when you pierce and slot together any or all of the planes?

VOLUME

In general terms, volume is the amount of space an object occupies. In three-dimensional design, **volume** refers to an enclosed area of three-dimensional space.

Cubes, cylinders, cones, and spheres are among the most common volumes that we find in both nature and architecture. Fascinated by such "biological structures," Kendall Buster has created entire exhibitions using large-scale, translucent volumes (9.31). By contrast, seemingly weightless organic volumes comprise Xiao Min's *Secret Room* (9.32). Using a twelfth-century Chinese sex manual as a source, he constructed a series of life-sized couples embracing. Made from translucent sheets

9.31 Kendall Buster, *New Growth*, 2007. Steel frame, cable ties, greenhouse shadecloth. Installation at Boise Art Museum. Size variable.

of steel mesh, the suspended figures are both dream-like and erotic.

Designers often create functional objects using **polyhedra**, or multifaceted volumes (9.33). Such volumes can be surprisingly strong. In beginning industrial design classes, students often use a variety of polyhedra to construct lightweight bristol board helmets. And in figure 9.34, Manuel Villa constructed an entire house based on a polyhedron.

Octahedron Net   Hexahedron Net   Dodecahedron Net

Octahedron   Hexahedron (cube)   Dodecahedron

9.33 A variety of polyhedra.

9.32 Xiao Min, *Secret Room #3*, 2008. Steel wire, 90 × 19 × 17 in. (127 × 48 × 43 cm).

9.34 Manuel Villa, *Polyhedron Habitable*, 2008. Bogota, Colombia. General construction materials, 9.8 × 8.2 × 8.9 ft (3 × 2.5 × 2.7 m).

9.35 Ettore Sottsass, *Ginevra Carafe*, 1997. Manufactured by Alessi, Crusinallo, Italy.

The specific amount of enclosed space is especially important when we create any kind of container, from architecture to glassware. *The Ginevra Carafe,* by Ettore Sottsass (9.35), easily holds a liter of wine. The elegant cylinder requires little table space, and an extra disk of glass at the base increases its weight and stability. An additional glass disk at the top ensures that the lid will remain firmly in place.

Linear networks, folding, and slotting are a few of the strategies artists and designers use to create volume. Defining an enclosed space while maintaining structural integrity is essential. If the structure fails, the volume will collapse and the space will be lost.

Each strategy has its advantages. As the fencer's mask in figure 9.27 demonstrates, woven structures can be elegant, lightweight, and remarkably strong. On the other hand, package designers generally create volume through folding. Sturdy Bristol paper can be printed while flat, then scored, cut, and folded. And surprisingly strong volumes can be created using slotted planes. Slotted structures can be

used to protect and separate fragile contents (such as wine bottles) and hold them in a specific position.

MASS

A **mass** is a solid three-dimensional form. A massive object can be as dense and heavy as a bar of gold or as light and porous as a sponge.

Massive sculptures are often carved from a solid block of plaster, clay, or stone or cast using bronze, glass, or other materials. Solid and imposing, they tend to dominate the environment in which they are placed.

Henry Moore's *Locking Piece* (9.36) gains power through a combination of mass and visual movement. Almost 12 feet tall, the interlocking bronze forms are as emphatic and muscular as a clenched fist. A dialogue between curves and angular forms adds variety and invites the viewer to experience the sculpture from every side.

Massive forms tend to suggest stability, power, and permanence. The ancient Olmec heads from Mexico combine the abstract power of a sphere

9.36 Henry Moore, *Locking Piece*, 1963–64. Bronze, 115 × 110¼ × 90½ in. (292 × 280 × 230 cm).

with the emotional power of a human head (9.37). Ledelle Moe's large-scale sculptures are equally powerful (9.38). Constructed from 200 or more puzzle pieces, when installed, these reclining heads seem to dream only tragic dreams. Even though they are hollow, the sculptures *appear* solid and imposing. Tom Friedman produced a very different type of mass in figure 9.39. He cut hundreds of pencils at various angles, and then reconstructed them to create an energetic maze.

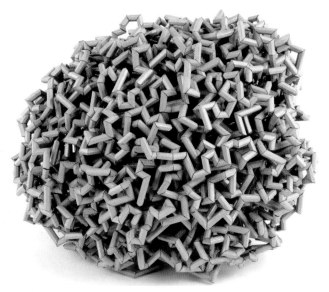

9.37 *Colossal Head*, **1300–800** BCE. Stone, 11 × 9⅝ × 9⅝ ft (3.4 × 3 × 3 m). Olmec culture, Jalapa, Veracruz, Mexico.

9.39 Tom Friedman, *Untitled*, **1995.** Pencils cut at 45-degree angles and glued in a continuous loop, 11 × 14 × 11 in. (28 × 35 × 28 cm).

9.38 Ledelle Moe, *Collapse V*, **2007.** Concrete and steel, 9 × 11 × 7 ft (2.7 × 3.6 × 2.1 m).

VOLUME AND MASS

- How can you use planar source materials (such as bristol paper and cardboard) to create sturdy volumes?

- What are the advantages of transparent versus opaque volumes?

- When is a mass more expressive than a volume?

SPACE

In three-dimensional design, **space** is the area within or around an area of substance. As soon as we position an object in space, we create a dialogue between a form and its surroundings. Space is the partner to substance. Without it, line, plane, volume, and mass lose both visual impact and functional purpose.

The proportion of space to substance triggers an immediate response. The space in Alice Aycock's *Tree of Life Fantasy* (9.40) seems fluid and weightless. Inspired by the double-helix structure of DNA and by medieval illustrations showing people entering paradise through a spinning hole in the sky, Aycock combined a linear structure with a series of circular planes. The resulting sculpture is as open and playful as a roller coaster. By contrast, Burden's *Medusa's Head* (see figure 9.23, page 190) presents a relatively solid mass of tangled cement, wood, and metal. With sculptures of this kind, the *surrounding* space becomes more important than any enclosed

space. Like a stone dropped into a glass of water, this large, heavy mass seems to displace the surrounding space, pushing it into the edges of the room.

Positive and Negative Space

Every area of three-dimensional design demonstrates the interrelationship between space and substance. A central void dominates David Smith's *Cubi XXVII* (9.41). The 10 gleaming metallic volumes are activated by the space they enclose. Space plays an equally important role in representational work. The open mouth in figure 9.42 really animates the mask. No facial expression, however extreme, would be as lively if this mouth were closed.

9.40 Alice Aycock, *Tree of Life Fantasy*, Synopsis of the Book of Questions Concerning the World Order and/or the Order of Worlds, 1990–92. Painted steel, fiberglass, and wood, 20 × 15 × 8 ft (6.1 × 4.6 × 2.4 m).

9.41 David Smith, *Cubi XXVII*, March 1965. Stainless steel, 111⅜ × 87¾ × 34 in. (282.9 × 222.9 × 86 cm).

9.42 Mochica, mask, c. 200 BC–AD 700. Ceramic, Peru.

Negative space is especially noticeable in designs that are dominated by positive form. Karen Karnes's *Vessel* (9.43) is a functional pot, with its internal bottom placed just above the vertical slit. In effect, the lower half of the design serves as a pedestal for the functional container at the top. This narrow slit of negative space presents a strong contrast to the solidity of the cylindrical form and helps to activate the entire vessel.

Compression and Expansion

Space is never passive or meaningless. It is just as important as the surrounding substance and can be manipulated very deliberately. The tangibility of space is especially apparent in Richard Serra's and Walter de Maria's artworks. Using four enormous steel plates, Serra created a sense of spatial compression in figure 9.44. Upon entering the piece, the viewer immediately becomes aware of the tilted planes' weight and of the claustrophobic compressed space between these planes. The space in de Maria's *The Lightning Field* (9.45) is equally clearly defined yet is wonderfully expansive. Arranged in a grid over nearly 1 square mile of desert, 400 steel poles act as a collection of lightning

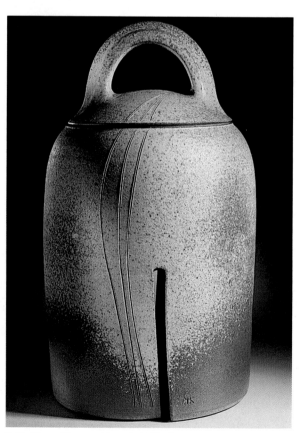

9.43 Karen Karnes, *Vessel*, 1987. Stoneware, wheel-thrown, glazed, and wood-fired, 16½ × 10½ in. (41.9 × 26.7 cm).

9.44 Richard Serra, *Betwixt the Torus and the Sphere*, **2001.** Weatherproof steel, 142 × 450 × 319 in. (361 × 1,143 × 810 cm).

9.45 Walter de Maria, *The Lightning Field*, **1977.** Stainless steel poles, average height 20 ft 7½ in. (6.1 m), overall 5,280 × 3,300 ft (1,609.34 × 1,005.84 m). Near Quemado, NM.

rods. Impressive even in daylight, the site becomes awe-inspiring during a thunderstorm. Lightning jumps from pole to pole and from the sky to earth, creating a breathtaking pyrotechnic display.

Activated Space

The space in an artwork may be contemplative, agitated, or even threatening. For example, a Japanese Zen garden is usually made from an enclosure containing several large rocks surrounded by carefully raked white sand. These simple objects create a contemplative space. By contrast, the space in Anish Kapoor's sculptures is often disorienting. Placed at the entrance to Millennium Park in Chicago, *Cloud Gate* reflects the surrounding buildings while the lower "gate" section visually pulls the viewer into a reflective interior chamber (9.46).

Entering Space

Some artists design their sculptures so that viewers can enter them physically, thus creating a unique experience. Lucas Samaras's *Mirrored Room* (9.47) multiplies and divides the reflection of each visitor who enters. Taking it even further, Yayoi Kasuma's *Fireflies on the Water* (see figure 9.12, page 185) surrounds the viewer with suspended lights and reflective water. Other artists create their works so that we can only enter them mentally. *Subway with Silver Girders* (9.48), by Donna Dennis, re-creates the architecture and lighting that we find in a subway station. Constructed at two-thirds the scale of an actual station, the sculpture presents a magical entry into a prosaic place. This subway station transports our minds rather than our bodies.

9.46 Anish Kapoor, *Cloud Gate*, Dedicated 2006. Millennium Park, Chicago. Stainless steel, 66 × 42 × 33 ft (20.12 × 12.8 × 10 m). The mirrorlike finish reflects visitors and the surrounding city.

9.47 Lucas Samaras, *Mirrored Room*, 1966. Mirrors on wooden frame, 8 × 8 × 10 ft (2.44 × 2.44 × 3 m).

9.48 Donna Dennis, *Subway with Silver Girders*, 1981–82. Wood, masonite, acrylic, enamel, cellulose compound, glass, electrical fixtures, and metal, 12 × 12 × 13.5 ft (3.6 × 3.6 × 4.11 m).

TEXTURE

Texture refers to the visual or tactile quality of a form. The increased surface area of a three-dimensional form heightens the impact of texture. The surface shifts and turns, presenting many opportunities for textural elaboration.

Degrees of Texture

Variations in the suface of a volume may be subtle or pronounced. In *Blackware Storage Jar*, by Maria Montoya Martinez and Julian Martinez (9.49), the artist combined a burnished, shiny surface with a

9.50 Walter Oltmann, *Caterpillar Suit I*, 2007. Anodized aluminum and brass wire, 46 × 23 × 17 in. (116.8 × 58.4 × 43.2 cm).

9.49 Maria Montoya Martinez and Julian Martinez, *Blackware Storage Jar*, 1942. Hopi, from San Ildefonso Pueblo, NM. Ceramic, 18¾ × 22½ in. (47.6 × 57.1 cm).

subtle matte surface. Geometric patterns enhance the jar's surface but never compete with the purity of the graceful globe. On the other hand, Walter Oltmann's *Caterpillar Suit* (9.50) is abuzz with exuberant texture. He combined wire mesh and hundreds of individual wires to create an oversized insect. Like an actual caterpillar, the result is both whimsical and threatening. Will we be tickled or stung when we touch this weird creature?

The Implications of Texture

On a compositional level, texture can enhance or defy our understanding of a physical form. In figure 9.51, the lines carved into the vessel's surface increase our awareness of its dimensionality. Concentric circles surrounding the knobs at the base of each handle create a series of visual targets that circle the globe, while additional grooves accentuate the surface of the sturdy handles. On a conceptual level, texture can add layers of meaning to art and design. In his *Alien Sculpture* series (9.52), Francesco

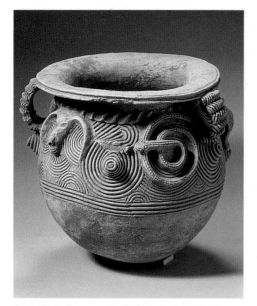

9.51 Globular vessel with inverted rim, tenth century, Igbo, Nigeria. Terra-cotta, 16 in. (40.6 cm).

9.52 Francesco Mai, *Boccosa with texture from 5D*, **2006.** Digital sculpture, Lambda print, 55 × 41 in. (139 × 104 cm).

Mai digitally created structures that combine mechanical with organic forms. Dramatic lighting in these images accentuates each knob and spike. Like improbable sea creatures, the resulting forms seem alive and ready to engulf or entrap their prey.

> ## key questions
>
> ### TEXTURE
>
> - How many textures can you create with the material you are using?
> - What happens visually when a surface gradually shifts from a polished, smooth texture to a very rough texture?
> - Can an unexpected use of texture enhance or expand the idea that you want to convey?

LIGHT

Light can enhance or obscure our understanding of form. It can entice us to enter a room, heighten our emotions, and create a mystery. It can even become a sculptural medium in its own right. Often overlooked, light is actually a pivotal aspect of three-dimensional design.

Value and Volume

Whenever light pours across a surface it produces a graduated series of highlights and shadows. These **values** (that is, variations in light and dark) are our primary means of perceiving space. As a result, lighting can greatly diminish the impact of a sculptural object. Giovanni Bernini's *Ecstacy of Saint Teresa di Avila* (9.53) depicts a mystical experience. As Saint Teresa described it, an angel plunged an arrow into her heart, overwhelming her with a love of God. Brightly illuminated from above with softer side lighting, the dramatic sculpture seems to glow. Product designers are equally aware of the importance of light. A badly lit form will lack definition and impact, while even the simplest form will attract attention when it is dramatically lit. In figure 9.54, highlights, gradations, and shadows give definition to each of Stan Rickel's *Teapot Sketches*.

Striking a Surface

Light is strongly affected by the surface it strikes. Light creates a continuous series of values when it strikes an opaque surface. Light behaves very differently when it strikes a **transparent** surface, such as clear plastic or glass. It is often **refracted** (or bent), creating a complex network of luminous shapes. **Reflective** surfaces can bounce light back into space. As a result, objects that are made from

9.53 Gian Lorenzo Bernini, *Ecstasy of Saint Teresa*, Cornaro Chapter, Santa Maria della Vittoria, Rome, 1645–1652. Marble, 138 in. (350.5 cm) tall.

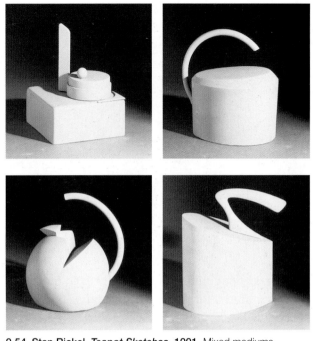

9.54 Stan Rickel, *Teapot Sketches*, 1991. Mixed mediums, 12 × 12 × 12 in. (30.5 × 30.5 × 30.5 cm).

polished steel, mirrors, and other reflective materials can appear to emit their own light. A **translucent** surface is partially transparent. Neither fully opaque nor fully transparent, translucent surfaces can be mysterious and evocative.

Each surface type can be used expressively. The movement of seven opaque figures in and out of light dominate *The Dance* (figure 9.10). Light and shadow accentuate the exuberant dancers' action. The same composition would dissolve into visual chaos if it were cast in transparent glass. Cast shadows further expand expressive potential. In Ruth Asawa's sculptures (9.55), suspended organic forms seem to float through the silent space. Spotlights illuminate the sculptures and create mysterious cast shadows.

9.55 Ruth Asawa, *Exhibition at de Young Art Museum in San Francisco*, 2005.

9.56 Robert Irwin, *Part II: Excursus: Homage to the Square³*. Installation at Dia Center for the Arts, New York, September 1998–June 1999.

Translucent materials can create even more complex effects. Robert Irwin's *Part II: Excursus: Homage to the Square³* (9.56) was installed at the Dia Center for the Arts in New York in 1998–99. This structure consisted of nine cubic rooms, defined by delicate translucent cloth walls. The fabric's translucency varied depending on the amount and location of the light. Two vertical fluorescent lights illuminated each cube, creating subtle changes in color from room to room.

Entering the installation was both inviting and disorienting. From any point, all of the rooms were visible yet veiled. The fabric layers and the variations in light made the most distant rooms appear to dissolve. The vertical fluorescent lights, which always remained visible, read first as individual, then as mirror images, creating a hallucinatory experience similar to a carnival funhouse. All activity within the space was created by the visitors themselves, who entered, explored, and left the installation like ghostly silhouettes.

Ambient and Directed Light

Ambient light encompasses an entire space or setting. For example, when we enter an open courtyard on a sunny summer afternoon, we are surrounded by warm ambient sunlight. Everything we see is colorful and brightly lit. **Directed light** is localized and focused, like a spotlight on a singer.

Exhibition designers are masters of light. They use directed light to focus the viewer's attention and increase visual drama. They use ambient light to create the underlying feeling. For example, the designers of a 1989 NASA exhibition used low ambient light to suggest the mystery of space travel. They then used bright pools of directed light to emphasize individual displays (9.57).

9.57 **NASA Exhibit at the 1989 Paris Air Show.** Designers: Bill Cannan, Tony Ortiz, H. Kurt Heinz. Design Firm: Bill Cannan & Co.

9.58 Stephen Knapp, installing *First Symphony*, 2006.

Light as Sculpture

Contemporary artists and designers use many types of sculptural light. Some shape neon tubes into sculptural forms. Others use commercial lighting fixtures and illuminated signs to convey aesthetic meaning. Still others project light onto various shapes and surfaces, creating effects ranging from the humorous to the tragic to the bizarre.

Projection and containment are two common ways to create sculptural light. The neon tubes in Robert Irwin's *Excursus* emit light, while Ruth Asawa used projected light to create expressive shadows. Stephen Knapp creates his light paintings (9.58 and 9.73, page 214) when light passes through shards of colored glass, producing an explosion of prismatic color. In all these cases, light is an essential component of the artwork.

The expressive possibilities increase when an image is projected onto a specific surface. On the anniversary of the bombing of Hiroshima, Krzysztof Wodiczko combined video interviews with a specific architectural structure—the Hiroshima Peace Memorial, one of the few buildings that remained standing after the explosion (9.59). Standing near the epicenter, over 5,000 spectators heard the stories of Japanese and Korean survivors from World War II.

With the increasing use of new media, light has become an eloquent and versatile addition to the elements of three-dimensional design. Moving beyond its traditional role in accentuating form, it has become a sculptural medium in itself. For example, in *The Veiling* (9.60), Bill Viola hung thin sheets of translucent fabric on parallel lines across the center of a darkened room. He projected a man's image from one end, while he projected a woman's image from the opposite

9.59 **Krzysztof Wodiczko,** *Hiroshima Projection*, **1998.** Public projection of video images at the Hiroshima Peace Memorial, Hiroshima, Japan.

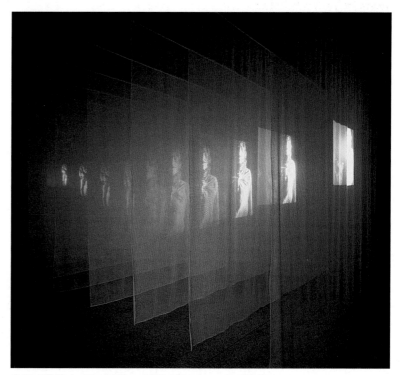

9.60 **Bill Viola,** *The Veiling*, **1995.** Video/sound installation.

end. These projections became increasingly diffused as they passed through the multiple layers of cloth. Finally, the two figures merged on a central veil as pure presences of light.

9.61A Hue.

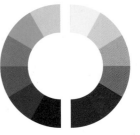
9.61B Value.

▶ key questions

LIGHT

- How can lighting direction diminish or accentuate your artwork's dimensionality?

- Does your artwork require special illumination, such as an internal light source, fiber optics, or a video screen?

- How can light enhance your artwork's expressive content?

- Can you redesign your project to use light and shadow more effectively? If so, how?

9.61C Intensity.

9.61D Temperature.

COLOR

Color definitions remain the same whether we are creating a three-dimensional or a two-dimensional composition. Each color has a specific **hue** (9.61A), based on its wavelength. **Value** (9.61B), the lightness or darkness of a color, helps determine legibility. **Intensity**, or **saturation** (9.61C), refers to a color's purity. **Temperature** (9.61D) refers to the physical or psychological heat suggested by a hue. For example, red is a warm color; blue is a cool color.

Degrees of Harmony

Selecting the right colors for a product and determining the degree of color **harmony** can make or break a design. The triadic harmony that Fisher-Price used in the Smartronics Learning System (9.62) creates an attractive educational toy for young children. The large red, yellow, and blue buttons are easy to push and invite even the most skeptical child to play. *Kita Collection*, by Toshiyuki Kita (9.63), offers a very different type of harmony. These simple chairs with their removable seats can be color-customized to fit any interior. The buyer can create his or her own sense of harmony.

9.62 Smartronics Learning System by Fisher-Price.

9.63 Toshiyuki Kita, *Kita Collection* **of chairs with removable seats for Stendig International Inc.** Beechwood frame and upholstered seat.

9.64 Do Ho Suh, *Reflection*, 2004. Nylon and stainless steel tubing, dimensions variable.

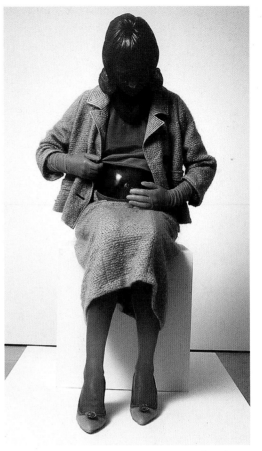

9.65 Keith Edmier, *Beverly Edmier*, 1967. Cast resin, silicone, acrylic paint, fabric.

Analogous colors, such as green, blue, and violet, can be especially harmonious. In *Reflection* (9.64), Do Ho Suh used such colors to produce a mysterious mirrored image. He combined an inverted gatelike form with its reflected counterpart to create an installation that was both magical and meditative.

We can also use clashing colors effectively. In figure 9.65, Keith Edmier portrays his pregnant mother on the day of President Kennedy's assassination. She is wearing the same Chanel suit pattern that Jackie Kennedy wore, and she pensively rubs her glowing belly. The artist himself appears as a fetus in the womb. The orange-reds and purple-reds suggest traditional monochromatic harmony but seem skewed and off-key. While the surface of normalcy remained intact, the substance of American politics shifted after Kennedy's death. Likewise, while the artist's mother seems calm, the colors and materials suggest an undercurrent of anxiety.

Contrast

Artists and designers often use contrasting colors to accentuate a product's function or to create a distinctive image. Contrasting colors and contrasting materials distinguish Michael Graves's *Alessi Coffee Set* (9.66). A metallic armor protects the fragile,

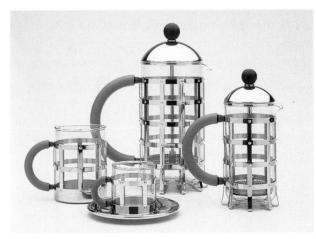

9.66 Michael Graves, *Alessi Coffee Set*, 1985. Glass, silver, mock ivory, and Bakelite.

9.67 **Kurt Perschke, *RedBall Taipei*, Bopiliao Street, 2009.** Vinyl inflatable, 15 ft (4.6 m) diameter.

Symbolic Color

Symbolic color is culturally based. Because each culture is unique, color associations vary widely. For example, yellow signifies the direction north in Tibet but represents the qualities of light, life, truth, and immortality to Hindus.[4] Blue represents mourning in Borneo, while in New Mexico it is painted on window frames to block evil spirits from entering. It represented faith and truth to the Egyptians yet was the color worn by slaves in Gaul.[5]

The blue face that dominates the Aztec mask of Tlaloc (9.69) is both symbolically and visually appropriate. Symbolically, the blue represents sky and the rain that Tlaloc calls forth to nourish crops. Visually, the contrast between the warm, reddish clay and the sky-blue paint enhances the impact of the ferocious face.

transparent glass. These metal bands emphasize the cylindrical forms, while the blue handles and bright red accents further animate the set.

The 15-foot-tall inflatable sphere Kurt Perschke uses in his *RedBall Project* (9.67) seems almost too simple. How can we call this art? However, when wedged into alleyways, under expressways, and in other tight spots, the cheery red sphere animates the surrounding gray building. It has traveled to over a dozen cities around the world, always attracting large audiences.

Color and Emotion

A visit to any car dealership demonstrates the emotional implications of color. Car manufacturers often market bright red, black, or silver sports cars as oversized toys for single drivers, while they often use more subdued colors for the minivans and station wagons, which families favor. Taking this idea a bit further, in a children's wheelchair design, Adele Linarducci used bright red, yellow, and blue to provide a sporty look—and add a psychological boost. On the other hand, it is the absence of color that brings power to the life-size figures in George Segal's installations. Despite their proximity to the viewer and their large scale, the white figures in *Walk, Don't Walk* (9.68) are drained of color, alienated, and emotionally distant.

9.68 **George Segal, *Walk, Don't Walk*, 1976.** Museum installation, with viewer. Plaster, cement, metal, painted wood, and electric light, 104 × 72 × 72 in. (264.2 × 182.9 × 182.9 cm).

9.69 Aztec vessel depicting the Rain God, Tlaloc, 1400–1521.
From the Templo Mayor, Tenochtitlan, Mexico. Polychrome ceramic vase, 13.8 × 13.8 × 12.4 in. (35.1 × 35.1 × 31.5 cm).

TIME

Every object occupies a position in time as well as space. In some cases, the specific temporal location is of minor importance. For example, *Locking Piece* (see figure 9.36, page 195) is as meaningful now as it was when Henry Moore constructed it in 1963. Constructed from durable bronze, it has effectively withstood the test of time. In other cases, temporal location gives the object its meaning. As noted on page 191, Nancy Holt's *Sun Tunnels* creates a kind of celestial observatory. Light pours through the holes in the curving walls, creating projections that mark the planet's movement. Without the element of time, the concrete tunnels would have no more meaning than drainage pipes at a construction site.

Two aspects of time are particularly important to sculptors. **Actual time** refers to the location and duration of an actual temporal event such as a bowling ball rolling along a track. By contrast, **implied time** is an event's suggested location or duration. The traffic light in Segal's *Walk, Don't Walk* changes, but the sculptural figures never move.

Actual motion and implied motion are equally important. In a brilliant use of actual time, actual motion, and natural forces, Ned Kahn constructed *Wind Veil* (9.70) from 80,000 aluminum panels.

 key questions

COLOR

- Which will better communicate your ideas—a limited range of hues or a wide range of hues?

- Are all the colors in your design similar in intensity? What would happen if you combined low-intensity colors with high-intensity colors?

- What is the proportion of warm and cool colors in your design? What would happen if these proportions were changed?

- What are the conceptual or symbolic implications of the colors you have chosen?

9.70 Ned Kahn, *Wind Veil*, 2000. 80,000 aluminum panels, total length 260 ft (79.25 m). Installation in Charlotte, North Carolina.

9.71 Claes Oldenburg and Coosje van Bruggen, *Shuttlecocks*, 1994. Aluminum, fiberglass-reinforced plastic, and paint. 230⁹⁄₁₆ × 191⅞ in. (585.63 × 487.36 cm).

9.72 **Jaume Plensa, *Crown Fountain*, 2000–04.** Glass, stainless steel, LED screens, light, wood, granite, and water, two 52½-ft-high towers, total area 7,217 ft² (2,200 m²).

Activated by each breath of wind, the wall shimmers with both energy and light. By contrast, *Shuttlecocks* (9.71), by Claes Oldenburg and Coosje van Bruggen, seems to capture the oversize game pieces just as they begin to hit the ground. In this case, the artwork depends on implied time and motion for its impact. A final example combines time and motion with anticipation. Positioned alongside Michigan Avenue in Chicago's Millennium Park, Jaume Plensa's *Crown Fountain* (9.72) attracts thousands of visitors each summer day. The work projects smiling images of everyday people from various city neighborhoods on the multiple video screens contained within each five-story tower. Every 15 minutes, the projected face purses its lips and a stream of water bursts forth, drenching the delighted children waiting below.

Viewing time is a final basic consideration. The multiple surfaces presented by any three-dimensional object require extended analysis. We walk around Rodin's *The Kiss* (figure 9.11A and B, page 185), noting every nuance in form and texture; we rotate a ceramic vessel in our hands, savoring every detail. *Fireflies on Water* (see figure 9.12, page 185), *Part II: Excursus* (see figure 9.56, page 206), and other installations require even more viewing time. To understand the artwork, the viewer must enter and fully explore the site.

key questions

TIME

- Is a "timeless" or a "timely" artwork more appropriate for the idea that you want to communicate?

- What compositional choices can you use to increase timelessness?

- How can actual, implied, or viewing time expand meaning in your design?

summary

- *Form* may be defined as the physical manifestation of an idea. *Content* refers to the idea itself, including the subject matter plus its emotional, intellectual, spiritual, and symbolic implications.

- In three-dimensional design, *form* also refers to dimensionality itself. Thus, a circle is a shape, while a sphere is a form.

- The first step in creating a design is to understand its purpose. An artist seeks to convey ideas and express emotions. A craftsperson or designer is equally concerned with the function and the beauty of an object.

- Height, width, and depth are the three dimensions in three-dimensional design.

- Artworks can vary in dimensionality from relief, which uses a flat backing to support dimensional forms, to environmental works that the viewer can enter and physically explore.

- A focal point can attract attention. An array is a collection of points. A line can connect, define, or divide a design. It can be static or dynamic, increasing or decreasing the form's stability.

- A plane is a three-dimensional form that has length and width but minimal thickness.

- In three-dimensional design, *volume* refers to an enclosed area of three-dimensional space.

- A mass is a solid three-dimensional form. A massive object can be as dense and heavy as a bar of gold or as light as a sponge.

- Space is the area within or around an area of substance. Space is the partner to substance. Without it, line, plane, volume, and mass lose both visual impact and functional purpose.

- *Texture* refers to a form's visual or tactile quality. The increased surface area of a three-dimensional form heightens the impact of texture.

- Light can enhance our perception of a three-dimensional form, attract an audience, or we can use it as a material in itself. Light behaves very differently when it hits a reflective or translucent surface.

- Hue, value, intensity, and temperature are the major characteristics of color.

- Every object occupies a position in time as well as space. We can combine actual time, implied time, actual space, and implied space in various ways to create compelling objects of great complexity.

key terms

actual lines	form	negative space	sight line
actual time	freestanding works	organic forms	site-specific
ambient light	function	orientation	space
array	geometric forms	orthographic	static forms
content	harmony	projection	symbolic color
continuity	hue	plane	temperature
directed light	implied lines	point	texture
direction	implied time	polyhedra	three-quarter
dynamic forms	installation	positive forms	work
earthwork	intensity	primary contours	translucent
elements	kinetic forms	reflective	transparent
environmental	line	refracted	value
work (or	mass	relief	viewing time
environment)	mechanical forms	saturation	volume

studio projects

To apply the concepts from this chapter in the studio, check out the Projects page in the Online Learning Center at www.mhhe.com/LTI5e. The following is a sample of the chapter-related assignments.

Calderesque Self-Portrait. A linear project using wire.

Spheres of Influence #1 and #2. Planar construction problems.

Discovering Mass. Modeling an object using foam rubber and carving a form from a plaster block.

Dominant and Subordinate. Exploring hierarchical composition.

9.73 Stephen Knapp, *Luminous Affirmations,* installed in the Tampa Municipal Office Building, Tampa, Florida, December 2005. Light, glass, stainless steel, 100 ft × 59 ft × 20 in.

Profile:
Marilyn da Silva,
Metalsmith
Metals and Metaphors

Professor Marilyn da Silva is program chair of the Jewelry/Metal Arts Department at California College of the Arts in Oakland. She was selected as "Master Metalsmith 1999" by the National Ornamental Metal Museum in Memphis, Tennessee, and her work has been displayed nationally and internationally, including at the Victoria and Albert Museum in London and the National Gallery of Australia.

MS: What is it that attracts you to metal?

MdS: I really love the resistance and permanence of metal. It only changes when I work it very deliberately: this gives me more control. If dropped, it will dent, but it will not break. It is inherently a "cool" medium, but using patinas and colored pencils, I can make metal appear "warm."

MS: How did you get started in this field?

MdS: From a very young age, I was always making things, such as furniture and clothing for my dolls. Working with my hands just came naturally. Other children enter into art through drawing; I entered through construction.

MS: You studied with Alma Eikerman, a particularly renowned metalsmith. What did you learn from her?

MdS: Alma emphasized both excellent craft and excellent design. She expected impeccable work: there were no excuses for weaknesses in either area. In one assignment, we made a black paper silhouette of our teapot body shape. We then designed 20 variations on handles and spouts using black paper. We then tried different combinations of handles, spouts, and pots, seeking the best solution. It sounds simple, but by generating dozens of variations, we were able to find the ideal combination.

MS: Your designs are charged with meaning. Please take us through your conceptual and compositional development of *Reap What You Sow*.

MdS: I designed this piece for a show devoted to pillboxes. The concept was based on three premises: (1) my recent discovery that I was allergic to penicillin, (2) the alarming amount of antibiotics in the foods we eat every day, and (3) the need for many to go over the border to acquire affordable prescriptions.

I did many drawings and decided to have a bird land on furrows found in fields. The bird would either be stealing a pill in its mouth or be placing it in the furrow. On all of my book pieces, the "leather" of the book turns into something else. In this case, it becomes the dirt and furrows of a field. I then selected the barn swallow as the bird of choice. It was an obvious solution because of its name "swallow" and the fact that this bird often builds its nest in barns, placing it in a farm environment.

The furrows have young plants sawed out of copper. If you look closer, you can see that the leaves look like small hands. The shadows of the hands are grasping at pills lying on the ground.

The book is made from heavy-gauge copper that has been hammered to give it texture. I used red oak flooring for the pages. The bird is carved out of basswood and has wings, feet, eyes, and beak made of metal. All of the metal parts of the book are colored with gesso and colored pencil. The title of the book, *Reap What You Sow: A Prescription for Life*, is etched into a brass plate and riveted to the book spine. Finally, an antique silver spoon with the name

"Grove" on it props up the book in the corner. You know, "just a spoon full of sugar helps the medicine go down. . . ."

MS: Conceptually, what do you seek in your work?

MdS: My artworks are layered with meaning. The viewer first sees the basic form and may respond to the beauty of the metal. Upon reflection, he or she may be drawn in by the storytelling and conceptual associations inherent in the work. For example, my *Rock, Paper, Scissors* refers to a children's game that is based on power dynamics and unpredictability. Likewise, *Reap What You Sow* can be read on many personal and environmental levels.

I avoid in-your-face polemics. It is better for viewers to respond to the work on the basis of their own experiences, and then return to the work for a second viewing.

Marilyn da Silva, *Reap What You Sow: A Prescription for Life*, 2004. Copper, sterling silver, brass, wood, plastic, gesso, colored pencil.

Principles of Three-Dimensional Design

To construct a successful composition, we must combine multiple parts to create a unified whole. Positive and negative forms create a lively dialogue and opposing forces add vitality rather than causing confusion. For example, Niels Diffrient combined graceful metal lines with contoured masses to create his *Freedom Chair* (10.1). In *Tree of Life Fantasy* (see figure 9.40, page 197) Alice Aycock combined lines, planes, and spaces to create an exuberant dance. Martin Puryear's *Seer* (10.2) consists of a closed volume at the top and an open volume at the bottom. The horn-shaped top piece is powerful and imposing, while the open construction at the bottom invites us to enter and visually explore the structure. Curving vertical "ribs" unify the top and bottom sections, while the contrast between open and closed forms adds a touch of mystery. In all three cases, every element is both dependent on and supportive of the other element.

10.1 Niels Diffrient, *Freedom Chair*, 1999. Die-cast aluminum frame with fused plastic coating; four-way stretch black fabric.

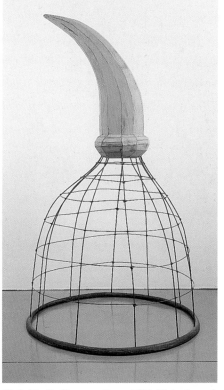

10.2 Martin Puryear, *Seer*, 1984. Water-based paint on wood and wire, 78 × 52¼ × 45 in. (198.2 × 132.6 × 114.3 cm).

In the previous chapter, we explored the elements (or building blocks) of three-dimensional design. This chapter will describe ways in which we can combine these elements.

UNITY AND VARIETY

We can define **unity** as similarity, oneness, togetherness, or cohesion. We can define **variety** as difference. Unity and variety are the cornerstones of composition.

Increasing Unity

We tend to scan an entire composition, then analyze the individual parts. When the parts fit together beautifully, the compositional puzzle can be highly expressive. When the parts don't fit, a great idea can become incoherent and confused. As we will see in the following section, grouping, containment, proximity, continuity, repetition, and closure are six common strategies for increasing unity.

Grouping

When we see a collection of separate visual units, we immediately try to create order and make connections. **Grouping** is one of the first steps in this process. As we noted in the discussion of Gestalt psychology in Chapter Three, we generally group visual units by location, orientation, shape, and color. *Towards the Corner* (10.3), by Juan Muñoz, demonstrates grouping by location. We first see a complete composition comprising seven figures. It is roughly triangular in shape, starting with the standing figure on the far left and ending with the seated figure on the right. The division between the two sets of bleachers creates two subgroups, composed of two figures on the right and five figures on the left. We can further group the three figures seated on the top bleachers and the three figures seated on the bottom, with the single standing figure providing a visual exclamation point for the sculpture as a whole.

Containment

Containment is a unifying force created by the outer edge of a composition or by a boundary within a composition. A container encourages us to seek connections among visual units and helps to define negative space. The room itself provides the container for Roni Horn's *How Dickinson Stayed Home* (10.4). Horn presents letters from the

10.3 Juan Muñoz, *Towards the Corner*, 2000. Seven figures, wood, resin, and mixed mediums, 6¾ × 12½ × 3¾ ft (2.1 × 3.79 × 1.13 m).

10.4 Roni Horn, *How Dickinson Stayed Home*, 1993. Installation. Solid aluminum and plastic. 26 cubes, each 3 × 3 × 3 in. (7.6 × 7.6 × 7.6 cm).

alphabet on 26 small cubes. Like Emily Dickinson's poetry, the installation is both economical and expansive. A minimal amount of information evokes a wide range of interpretations. Contained by the room's white walls and dark floor, the blocks create a unified statement, despite their seemingly random distribution.

Proximity

In design, the distance between visual units is called **proximity**. Even very different forms can become unified when we place them in close proximity. For example, Louise Nevelson constructed *Wedding Chapel IV* (10.5A) from an improbable collection of wooden crates, staircase railings, dowels, chair legs, and other scrap. She organized them into 14 stacked boxes, creating a unified and energetic composition.

Continuity

A fluid connection among compositional parts creates **continuity**. When we place objects in close proximity, continuity often happens naturally.

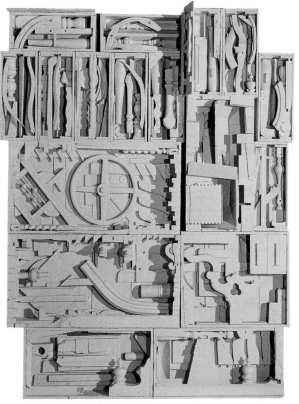

10.5A Louise Nevelson, *Wedding Chapel IV*, 1960. Painted wood, height approx. 9 ft (2.7 m).

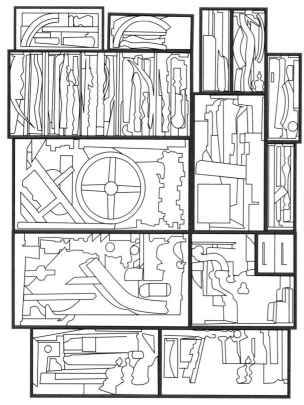

10.5B Line drawing of Figure 10.5A, showing containers in red and overall continuity in black.

As figure 10.5B demonstrates, each form in *Wedding Chapel IV* touches several other forms. As a result, our eyes move easily from section to section, increasing the connections among the parts.

Repetition

Repetition occurs when we use the same visual element or effect any number of times within a composition. Aaron Macsai used similar lines, shapes, textures, and colors in each of the *Panels of Movement* (10.6) segment. A spiral shape, a wavy line, a sphere, and at least one triangular shape appear repeatedly. Despite their variations in size, texture, and location, these repeated forms create a strong connection from panel to panel.

Closure

In an attempt to make sense of the world, our minds tend to connect fragmentary information into completed forms. We call this process **closure**. In Zac Freeman's *Steve* (10.7), we must visually connect hundreds of washers, screws, and other hardware to create a man's face. Closure makes it possible to communicate using implication. Freed of the necessity to provide every detail, the artist

10.6 Aaron Macsai, *Panels of Movement*. Bracelet, 18K gold, sterling, copper, ⅞ × 7 in. (2 × 18 cm).

10.7 Zac Freeman, Detail of *Steve*, 2006. Found objects on board, 60 × 48 in. (152 × 122 cm).

or designer can convey an idea through suggestion rather than description. When the viewer completes the image in his or her mind, it is often more memorable than a more obvious image.

Combining Unifying Forces

James Ingo Freed used all these unifying forces to create the *Tower of Photos* in the Holocaust Memorial Museum in Washington, DC (10.8). His design team wanted to demonstrate the number of lives lost in one Polish village while honoring the individuality of the inhabitants. They collected and framed thousands of

10.8 *Tower of Photos* from Ejszyszki, completed in 1993. United States Holocaust Memorial Museum, Washington, DC. James Ingo Freed, lead designer.

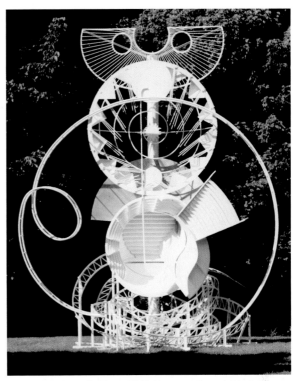

10.9 Alice Aycock, *Tree of Life Fantasy*, Synopsis of the Book of Questions Concerning the World Order and/or the Order of Worlds, 1990–92. Painted steel, fiberglass, and wood, 20 × 15 × 8 ft (6.1 × 4.6 × 2.4 m).

photographs, including groups of schoolchildren, weddings, and family snapshots. Placed in close proximity, the photographs personalize the victims while emphasizing their connection to the lost community. Based on the chimneys that released smoke from the burned bodies to the heavens, the tower itself provides the dominant framework for the exhibition, both structurally and emotionally.

Increasing Variety

Difference in any aspect of a design increases variety. By reviewing the elements of design that we described in Chapter Nine and the principles of design described in this chapter, you can quickly create a checklist of areas for variation, such as:

- *Line variation.* Alice Aycock used lines of different diameter and texture in *Tree of Life Fantasy* (10.9).

- *Variation in texture.* Combining smooth and textured surfaces can add energy and interest to even the simplest form.

- *Variation in pattern.* The Pacific island mask in figure 10.10 is unified through symmetrical balance. This underlying order freed the artist to experiment with many colors and patterns.

10.10 Mask (Wanis), New Ireland. 37 × 20⅞ × 19 in. (94 × 53 × 48.3 cm).

Degrees of Unity

As noted in Chapter Eight, our compositional choices must support our conceptual intentions. Some designs require a high level of unity. For example, Eva Hesse's *Accession II* (10.11) consists of a single cube. Dramatic contrast between the methodical exterior and the fiercely textured interior is the only significant variation. Other designs require a high level of variety. The lines, shapes, volumes, and masses in Sarah Sze's *Hidden Relief* (10.12) ricochet off the floor, walls, and ceiling with a chaotic energy.

Grid and Matrix

We can create a **grid** through a series of intersecting lines. A **matrix** is a three-dimensional grid. Both can unify a design by creating containment, continuity, proximity, and repetition.

In *Number 56* (10.13), Leonardo Drew poured rust into hundreds of plastic bags,

10.11 Eva Hesse, *Accession II*, 1967. Galvanized steel, rubber tubing, 30.5 × 30.5 × 30.5 in. (77 × 77 × 77 cm).

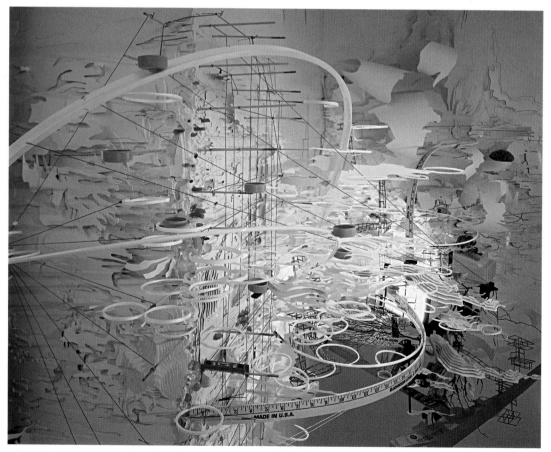

10.12 Sarah Sze, *Hidden Relief*, 2001. Exhibition at Asia Society, New York, 2004. Mixed mediums, 168 × 60 × 12 in. (426.7 × 152.4 × 30.1 cm).

10.13 Leonardo Drew, *Number 56*, 1996. Rust, plastic, wood, 113 × 113 in. (287 × 287 cm).

which he then connected to a wooden support. The rust and the methodically numbered plastic bags create a dialogue between the orderly grid and the decaying metal. This combination of order and disorder balances monotony with mystery.

Daniel Buren's *The Two Plateaus* (10.14) offers another variant on the grid. This public art project, located in the Palais Royal in Paris, covers a 1,000-square-foot plaza. The striped cylinders range in height from about 2 to 5 feet. Mimicking the columns in the building and organized on the pavement like players on a checkerboard, they bring both energy and humor to the site.

10.14 Daniel Buren, *The Two Plateaus*, 1985–86. 1,000-square-foot sculpture for the Cour d'Honneur, Palais Royal, Paris. Black marble, granite, iron, cement, electricity, water.

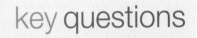

key questions

UNITY AND VARIETY

- What strategies have you used to unify your composition?

- What gives your composition variety?

- Is the balance between unity and variety appropriate for the ideas that you want to express?

- What would happen if you constructed your composition using a grid or matrix?

- How can you use space to increase unity or increase variety?

BALANCE

The distribution of weight or force among visual units creates **balance**. Like physical balance, visual balance requires equilibrium in size, visual weight, and force. An evenly balanced composition such as *The Two Plateaus* (10.14) tends to be stable. This is a peaceful space for us to enter. By combining balance with the illusion of movement, Claes Oldenburg and Coosje van Bruggen created a much more dynamic sculpture in figure 10.15. Nearly 19 feet tall, *The Typewriter Eraser* seems to whirl forward like a crazed unicycle that is on the verge of collapse.

There are three major types of balance. In **symmetrical balance**, forms are mirrored on either side of a central axis. The resulting artwork generally is physically and visually stable. The central face in figure 10.16A is an example of symmetrical balance.

With **radial symmetry**, design elements extend out from a central point, like the spokes of a wheel. Radiating in all directions while remaining anchored at the center, this type of balance tends to generate considerable energy while retaining unity. As shown in diagram 10.16B, figure 10.16A combines symmetrical balance (in the central face) and radial balance (in the outer ring).

Asymmetrical balance creates equilibrium among visual elements that do *not* mirror each other on either side of an axis. As *The Typewriter Eraser* shows, the resulting design may be very dynamic.

10.15 Claes Oldenburg and Coosje van Bruggen, *The Typewriter Eraser*, 1998–99. MGM Mirage, Las Vegas. Aluminum, fiberglass, urethane paint, size variable.

10.16A Bella Coola Mask Representing the Sun, from British Columbia, before 1897. Wood, diameter 24¾ in. (63 cm).

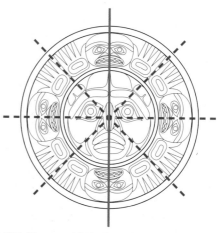

10.16B Diagram of Bella Coola mask. The central face is symmetrically balanced. The outer ring is an example of radial symmetry.

We can use many strategies to create asymmetrical balance:

- Place a large form close to the fulcrum, and a small form farther away. Just as a child at the end of a seesaw can balance an adult near the center, so large and small forms can be balanced in a design (10.17A).

- Multiple small forms can balance a single large form (10.17B).

- A small, solid form can balance a large, open form. The square's solidity and stability give it visual weight as well as physical weight (10.17C).

We construct most artworks from multiple parts. Size variations among the parts affect both the physical balance and the expressive impact. One or more **subordinate**, or secondary, forms often balance a **dominant**, or primary, form. For example, in Theodore Gall's *Plaza Facets* (10.18),

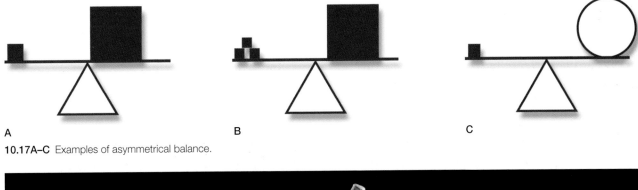

10.17A–C Examples of asymmetrical balance.

10.18 Theodore Gall, *Plaza Facets*, 2001. Cast bronze, 6 × 6 × 6 in. (15.2 × 15.2 × 15.2 cm).

the column and fragmentary heads on the right balance the large head on the left. The seven smaller figures create yet a third compositional level. Using these compositional hierarchies, artists and designers can create unified designs from distinctly individual parts.

Two contrasting interpretations of a single figure further demonstrate the expressive power of balance. Figures 10.19 and 10.20 show St. Bruno, an eleventh-century Catholic saint. His followers, known as the Carthusian Order, lived in caves and devoted their time to manuscript transcription, meditation, and prayer.

The first statue, completed by Michel-Ange Slodtz in 1744, dramatizes a pivotal moment in Bruno's life. Preferring meditation in a monastery to the power and prestige of public life, Bruno rejected promotion to the office of bishop. Slodtz used asymmetrical balance to express this dramatic moment. The small bishop's hat,

offered by the angel in the lower-right corner, is the focal point of the entire sculpture. The much larger figure of St. Bruno recoils when confronted by this symbol of authority. As a result, the small hat is equal in compositional weight to the frightened monk.

The second sculpture depicts a different interpretation of St. Bruno's life. Completed by Jean-Antoine Houdon in 1766, it emphasizes the Carthusian Order and its founder's contemplative nature. Using symmetrical balance, Houdon presents a dignified, introspective man. If we divide the figure in half from top to bottom, the two sides basically mirror each other. This saint is a philosopher, very much at peace with his choices. Just as asymmetrical balance is appropriate for the dramatic moment represented by Slodtz, so symmetrical balance is ideal for the serenity shown by Houdon.

Exaggerated weight or buoyancy can shift the balance in an artwork and expand meaning. In

10.19 Michel-Ange Slodtz, *St. Bruno*, 1744. Marble.

10.20 Jean-Antoine Houdon, *St. Bruno of Cologne*, 1766. Stucco.

Chuichi Fujii's *Untitled* (10.21), the weight of a second log seems to have crushed a cedar log. At the other extreme, Todd Slaughter's *Mortarboard* (10.22) seems to fly through the air with exuberant energy. This effect is especially noticeable at night. This artwork derives its power from the denial of gravity, while figure 10.21 derives its power from exaggerated gravity.

▶ key questions

BALANCE

- Which form of balance is most appropriate to the ideas that you want to express?

- What happens when an unexpected part of the design plays the dominant role?

- How can space and lighting affect compositional balance?

10.21 Chuichi Fujii, *Untitled*, 1987. Japanese cedar, 10 ft 6 in. × 13 ft ½ in. × 11 ft 6 in. (320 × 400 × 350 m).

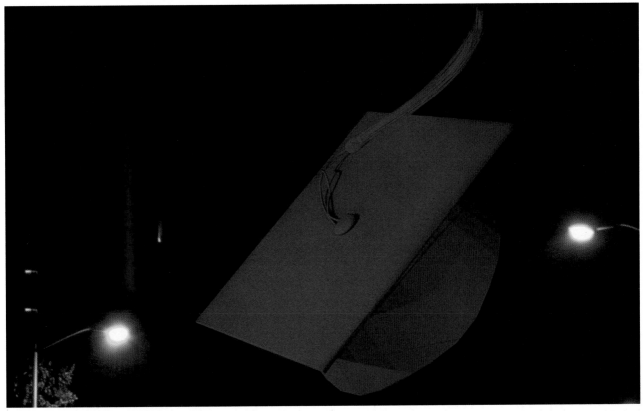

10.22 Todd Slaughter, *Mortarboard*, 2003. Commissioned in commemoration of Franklin University's 100th anniversary, Columbus, Ohio. Steel, aluminum, 20 × 20 × 9 in. (50.8 × 50.8 × 22.9 cm) and five support columns.

SCALE AND PROPORTION

Scale

Scale commonly refers to the size of a form when compared with human size. Using our body as a constant, we can identify three major types of scale relationships. Small-scale objects can be **handheld**, while **human scale** refers to designs that are roughly our size. Very large objects and installations are **monumental** in scale.

Inspired by Theodore Gall's sculpture (figure 10.18, page 225), we can explore the implications of each scale type. The actual artwork is roughly 6 × 6 × 6 inches and can be handheld. At this scale, we are invited to enter and explore the artwork mentally rather than physically (10.23A).

At triple this size (18 × 18 × 18 in.), the dominant head in the design would be about the size of our own head (10.23B). This would create a very different dialogue between the audience and the artwork. Expanded to monumental scale—say, 32 × 32 × 32 feet—the artwork would invite physical entry (10.23C). We could now stand beside the sculptural figures in the piece. Simply by changing the scale, the artist could create three different responses to the same composition.

Proportion

Proportion refers to the relative size of visual elements *within* an image. When we compare the head's width with its height, or divide a composition into thirds, we are establishing a proportional relationship.

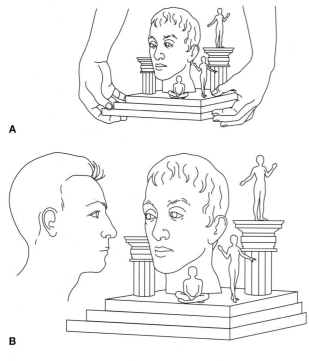

A

B

C

10.23A–C Scale variations, from handheld to monumental.

10.24 Home Pro garden tool line. Designers: James E. Grove, John Cook, Jim Holtorf, Fernando Pardo, Mike Botich. Design Firm: Designworks/USA.

10.25 Teapot vector drawings.

In industrial design, changes in proportion can enhance or diminish function. The five gardening tools in figure 10.24 are all based on the same basic combination of handle, blades, and a simple pivot. The short-handled pruner in the lower-left corner is for trimming twigs and small branches from shrubs. It must fit comfortably in a single hand. The proportions of the lopper in the lower-right corner are much different. Its 20-inch-long handle provides the required leverage to cut heavier branches from small trees. Figure 10.25 presents another example of proportional variation. Each of the 20 teapots has a distinctive height and width. As with the gardening tools, these variations affect each teapot's function.

In sculpture, variations in proportion can increase aesthetic impact. Figures 10.26 through 10.28 show three proportional variations on Constantin Brancusi's *Bird in Space*. In *Maiastra* (10.26), the abstract bird form is dominated by the egg-shaped torso, which tapers into the folded wings at the bottom and the raised head at the top. This bird is approximately three times taller than it is wide. Brancusi further abstracted *Golden Bird* (10.27) and elongated the body. The bird is now seven times taller than it is wide, and an elaborate base adds even more height to the sculpture. With *Bird in Space* (10.28), Brancusi elongated the form even more and added an expanding "foot" below the folded wings. This bird is almost 10 times taller than it is wide. By lengthening the columnar structure in this final version and carefully tapering the sculpture near the base, Brancusi made this simple sculpture fly.

As with all design decisions, choosing the right scale and proportion greatly increases expressive power. Giovanni Bologna scaled *Apennine* (10.29) to overwhelm the viewer with a sense of the mountain spirit's presence. His human frame is monumental, and the surrounding trees and cliff appear to diminish by comparison.

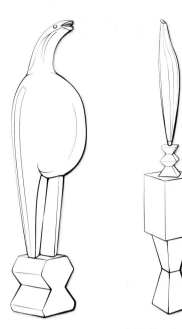

10.26 Rendering of Constatin Brancusi's *Maiastra*.

10.27 Rendering of Constantin Brancusi's *Golden Bird*.

10.28 Rendering of Constantin Brancusi's *Bird in Space*.

10.29 Giovanni Bologna, *Apennine*, 1580–82. Stone, bricks, mortar. Villa di Pratolino, Florence region, Italy.

Proportional extremes can be equally expressive. Less than 5 feet tall, Alberto Giacometti's *Chariot* (10.30) offers a somber analysis of the human condition. The solitary figure is delicately balanced on gigantic wheels, which rest on two small pedestals. The entire form is linear, as if distilled down to the barest essentials. Both the chariot and the life it transports are precariously balanced and seem fragile and vulnerable.

▶ key questions

SCALE AND PROPORTION

- What would happen to your composition if you dramatically changed its scale?

- What would happen conceptually if you dramatically changed its proportions?

- Imagine that you can stretch or compress your design in any direction. What are the advantages of a very tall, thin composition compared to a short, cubic composition?

- How does a change in scale or proportion affect balance?

10.30 Alberto Giacometti, *Chariot*, 1950. Bronze, 57 × 26 × 26⅛ in. (144.8 × 65.8 × 66.2 cm).

Degrees and Forms of Contrast

Contrast can appear in many forms and in varying degrees. In Arnaldo Pomodoro's *Sphere Within Sphere* (10.31), an external force seems to have eaten

CONTRAST

Contrast is created when two or more forces operate in opposition.

Opposing Forces

By reviewing the elements and principles of design discussed thus far, we can quickly create a long list of potential adversaries, including static/dynamic, smooth/textured, small/large, and curvilinear/rectilinear. When the balance is just right, we can create powerful compositions from any such combination. Many artists and designers devote two-thirds of their compositional area to one force and roughly one-third to a contrasting force. The larger force sets the standard, while the smaller force creates the exception.

10.31 Arnaldo Pomodoro, *Sphere Within Sphere*, 1965. Bronze, 45 × 46½ × 47⅝ ft (114.2 × 118.1 × 121.0 m). Dublin, Ireland.

A Full View

B Detail

away at the imposing spherical form, revealing a pattern of rectilinear teeth and a second sphere inside. This creates a strong contrast between the massive structure and the invading space.

In *Plan, Prepare, Execute* (10.32A and B), Liza Lou also used contrast to suggest an existing form's metamorphosis into a new configuration. It is hard to tell whether the dominant field of dark gray is "eating" or "being eaten" by the colorful patterns around the edge and the lines at the bottom. This uncertainty makes the artwork even more intriguing.

Contrast and Connection

Effective use of opposing forces can create a new form of dynamic unity. Like complementary colors, contrasting forces can simultaneously increase both unity and variety in a design.

Loops (10.33), by Mary Ann Scherr, presents a contrast between movement and constraint. A curving plane encircles the wearer's throat, providing protection but restricting motion. Below, the suspended rings sway with every movement

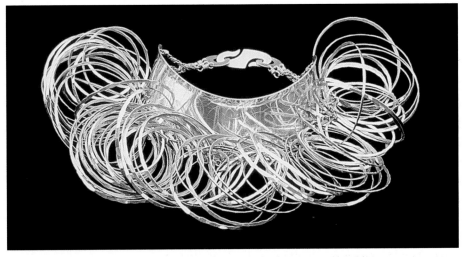

10.33 Mary Ann Scherr, *Loops,* **1988.** Sterling silver neckpiece, 8½ × 4¾ × 5 in. (21.6 × 12.1 × 12.7 cm).

10.34 Pol Bury, *Fountains at Palais Royal*, Paris, 1985.

of the body, creating a dynamic counterpoint to the constraining collar.

Water animates Pol Bury's *Fountains at Palais Royal* (10.34). The design relies on three major elements. The regularly spaced columns so characteristic of neoclassical architecture dominate the site itself. Placed on top of each circular fountain, the polished metal spheres reflect these columns and the shimmering water. In a sense, the spheres serve as mediators between the rigid columns and the silvery water. Like the columns, they are simple volumes arranged in a group. Like the water, they seem fluid as they reflect the rippling pool and the passing clouds. In this project, Pol Bury combined unity and variety to create an elegant and ever-changing sculpture.

 key questions

CONTRAST

- Consider all of the contrasting forces that you might use in your composition. How can contrast enhance your idea?

- How many contrasting forces can you use effectively in a single artwork? Two? Three? Six?

- What would happen to your composition if you dramatically increased the amount of contrast?

EMPHASIS

Emphasis gives particular prominence to part of a design. A **focal point** is a compositional device used to create emphasis. For example, the bishop's hat in Slodtz's version of St. Bruno (figure 10.19, page 226) is the composition's focal point. Both emphasis and focal point can attract attention and increase visual and conceptual impact.

Emphasis by Isolation

Any **anomaly**, or break from the norm, can emphasize an idea. Because we seek to connect the verbal and visual information that we receive, a mismatched word or an isolated object immediately attracts attention. Do Ho Suh's *Fallen Star* (10.35) is a three-quarter sized cottage based on an actual house in Providence, Rhode Island. Placed

10.35 Do Ho Suh, *Fallen Star*, 2012. House construction materials and furniture, roughly 15 × 18 ft (4.6 × 5.5 m). Stuart Collection, University of California at San Diego.

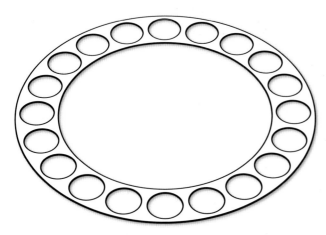

10.36 Rendering of David Watkins' *Torus 280 B2*.

on the ground in a suburban setting, it would simply read as a very small house. Tilted and precariously perched on the side of a campus building, it is isolated and thus stands out.

Emphasis through Color

Color attracts attention, especially when it is unexpected or hard to explain. Color plays an especially important role with public art projects. The reds and violets in Janet Echleman's *Tsunami 1.26* (9.28 on page 192) enhance the magical floating form. The white lines and planes in Alice Aycock's *Tree of Life Fantasy* on page 221 increase this sculpture's psychological buoyancy. And, as we noted on page 210, Kurt Perschke has installed his inflatable *RedBall Project* at various sites in more than a dozen cities. In stark contrast to the grays and greens that we expect in urban settings, the 15-foot-tall ball immediately engages even the most distracted pedestrian.

> ## key questions
>
> ### EMPHASIS
>
> - Is there a focal point in your composition? If not, should there be?
>
> - What is the dominant form in your composition? Is it the form you most want to emphasize?

REPETITION AND RHYTHM

As we noted at the beginning of this chapter, repetition occurs when we use the same visual element or effect any number of times within a composition. **Rhythm** can be defined as the organization of these multiple elements or effects into a deliberate pattern. Just as a musician creates a rhythmic pattern by connecting sound and silence, so the artist can create rhythm using positive form and negative space.

Variations in volume can accentuate rhythm. For example, when every fourth beat is accented in a musical composition, a clear rhythm emerges. Repeated accents in an artwork have a similar effect. And the number of beats within a given space creates the **tempo**, or rate of change. In David Watkins's *Torus 280 (B2)* (10.36), the large circular shapes create a slow, regular pattern. Increasing the number of circles would accelerate the tempo.

Rhythm plays an even greater role in figure 10.37. The woven herringbone pattern at the bottom suggests a clockwise and then a

10.37 Tanija & Graham Carr, *Untitled*, 2001. Wet-formed leather, acrylic paint, 13¾ × 29¼ × 29¼ in. (35 × 74 × 74 cm).

counterclockwise visual movement. A similar pattern at the top accentuates spatial depth. Tapered rectangles create a border around both the interior and the exterior edges. Like a complex musical piece, the artists have skillfully woven together three types of rhythm.

Because sculptures can be viewed from all sides, three-dimensional rhythm is especially powerful. The movement of four women around an exuberant musician creates a joyous dance in Jean-Baptiste Carpeaux's *The Dance* (10.38). Our eyes follow the turning heads, clasped hands, and swirling arms as they move in, out, and around in space. A similar rhythm animates Steve Woodward's *Model of Proposal for Concourse Commission*

(10.39). The plywood vortex seems to rise out of the floor to collect in a spinning disk at the top, and then descend again, in perpetual motion. When combined with the spinning effect, this ascending and descending movement gives the design great vitality.

Artists and designers often use repetition to increase compositional unity and conceptual impact. For example, the 30 statues in Magdalena Abakanowicz's *Standing Figures (30)* (10.40) are unified by their similarity in size, shape, and solemnity. Variations in each cast bronze surface provide a degree of individuality. Often interpreted as victims of war, the hollow, headless figures seem frozen in time, offering silent

10.38 Jean-Baptiste Carpeaux, *The Dance (After Restoration)*, 1868–69. Marble, 7 ft 6½ in. (2.3 m).

10.39 Steve Woodward, *Model of Proposal for Concourse Commission*, 1987. Wood, 13¾ × 8 × 7 in. (34.9 × 20.3 × 19 cm).

10.40 Magdalena Abakanowicz, *Standing Figures (30)*, 1994–99. Bronze, overall 54 ft 3 in. × 19 ft 8 in. (16.55 × 6 m).

testimony to a tragic past. The 6,000 clay soldiers filling the tomb of Emperor Shih Huang Ti (10.41) demonstrate a different use of repetition. As he faced his death, the emperor may have sought companionship or protection from his army. In each case, repetition and rhythm have been used deliberately in order to strengthen the artwork's visual impact and conceptual strength.

10.41 **Tomb of Emperor Shih Huang Ti, 221–206 BCE.** Painted ceramic figures, life-size.

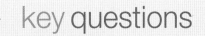

key questions

REPETITION AND RHYTHM

- Try repeating any element in your design. What does this repetition contribute, conceptually and compositionally?

- What happens when you change simple repetition to specific rhythm?

- Does the rhythm remain constant in your design, or is there a change in tempo? What is the advantage of each approach?

summary

- Through composition, we can combine multiple parts to create a unified whole.

- Grouping, containment, proximity, continuity, repetition, and closure are six common strategies for increasing unity. Difference in any aspect of a design increases variety.

- We can create a grid through a series of intersecting lines. A matrix is a three-dimensional grid.

- Symmetry, radial symmetry, and asymmetry are three common forms of balance. One or more subordinate, or secondary, forms often balances a dominant, or primary, form.

- Scale and proportion are two types of size relationships. Proportion refers to size relationships within an image, while scale involves a size comparison with our physical size.

- Emphasis gives prominence to a specific part of a design. A focal point is a compositional device that an artist often uses to create emphasis.

- We create contrast when two or more forces operate in opposition. Many artists and designers devote most of their compositional area to one force and a much smaller area to a contrasting force. The larger force sets the standard, while the smaller force creates the exception.

- Repetition occurs when we use the same visual element or effect any number of times within a composition. Rhythm is the organization of these multiple elements or effects into a deliberate pattern. Just as a musician creates a deliberate pattern connecting sound and silence, so the artist can create rhythm using positive form and negative space.

key terms

anomaly
asymmetrical
 balance
balance
closure
containment
continuity
contrast

dominant
emphasis
focal point
grid
grouping
handheld
human scale
matrix

monumental
proportion
proximity
radial symmetry
repetition
rhythm
scale
subordinate

symmetrical
 balance
tempo
unity
variety

studio projects

To apply the concepts from this chapter in the studio, check out the Projects page in the Online Learning Center at www.mhhe.com/LTI5e. The following is a sample of the chapter-related assignments.

Negative and Positive. Creating a dialogue between substance and space.

Three-Dimensional Balancing Act. Increasing compositional complexity, using curvilinear and rectilinear forms.

Myths and Masks. Working with many elements of 3-D design to create a wearable mask for a new ceremonial occasion.

Materials and Methods

We can use an incredible range of materials and methods to produce three-dimensional objects. Paper, metal, fibers, clay, glass, and plastic are among the most versatile materials; folding, casting, carving, weaving, and stamping are just a few of the production methods. We would need a separate course specially devoted to materials if we were to explore this subject in depth.

Fortunately, our purpose is more pragmatic. As a beginner, you need both straightforward advice and a basic introduction to the meanings that we assign to various materials. In this chapter, we explore the essential characteristics of all materials, and then consider ways in which contemporary artists use different materials to communicate their ideas. The chapter ends with an overview of basic materials commonly used in beginning courses.

CHOICE OF MATERIALS

Each material has specific strengths and limitations. For example, rubber cement is a temporary adhesive for ordinary paper, while white glue is a permanent adhesive for heavier paper and cardboard. Carpenter's glue works well with wood, while hot glue works well with rough cardboard and other unconventional materials. Misuse of any material can ruin a great design. By understanding the physical characteristics of common materials, we can produce better work in less time and at less cost. The following considerations are crucial:

- *Strength.* How much weight can a given material support? What is its breaking point when we twist, fold, or bend it?

- *Workability.* How difficult is it to alter a material's shape? Does it cut and bend easily? Can we melt and cast or drip it to create a new form? Does it retain its shape when bent?

- *Durability.* What range of forces can this material withstand and for how long? Is it impervious to heat, water, wind, and ultraviolet light?

- *Weight.* A material that is too light for a given purpose can be as problematic as a material that is too heavy. What is the function of the project, and how heavy does the material need to be?

- *Cost.* Can the material chosen be obtained easily and at a reasonable cost? Are cheaper alternatives available?

- *Toxicity.* Many plastics produce toxic gases when they are cut, etched, or burned. Paints and solvents may require us to use masks and gloves. They also present significant disposal problems. Is the studio ventilation adequate for the materials we want to use? How can we effectively dispose of toxic waste?

- *Function.* How appropriate is a given material for a particular purpose? A teapot will be useless if we make it from a porous, leaking material, and we can never mass produce a chair that is too difficult to build. The materials that we choose must effectively serve the structural and aesthetic needs of the objects we create.

Increasing Material Strength

Composites

A **composite** is created when we fuse together two or more materials of differing strengths. Two common composites are Fiberglas and ferro-concrete. Fiberglas combines glass filaments with a plastic resin while ferro-concrete is made from metal mesh embedded in concrete. Foamcore (which is made from a sheet of polystyrene sandwiched between sheets of coated paper) and duct tape (constructed from three layers of "skin") are composites that we commonly use in three-dimensional design classes. Composites are often cheaper, stronger, and lighter in weight than other materials.

Structural Strength

After millions of years of experimentation, nature has developed an amazing array of effective structures. Two major types are skeletons and exoskeletons. A **skeleton** (or **endoskeleton**) provides the internal structure that mammals and fish require. An external **exoskeleton** provides the structure that insects, crabs, and lobsters use.

Architects are masters of both skeletal and exoskeletal structures. In *Guggenheim Museum Bilbao* (11.1), architect Frank Gehry created a complex "skeleton" to support the building's gleaming titanium skin. The Gothic cathedral in figure 11.2 demonstrates the use of an exoskeleton. To increase building height while reducing mass, medieval architects developed the **flying buttress** used in hundreds of cathedrals throughout

11.1 Frank Gehry, *Guggenheim Museum Bilbao*, 1997. Computer-generated Catia image.

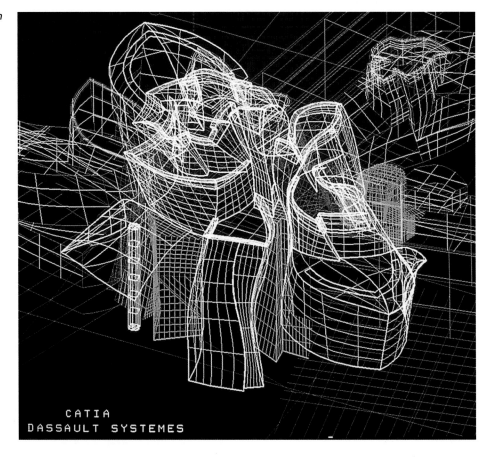

Europe. These external structures distributed the force exerted by the heavy stone and made it possible for the builders to create very high ceilings.

Artists and designers often use an **armature** to create internal structure. For example, a wire or wooden armature can support the cloth or paper commonly used in lampshades (11.3). Engineer Alexandre-Gustave Eiffel developed a much more elaborate armature to support Auguste Bartholdi's *Statue of Liberty* (11.4). Standing over 150 feet tall and weighing 225 tons, this monumental sculpture has to withstand wind, rain, and brisk sea winds. Without a strong internal structure, the statue could never have been built.

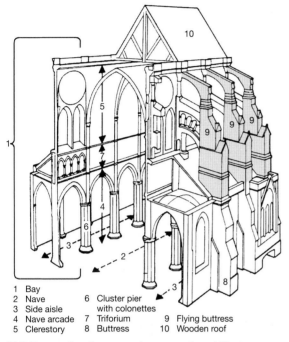

1	Bay		
2	Nave	6	Cluster pier
3	Side aisle		with colonettes
4	Nave arcade	7	Triforium	9	Flying buttress
5	Clerestory	8	Buttress	10	Wooden roof

11.2 Perspective diagram and cross-section of Chartres Cathedral, 1145–1220.

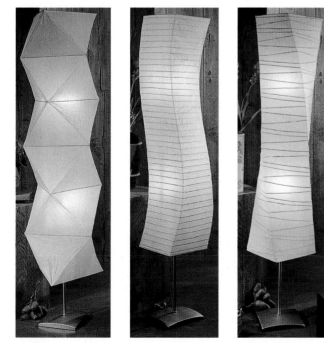

11.3 Shoji Design. Three Japanese floor lamps. Steel, bamboo, paper, size variable.

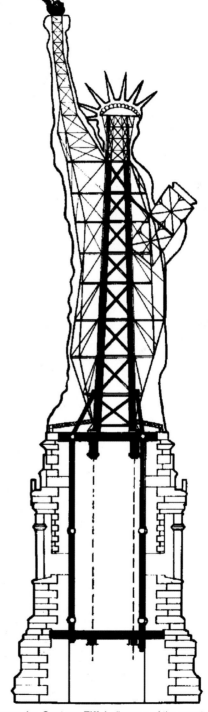

11.4 Alexandre-Gustave Eiffel, diagram of the construction of the Statue of Liberty.

Distributing Force

As figure 11.5A–E shows, the five major forces are compression, tension, bend, torque, and shear. **Compression** occurs when we push a material inward; **tension** occurs when we pull a material outward; direct pressure at one point causes a material to **bend**; **torque** is a twisting motion; **shear** can occur when we apply force to the opposite sides of a material.

An equilateral triangle is the linear shape that best resists deformation caused by each of these forces, and the tetrahedron, or pyramid, is the strongest three-dimensional form. A triangular support, such as a corner brace on the back of a painting, can distribute force effectively and greatly increase strength. On a larger scale, a network of crossbeams in Thorncrown Chapel (11.6) adds both strength and beauty to a sacred space.

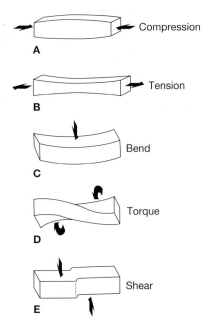

11.5A–E Major physical forces.

11.6 E. Fay Jones & Associates, Thorncrown Chapel, Eureka Springs, Arkansas, 1981.

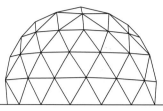

R. Buckminster Fuller's geodesic dome (11.7) expands this idea even further. Typically constructed using hundreds of tetrahedrons, the dome is relatively easy to build and creates a large volume using a minimal amount of mass. A model of beauty and efficiency, architects have used the geodesic dome for large, open buildings, such as greenhouses and exhibition spaces.

Methods of Construction

Various methods of construction strongly influence our compositional choices. The two most common methods of construction are addition and subtraction.

In **additive sculpture**, the artwork is created from separate parts that have been connected, usually using glues, joints, stitching, or welds. **Assemblage** is one additive method. Using objects and images originally designed for another purpose, Joseph Cornell created a whole series of evocative box structures (11.8). He designed many of these assemblages to honor specific people, past and present. On a more playful note, Larry Fuente combined wood, plastic, beads, buttons, poker chips, dice, ping-pong balls, and other materials in his *Game Fish* (11.9). **Modeling** is an additive process that ceramicists often use. Pinching and pushing the pliable clay, skillful ceramicists can make

11.8 Joseph Cornell, *Untitled (Medici Princess)*, c. 1948. Construction, 17⅝ × 11⅛ × 4⅜ in. (44.8 × 28.3 × 11.1 cm).

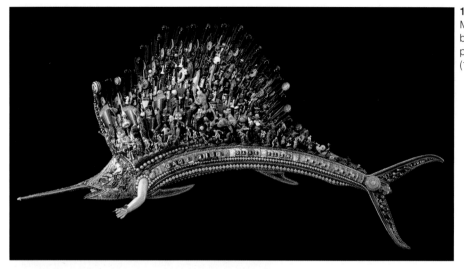

11.9 Larry Fuente, *Game Fish*, 1988.
Mixed media: wood, plastic, beads, buttons, poker chips, badminton birdies, ping-pong balls. 51 ½ × 112 ½ × 10 ¾ in. (131 × 285.8 × 179.7 cm).

11.10 Jean-Pierre Larocque, *Untitled (Head Series)*, 2002. Stoneware, 36¾ × 21 in. (93.3 × 53.3 cm).

both functional and sculptural objects of great complexity. To create his *Head Series* (11.10), Jean-Pierre Larocque stamped slabs of clay with various textures from cloth, then modeled and carved a head that is both activated and imposing.

In **subtractive sculpture**, the artist removes materials from a larger mass. Carving, drilling, cutting, and turning on a lathe are all subtractive processes. The Tlingit woodcarver in figure 11.11 follows a methodical process, beginning by drawing on the cedar pole, making a rough cut, then refining and finishing the totem pole.

Plastic and metal forms are often produced using two additional methods. In **solidification**, a liquid material is poured into a mold or extruded through a pipe and then allowed to harden. For example, when we squeeze cake frosting through a shaped nozzle, we can create a wide range of extruded forms. We can apply this basic

11.11 Tlingit totem carver, 1996. Southeast Alaska.

principle to materials that are more permanent and less tasty. In **displacement**, a solid material is physically forced into a new configuration. The stamping process used to mint coins is a familiar example of displacement.

> ## ▶ key questions
>
> ### CHOICE OF MATERIALS
>
> - Test the limits of the materials that you plan to use. Note especially their strength, workability, toxicity, and cost.
>
> - Are there "greener" materials that you might use for your project?
>
> - Make a model from an unfamiliar material. Does it offer any conceptual or technical advantages over the material that you usually use?

CONNECTIONS AND TRANSITIONS

Connections

Physical and visual connections are equally important in three-dimensional design. Visual connections compositionally unify multiple surfaces, while physical connections can increase strength, flexibility, functionality, and stability. We typically make connections through

- *contact* (11.12A)
- *junctions* (11.12B)
- *joints* (11.12C)

Physical connections are especially important to woodworkers. Carpenters and furniture designers learn dozens of specific joints, hinges, and splices. Mary Miss constructed *Pool Complex: Orchard Valley* (11.13A) using many types of joints (11.13B). Nails, screws, bolts, and glue are needed for lap or butt joints. Interlocking joints can often create a simple connection without this additional reinforcement.

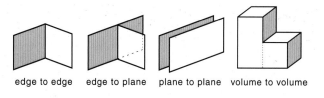

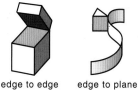

edge to edge   edge to plane   plane to plane   volume to volume

edge to edge   edge to plane   plane to plane   mass to mass

11.12A Examples of connections through contact.

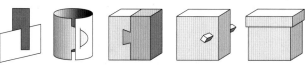

11.12B Examples of connections through junctions.

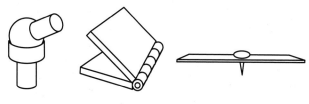

ball and socket   hinge   pivot

11.12C Examples of connections through joints.

Employed to create functional objects, industrial designers pay particular attention to all types of connections. Take, for example, a simple camera tripod. Because of the various joints it includes, we can expand or collapse it and we can rotate and reorient its top. Elizabeth King's self-portrait figure (11.14) presents an even wider array of possibilities. Ball-and-socket joints at the shoulders and hips create rotating forms, while hinge joints in the fingers, knees, and elbows permit a folding and unfolding movement.

Visual connections are just as important as physical connections. A split yellow circle dominates John Okulick's *Wind Wizard* (11.15). Through closure, we mentally connect the halves, despite their physical separation. A second broken circle echoes the interior circle and creates a dynamic boundary for the composition as a whole. The two gold spheres at the upper left and lower right seem poised for movement. The work creates a strong sense of unity through connections between the forms and the implied circular motion.

11.13A Mary Miss, *Pool Complex: Orchard Valley at the Laumeier Sculpture Park, St. Louis*, 1983–85. Wolmanized pine, stone, galvanized steel, concrete, size variable.

butt joint

lap joint

interlocking joint

11.13B Three types of joints.

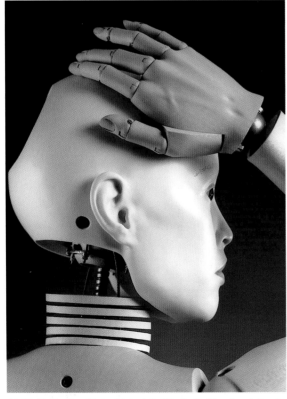

11.14 Katherine Wetzel (photo), Elizabeth King (sculpture), *Pupil* from *Attention's Loop*, 1987–90. Porcelain, glass eyes, carved wood, brass, one-half life size.

11.15 John Okulick, *Wind Wizard*, 1987. Painted wood, gold leaf, oil stick, 22 × 25 × 6 in. (55.9 × 63.5 × 15.2 cm).

Transitions

We can create many types of transitions in three-dimensional design. The various angles and joints in Eduardo Chillida's *Asbesti Gogora III* (11.16) create an abrupt transition from surface to surface. The resulting sculpture pulls to the right then the left, as if it were at war with itself. Gentler, more fluid transitions help to unify the various sections of Liv Blåvarp's *Bird* (11.17). As figure 11.18A–F shows, gradual change tends to create a fluid transition. Such **gradation** creates sequential change within a consistent pattern. Figure 11.18A shows examples of gradation.

> ▶ ## key questions
>
> ### CONNECTIONS AND TRANSITIONS
>
> - How can physical and visual connections strengthen your artwork—both structurally and conceptually?
>
> - Which type of transition is most appropriate to the idea or emotion that you want to convey?
>
> - Are the transitions in your artwork deliberate and effective?

11.17 Liv Blåvarp, *Bird*, 1991. Neckpiece, bird's-eye maple, satinwood, whale tooth, 12½ × 10¼ in. (32 × 26 cm).

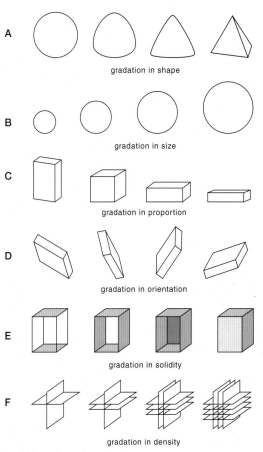

A — gradation in shape

B — gradation in size

C — gradation in proportion

D — gradation in orientation

E — gradation in solidity

F — gradation in density

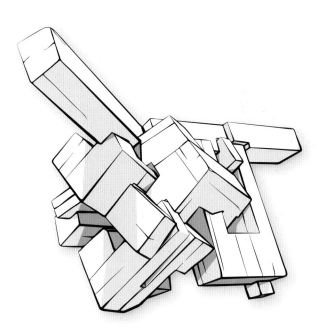

11.16 Rendering of Eduardo Chillida, *Asbesti Gogora III*.

11.18A–F Examples of gradation.

TRADITIONAL AND TRANSFORMATIVE MATERIALS

Stone

Limestone, basalt, marble, and other dense, fine-grained stones have been used since prehistory to create durable and imposing objects. Handheld stone amulets have been worn to ward off evil, while monumental sculptures, such as the Egyptian pyramids at Giza, have been constructed to commemorate political as well as religious beliefs. Using chisels, mallets, and rasps, stone carvers can create remarkably delicate forms with an amazing array of textures.

In *Blind Man's Bluff* (11.19), Louise Bourgeois used traditional methods to make a very contemporary statement. Spherical and cylindrical forms seem to bubble up from the bottom of the sculpture. A block of rough stone caps these bubbly forms. This contrast, which Bourgeois describes as "polarization," creates tension between the animated and sexually suggestive forms and the heavy stone cap. Surrounded by sexual promiscuity as a child, Bourgeois has often described the emotional blindness that she developed as a coping strategy.

Clay

Clay is perhaps the most basic and versatile of all materials. Essentially made from refined earth, it can be hand-formed using coil, slab, and carving techniques. We can pour it into molds and "throw" it using a potter's wheel. When fired, it becomes extremely durable and we can decorate it with beautiful colored glazes.

Contemporary ceramicists fully exploit all these qualities. Born into a family of traditional Cochiti potters, Virgil Ortiz began making pottery at the age of six. Creating a fusion between traditional Native American methods and contemporary life, Ortiz

11.19 Louise Bourgeois, *Blind Man's Bluff*, 1984. Marble, 36 × 35½ × 25 in. (91.4 × 90.2 × 63.5 cm).

11.20 Virgil Ortiz, *Untitled*, 2002. Cochiti red clay, white and red clay slip, black (wild spinach) paint, 28 × 29 in. (71 × 74 cm).

combines bold surface decoration with animated figurative forms (11.20). The malleability of clay is strongly evident in Jean-Pierre Larocque's *Head Series* (see figure 11.10, page 242). Adding and subtracting textural layers, Larocque combined the fluidity of gesture drawing with the solidity of fired clay. Carving into "leather-hard" clay, David MacDonald (see Profile, page 258) activates his simple forms with parallel and intersecting bands of texture.

Metals

Artists have traditionally used bronze casting for all kinds of large-scale sculptures. Gold, silver, copper, pewter, and brass are more commonly used for jewelry and utensils. We can cast, forge, solder, etch, and stamp most metals.

Mariko Kusumoto used copper, nickel silver, sterling silver, resin, bronze, and brass to create *Tansu no Oku* (11.21). A lotus blossom, seashells, butterflies, and an open hand extend out from an etched sheet of turn-of-the-century advertisements. A plastic resin adds color and sparkle to the butterflies. Kusumoto based the structure on a children's pop-up book, while the images recall the Victorian fascination with mechanical and natural objects.

Nature also inspired Crystal Kwan's Diamond Insect-Gold Moth (11.22). Skillful construction combined with precious materials transformed an insect into an artwork.

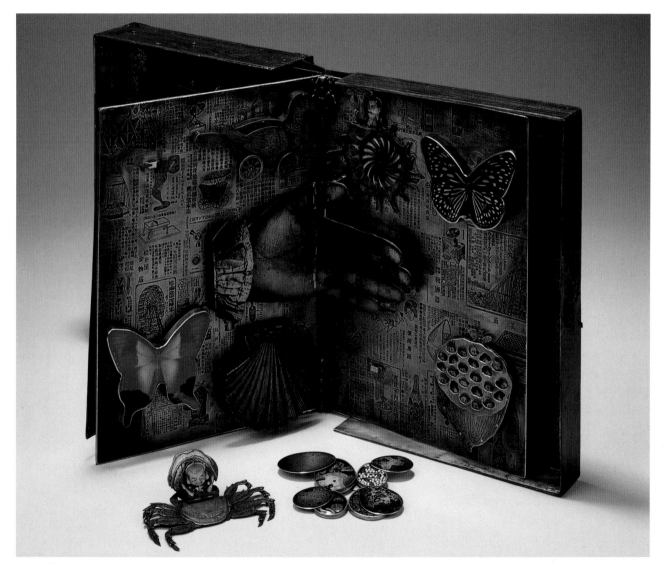

11.21 Mariko Kusumoto, *Tansu no Oku*. Copper, nickel silver, sterling silver, resin, bronze, and brass, 15½ × 14 × 14 in. (39.4 × 35.6 × 35.6 cm) open.

Wood

Traditional cultures worldwide use wood to create functional structures, such as buildings, furniture, and utensils, as well as sculptural objects, such as masks, ancestor poles, and walking sticks. Readily available in most areas, wood is inherently beautiful, easily painted, relatively lightweight, and surprisingly versatile. We can carve, steam form, and assemble it using various hinges and joints.

Traditional examples of wood sculpture appear on pages 244 and 245. Figure 11.23 demonstrates the power of wood in a nontraditional setting. Constructed from pliable strands of bamboo, Patrick Dougherty's large-scale artwork seems to arise directly from nature.

Glass

Glass, which is made primarily from silica, has been used for containers of all kinds since the time of the pharaohs. It can be transparent or opaque and, with the addition of copper, cadmium, cobalt, and other materials, can take on a complete range of colors. In its molten state, the artist can pour, blow, press into molds, draw into threads, stamp, and extrude.

Eric Hilton based his *Innerland* (11.24) on the transparency of glass. Constructed from 25 cubes of clear glass, the sculpture appears to shift with each change in the viewer's position. Hilton combined the transparency and brilliance of glass with its density and mass to create an evocative artwork.

In a very different approach, Gene Koss's *Hay Loader* (11.25) transforms a piece of farming equipment into a sculpture that is both fragile and imposing. Because we know that the heavy sheets of glass will shatter if the tower topples, the entire sculpture is charged with energy.

11.22 **Crystal Kwan, Diamond Insect-Gold Moth, 2009.** Gold, diamonds, rubies, 1¾ × 1½ × ½ in.

11.23 **Patrick Dougherty, *Untitled*, 1992.** Bamboo, height 25 ft (7.6 m), diameter 10 ft (3 m). Temporary installation.

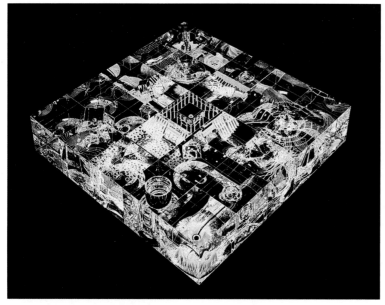

11.24 Eric Hilton, *Innerland*, 1980. Engraved by Ladislav Havlik, Lubomir Richter, Peter Schelling, and Roger Selander, cut by Mark Witter. Cast, cut, engraved, sandblasted, and polished, 3⅞ × 19⅜ × 19⅜ in. (9.9 × 49.3 × 49.3 cm).

Fibers

The term *fibers* covers a wide range of linear materials, including strips of willow, bamboo, and reeds, as well as the more familiar cotton, linen, silk, and wool. Like the other traditional materials, artists and designers have used fibers for basketry, quilts, clothing, and other commonplace objects, as well as for prayer rugs and ritual clothing from shrouds to wedding dresses. Most fibers readily accept paint or dyes and can be woven, braided, knotted, and knitted.

Nick Cave's *Soundsuit* (11.26) combines technical mastery with whimsical inventiveness. Used in both solo and group performances, it creates various

11.25 Gene Koss, *Hay Loader*, 2006. Cast glass, steel, and neon, 13 × 2 × 10 ft (4 × 0.61 × 3 m).

11.26 Nick Cave, *Soundsuit*, 2009. Mixed mediums, 90 × 40 × 32 in. (229 × 102 × 81 cm).

11.27 *Hyperbolic Coral Reef*, an ongoing collaborative project organized by the Institute for Figuring. Crocheted fibers, size variable.

sounds as the dancer moves. A very different approach is used in the continuing development of the *Hyperbolic Coral Reef* (11.27). Organized by the Institute for Figuring, this collaborative project is designed to encourage people from around the world to protect fragile oceanic reefs. Participants in the project crochet "coral" structures that they display in their own communities.

Three qualities most distinguish contemporary fibers. First, the traditional separation between sculpture and fiber arts has largely disappeared. As demonstrated by Janet Echelman's *Tsunami 1.26* (figure 9.28, page 192), artists often use fibers for large-scale designs. Second, the definition of *fibers* has become increasingly broad. For example, Cathy Strokowsky wove together glass, wire, artificial sinew, and horsehair to create *Glass Pod with Hair* (11.28). Third, the relationship between fiberworks and the human body continues to evolve through performance art and installations.

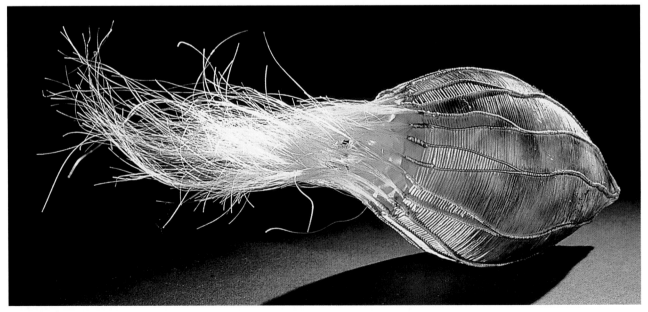

11.28 Cathy Strokowsky, *Glass Pod with Hair*, 2001. Blown glass, sandblasted, woven artificial sinew, wire, horsehair, 4¾ × 12½ × 4¾ in. (12 × 31.75 × 12 cm).

Plastics

Transparent, translucent, or opaque, plastics can be formed into sheets and then cut and assembled. We can also extrude, cast, vacuum-form, and stamp many types of plastic. Lightweight, varied in color, and relatively cheap to produce, plastics have fueled a revolution in household product design and distribution.

Using a variety of plastics, Ron Mueck has created many large-scale sculptures of human figures. One of the most compelling is *The Boy* (11.29), installed in London's Millennium Dome. The crouching adolescent boy seems vulnerable and defensive, despite (or perhaps because of) his enormous size. As with all of Mueck's work, the details are astounding: every hair is defined, and the eyes seem to glisten with moisture as well as apprehension.

Ephemeral Materials

One of the most notable characteristics of postmodern art is its emphasis on concept combined with a de-emphasis on traditional materials and methods. Many artists today deliberately use **ephemera** (materials that rapidly decay) or trash (which is already in a state of decay). In some cases, the transient nature of the material is part of the concept. In other cases, conceptual punch simply trumps material value.

Time Bomb (11.30) by Ernest Daetwyler is a dramatic example. Constructed from fragments of broken furniture supported by a steel armature, the nearly 10-foot-tall sphere is ominous and imposing. Precariously balanced and displayed in a lovely forest, this wooden bomb seems on the verge of exploding.

11.29 Ron Mueck, *The Boy*, 1999. Site-specific work installed in the Mind Zone at the Millennium Dome, London, United Kingdom. Mixed media, 16.8 × 16.8 × 7.9 ft (490 × 490 × 240 cm).

11.30 Ernest Daetwyler, *Time Bomb (Im Hölzernen Himmel)*, **2008.** Old furniture parts, steel substructure, 11.8 ft (3.6 m) diameter.

Tara Donovan uses commonplace materials in a very different way. From hundreds of mass-produced cups, drinking straws, plastic forks, and other lightweight materials, she creates elegant structures and installations that seem to defy their humble origins. The installation in figure 11.31 suggests both cloud formations and biological structures.

Rick Paul also used nonprecious materials in many of his installations. He created *Querschnitt* (11.32) from an especially strong type of foam board and translucent fabric supported by a wooden armature. Filling a room nearly the size of a basketball court, this temporary artwork had to be both strong and inexpensive to produce.

▶ **key questions**

TRADITIONAL AND TRANSFORMATIVE MATERIALS

- Research the material that you plan to use. How has it been used traditionally? Do contemporary uses expand its physical and conceptual potential?

- What are the conceptual and environmental advantages of ephemera? What are the challenges in terms of construction and longevity?

11.31 Tara Donovan, *Untitled (Styrofoam Cups)*, 2008. Styrofoam cups and glue. Installation dimensions variable. Installation view, The Institute of Contemporary Art, Boston.

11.32 Rick Paul, *Querschnitt*, 1994. Installation, Gatorfoam™, wood, fabric, 24 ft × 12 ft (7.31 × 3.6 m).

STUDENT MATERIALS

To minimize cost and expedite exploration, we can construct three-dimensional design projects from common materials, such as bristol board, corrugated cardboard, plywood, wire, plaster gauze, and plaster. This section describes the characteristics of the most basic types of boards and adhesives.

Boards

Many types of board are remarkably strong as well as inexpensive. *Bristol board* is like thick, stiff paper. It is available in various thicknesses from 1-ply (similar to drawing paper in weight) to 5-ply (similar in weight to illustration board). A *cold-pressed* (or vellum) surface is slightly textured, while a *hot-pressed* (or plate) surface is very smooth. The vellum surface is best for graphite, charcoal, pastels, and colored pencils. The smooth surface is good for felt markers and for pen and ink. We can use either for model building, book arts, and planar structures.

Chipboard is a dense, gray, uncoated board made from recycled paper. Most drawing pads have a chipboard backing. Single-thickness chipboard can be cut with an X-Acto knife or a heavy-duty paper cutter; use a utility knife to cut all heavier board.

Foamcore is light, strong, and rather unforgiving. It must be cut with a very sharp X-Acto knife or a scroll saw, and dents in the surface or cutting errors are difficult to repair.

Corrugated cardboard is strong, lightweight, cheap, and amazingly versatile. It is often used for large-scale projects. Through careful planning, you can use the grain (corrugation direction) to create curving planes or even expose it to add texture.

Glues

White glue is nontoxic and water-soluble when wet. It can be used with most porous materials, including all the boards that we have described previously. It is not suitable for paper-to-paper adhesion, as most papers will buckle as they dry.

Glue stick is water-soluble, acid-free, and nontoxic. Designed as an adhesive for thin paper, glue stick is ineffective for gluing any kind of board.

Rubber cement is a traditional paper adhesive that you can "erase" when you misapply it. However, because rubber cement is highly toxic, flammable, and impermanent, it isn't very useful in three-dimensional design.

Hot glue is a wax-based, translucent material that is heated in a gun and applied as a hot, viscous fluid. It is most effective in adhering nonporous materials, and it provides a quick way to create an assemblage. You can also use it to tack cardboard structures together while the white glue dries.

Dry mounting tissue is distributed in clear, thin sheets. Adhesion occurs when you heat this material, either in a drymount press or using an iron. This is an excellent adhesive for most papers and lightweight cloth, and it is widely used in photography and book arts.

Tapes

Transparent tape ("Scotch tape") is an all-purpose, lightweight, temporary adhesive for paper. It is not an effective adhesive for boards.

Masking tape is tough, flexible crepe-paper tape. It is designed to mask off unpainted areas, as when painting a car. It is a good temporary adhesive for boards, especially during the model-building stage.

Drafting tape and *artist's tape* are like masking tape but have less glue. They can be removed without damaging the surface to which they are applied.

Double-sided encapsulating tape has acrylic adhesive on both surfaces. A layer of thin paper protects one side until you apply the tape. An archival version of this material is sold by bookbinding stores, and it can be used for well-crafted final projects.

▶ key questions

STUDENT MATERIALS

- Why did you choose a particular material for your project? Considering its strength, workability, and cost, is it really the best material for your purpose?

- How would a change in material affect the meaning of your project?

- What nontraditional materials might you use? How can they expand meaning?

MEANINGFUL MATERIALS

Whether we are creating a sculpture or designing a teapot, all materials have meaning. For example, the thorny branches at the base of Michele Oka Doner's *Terrible Table* (11.33) are sure to change the emotional atmosphere of any room. And, the wood and wire Deborah Butterfield used to create *Large Horse #4* (11.34) force us to reconsider our understanding of both horses and nature.

Furthermore, every material has its own distinctive properties. We can saw, carve, sand, and glue

11.33 Michele Oka Doner, *Terrible Table*, 1988. Bronze and glass, 16½ × 26 × 22 in. (42 × 66 × 56 cm).

11.34 Deborah Butterfield, *Large Horse #4*, 1979. Steel, wire, sticks, 77 × 124 × 33 in. (195 × 315 × 84 cm).

wood. We can hammer, cast, and solder gold, which occurs in nature as dust, in nuggets, or in veins. We can sew, weave, knot and knit most fibers.

Despite the adaptability of most materials, however, we are *accustomed* to using them in specific ways. For example, a steel teapot's reflective surface, a glass's transparency, and clay's earthy functionality fulfill our expectations.

When we use a material in an uncharacteristic way or when we add strange textures to familiar forms, the viewer must reappraise both the material and the object it represents. Except for the wooden platform and brass screws, Richard Notkin has created his *Vain Imaginings* (11.35) from clay. He skillfully imitated many other materials, such as wood, plastic, and bone.

Clay is very unlike any of these materials, and a purist might argue that such mimicry violates its inherent nature. On closer examination, however, we can see a perfect match between the image and the idea. The table, which symbolizes the world, supports a chess set, which suggests risk, and a television set, which presents an illusion. Notkin has placed the ceramic skull on top of four books titled *The Shallow Life, Moth and Rust, Vain Imaginings*, and *By Bread Alone*. The image on the screen repeats the skull. The clay itself suggests impermanence (as in "he has feet of clay") and mortality (as in "earth to earth, dust to dust," which is often said during

funerals). In this masterwork of metaphor, Richard Notkin has created a "fake" ceramic sculpture for a false world.

A love of materials and an understanding of their characteristics are essential aspects of all three-dimensional work.

11.35 Richard Notkin, *Vain Imaginings*, 1978. White earthenware, glaze, brass, redwood, white cedarwood, 16 × 13½ × 16½ in. (40.6 × 34.3 × 41.9 cm).

summary

- Choice of material substantially affects both the structure and the meaning of a three-dimensional object.
- Strength, workability, durability, weight, cost, toxicity, and function are major considerations when an artist or a designer chooses a material.
- We can strengthen materials by using composites, skeletons, or exoskeletons, and by distributing force.
- Common construction methods include addition, subtraction, solidification, and displacement.

- Connections and transitions can increase visual impact as well as structural strength.
- Contemporary artists use traditional materials, such as stone, wood, metal, clay, glass, fibers, and plastics, to express a wide range of ideas.
- Ephemeral materials can expand meaning, reduce cost, and minimize environmental impact.
- Student materials, including various types of boards and adhesives, work best when we use them for the intended purpose.

key terms

additive sculpture	compression	modeling	subtractive sculpture
armature	displacement	shear	tension
assemblage	ephemera	skeleton (endoskeleton)	torque
bend	exoskeleton	solidification	
composite	flying buttress		
	gradation		

studio projects

To apply the concepts from this chapter in the studio, check out the Projects page in the Online Learning Center at www.mhhe.com/LTI5e. The following is a sample of the chapter-related assignments.

Wooden Wizardry. Transforming a standard wooden plank into an extraordinary wizard's staff.

Book Transformed. Transforming an old or used book into a new content-based sculpture.

Material and Immaterial. Investigating physical and conceptual properties of a wide variety of materials.

Linear Athlete. Exploring implied volume and motion with wire.

Discovering Mass. Transforming a plaster block into a dynamic sculpture.

Becoming Borg. Investigating the transition from human to machine.

Profile:
David MacDonald,
Ceramicist
A Passion for Pottery

Internationally renowned ceramicist David MacDonald is best known for his work with utilitarian vessels. His work has been included in over 60 exhibitions, including the Torpedo Factory Art Center in Alexandria, Virginia; the Studio Museum in Harlem; and the Afro-American Historical and Cultural Museum in Philadelphia. He is also a renowned community leader, having worked in an adult literacy program, in a summer ceramics intensive program for high school students, and with inmates at the Green Haven Maximum Security Correctional Facility in New York State.

MS: How did you start making art?

DM: Initially, it was a way to create some private space. As the third in a family of nine children, I always shared a bedroom with at least three of my brothers. I would help my parents unpack the groceries, then unfold the paper bags so that I could use the inside as drawing paper. Through hours of drawing, I was able to create my own little world.

MS: In our conversations and in viewing your work, I am struck by your passion for ceramics in general and functional vessels in particular. What is special about clay?

DM: I was introduced to ceramics during my second year in college. I was immediately fascinated by clay: it is responsive to the slightest pressure and can record the finest impression. After my first mug came out of the kiln and I made my first cup of tea, I was hooked. The idea of turning a lump of dirt into a useful object amazed me. Since I grew up with very little material wealth, I loved the idea of transforming nothing into something.

Now, I am drawn to functional ceramics because I like playing with the interaction between the object and the user. Having to produce a functional object makes the creative act much more interesting and challenging for me. When a teapot has just the right weight, balance, and proportions, it makes the act of pouring tea a celebration of the physical world.

MS: What is the source of your ideas?

DM: Anything can become a conscious or unconscious inspiration. I can get lost in the produce section of the supermarket: the shapes and colors of the vegetables give me all sorts of ideas.

On a more scholarly level, I was influenced by Japanese and Chinese ceramics during college, and for the past 30 years I have been strongly influenced by African art and culture.

MS: Yes, I notice that a dramatic change in your work occurred around 1978. Before that time, your work was sculptural, representational, and highly charged politically; afterward, it became more utilitarian and abstract. What happened?

DM: At the opening for a solo show in Syracuse, I was asked a question by an elderly white woman that dramatically changed my attitude about my work. She innocently asked if there was anything positive about being black in America or was it just one frustration and humiliation after another. The question haunted me for months afterward. I realized that my creative work had been based on anger and a feeling of victimization. As I matured as an individual, I realized that my experiences weren't limited to anger—there is much more to my life than that! I then decided to tap the rich and varied cultural and artistic tradition to which I am heir. Now I am most interested in expressing the magnificence and nobility of the human spirit and in celebrating my African heritage.

MS: What distinguishes a great pot from a mundane pot?

DM: There is no simple answer to this question. We can talk endlessly about form, surface, line, and so forth and still not gain any real insight into what makes one pot great and another mundane, yet we immediately feel it when the mixture of physical elements is just right. Out of the 30 similar bowls a potter produces, two or three always seem to stand apart, as something special.

The search for this elemental quality makes my art magical and compels me to make the next piece. Ironically, if I ever identify exactly what it is that makes an exceptional piece, the excitement will be sucked out of the creative process. The search is as compelling as the solution.

MS: Tell me about the vessel pictured here.

DM: *Carved Stoneware Storage Jar* was inspired by the bulbous form of a melon or gourd. The body is full and round and the lid handle is suggestive of a stem. I like the sense of an internal force or energy stretching the outer shell almost to the point of bursting.

First, I considered the function of the jar. To a large extent, the function determines the form. A certain size range facilitates everyday use. If the size is increased, the object is more suitable for ceremonial use, or as a decorative object. Certain shapes offer more storage capacity and better accessibility to whatever is being stored. Finally, the base must be big enough to provide stability.

The surface was carved when the jar was leather-hard, a couple of days after being thrown on the potter's wheel. A form this large can "carry" a fairly complex pattern, composed of smaller shapes in combination with larger design areas. By leaving some areas uncarved, I was able to create an overlapping effect and increase the illusion of space. The slashing diagonal lines help to unify the design and move the viewer's eye around the form, reinforcing the spherical volume.

MS: What were the most valuable lessons you learned from your teachers?

DM: From Joseph Gilliard at Hampton University, I learned the history and technique of ceramics and gained greater patience and self-control. I developed my self-awareness and passion for communication through my work with Robert Stull at the University of Michigan. From Henry Gernhardt, my Syracuse University colleague for 24 years, I learned that teaching is also an art. In nearly 40 years of teaching, Henry's commitment to his art and his students never faltered.

MS: Is there any advice you would like to give to my students?

DM: An artist has to believe in him- or herself. The dedication, courage, and energy my students bring to the classroom are more important than anything I can offer. If you want to stand above the crowd, your passion for your art must be manifest through a willingness to work harder than anyone else. The students who succeed see their art as a way of life and not simply as a way of earning a living. My job as a teacher is to help my students realize their potential and to bring eloquence to their unique voice.

David MacDonald, *Carved Stoneware Storage Jar*, 1997. 15 in. (38.1 cm).

Physical and Cerebral

What is the difference between the pile of wood in figure 12.1 and the sculpture in figure 12.2? The size, orientation, and location of the pile of wood are based on its purpose. It provides the raw material needed for building a house. Positioned at the edge of a construction site, the boards are arranged in a roughly parallel position so that workers can easily grasp and remove individual planks. This pile of wood is purely functional. Its organization has no aesthetic intention.

At first glance, figure 12.2 may seem very much like a pile of wood. The rough planks are clustered together, in close proximity to the house and in a parallel position. On closer examination, we see that the vertical beams support a raised structure. Balanced on stilts, the mass of wood seems suspended and in transition. It continues around the house and into the windows. Is the house expelling or inhaling the boards? The entire structure seems poised, ready to shift at any moment.

How and why was this sculpture made? Tadashi Kawamata begins by collecting scrap wood from demolished buildings. He then constructs temporary installations, which he describes as "cancers," on conventional buildings. With no predetermined end point, the structures grow like weeds, often enveloping the building. When the exhibition ends, Kawamata continues onward, dismantling the construction to create another sculpture elsewhere. Using scrap material to build temporary structures, his work demonstrates the fluidity and circulation of urban structures. His intention is aesthetic rather than functional.

12.1 Wood pile at a construction site.

12.2 Tadashi Kawamata, *Apartment project Tetra House N-3 W-26*, **August-September, 1983.** Installation in situ, Mr. and Mrs. Endo's house, Sapporo Bois, Japan.

As we noted at the beginning of this section, physical presence gives any three-dimensional artwork a distinctive power. That the artwork exists in our reality changes our perception. Sculpture, however, is much more than brute force. A sculpture gains significance when its creator transforms tangible materials into an aesthetic experience. The planks in figure 12.1 begin and end as physical material. A pile of wood is just a pile of wood. By contrast, sculpture, such as *Tetra House N-3, W-6 Project,* uses physical material to explore and express ideas.

CONSTRUCTED THOUGHT

From Life to Art

As we can see from figure 12.2, contemporary sculpture invites new connections between art and life and challenges our aesthetic expectations. Unconventional materials may be used, including ice, soil, plants, fire, blood, spools of thread, and crushed automobiles. For example, in her *Ceremonial Arch* (12.3), Mierle Ukeles combined traditional materials, such as metal and wood, with light bulbs, metal springs, and sanitation workers' gloves. Sculpture is now shown in parks, subway stations, and public plazas, in addition to galleries and museums. Boundaries between fine art and everyday experience may dissolve.

This can be an advantage or a disadvantage. Connection to life gives art its vitality. For example, when a play expresses actual feelings in a compelling way, it connects to our personal experience. Too direct a connection is deadly, however. A pile of wood is just a pile of wood. For art to have meaning, commonplace

12.3 Mierle Laderman Ukeles, *Ceremonial Arch Honoring Service Workers in the New Service Economy*, 1988. Steel arch with materials donated from New York City agencies, including gloves, lights, grass, straps, springs, and asphalt; overall structure 11 ft × 8 ft × 8 ft 8 in. (3.35 × 2.43 × 2.44 m), plus glove branches ranging from 2 to 4 ft (61 to 122 cm) long.

experiences must be distilled, reexamined, or transformed. It has often been said that a play is "life with the boring parts left out." A play that simply replicates everyday experience can never transport an audience beyond the commonplace. Likewise, sculpture requires a heightened experience *beyond* everyday life. Through a combination of insight and hard work, the sculptor transforms even the most resistant material into compelling communication. When all elements in a sculpture support the central concept, the viewer is simultaneously connected by the reality of the material and transported by the power of the idea.

Degrees of Representation

Representational artworks often depict persons or objects in such exquisite detail that they seem to come to life. Michelangelo's *Pietà* (12.4) is a good example. In this massive sculpture, Mary grieves as she cradles the dead Jesus. We can clearly see every crease in the fabric and every gestural nuance. Mary's right hand extends Jesus' flesh as she gently lifts his right shoulder. She tilts her head slightly, and her left hand echoes the diagonal position of his feet. Sculptures such as the *Pietà* seem to embody life. They engage our thoughts and emotions through their compelling realism and narrative implications.

Nonobjective artworks can be appreciated for their pure physical beauty. For example, the simple metal rings that Sandra Enterline constructed for her *Caged Sphere Bracelet Series* (12.5) work beautifully as ends in themselves. We can appreciate their economy and grace without knowing a story or pursuing any additional ideas that they may suggest.

Most sculptural objects fall somewhere between these two extremes. These **abstract artworks** have been distilled down from a recognizable source. Myra Mimlitsch-Gray's *Timepiece* (12.6) simultaneously suggests the mechanism and movement of a clock, a pendulum, and a musician's metronome. By reducing these familiar timepieces to their essential form, she was able to create an economical design that conveys a universal sense of time.

12.4 Michelangelo, *Pietà*, 1498–1500. Marble, 5 ft 8 in. × 2 ft 3 in. (1.74 × 0.69 m).

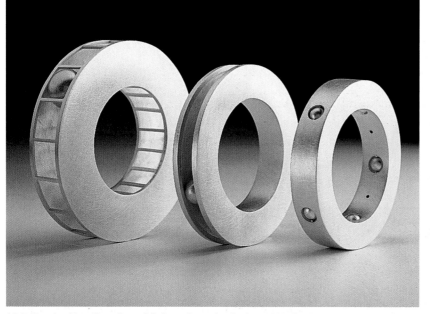

12.5 Sandra Enterline, *Caged Sphere Bracelet Series*, 1992. Sterling silver, 18-karat gold, hollow-formed, fabricated. Left to right: 5 × 5 × 1⅛ in. (12.7 × 12.7 × 3 cm), 4 × 4 × ¾ in. (10.2 × 10.2 × 1.9 cm), 4 × 4 × ¾ in. (10.2 × 10.2 × 1.9 cm).

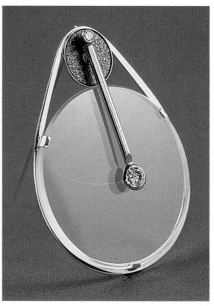

12.6 Myra Mimlitsch-Gray, *Timepiece*, 1988. Kinetic brooch, 14-karat gold, lens, diamonds, abrasive disk. Fabricated, 2¼ × 1½ × ¼ in. (6 × 4 × 0.5 cm).

12.7 Barnett Newman, *Broken Obelisk*, 1963–67. Cor-Ten steel, 26 × 10½ × 10½ ft (66 × 26.7 × 26.7 m).

12.8 Walter Martin and Paloma Muñoz, *Of Bodies Born Up by Water*, 1987. Plaster, oil paint, sheet metal, wood, 111½ × 20 × 16½ in. (283 × 51 × 42 cm).

Each approach has its advantages. Artists and designers often use nonobjective forms in situations that require universality or simplicity. Barnett Newman's *Broken Obelisk* (12.7) is a monochromatic structure constructed from a simple pyramid and an inverted obelisk. The point of contact between the two sections becomes charged with energy, as the top half seems to balance on the top of the pyramid. Caught in this moment of equilibrium, the sculpture is as carefully balanced as a ballerina on her toes.

On the other hand, a representational approach can stimulate the imagination by providing a fresh interpretation of a familiar object. In *Of Bodies Born Up by Water* (12.8), Walter Martin and Paloma Muñoz used a similar structure to create a very different effect. The poised obelisk is now a grandfather clock. When it topples, it may erase time, memory, and family history.

12.9 James Lee Byars, *The Perfect Thought*, 1990 (installation shot). Various objects covered with gold leaf, composed in one of two circles of gold leaf, large circle 40 ft (12.2 m) diameter, small circle 27 ft (8.2 m) diameter.

Boundaries

Because the art/life connection is so important, sculptors must be especially attentive to the physical and psychological boundaries in each piece. As a dividing line between objects, images, or experiences, the boundary is charged with energy. It can serve three major purposes.

Boundaries Can Connect

A simple shape can create a boundary. To define *The Perfect Thought* (12.9), James Lee Byars placed two gold-leaf circles on the floor. The larger circle enclosed 23 separate works from earlier exhibitions, while the smaller circle remained empty. This simple strategy unified a collection of individual artworks while leaving a second space open, to be filled by the viewer's imagination.

Dwelling (12.10) by Yong Soon Min focuses on psychological boundaries. Born in Korea and raised in the United States, Min explores issues of alienation and disorientation. In *Dwelling*, she

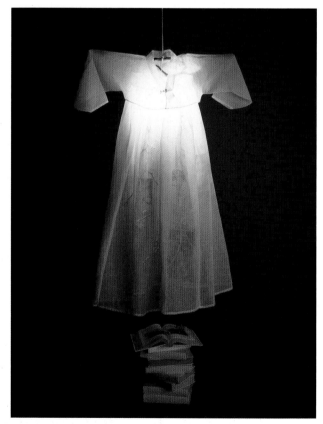

12.10 Yong Soon Min, *Dwelling*, 1994. Mixed mediums, 72 × 42 × 28 in. (183 × 107 × 72 cm).

combined a brightly lit Korean dress with a pile of maps, photographs, and books. A fragment of poetry, inserted in the dress, describes the loss of identity. In this type of sculpture, boundaries between the personal and the public begin to blur.

Boundaries Can Separate

Constructed from nine 12-foot-wide bushes within the median of a busy highway, Maya Ying Lin's *Topo* (12.11) uses a boundary to separate as well as to connect. Enclosed within the mile-long median, the bushes provide a series of diagonal stepping-stones. Shifting circles at either end of the sculpture appear to rotate the last two bushes, directing our attention back down the line. This illusion of perpetual motion activates the simple design. Bound on either side by highways, this artwork is contained within the median yet connected to the motorists whizzing past.

Psychological separation adds power to George Segal's *Walk, Don't Walk* (figure 9.68, page 210). The combination of the life-sized figures with an actual pedestrian sign suggests that these ghostly figures are part of our world. They are familiar, yet remain distant. The platform on which they stand, their immobility, and their absence of color separate them from our reality.

12.11 Maya Ying Lin, *Topo*, 1991. 1,600 × 40 ft (487.7 × 12.2 m).

Boundaries Can Enclose

Increasingly, sculptors are using every square inch of gallery space and surface to create complex installations. In *Blue Skies* (12.12), Susan Trangmar

12.12 Susan Trangmar, *Blue Skies*, 1990. Installation view, size varies.

12.13 Olafur Eliasson, *The Parliament of Reality*, 2006–09. Concrete, stone, stainless steel, water, trees, other plants. Dimensions variable. Installation at The Center for Curatorial Studies (CCS Bard), New York. The Center for Curatorial Studies and the Luma Foundation.

used the gallery walls as four large projection surfaces. Surrounded by the projections and by his or her own cast shadow, the viewer becomes a participant in the installation.

The sculpture itself can also envelop the viewer. Olafur Eliasson's *The Parliament of Reality* is composed of multiple units, including a man-made island surrounded by a circular lake, grasslands, and two dozen trees. Figure 12.13 shows a 20-foot-long bridge loosely enclosed by latticework. As visitors cross the bridge, they become part of the sculpture.

Bases and Places

Traditional sculpture is generally mounted on a **plinth**, which provides a horizontal base, or on a **pedestal**, which provides a vertical base. Either can serve three purposes:

- To physically separate the sculpture from the surrounding space
- To provide strength and structural stability

12.14 Barbara Chase-Riboud, *Malcolm X #3*, 1970. Polished bronze and silk, 118 × 47 × 10 in. (300 × 120 × 25 cm).

- To elevate an object psychologically, distinguishing it from its surroundings and increasing its impact

Seemingly insignificant, the plinth or pedestal is actually a crucial component of sculpture, both physically and aesthetically. In figure 12.14, the marble base adds elevation as well as a marked contrast in material. As a result, Barbara Chase-Riboud's *Malcolm X #3* now has a solid platform from which to speak. The plinth in *Horse Galloping on Right Foot* (12.15), by Edgar Degas, provides a visual context for the galloping horse, as well as physical stability. The sculpture would collapse (both physically and aesthetically) if the base were removed. The pedestal for Benvenuto Cellini's *Perseus and Medusa* (12.16) elevates the heroic statue and creates an architectural connection to the surrounding buildings.

12.15 Edgar Hilaire Germain Degas, *Horse Galloping on Right Foot*,
c. 1881. Bronze cast of wax model, 11⅛ in. (30 cm).

For Constantin Brancusi, the base was an aesthetic element rather than a passive support. He used a specific pedestal form to enhance the power and grace of each of his variations on birds (figures 10.26, 10.27, and 10.28, page 229). Seeking dynamism rather than stability, Umberto Boccioni split the base in half when he composed *Unique Forms of Continuity in Space* (12.17). The abstracted figure strides forward in space, too energetic to be constrained by conventional boundaries.

In contemporary sculpture, the base often extends to include an entire architectural site. Resting directly on the surface of the plaza, the granite boulders in Elyn Zimmerman's *Marabar* (12.18) become "continents" while the channel of water suggests the ocean. Combining large scale with a "baseless" design, the artist has dissolved the traditional boundary between the stones and the surroundings. As a result, Zimmerman transformed the entire plaza into a sculptural site.

12.16 Benvenuto Cellini, *Perseus and Medusa*, 1545–54. Bronze, 18 ft (5.5 m) h.

12.17 Umberto Boccioni, *Unique Forms of Continuity in Space*, 1913. Bronze (cast in 1931), 43⅞ × 34⅞ × 15¾ in. (111.2 × 88.5 × 40 cm).

12.18 Elyn Zimmerman, *Marabar*, 1984. Boulders (natural cleft and polished granite) and water. Plaza: 140 × 60 ft (42.7 × 18.3 m).

▶ key questions

CONSTRUCTED THOUGHT

- How is your artwork similar to everyday life? How is it different?

- What can a boundary or base contribute to your design?

- How will the meaning change if you place your project in a specific setting?

PHYSICAL FORCES

Weight and Gravity

Of the forces of nature, gravity is the most immediately noticeable when we begin to construct a three-dimensional structure. We must organize lines, spaces, and volumes according to the laws of physics while simultaneously meeting our aesthetic objectives. Balance is a structural necessity as well as a compositional force. After watching several prototypes collapse, it is easy to conclude that gravity is our enemy, to be conquered at all costs. But is it?

When we begin to analyze the uses of gravity in sculpture, we soon find that it is an asset rather than a liability. Just as a ballet dancer relies on gravity to provide a solid launching pad for each leap and a predictable support for each landing, so the sculptor uses gravity to express ideas and generate emotions.

Downward gravity animates *Device to Root Out Evil* (12.19). The inverted church structure seems to have fallen from the sky, driving into the ground upon landing. As sculptor Dennis Oppenheim noted, this inversion of a familiar structure creates a reversal of content. The steeple is now pointing to hell rather than to heaven. Even without any cultural associations, however, we would still respond to the improbable balance and intense color in this large piece.

A combination of weight and weightlessness gives Antony Gormley's *Learning to Think* (12.20) its impact. Constructed from a mold made from the artist's own body, the hollow lead figures are basically identical. Hovering roughly 10 feet off the ground, they seem weightless. At the same time, because they are suspended from the ceiling, each figure seems as heavy as a convict at the end of a hangman's noose. This paradox gives the

12.19 Dennis Oppenheim, *Device to Root Out Evil*, **1997.** Galvanized structural steel, anodized perforated aluminum, transparent red Venetian glass, concrete foundations, 20 × 15 × 8 ft (6.1 × 4.57 × 2.44 m).

sculpture great physical force and communicates an elusive concept. Clearly, the knowledge embodied in this sculpture is not easy to attain!

Compression and Expansion

Most materials tend to compress as weight increases. In figure 10.21 (page 227), Chuchi Fujii

12.20 Antony Gormley, *Learning to Think*, **1991.** Lead, fiberglass, air, five figures, each 68 × 41¾ × 122 in. (173 × 106 × 310 cm).

used such physical compression to evoke a visceral response. We feel the pressure as the top log pushes down on the log below. Compression also plays an important role in John Chamberlain's sculptures. In *The Hedge* (12.21), he transformed crushed automotive pieces into an improbable garden. The contradiction between the materials and the meaning suggests a new definition of nature.

12.21 John Chamberlain, *The Hedge*, **1997.** Painted milled steel, chromium-plated steel, stainless steel; overall installed 44½ in. × 44½ in. × 46 ft 4 in. (113 cm × 113 cm × 14.12 m); 16 units, each 44½ × 44½ × 12 in. (113 × 113 × 30.5 cm).

Expansion is an equally compelling force. Constructed from the charred fragments of a church that had been struck by lightning, Cornelia Parker's *Mass* (12.22) seems to present the event in suspended animation. Supported by fine steel wire and cotton thread, the hovering sculpture appears weightless, caught at the moment of explosion.

Tension and Torsion

Tension can be used to stretch or bend an object, while torsion creates a twisting movement. Either can add physical and cerebral strength to a sculpture. Stretched taut, the steel cables in Kenneth Snelson's *Free Ride Home* (see figure 9.18, page 188) provide the force needed to elevate the aluminum tubes that dominate the sculpture. Tension is equally important for the designer. The *Peregrine Tent* by The North Face (12.23) is constructed through the tension in its bent, metal poles.

12.23 *Peregrine Tent* by The North Face, San Leandro, CA.

To create *12 Trees No. 2* (12.24), Maren Hassinger twisted cables and wires together, and then clamped them at the top. Based on our experience in the physical world, we can feel the force in the twisted strands and imagine the explosive result if this power were released.

12.22 Cornelia Parker, *Mass (Colder Darker Matter)*, 1997. Charcoal retrieved from a church struck by lightning, suspended from steel wire and cotton thread, 10 × 10 × 10 ft (3.5 × 3.5 × 3.5 m).

12.24 Maren Hassinger, *12 Trees No. 2*, 1979. Galvanized wire rope, 10 × 150 × 5 ft (3.1 × 45.7 × 1.5 m).

Presence and Absence

Presence is another important aspect of physicality. When we confront a massive sculpture, such as Chris Burden's *Medusa's Head* (figure 9.23, page 190) it exudes a strength that is far beyond anything a small photograph can convey. Equally, the space surrounding a sculpture or the absence of an anticipated object can have great impact.

Many sculptors have used this quality of presence and absence to explore the passage of time and the nature of memory. British sculptor Rachel Whiteread explores presence and absence in many of her works. In her *Vienna Holocaust Memorial* (12.25), Whiteread used hundreds of gallons of cement to create her "nameless library," with the spines of the books facing outward. These immobilized books represent the lives snuffed out by the Nazis during World War II. She accentuated *absence* by making the massive memorial so physically *present*. The next image provides another approach to the same subject. In *The Writing on the Wall* series,

12.25 Rachel Whiteread, *Vienna Holocaust Memorial*, 2000. Steel and concrete, 10 × 7 × 10.7 × 3.8 m.

Shimon Attie used slide projections to remind us of shops and families destroyed during the Holocaust. Figure 12.26 shows one of the many slides from the 1930s that he projected onto various buildings in Berlin. The actual bookstore depicted disappeared long ago.

12.26 Shimon Attie, *Almstadtstrasse 43 (formerly Grenandierstrasse 7): Slide Projection of Former Hebrew Bookstore, Berlin, 1930*, from the series *The Writing on the Wall*, 1992. Ektacolor print of site-specific slide-projection installation, 20 × 24 in. (50.8 × 60.9 cm).

12.27 **Todd Slaughter**, *Grinding Knuckles*, **1993.** One RPM graphite and motors, 12 × 20 × 12 in. (30.5 × 51 × 30.5 cm).

Process and Product

In the past 50 years, sculptors have expanded their choice of materials to include many physical and chemical processes:

• *Friction.* The graphite hands in Todd Slaughter's *Grinding Knuckles* (12.27) slowly rotate, grinding the sculpture away every time this artwork is displayed.

• *Condensation.* Sealed inside the Hans Haacke *Weather Cube* (12.28), water evaporates or condenses based on the ambient temperature inside the gallery.

• *Oxidation.* Cai Guo Qiang transformed the entrance to

12.28 **Hans Haacke**, *Weather Cube*, **1963–65.** Acrylic plastic, water, climate in area of display, 12-in. (30.5-cm) cube.

a very traditional building when he ignited Fallen Blossoms: Explosion Project (12.29). Inspired by the memory of Anne d'Harnoncourt (1943–2008), the late director of the Philadelphia Museum of Art, this commissioned artwork addressed personal themes of loss and renewal on a very public level.

- *Filtration.* Located next to a wastewater treatment plant, Lorna Jordan's *Waterworks Gardens: The Grotto* (12.30) purifies up to 2,000 gallons of oil-laced storm water per minute. The 8-acre site includes stone mosaics, natural filtration systems, and colorful bands of sedges, yellow irises, and red-twig dogwoods.

12.29 Cai Guo-Qiang, *Fallen Blossoms: Explosion Project*, Philadelphia Museum of Art, December 11, 2009, 4:30 p.m., 60 seconds. Gunpowder fuse, metal net for gunpowder fuse, scaffolding, explosion area (building facade) approximately 18.3 × 26.1 m. Commissioned by the Philadelphia Museum of Art.

▶ key questions

PHYSICAL FORCES

- How can weight or gravity add meaning to your artwork?

- What are the compressive and expansive limitations of the material(s) that you are using? How might these forces enhance your concept?

- Tension and torsion create pent-up energy, like a spring ready to release. How might these forces add meaning or a feeling of suspense?

- What happens when the absence of an object or the residue after an event becomes the artwork?

- All materials and actions eventually decay. Can this process of decay become part of your concept?

12.30 Lorna Jordan, *Waterworks Gardens: The Grotto*, 1996. Third of five public garden rooms in King County East Division Reclamation Plant, Renton, WA.

CONTEMPORARY QUESTIONS, CONTEMPORARY ANSWERS

Building on a Tradition

Four qualities characterize traditional sculpture. First, mass, or solid substance, rather than open space, is the primary concern. Traditional sculptures, such as Michelangelo's *Pietà* (see figure 12.4, page 262), are relatively solid. In this masterpiece, the artist creates a sense of profound resignation through the use of gravity. The mother has fully accepted her grief. The position of the limbs and the folds in the fabric create a dynamic surface on a stable pyramidal mass. Second, the human figure is the primary subject. Sculptors have long sought to capture in wood, metal, or stone the vitality of a living person. Third, as a means to this end, traditional sculpture is overwhelmingly representational. Indeed, attention to detail and the ability to animate marble have long been the hallmarks of Western sculpture, from the Renaissance to Romanticism. Even a playful Meso-American Colima Jar (12.31) gains eloquence from the use of representation.

Finally, traditional sculptures often tell stories. Kings or communities of ordinary people have frequently commissioned public monuments to tell national stories. For example, French artist and sculptor Frederic-Auguste Bartholdi designed the Statue of Liberty to embody the democratic ideal that France and the United States shared. It was financed through a public lottery, theatrical events, and even prizefights. The poem describing "huddled masses yearning to breathe free," combined with the heroic figure, distills the history of immigration to America into a few words.

Reinventing Sculpture

In Europe, these four qualities of traditional sculpture reached their climax during the nineteenth century. Seeking fresh ideas and new approaches, artists in Russia, Italy, and France then began a process that would transform sculpture forever.

Four major changes followed. First, space became a major concern. Sculptors began developing their works from the inside out, rather than carving them from the outside in. Second, abstraction and transformation became more important than description and representation. For example, Raymond Duchamp-Villon's *The Great Horse* (12.32), constructed from a mix of organic and mechanical parts, bears little resemblance to an

12.31 Colima Rabbit Jar, c. 200 BCE–200 CE. Ceramic, 13¼ × 9 in.

12.32 Raymond Duchamp-Villon, *The Great Horse*, 1957 version of a 1914 work. Bronze, 39¼ × 24 × 36 in. (99.7 × 60.9 × 91.4 cm).

actual horse. Third, while the human figure continued to dominate early-twentieth-century sculpture, by mid-century sculptors were using almost any subject matter. Many significant artworks from this period, including Mark di Suvero's

12.33 Marcel Duchamp, *Bicycle Wheel*, 1951. (Third version, after lost original of 1913.) Assemblage, metal wheel, 25½ in. (63.8 cm) diameter, mounted on painted wood stool 23¾ in. (60.2 cm) h.; overall 50½ × 25½ × 16⅝ in. (128.3 × 63.8 × 42 cm).

Are Years What? (see figure 9.20, page 189), are largely nonobjective, having no external subject matter. Weight, balance, and the dynamics of space are the only content such works require. Most importantly, sculptors began to break down the traditional separation between art and life. Commonplace objects, such as Marcel Duchamp's *Bicycle Wheel* (12.33), appeared in galleries and were defined as art. Finding a sculptural *idea* became as important as forming a sculptural *object*.

Contemporary Directions

The evolution of sculpture has accelerated in the past 30 years. Earthworks, which transform natural sites into sculptural settings, have become a powerful force in both art and ecology. An installation, which may combine time, space, and sound, can present both artist and audience with new opportunities for communication and expression. Performance art (which we discuss at greater length in Chapter Fifteen), combines art, technology, and theater. The traditional has become the transformative. Four manifestations of this change follow.

Sculpture as Place

Throughout history, sculpture has played a significant role in a variety of settings. Stonehenge (12.34), constructed from massive limestone blocks weighing up to 50 tons, may have been used as a gigantic sundial by its Neolithic builders. The avenue approaching the stone circle aligns accurately to the summer solstice, while stones within the circle align with the northernmost and southernmost paths of the rising moon.

Likewise, contemporary sculptors add meaning to their work by exploring the physical, psychological, and temporal characteristics of each site. Glen Onwin's *Nigredo* (12.35) is one of four works in a series titled *As Above, So Below*. Placed in an abandoned chapel, this concrete pool, filled with water, black brine, and wax, seems especially ominous in the once-sacred site. In a very different investigation of place, David Adjaye's *Europolis* (12.36) traces transportation networks between various European capitals. Sandwiched between panes of glass, the brilliant red lines resemble both pulsating blood vessels and a teeming microscopic world.

12.34 Stonehenge (aerial view), Salisbury Plain, England, c. 2800–1500 BCE.

12.35 Glen Onwin, *Nigredo*, 1992. Installation view of exhibition *As Above, So Below*, at the Square Chapel, Halifax, May 9–June 15, 1992. Exposed timbers of the roof reflected in an artificial concrete pool filled with black brine and wax.

12.36 David Adjaye, *Europolis*, 2008. Metallic foil laminated in clear float glass, 6 ft × 4 ft × 2 ft.

Karin Giusti combined the personal and the political in her work *White House/Greenhouse* (12.37). Placed in Battery Park in New York City, the transparent one-quarter scale White House model had both Wall Street and the Statue of Liberty in the background. Constructed from recycled steel beams, clear vinyl, and large paintings on Plexiglas, the structure presented a strong commentary on American politics while providing a greenhouse for 200 rosebushes.

Sculpture as Journey

As sculptures have expanded in size, the manner in which the viewer enters, exits, and explores the site has become increasingly important. When the audience participates, a sculpture can be transformed from an object into an experience.

Christopher Janney's *Sonic Plaza* (12.38) at Eastern Carolina University is an especially enticing example. Composed of four distinct sculptures, the site offers a variety of sensory experiences. Various melodic sounds greet participants at the *Sonic Gates*. The 64 water jets on the *Percussion Water Wall* spew forth complex water patterns to a percussive accompaniment. Four smaller sculptures emerge each day from the large doors of the *Media Glockenspiel*. Finally, *Ground Cloud* creates a water vapor cloud that hovers over the plaza. This responds to pedestrian movement as well as wind direction.

Sculpture as Time

A fascination with time pervades contemporary sculpture. Many sculptures demonstrate the changes that occur as time passes. Combining his background in sculpture with a fascination with time and movement, Leo Villareal has created both small-scale artworks and large-scale installations using thousands of programmable lights. The array of lights in *Big Bang* (12.39) flash in a variety of colorful patterns, suggesting the formation of the universe.

Christian Marclay often combines sound with sculpture to expand our experience and

12.37 Karin Giusti, *White House/Greenhouse*, New York City, 1996. Recycled steel beams, vinyl, Plexiglas, and rosebushes, 40 × 15 × 14 ft (12 × 4.5 × 4.3 m).

12.38 Christopher Janney, *Sonic Plaza*, Eastern Carolina University, 1998. Sound, light, water, and interactive elements, total length 400 ft (122 m). Top: *Sonic Gates*; middle row left to right: *Media Glockenspiel* and *Percussion Water Wall*; bottom, *Ground Cloud*.

understanding of time. In *Amplification* (12.40), he installed large-scale translucent reproductions of six anonymous flea-market photographs in San Stae, a Baroque church in Venice, Italy. Each photograph captures a nonprofessional musical performance. An old woman plays a piano; a small girl plays a recorder; a group of men on various instruments compose an informal band. Fragments of audio recordings combined with each visitor's muted footsteps create a somber evocation of the past while simultaneously emphasizing the present.

Sculpture can also demonstrate the impermanence that is an essential characteristic of time. To create *curcuma sul travertino* (12.41), Shelagh Wakely covered the entrance hall to a British school with a thin layer of yellow turmeric spice. As visitors passed through the room, they gradually erased

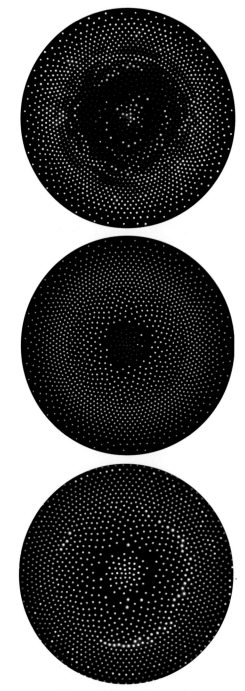

12.39 Leo Villareal, *Big Bang*, 2008. 1600 LEDs, aluminum, custom software, and electrical hardware, 59 × 59 × 8 in. (150 × 150 × 20.3 cm).

the dust. Thus, during the week-long exhibition, visitors were marked by their passage through the room, and, with spice on their shoes, subsequently marked each new room that they entered.

Sculpture as Self

It has often been said that all artwork is autobiographical. This is especially true of sculpture. As the physical manifestation of thought, sculpture has an immediacy similar to that of a living person.

12.40 **Christian Marclay,** *Amplification*, **1995.** Mixed mediums with six found prints and six photographic enlargements on cotton scrim, size varies.

12.41 **Shelagh Wakely,** *curcuma sul travertino*, **1991.** Turmeric powder on travertine marble floor (smell of turmeric filled the space), swept up after three weeks, 46 ft × 11 ft 6 in. (14 × 3.5 m).

Both traditional and contemporary sculptors have explored this theme in many marvelous ways. New Zealand's indigenous people, the Maori, have often combined sculpture with architecture to create a genealogical self-portrait. It is not uncommon for the Maori to place a prominent ancestor's face on the sacred meeting house's front gable (12.42). The rooftop's ridge is the ancestor's backbone, the rafters form his ribs, and the four corner posts symbolize his arms and legs. The Maori carve other ancestors on the building's exterior and on interior posts. Finally, they place carvings of the Earth Mother and Sky Father over the porch. Through a combination of representation and symbolism, the Maori design every aspect of the building to honor the past and inspire the present people.

Attention's Loop (11.14, page 244), by Elizabeth King, offers another type of self-portrait. In this installation King presents six highly detailed mannequins in a variety of poses. Carefully articulated arms and hands in three additional display cases line the back wall of the gallery, while an 11-minute video loop shows the mannequins moving. The combination of supreme craftsmanship, robotic machinery, and fluid animation communicates a complex range of ideas. The mannequins are both fascinating and disturbing. Human consciousness seems to be trapped in a sculptural form.

Kiki Smith infused her *Virgin Mary* (12.43) with a very different energy and insight. Completed during a tragic period in her life that included the death of both her sister and her father, the figure appears flayed and exposed. Built from wax, cheesecloth, and wood, the woman is physically and emotionally fragile.

12.42 *Maori Meeting House*, **called "Rautepupuke," New Zealand, 1881.** 56 ft × 13 ft 10 in. (17 × 4 m).

12.43 Kiki Smith, *Virgin Mary*, 1992. Wax, cheesecloth and wood with steel base, 67½ × 26 × 14½ in. (171.5 × 66 × 36.8 cm).

Eva Hesse's *Laocoön* (12.44) is a more abstract self-portrait. As noted in Chapter Nine, the ancient Greek sculpture *Laocoön and His Two Sons* (see figure 9.24, page 191) depicts a scene from the Trojan War. Laocoön warns against accepting the large wooden horse that the Greeks offer as a gift. The Greek goddess Athena sends two serpents to attack and kill Laocoön, thereby gaining entry into Troy and victory for the Greeks who are hiding in the horse. Like the snakes that bind Laocoön and

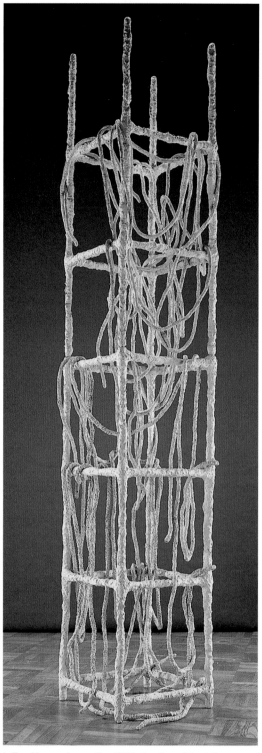

12.44 Eva Hesse, *Laocoön*, 1966. Acrylic paint, cloth-covered cord, wire, and papier-mâché over plastic plumber's pipe, bottom 130 × 23½ × 23 in. (330.2 × 59.7 × 58.4 cm), top 130 × 21½ × 21½ in. (330.2 × 54.6 × 54.6 cm).

his sons, the cords in Hesse's sculpture are messengers of death. They choke the ladder structure and foreshadow Hesse's own tragic death at age 34 from a brain tumor. As she noted, "My life and art have not been separated."

Ideas in Physical Form

The combination of tangible material and aesthetic complexity gives sculpture a unique power. Like an alchemist, the sculptor transforms ordinary materials into conceptual gold. Tadashi Kawamata's pile of wood becomes a metaphor for urban change. Mierle Ukeles transforms sanitation workers' gloves and lightbulbs into a sculpture in her *Ceremonial Arch*. A colorful explosion becomes a memorial to a museum curator in Cai Guo-Qiang's *Fallen Blossoms*. Through a miracle of invention, the best sculptures simultaneously embrace and transcend their physical nature.

► **key questions**

CONTEMPORARY QUESTIONS, CONTEMPORARY ANSWERS

- What are the historical antecedents for your idea?
- How can contemporary materials and methods strengthen your idea?
- What does your artwork reveal about yourself and the world around you?

► # summary

- A wood pile at a construction site is stacked for convenience and accessibility. A wood pile in a sculpture serves to communicate ideas and emotions.
- Art gains power from its connection to life. Through their creative expression, artists distill, reexamine, and transform commonplace experiences.
- Physical and psychological boundaries can connect or separate art and life.
- A base can separate a sculpture from its surrounding space, provide structural stability, and expand aesthetic content.
- An artist can use physical forces, such as gravity, compression, expansion, tension, and torsion to express ideas while providing structural strength.
- The materials a sculptor selects can heighten and deepen the artwork's meaning.
- Traditional Western sculpture is massive, representational, figurative, and narrative.
- Contemporary sculpture is often more spatial, abstract, and nonfigurative than traditional sculpture. It often breaks down the traditional separation between art and life.
- Many contemporary sculptors use specific sites, audience participation, temporal change, and explorations of the self to create powerful artworks.

► # key terms

abstract artworks	**pedestal**	**representational artworks**
nonobjective artworks	**plinth**	

► # studio projects 🌀

To apply the concepts from this chapter in the studio, check out the Projects page in the Online Learning Center at www.mhhe.com/LTI5e. The following is a sample of the chapter-related assignments.

Becoming Borg. The skin and skeleton of human and machine.

Time Piece. Expanding upon kinetic time.

Charles and Ray Eames, *Powers of Ten*, **1977.** Film frame.

Time
Design

From prehistory to the present, artists and designers have sought to create images, objects, and architectural works that embody and express the most profound aspects of human experience. Visions of love and hate, life and death, and the beauty of nature fill the walls of any art museum or gallery.

This compulsion to create has always inspired artists and designers to seek new avenues of expression. In contemporary art, innovation and experimentation have become the rule rather than the exception. Amazing new digital projects can distribute ideas to a global audience. Images and ideas that we once considered taboo dominate many exhibitions. Through performance art, separations among music, theater, and art become blurred.

In this final major section, we consider time as a dimension of art and design. Although all areas of visual communication are affected by time, sequential arts — such as photography, digital media, visual books, and performance art — most depend on its power.

Chapter Thirteen offers an overview of time design and a description of its basic aspects and elements. We discuss various forms of storytelling in Chapter Fourteen. We conclude with an exploration of interdisciplinary art and design, including an extended discussion of visual books, installation art, and performance art.

Part
Four

Aspects and Elements of Time

Abe Morell quietly sets up a large camera in an empty New York apartment. Except for a single small opening, he has blocked the light coming in the windows. Ghostly and inverted images of the surrounding city begin to appear on the walls. At just the right moment, he releases the shutter.

In 1998, Nancy Callahan and Diane Gallo created *Storefront Stories* in Cherry Valley, New York. They installed a combination of words, images, and everyday objects in an unused storefront window. Every 10 days, they changed the installation and presented the next chapter in a story. Over a six-week period, they revealed an entire narrative to the townspeople.

During the 1984 Super Bowl, a feisty start-up company aired an unusual commercial. The 60-second commercial begins as gray-faced workers in a futuristic city trudge to a huge theater and shuffle to their seats (13.1). From the screen, a grim "Big Brother" intones: "From today we celebrate the first anniversary of the information purification directions." A woman athlete then appears carrying a sledgehammer and sprinting toward the theater, with guards in hot pursuit. On arrival, she hurls the hammer into the screen, which explodes. As the words appear on the screen, an announcer reads, "On January 24, Apple Computer will introduce Macintosh. And you'll see why 1984 won't be like *1984*." Through this ad, Apple offered an alternative to George Orwell's dystopian vision of the future. From 1984 onward, computers have expanded into every aspect of our lives, from laptops to smartphones and beyond.

13.1 Apple Computer television ad introducing the Macintosh computer. Televised during the 1984 Super Bowl.

What is the connection? What do these artworks have in common? In each case, an understanding of time is an essential aspect of the work. Like gravity, time itself is intangible. We cannot see time, yet it affects every aspect of our lives. An illustrator working on a track meet poster seeks the most dramatic moment in each event. Theodore Gericault composed *Raft of the Medusa* (13.2) to capture the most dramatic moment in time. And, through variations in texture and color, a ceramicist invites us to examine a bowl slowly, revealing each nuance as we rotate the form.

Photographers, illustrators, and digital media artists are especially sensitive to the importance of time. When news photographer Sam Shere captured the moment at which the dirigible *Hindenburg* exploded, he created an indelible image (13.3). In *The Mysteries of Harris Burdick*, illustrator Chris Van Allsburg suggested a series of complex stories using a single drawing and a fragment of text (see figure 4.22, page 99). Christian Marclay's *The Clock* (13.4) presents excerpts from thousands of film clips. The film includes car chases, bank heists, burning candles, and every conceivable form of clock. Synchronized to the actual passage of time over a 24-hour period, this artwork blurs the line between film and everyday reality. Time itself is its subject.

Meanings unfold through the passage of time. By selecting and composing each moment, we can turn the most mundane event into a memorable experience. Connections that we make through the juxtaposition of images can create a visual rhythm, express an idea, or tell a story. While film, video, and photography most clearly demonstrate these aspects of time, the implications for all areas of art and design are profound.

13.2 Théodore Géricault, *Raft of the Medusa*, 1818–19. Oil on canvas, 16 ft 1 in. × 23 ft 6 in. (4.9 × 7.2 m).

13.3 Sam Shere, *Explosion of the* Hindenburg, *Lakehurst, NJ*, 1937. Photograph.

13.4 Christian Marclay, *The Clock*, 2011.

13.5A Single frame, close-up.

13.5B Single frame, medium shot.

13.5C Single frame, long shot.

BUILDING BLOCKS

Artists generally compose the sequential structures in film, video, and graphic novels using four basic units: frame, shot, scene, and sequence.

The **frame** is a single static image. Projected onto a flat screen, the same compositional forces that we explored in Part One govern a film frame. As figures 13.5A, 13.5B, and 13.5C show, the boundaries of the frame determine the image's meaning. The **close-up** in the first frame shows the gasoline can that starts the fire. The **medium shot** in the second frame shows the parking lot where the fire has been set. The **long shot** in the final frame shows the fire in a larger context. We now see that this fire in a parking lot could spark an explosion at a nuclear power plant.

In filmmaking, a **shot** is a continuous group of frames. In figure 13.6, the first shot consists of eight frames, the second shot consists of six frames, and the third shot consists of four frames. In traditional films, the eight-frame shot would last for one-third second, while the six-frame shot would last for one-quarter second.

By combining these shots, we can create a scene. Filmmakers usually construct a **scene** from continuous action in continuous time and continuous space. They often combine shots of various length to strengthen expression.

A **sequence** is a collection of related shots and scenes that constitute a major section of action or narration. To understand the expressive potential of a sequence, we will examine four major ways in which shots can be related.

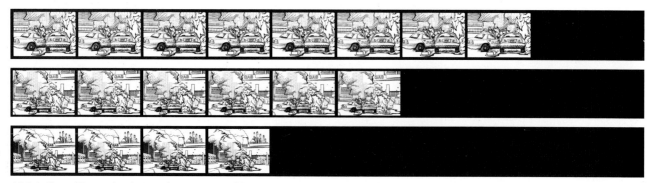

13.6 In filmmaking, a shot is a continuous group of frames.

Relationships

In *Film Art: An Introduction,* David Bordwell and Kristin Thompson describe four types of shot-to-shot relationships.

A **graphic relationship** connects two or more images through visual similarity. Because the images of doves, airplanes, and crosses in figures 13.7A, 13.7B, and 13.7C are graphically similar, we can make a visual connection when we view them sequentially. In this case, a visual connection communicates a political idea. Doves symbolize peace, bombers symbolize war, and crosses symbolize death. The juxtaposition of these shots shows that the transition from peace to war leads to death.

A **spatial relationship** can expand or compress the stage on which an action occurs. Through a combination of close-ups and distance shots, the filmmaker can increase or decrease the emotional connection between the actor and the audience

(13.8A–C). In the final close-up in this series, the actor can speak to us directly.

A **temporal relationship** can establish **chronology**, the order in which events occur. We may tell a story through a simple sequence of events or organize it using **flashbacks**, which refer to previous events. The 1993 movie *The Fugitive* uses flashbacks extensively. The film begins with the murder of Dr. Kimball's wife. Wrongly accused of the crime and sentenced to death, Kimball must discover the actual killer if he is to clear his name. Flashbacks to the murder (which occur throughout the film) show Kimball's recollection of the event that shattered his life.

When a filmmaker combines many shots he or she can create a deliberate **rhythmic relationship**. Rhythm is often based on an interplay between static and dynamic, on a contrast between light and dark, or on a combination of shots of different duration.

13.7A Doves symbolize peace.

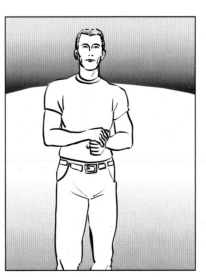

13.7B Bombers symbolize war.

13.7C Crosses symbolize death.

13.8A Long shot.

13.8B Medium shot.

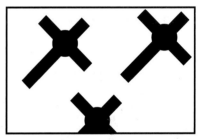

13.8C Close-up.

A   B   C

D   E   F

G   H   I

J   K

13.9A–K Alfred Hitchcock, *The Birds*, 1963.

In *The Birds,* Alfred Hitchcock used all these relationships to create a suspenseful sequence that builds to an explosive climax (13.9A–K). In *Film Art,* David Bordwell and Kristin Thompson describe this example in detail.[1] Melanie, the central character in the sequence, watches in horror as a line of flaming gasoline advances across the pavement, and then ignites a gasoline station. The shots of her face create one graphic relationship, while the shots of the flame create a second. By **crosscutting**, or alternating between the two, Hitchcock created a powerful rhythm and established a simultaneous temporal relationship: Melanie is watching the gasoline as it advances toward the gas station. In a final aerial view (13.9K), we shift our spatial position to watch the final explosion from a seagull's point of view. Hitchcock combined graphic, rhythmic, temporal, and spatial relationships to create a cinematic tour de force.

Transitions

Four common transitions are the cut, fade, dissolve, and wipe (13.10). A **cut** is an abrupt transition that may connect very different images or very similar images, depending on the desired effect. Fades and dissolves are gradual transitions. In a **fade**, the shot slowly darkens or lightens. In a **dissolve**, as one shot

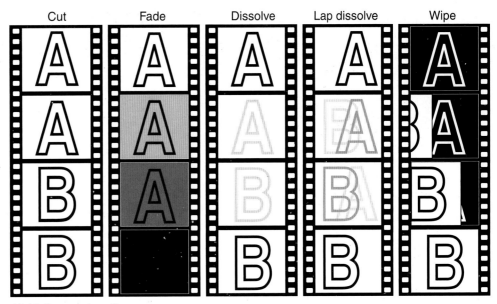

13.10 Common transitions.

fades, another appears. Two shots are superimposed briefly in a **lap dissolve**. A **wipe** is more abrupt than a fade but softer than a cut. In a wipe, the first shot seems to be pushed off the screen by the second.

Our next section will illustrate four additional transitions that are often used in graphic novels. This information is derived from Scott McCloud's *Understanding Comics*.[2] An **action-to-action transition** (13.11) simply illustrates sequential movement within an event. Here, the villain leans back and then throws the bomb. In a **subject-to-subject transition** (13.12), two shots within the same scene are juxtaposed. The villain lights the match and then hurls the bomb. A **scene-to-scene transition** (13.13) requires more viewer involvement. Here, we move from a party to a display of fireworks. Our final example, a **non-sequitur transition** (13.14), requires the reader to work even harder. Since there is no logical relationship between the juggler and the bridge, we must invent our own meaning.

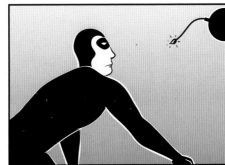

13.11 Capturing sequential moments within a single event, the **action-to-action transition** is clear and straightforward.

13.12 In a **subject-to-subject transition**, two shots within the same scene are juxtaposed. The combination may provide crucial information, as in this explosive story.

13.13 We must work a bit to understand a **scene-to-scene transition**. Depending on the images that the filmmaker uses, this type of transition can transport us across great distances in time and space. In this example, we must connect a New Year's party to fireworks bursting over a bridge.

▶ key questions

BUILDING BLOCKS

- Can a graphic or temporal relationship add meaning to your artwork?

- Where are you using close-ups, medium shots, and long shots? What purpose does each shot serve?

- How might crosscutting affect rhythm and meaning in your artwork?

- Try cuts, fades, and other types of transitions. How does the transition type affect the meaning of your artwork?

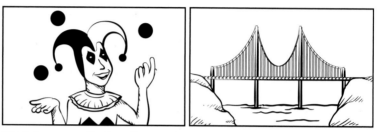

13.14 A **non-sequitur transition** requires even more reader involvement. Because there is no logical relationship between shots, the filmmaker must invent meaning.

10-second rocket launch will make it boring rather than gripping. Every moment has its own power. A 15-second advertisement uses time just as carefully as a 2-hour film.

Determining the plot duration is especially important. Following the principles of drama described by Aristotle, ancient Greek plays (such as *Oedipus Rex*) generally occur over a one- or two-day period. While the characters may refer to previous events, the action on stage is brief. *Hamlet, Romeo and Juliet,* and other Shakespearean plays are equally brief. By limiting the time frame, the playwright focuses our attention on a few events and thereby increases the play's impact.

DURATION

Duration refers to three things: the running time of a film, video, or performance; the time covered by the events that the story depicts; and the overall span of time that the story encompasses. For example, the viewing time of *Star Wars* is 118 minutes. The **plot duration** (from the capture of Princess Leia to the destruction of the Death Star) is about a month. The overall **story duration**, however, extends back to Darth Vader's betrayal of the Jedi warriors and his alliance with the dark side of the Force.

Matching all three aspects of duration to the intended message is essential. A 15-minute film cannot fully communicate Tolstoy's Russian novel *War and Peace*. Equally, expanding the duration of a

▶ key questions

DURATION

- What is the actual duration of the event on which you have based your artwork? What is the duration of your edited version?

- What did you cut from the raw footage and what did you add? Why?

- What strategies can you use to expand or compress duration?

- Will expanded or compressed duration add meaning to your artwork?

13.15 George Lucas, *Star Wars*, 1977. Film frame.

TEMPO

Tempo refers to the speed at which time passes. Despite the apparent constancy of real time, our perception of events in our lives varies widely, depending on the nature of the activity and the rate of change. Consider this story. Six coal miners were trapped by the collapse of a mine shaft. Based on the size of their shelter and the number of trapped men, the miners determined that there would be enough oxygen for a four-hour wait. Beyond that point, rescue would be futile: they would run out of oxygen. A miner with a fluorescent watch called out the hours as the time passed. He modified his report, cutting in half the actual length of time passed. Six hours passed. All of the miners survived, except the man with the watch. He alone knew that they were out of oxygen!

Actors' movement and film editing both affect tempo. In *Star Wars,* the fight between Darth Vader and Obi-Wan Kenobi began as staged combat between two actors (13.15). To provide enough raw material, director George Lucas filmed many versions, or **takes**, using multiple cameras. He was able to create the final tempo through editing. By connecting fragments from many different views,

Lucas was able to increase or decrease the fight tempo.

In a visual book, the artist or designer commonly creates tempo in two ways. First, by increasing the number and frequency of images, the artist or designer can increase the tempo. Second, by turning the page, the reader controls the viewing speed.

In a flip book, actions can pass slowly or quickly, depending on the pace set by the viewer. In a more elaborate book called *Cover to Cover*, Michael Snow presented multiple views of a room interior and the surrounding landscape. There is no text—photographs of walls, doorways, and streets re-create the environment within the book format. The viewer can run or stroll through this house, depending on how fast he or she turns the pages.

As with film, the organization of multiple images largely determines tempo in a comic book. Vertical panels placed in close proximity tend to speed up the tempo, and horizontal panels tend to slow it down. Figure 13.16 shows interactions among various superhero characters. The horizontal panels emphasize the speed of the flying figures, while the vertical panels slow down the action. Close-ups in the final sequence of images emphasize each character's fierce determination.

13.16 Captain America, Silver Surfer, *Infinity Gauntlet #4*, **Cover Date: October 1991.** Writer: Jim Starlin. Penciler: Ron Lim. Inker: Josef Rubinstein. Characters featured: Captain America, Thanos, Adam Warlock, and Silver Surfer. © 2010 Marvel Characters, Inc. Used with permission.

key questions

TEMPO

- How quickly does time pass in your artwork?

- What are the advantages of a slow tempo? Of a fast tempo? Of variations in tempo?

- How does tempo affect meaning? Or heighten emotion?

INTENSITY

Intensity refers to the level of energy in a performance or the quality of observation of an event. For example, to win an Olympic gold medal, an ice skater must spin rapidly, fully extend each move, and exude both athletic skill and emotional conviction. Likewise, even an ordinary glass of water becomes fascinating when we observe it closely. The glass itself offers a graceful interplay between line and shape, while light passing through droplets of water breaks into a prismatic array of color.

Intensity of performance is an essential aspect of theater. We can feel the concentration that the actors bring to the stage. When a dramatic or dangerous event occurs, we can share their emotion. In *Cleaning the House* (13.17), Yugoslavian artist Marina Abramovic combined intensity with metaphor to make a political statement. Wearing a white dress and sitting in a poorly lit New York City basement, she scrubbed the dirt and blood off a collection of massive cow bones. Like the bones, various ethnic groups in her homeland had been "cleansed," through expulsion from their homes, bringing trauma and bleached bones to the shattered country.

Artists often use video first to record, and then to intensify everyday experience. In *Migration*

13.17 Marina Abramovic, *Cleaning the House*, 1995. Performance at Sean Kelly Gallery. Duration, two hours.

13.18 Mary Lucier, *Migration (Monarch)*, 2000. Video projection, Times Square.

(Monarch) (13.18), Mary Lucier photographed a monarch butterfly, which alights on a human hand, then dies. Capable of migrating thousands of miles, Lucier shows the beautiful creature as fragile and transient. The very act of filming the insect's death focuses our attention on the event, while the subsequent video projection in the middle of Manhattan increases its poignancy and significance.

▶ key questions

INTENSITY

- What is the intensity level of your artwork or performance? How will a change in intensity affect your artwork's expressive power?

- How are you communicating this intensity to the audience?

- What is the most important moment in your work? Is it the most intense moment?

SCOPE

We can define **scope** in two ways. Conceptually, it is the extent of our perception or the range of ideas that our minds can grasp. Temporally, scope refers to the amount of action that occurs within a given moment.

The earliest films, such as *The Arrival of a Train at La Ciotat Station* (13.19), are limited in scope. We see a single event from a fixed viewpoint. By positioning his camera carefully, director Louis Lumière created a dynamic, diagonal composition. The train and passengers seem to come out of the screen and into the theater. Some audience members were so convinced of the illusion that they were afraid they would be hit by the train. In the early days of cinema, *any* moving image fascinated the audience, and this simple film became very popular.

As directors gained experience, they expanded the temporal scope of their films. In *The Great Train Robbery* (1903), a gang of bandits holds up a train; a telegraph operator alerts the authorities; a posse is gathered from men at a local dance; the posse captures the thieves. Director Edwin S. Porter used only 11 shots with simple editing.

13.19 Louis Lumière, *The Arrival of a Train at La Ciotat Station*, 1897. Film frame.

13.20A D. W. Griffith, *Intolerance*, 1916. Film frame.

13.20B D. W. Griffith, *Intolerance*, 1916. Film frame.

Nonetheless, it is clear that the robbery, the telegrapher's message, and the dance are roughly simultaneous events.

With *Intolerance,* director D. W. Griffith expanded conceptual scope much further. Using intolerance throughout history as a theme, Griffith developed four simultaneous stories: the fall of Babylon, Jesus' final days, the St. Bartholomew's Day Massacre in France, and a labor strike in modern-day America. These stories are intercut throughout the film, with the image of a woman rocking a cradle as a recurrent motif that increases the sense of connection. Each story concludes in an attempted rescue. Weaving the four narratives together in an accelerating rhythm (13.20A and B), Griffith brought the film to a breathtaking conclusion.

Complex stories often require complex editing, and Griffith became a master of the art. By alternately showing two or more events, he created a connection between simultaneous actions. Comic book artists use many of the same devices. Paul Jenkins and Jae Lee repeatedly use this technique of crosscutting in *Inhumans* (13.21). Because we move back and forth between a firing cannon and a quiet conversation, we realize that these are simultaneous events.

Scope is equally important in traditional narrative painting. Nicolas Poussin's *The Rape of the Sabine Women* (13.22) presents a complex event in a single image. Seeking wives, the Romans have invited the Sabines to a festival. They then attack their guests and abduct the women. Many actions occur at once. In the upper-left corner, Romulus raises his cloak as a signal to attack. As the courtyard swirls with struggles between the women and their captors, an old woman and two children at the center of the painting watch in terror.

▶ key questions

SCOPE

- Is your artwork limited or broad in scope?

- If it is broad in scope, how can you create continuity among multiple events?

- If it is narrow in scope, how can you make the "small" story become meaningful?

- Consider moving from broad scope to narrow scope within your movie. How does this affect communication?

13.21 Paul Jenkins (Writer) and Jae Lee (Artist), *Inhumans: "First Contact,"* Volume 2, Issue 5, March 1999.
© 2010 Marvel Comics, Inc. Used with permission.

13.22 Nicolas Poussin, *The Rape of the Sabine Women*, 1634. Oil on canvas, 5 ft ⅞ in. × 6 ft 10⅝ in.
(154.6 × 209.9 cm).

SETTING

Setting is one of the most complex aspects of time. It includes the physical and temporal location of a story, its props and costumes, and the use of sound.

Physical and Temporal Location

The physical setting of an event has an extraordinary impact on meaning. An action that is appropriate in one context may be appalling in another. As a drum major, the crowd will applaud you when you strut down Main Street during a

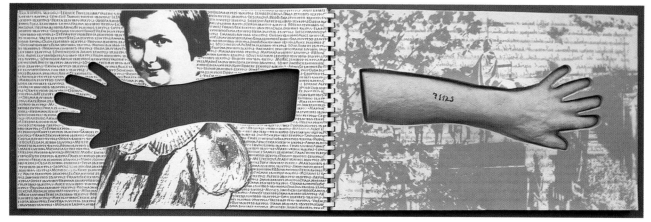

13.23A Tatana Kellner, *Fifty Years of Silence*, 1992. 12.2 × 19.7 × 2 in. (31 × 50 × 5 cm).

13.23B Tatana Kellner, *Fifty Years of Silence*, 1992. 12.2 × 19.7 × 2 in. (31 × 50 × 5 cm).

13.23C Tatana Kellner, *Fifty Years of Silence*, 1992. 12.2 × 19.7 × 2 in. (31 × 50 × 5 cm).

Fourth of July parade. At a different time of day (such as Monday morning rush hour) or in a different location (such as an airport), you are likely to get arrested.

The temporal setting is equally significant. Most of the action in *Gone with the Wind* is derived from romantic conflict involving Scarlett O'Hara, Ashley Wilkes, and Rhett Butler. While each of the three characters is interesting, the love triangle itself is commonplace. It is the film's temporal setting during the American Civil War that shifts the story from soap opera to epic.

Likewise, Nancy Holt's *Sun Tunnels* (9.26A–B, page 191) would be meaningless if removed from its site in western Utah. Constructed from four 22-ton concrete tunnels, this sculpture aligns with the rising and setting sun on the winter and summer solstices. Holes cut in each tunnel's walls show the arrangement of stars in four constellations. Designed to heighten awareness of our place in the universe, this work relies on both time and place for its impact.

Props and Costumes

Props and costumes can have an equally dramatic effect in a narrative. When performing an elegant ballroom dance, Fred Astaire wore a top hat and tuxedo. When dancing down a gritty city street, Michael Jackson wore a leather jacket and jeans. In Peter Jackson's *The Lord of the Rings*, the one ring of power is as important a character as Frodo himself.

Fifty Years of Silence (13.23A–C), a visual book by Tatana Kellner, is even more dependent on objects and their meanings. The simple pine crate that protects the book seems innocuous until we see the small, five-digit number burned into the lid. Removing the lid reveals a papier-mâché arm that bears the same number. It is a cast of the arm of Kellner's mother, an Auschwitz concentration camp survivor. The book pages, cut out around the arm, tell the family's story before and during the Holocaust. As we turn the pages, the actual arm and the cutout arm are as inescapable as the Holocaust survivor's repressed memories. By placing it in such a prominent position in the book, Kellner provides us with a sculptural close-up of the indelible tattoo. Using the crate and the arm as "props," Kellner transformed the story of a Holocaust survivor into a highly personal event.

Setting and Actor

Relationships between an actor and a setting can substantially affect our interpretation of an action or event. As we will see in the next section, placement of a single figure within a setting offers a wide range of possibilities.

First, we must decide where to place the dancer within the frame. Figure 13.24 shows three alternatives. Positioned at the far left edge, the dancer faces an empty stage, which invites her to enter. Positioned in the center, she commands attention. She can move to the right, to the left, forward, or back with ease. She is now in a more commanding position. Facing right, and positioned at the right, she seems ready to leave the frame, perhaps to join other dancers offstage.

13.24

What happens when the dancer's size is varied? Figure 13.25 shows that changing her size relative to the frame helps to define the distance between the dancer and the viewer. When we reduce her size and place her in the upper half of the frame, she seems distant, far from the viewer. When she moves far into the foreground, with her torso filling the frame, she seems to push past the boundary and into our space.

13.25

The addition of an illusionistic setting (13.26) dramatically changes the amount of space available to our dancer. We can even use a simple line in various ways. It may be the ground, providing her with a resting place. When the dancer overlaps the line, it recedes, suggesting a horizon. The addition of a second line can expand the space even further. We can now show two grounds at the same time: the foreground and the background.

13.26

In figure 13.27, the addition of perspective lines further enhances the space. A long corridor in one-point perspective gives the dancer more room. She can now dance toward us or away from us. The space is extended beyond the edge of the frame by the repeating chairs and the lines in the floor. Despite her small size, the dancer's central placement makes her the focus of both images.

13.27

The setting can become even more significant when we view the dancer from above or below (13.28). Looking up from the front row gives the figure a commanding presence. Looking down from the balcony makes her seem insignificant.

13.28

Adjusting the lights (13.29) increases the compositional and emotional possibilities. Sidelighting accentuates the dimensionality of both the figure and the setting. When we backlight the dancer, she becomes a silhouette. We lose information about her volume but gain a striking graphic image and an impressive cast shadow. Spotlighting the dancer can direct attention to a specific part of her body or eliminate the rest of the stage altogether.

13.29

Variations in focus (13.30) can affect both spatial location and emotional impact. When the foreground figure is out of focus, she is less dominant, and we quickly look past her into the more tightly focused audience. The middle drawing presents a more traditional use of focus. Clear focus in the foreground gradually diminishes as we approach the distant stage. However, do we really want to focus on the back of the audience? By focusing on the distant stage, we can watch the dancer as she ends her performance and accepts the applause.

13.30

▶ key questions

SETTING

- Start with a single actor. Who is this person? An eight-year-old boy? A pregnant woman? A soldier in a wheelchair? What objects relate to this character?

- How many ways can you position the actor in the setting? How does each position affect meaning?

- What is the viewer's position relative to the actor?

Sound: The Hidden Dimension

During the 1996 Academy Awards ceremony, the presenters showed two versions of a clip from *Chariots of Fire*. This story of the British track tream that won many medals during the 1924 Olympic Games showed the transformation of idealistic men into heroic athletes. In the first version, a group of young men ran along a beach, accompanied by the sounds of their feet splashing in the water. They were ordinary men on an ordinary beach. The same footage was then shown as it appeared in theaters around the world. Accompanied by the heroic, Oscar-winning theme music, these Olympic runners became graceful, even godlike. They were transformed by the music.

Despite its invisibility, the soundtrack is as important to a film as the images that we see. Sound engages another of our senses and heightens our emotion. A well-written score can set the stage for an action and help unify a complex film. Sound also heightens our expectations. Consider the importance of squeaky doors in a horror movie or our feeling of expectation when we hear the *Star Wars* theme. As we begin to study film, we find that this example from *Chariots of Fire* is not an isolated case. Sound can make or break a film.

Four types of sound dominate time design: speech (as delivered by an actor or generated by the audience), music, ambient sound, and sound effects. Each sound has the following seven qualities.

Loudness is determined by the size of the oscillations in a sound wave. Just as Beethoven varied the volume (or loudness) within his symphonies, so an astute filmmaker or performance artist learns to use a full range of sound, from a whisper to a scream.

Pitch is determined by wave frequency, as compression and expansion occur within the sound wave. The higher pitch of most female voices generally is less threatening than the lower pitch of most male voices. Not surprisingly, the hero is a tenor, while the villain is a baritone in most operas.

Timbre refers to each instrument's unique quality. When we play the same note on a violin and a trumpet, it sounds very different.

Duration refers to the length of time that we can hear a sound. A sound that persists over a long period of time can serve as a bridge between two or more film clips, while a brief, explosive sound may jolt us out of our seats.

Three qualities define **rhythm**: the **beat**, or pulse, of the sound; the **pace** (or tempo) at which the sound is played; and the **accents**, or areas of emphasis, within the sound. We encounter rhythm in every conversation as we listen to the speed of our friend's speech and note his or her emphasis on particular words. Rap music, which in some ways is a heightened form of speech, greatly emphasizes the beat through both a rhythmic use of words and the strong definition of each syllable.

In film, **fidelity** refers to the connection between a sound and its source. The insistent sound of a churning propeller accompanies the arrival of a helicopter at the end of the musical *Miss Saigon*. Here, the sonic information and the visual information match. In Francis Ford Coppola's *Apocalypse Now,* we hear Richard Wagner's famous "Ride of the Valkyries" as a group of helicopters arrives. As in *Chariots of Fire,* this mismatch between the visual and sonic information substantially changes our interpretation of the event.

Finally, all forms of sound operate within a **spatial context**. The bagpipe, designed to rally troops in war, is an excellent instrument to play outdoors. When played in a small room, the same instrument can very nearly blast plaster off a wall. Likewise, a whispered conversation in a closet may be more compelling than a shouted conversation on a beach. Even when we have no image at all, sound alone can define space and create a sense of anticipation or dread.

In a film, the spatial dimension of sound becomes even more significant. An onscreen event or an invisible, offscreen source generates a **diegetic** sound. Diegetic sounds seem to emanate directly from the world of the film. Both onscreen and offscreen sound are critically important, and in many cases a director will shift between the two. For example, in James Cameron's *Titanic,* a quartet of musicians plays "Nearer My God to Thee" as the ship sinks lower and lower. The music continues as we see an elderly couple in their cabin, embracing (13.31), and a mother comforting her child. The combination of the

13.31 James Cameron, *Titanic*, 1997.

sorrowful music and the tragic images heightens our sense of loss.

Composer Aaron Copland was a master of film music. In 1949, he wrote "Tip to Moviegoers: Take Off Those Earmuffs," an essay describing ways that music can enhance a film.[3] While his comments are most applicable to music, we can also apply them to other types of sound. Copland emphasized five points, paraphrased below.

- *Sound can create a more convincing atmosphere of time and place.* For example, harpsichord music may be effective in a film set in seventeenth-century Paris while jazz may be appropriate for a detective story set in contemporary New Orleans.

- *Sound can communicate a character's unspoken thoughts or a situation's unseen implications.* A cheerful family picnic film can quickly become threatening and claustrophobic if the filmmaker adds an accelerated heartbeat.

- *Sound can serve as a neutral background, filling space between bits of dialogue.* Copland considered this the "composer's most ungrateful task" yet noted its value in helping create a unified film. Background sounds can subtly season the overall temporal stew.

- *Sound can increase continuity.* As we noted in Chapter One, a collage of visual fragments is difficult to unify. Similarly, a **montage**, or collection of temporal fragments, can quickly become chaotic and incomprehensible. The addition of sound helps connect the parts and can add a unifying rhythm.

- *Sound often heralds the beginning of an event or rounds it off with a sense of finality.* John Williams, one of the most successful and prolific of contemporary composers, is renowned for his memorable introductions as well as his grand finales. For examples of his work, watch and listen to *Harry Potter and the Sorcerer's Stone, Jaws, Star Wars, Raiders of the Lost Ark, Superman,* and *Schindler's List.*

For clarity, all of these examples are emphatic and familiar. In your own work, consider less obvious and more inventive solutions. The interplay between sound and image is extremely rich, and experimenting with the least familiar combinations may lead you to the most powerful results.

▶ key questions

SETTING

- Consider all aspects of setting: sound, props, physical space, and lighting. Have you used each aspect fully?

- To what extent should various aspects of setting match? What happens when you create a deliberate mismatch between one or more setting components?

- Consider various settings. What will happen if the setting changes during the performance from a deserted train station to a factory? To a doctor's office? To a lecture hall?

CHRONOLOGY

Chronology refers to the order in which events occur. In real time, a foot race begins with the athletes lining up in position (action A), followed by the firing of the starting gun (action B), the running of the race (action C), and the conclusion at the finish line (action D). We can organize these actions in various ways, from a disorienting ABACADA pattern to the familiar ABCD pattern of the actual race.

In *Structure of the Visual Book,*[4] Keith Smith demonstrates the narrative possibilities of multiple images (13.32–13.38, page 302). Changes in chronology completely change meaning. In each case, relationships among the images create the sequence of events needed to tell a story.

Combining shots creates chronology. A filmmaker combines shots through **editing**. Editing serves six basic purposes.

1. The film editor must select the most compelling images from the total footage shot. No matter how carefully actors rehearse a scene, variations in performance quality occur. Documentary films require even more footage. Before editing a film about the 1936 Olympic Games in Berlin, director Leni Riefenstahl devoted 10 solid weeks of work to just watching the raw footage. Editing this material down to a 3½-hour film took another two years!

2. The filmmaker must organize the raw film into a cohesive whole. Directors often use multiple cameras to provide plenty of rough footage. Constructing a coherent composition using both close-up and distant shots is often the first step.

3. Through editing, the filmmaker can develop a temporal framework. Time can expand, contract, or move in a dizzying spiral. When using crosscutting, the editor shifts back and forth between two or more events, thereby suggesting the simultaneous occurrence of multiple actions. *A Tale of Two Cities,* by Charles Dickens, is a literary example of crosscutting. The narrative reaches a climax as Sydney Carton, in Paris, is led to the guillotine, while his double, who was actually condemned to die, is drugged and transported to London. Chapter after chapter, the story shifts between the two men, increasing the sense of urgency while presenting the simultaneous events. This novel offers simultaneous action at its best. Pioneer film director D. W. Griffith used Dickens as an example when he was criticized for his innovative editing of *Intolerance.*

4. Filmmakers determine tempo largely by the number of cuts. For example, a filmmaker can construct an introspective drama from 1,000 shots, while an action film may require 2,000

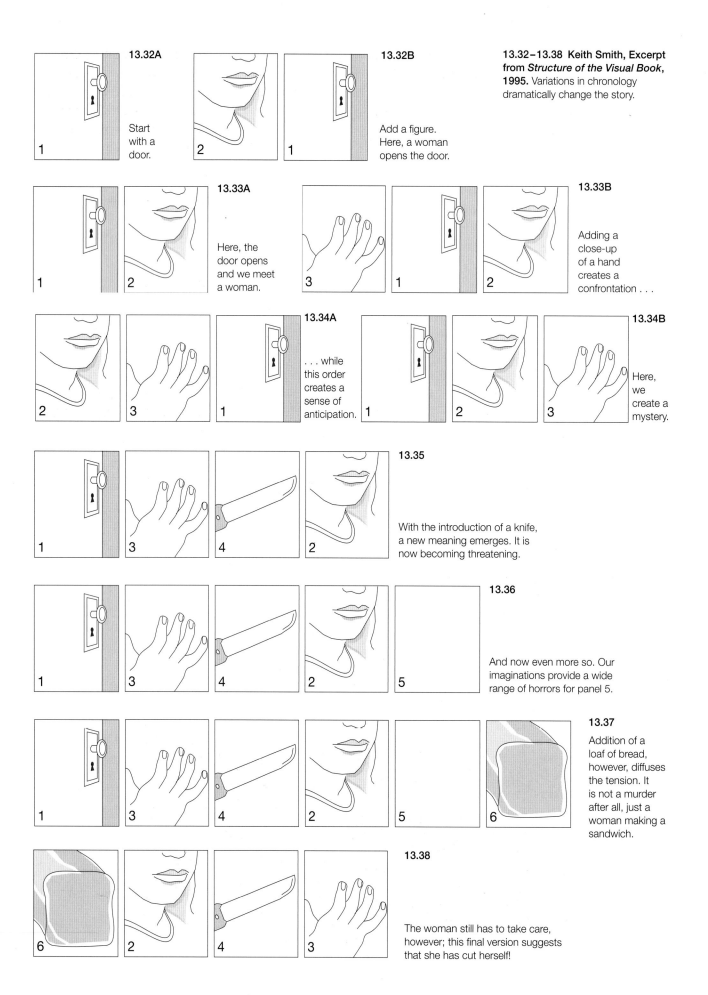

13.32A

1 Start with a door.

2 1 Add a figure. Here, a woman opens the door. **13.32B**

13.32–13.38 Keith Smith, Excerpt from *Structure of the Visual Book*, 1995. Variations in chronology dramatically change the story.

13.33A

1 2 Here, the door opens and we meet a woman.

3 1 2 Adding a close-up of a hand creates a confrontation . . . **13.33B**

13.34A

2 3 1 . . . while this order creates a sense of anticipation.

1 2 3 Here, we create a mystery. **13.34B**

13.35

1 3 4 2 With the introduction of a knife, a new meaning emerges. It is now becoming threatening.

13.36

1 3 4 2 5 And now even more so. Our imaginations provide a wide range of horrors for panel 5.

13.37

1 3 4 2 5 6 Addition of a loaf of bread, however, diffuses the tension. It is not a murder after all, just a woman making a sandwich.

13.38

6 2 4 3 The woman still has to take care, however; this final version suggests that she has cut herself!

shots or more. Variations in tempo help sustain interest. If there is too little variation, a fast-paced film is just as monotonous as a slow-paced film. To develop momentum gradually, many filmmakers use a slow-paced beginning, which builds to a fast-paced climax.

5. Connections that filmmakers make through editing can heighten emotion and suggest the real motivation for a character's actions. In a famous experiment, early Soviet filmmaker Lev Kulesov demonstrated the emotional impact of editing. He combined a neutral shot of an actor's face with four very different images: a bowl of soup, scenes from nature, a baby, and a dead woman. When the film was shown, the audience praised the actor's skill: he looked hungry when the soup appeared, longed for freedom when the landscape was shown, was filled with joy at the sight of the baby, and felt grief at the sight of the woman. In each case, however, the shot of the actor's face was *exactly* the same. The emotions were created by the audience's response to the editing, not by any change in the actor's expression.

6. Connections that occur through editing can substantially alter or enhance a film's meaning. By cutting from a bone spinning in the air to a space station orbiting the earth (13.39), Stanley Kubrick connected prehistory to space travel in *2001: A Space Odyssey.*

▶ key questions

CHRONOLOGY

*   Do events in your project occur in a traditional linear (ABCD) order?

*   What would happen if you changed this order? Would ADBDCCC be more powerful?

*   What would happen if you deleted half the information in your project? Would the artwork as a whole gain or lose power?

*   What would happen if you added more material from a different source?

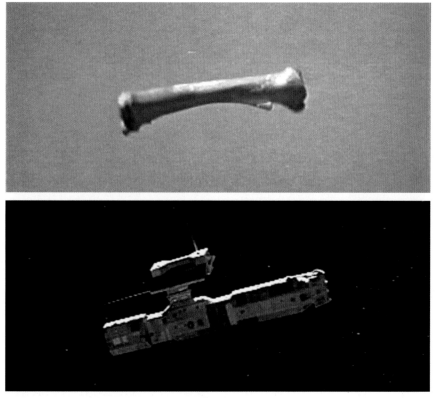

13.39 Stanley Kubrick, *2001: A Space Odyssey*, 1968. Juxtaposing the whirling bone and the floating space station connects prehistory to the space-age.

SCHINDLER'S LIST: CONTENT AND COMPOSITION

Director Steven Spielberg used all these aspects of editing in *Schindler's List*. Mixing contemporary images with black-and-white images of wartime Poland, Spielberg tells a harrowing tale of the survival of over 1,000 Jews during the Holocaust. Based on historical events, the film shows the transformation of Nazi Oskar Schindler from a single-minded war profiteer to a compassionate man who eventually bought the lives of his enslaved workers. It is an incredible story, and any skillful filmmaker could have made a good film based on this event. However, to show the complexities of each character and to turn the story into a truly compelling film required another level of insight. Spielberg and his collaborators had that insight.

The critical importance of editing is apparent from the start. A contemporary scene of a Jewish family at home ends with a trail of smoke rising from an extinguished candle (13.40). We cut to the smokestack on a train in wartime Krakow (13.41) and are transported back in time.

Editing also establishes Schindler's motivation and gives us insight into his personality. When he arrives at a cafe favored by Nazi officers, the maitre d' seats him, then asks a waiter who he is. Neither one knows his name. Schindler carefully positions himself at the center of the room. Through a series of close-ups, we follow his gaze as he notes the SS insignia on an officer's uniform and assesses the importance of the reserved table across the room. Using Schindler as the axis, the camera pans around the room (13.42). Positioned just over his shoulder, we watch Schindler as he observes the soldiers. He did not come to this restaurant to eat. He intends to meet the most influential Nazis in the area and establish himself as a man of consequence.

As the scene continues, Schindler joins the Nazis and leads a song. Finally, the highest-ranking officer asks the maitre d' about this newcomer. He now enthusiastically replies, "Why, that is Oskar Schindler!" (13.43). Schindler (who entered the restaurant as a nobody) is now well defined: he has become the center of attention (13.44). The evening has been a success.

13.40 Steven Spielberg, *Schindler's List*, 1993. Extinguished candle.

13.41 *Schindler's List*, 1993. Train's smokestack.

13.42 *Schindler's List*, 1993. Schindler in a cafe.

Spielberg uses crosscutting throughout the film, both to establish a connection and to emphasize separation. Eviction of a Jewish family from their spacious home is immediately followed by images of Schindler surveying the same space, now his new home. He reclines on a large bed and exclaims, "It couldn't be better!" (13.45). We then cut to the evicted family, struggling up the stairs of their new dwelling, which they will share with many other families. As they sit down in the single room, the wife notes, "It could be worse." Her angry husband replies, "How could it *possibly* be worse?" (13.46). Just then, another large family apologetically moves into the cramped space. It is now worse.

The destruction of the Krakow ghetto is a masterpiece of storytelling. Sound is especially important in this sequence, and variations in pacing substantially increase the visual impact. The sequence begins as Nazi commandant Goeth gives his assembled troops a brief history lesson (13.47). As he describes the arrival of the Jews in Poland in the fourteenth century, we cut from the soldiers to scenes of ghetto families quietly eating and preparing for the day ahead, unaware of the terror to follow. We return to Goeth as he concludes his speech, noting that "by this evening, those six centuries are a rumor. They never existed."

An explosion of violence follows. The family at breakfast is now wrapping jewels in bread and eating them, in the hope of retaining something of value when the attack ends. Itzhak Stern, the overworked accountant upon whom Schindler depends, desperately searches his pockets for his identity papers as a soldier screams in his face. The camera is jostled as terrified people are evicted from their apartments. Diagonal staircases and extreme camera angles increase compositional dynamism (13.48).

A contrast between violence and compassion, fast and slow pace, heightens the impact of this sequence. Running soldiers ignore an old woman who walks slowly down a foggy street, yet mercilessly kill other people. A doctor methodically adds poison to cups of water, then gently administers it to his patients (13.49) rather than leave them for the soldiers to kill. A young Polish boy,

13.43 *Schindler's List*, 1993. Officer asks maitre d' about Schindler.

13.44 *Schindler's List*, 1993. Focus shifts to Schindler as he is identified.

13.45 *Schindler's List*, 1993. New home.

13.46 *Schindler's List*, 1993. New home, shared by three families.

13.47 *Schindler's List*, 1993. Commandant Goeth.

13.48 *Schindler's List*, 1993. Staircase.

13.49 *Schindler's List*, 1993. Doctor administering poison.

assigned to report any survivors, instead saves the life of a woman and her daughter.

We now see a small girl in a red coat walking through the streets (13.50) and observed by Schindler, who surveys the action from a nearby hill. Accompanied by angelic music, she is the symbol of all the innocent deaths on this horrible day. We last see her as she scoots under a bed, seeking a place to hide. We will not see her again until much later in the film, when her red coat appears as the corpses from the ghetto liquidation are gathered to be burned.

Quiet finally descends on the city. The soldiers are now using stethoscopes to listen for

13.50 *Schindler's List*, 1993. Girl in a red coat.

survivors who may have hidden in apartment walls. In a final burst of violence, one soldier plays a vigorous Bach fugue while other soldiers explode into action, firing their machine guns into the walls and commanding their dogs to attack.

The calm before the storm makes this sequence even more frightening. It would be impossible to sustain a fast pace throughout the film. Incessant horror would have simply left us numb. The editing and use of contrast have greatly enhanced the power of the ghetto sequence, leaving an indelible impression.

summary

- An understanding of time is an essential aspect of any artwork. Photographers, film-makers, and performers use time directly; painters, illustrators, ceramicists, and other artists generally use time indirectly.
- The building blocks of film are the frame, the shot, the scene, and the sequence.
- We can relate shots graphically, spatially, temporally, and rhythmically.

- The cut, fade, dissolve, and wipe are the most common transitions in film.
- Comic books use four additional transitions: action-to-action, subject-to-subject, scene-to-scene, and non-sequitur.
- Duration, tempo, intensity, scope, setting, and chronology are the six major elements of time design.

key terms

accents	fidelity	pace	spatial context
action-to-action	flashbacks	pitch	spatial
transitions	frame	plot duration	relationship
beat	graphic	rhythm	story duration
chronology	relationship	rhythmic	subject-to-subject
close-up	intensity	relationship	transition
crosscutting	lap dissolve	scene	takes
cut	long shot	scene-to-scene	tempo
diegetic	loudness	transition	temporal
dissolve	medium shot	scope	relationship
duration	montage	sequence	timbre
editing	non-sequitur	setting	wipe
fade	transition	shot	

studio projects

To apply the concepts from this chapter in the studio, check out the Projects page in the Online Learning Center at www.mhhe.com/LTI5e. The following is a sample of the chapter-related assignments in step-by-step detail.

Time Observed. Increasing awareness of time through careful attention.

Arrested Time. Implied time and captured moments.

Tempo. Exploring variations in the rate of change.

Chronology. A quick, simple demonstration of the impact of chronology on narrative.

Narrative and Nonnarrative

Just as a poet uses a few words to evoke a complex idea, so an artist or designer can communicate complex thoughts and feelings through a single image. By contrast, when we use multiple images, we can act like novelists. Because the verbal and visual information is distributed over many images, we can elaborate and expand our ideas sequentially. In this chapter, we explore the uses, characteristics, and construction of multiple-image structures.

STORYTELLING

Storytelling is one of the most ancient and effective forms of sequential communication. It can serve four basic purposes:

- *Stories can increase self-awareness.* When we record our own story in an autobiography, we become more conscious of the patterns in our lives. We can also gain a better understanding of the individual events that break or reinforce these patterns.

- *Stories can provide inspiration.* By researching the life of another artist or discussing the past with an older relative, we find that our personal problems and conflicts are not unique. Everyone experiences a wide range of emotions, from exhilaration to despair. In reading another person's story, we can learn from his or her solution to a problem.

- *Stories can supply information.* News stories and documentary films provide us with information on current events and analysis of their implications. Art never occurs in a vacuum. Developing an understanding of the world around us can strengthen our ideas.

- *Stories can encourage understanding.* Abstract numbers and dry statistics are rarely as compelling as human experience. When we hear the story of a particular refugee in a specific war, the effect of combat on civilians becomes personal.

To increase our understanding even further, we may explore the biggest questions of all, through myths. A **myth** is a traditional story collectively composed by many members of a society. Authors explain the creation of the world, sources of evil, the power of knowledge, and even the nature of reality through these grand expressions of the imagination. The *Star Wars* series, most comic books, and many types of performance art are inspired by myths.

From Singular to Multiple Images

In all forms of storytelling, multiple images can provide many advantages over an individual image. Jacques-Louis David expresses both action and emotion within a single frame in his *Oath of the Horatii* (14.1). To avoid mass slaughter, two warring Roman clans, the Horatii and the Curatii, have each agreed to send three warriors into a fight to the death. The three young Horatii warriors on the left demonstrate this heroic moment of self-sacrifice. The plan is tragically complicated by the warriors' wives who are huddled in a triangular shape on the right. They are members of the opposing Curatii clan and will lose either their brothers or their husbands in the battle. The children to the left of the women are caught in the middle.

Through skillful composition and careful selection of an emotionally charged moment in the narrative, David created a masterpiece that caused a sensation when it was first shown in 1786. The dramatic gesture, the composition, and the technique in this painting are stunning. Nonetheless, it is difficult to appreciate the painting fully or to understand the story without explanation. Employing only a single image, David had to rely on his audience for some knowledge of the story.

By contrast, in *Division Street* (14.2), Jerome Witkin used three paintings to tell a story. Like David, he selected the colors, gestures, and actions most appropriate to the narrative and composed each frame with great care. Unlike *Oath of the Horatii*, however, *Division Street* requires little explanation. We can clearly see the argument in the first frame, the father's departure in the second, and the determined mother in the third. This multiple-image narrative speaks for itself.

14.1 Jacques-Louis David, *Oath of the Horatii*, 1784–85. Oil on canvas, 14 ft × 10 ft 8¼ in. (4.27 × 3.26 m).

Group, Series, and Sequence

In *Structure of the Visual Book,* Keith Smith describes three multiple-image structures commonly used by printmakers, photographers, and book artists.[1] A **group** is a collection of images that are related by subject matter, composition, or source. In figure 14.3, images of a pyramid, the letter *A,* a meditating man, and a pair of praying hands can be grouped by shape. A triangle dominates each. By contrast, we can group the three illustrations in figures 14.4, 14.5, and 14.6 by subject. All are part of the *Frog Folio,* a calendar produced by Dellas Graphics to showcase the work of contemporary illustrators. In a group, the image order is unimportant.

A **series** links multiple images together sequentially. Each image builds on the previous image and leads to the subsequent image. *Chance Meeting,* by Duane Michals (14.7, page 312), is a series of photographs. Like a short film, it tells the simple story of a chance meeting.

Simple narratives, such as fairy tales and fables, often use serial construction. Numerical repetition may be an essential part of the story. For example, when Goldilocks enters the house of the three bears, she samples three bowls of porridge. One is too hot, the second is too cold, the third is just right. She tries sitting on the three chairs, with a similar result. Finally, when she decides to take a nap, she finds the first bed too hard, the second too soft, and the third just right. As a story for children, "Goldilocks" and other such tales are simple and straightforward. Storytellers rarely use flashbacks, crosscutting, or other complex narrative structures in fairy tales.

As defined by Smith, a **sequence** is the multiple-image structure used by most popular filmmakers and comic book artists. In a sequence, they organize multiple images by *cause and effect.* In a simple sequence, the first action causes the second, which then causes the third. Like cars in a train, events are clearly linked. In a complex sequence, there may be a considerable delay between the cause and the effect. For example, a childhood trauma may influence an adult's decision. Returning to our train analogy, in a sequence we may move among the cars, showing the

14.2 Jerome Witkin, *Division Street* **[A Story Told in 3 Panels], 1984–85.** Oil on canvas, triptych. Top panel 75⅛ × 63¼ in. (190.9 × 160.7 cm), middle panel 81⅛ × 63 in. (206.2 × 160 cm), bottom panel 87⅛ × 63 in. (221.3 × 160 cm).

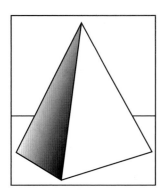

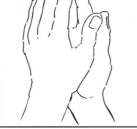

14.3 Grouping by shape.

14.4 Bart Forbes, *Landmark*, 1999. Oil on canvas, 14 × 19 in. (35.6 × 48.3 cm).

14.5 Charles Santore, *Cover of William the Curious, Knight of the Water Lilies*, 1997. Watercolor, front cover 9 × 12 in. (22.8 × 30.5 cm).

14.6 Murray Tinkelman, *The Frog Jumps over the Moon*. Colored ink crosshatch, 9 × 12 in. (22.9 × 30.5 cm).

14.7 Duane Michals, *Chance Meeting*, 1969. Six prints, each 4⅞ × 3¼ in. (12.4 × 8.3 cm).

conductor napping, two passengers playing cards, the engineer steering, and another passenger reading. We may combine these human actions with images of the landscape through which the train is traveling, the setting sun, or other images that are related to the journey. To understand a sequence, viewers may have to mentally connect many fragments of information.

From Scene to Screenplay

With a run time of an hour or more, screenwriters construct a film or a television show from many sequences, each building the story using cause and effect. Let's analyze one example.

> Jeremy and Angela are spending their honeymoon traveling on the luxurious Blue Train through South Africa. On the third morning of the trip, they awake to the sound of drunken singing in the adjoining cabin. Angela wants to confront the revelers, while Jeremy cautions her against

getting involved. They begin to argue. Angela accuses Jeremy of indifference, while Jeremy says Angela is overreacting. Now focused on their own quarrel, they ignore the singers and instead continue their argument over breakfast in the dining car. Finally, Angela threatens to leave. Jeremy ridicules her threat, saying that she isn't capable of traveling alone in a foreign country. Angela punches Jeremy in the nose. Jeremy shoves his grapefruit into her face. Their fight disrupts the dining car. At the next stop, the conductor throws both of them off the train. Sitting in a deserted train station, they both begin to laugh at their ridiculous overreaction to the drunken singers.

In Robert McKee's *Story*, the **beat** is the most basic narrative element.[2] A beat is an exchange of behavior based on action and reaction. There are six beats in this story.

1. Angela responds to the singers: "I am not going to listen to those drunken louts for one more

minute!" Then Jeremy responds to Angela: "Oh, take it easy. Let's get some breakfast; I bet they will pass out before we return."

2. As they walk to the dining car, Angela says to Jeremy: "You really don't care, do you? If someone punched you in the nose, you would just walk away." Jeremy responds to Angela: "Don't be such a hothead. There is no reason to get angry about every little thing."

3. Over breakfast, Angela retorts: "If you can't take the heat, get out of the kitchen! I suggest we split up at the next station." Jeremy responds: "Are you kidding? You wouldn't last a day on your own."

4. Angela punches Jeremy, who shoves his grapefruit into her face.

5. The conductor reacts by throwing both of them off the train.

6. Sitting on their suitcases in the empty station, they finally respond to the situation by laughing.

Beats build **scenes**. Scenes generally occur in a single space in continuous time. Scenes build sequences. In filmmaking, a sequence is made from a series of scenes, which generally increase in emotional impact. In this story, a minor disagreement escalates into a major battle. Each action results in a stronger reaction, culminating in the couple's ejection from the train. Sequences build **acts**. An act is an even longer sequential structure. The **screenplay**, which is the written blueprint for the film, is constructed from multiple acts.

▶ key questions

STORYTELLING

- How many ways might you use storytelling to expand or enhance an idea?

- What are the advantages of a single-image narrative versus a multiple-image narrative?

- How can a series of increasingly powerful beats heighten emotion in your narrative?

ESTABLISHING BOUNDARIES

When just starting college, few of us have the time, money, or expertise necessary to write a screenplay or direct a film. However, we can use the same principles to develop storyboards, videos, and visual books.

Conceptual Boundaries

We can begin by defining the conceptual breadth of an idea. An idea that is overly ambitious or ill defined will be impossible to communicate well.

You already have extensive experience with conceptual boundaries. Just consider the questions that you face when planning a 10-page art history paper:

- *What is the topic?* What historical period interests you most? In a course devoted to Western art from the Renaissance to Impressionism, you have many excellent choices and a dazzling array of images. It makes sense to choose a topic that is manageable and interesting.

- *How should you approach the topic?* If the paper is on Impressionism, you could:

  - Analyze the work of a single artist, such as Mary Cassatt or Edgar Degas

  - Compare and contrast paintings by Cassatt and Degas

  - Explore the impact of photography on Impressionist painters

By focusing on one aspect of a complex topic, you can develop an effective research strategy and complete the paper on time.

Defining conceptual boundaries is equally important in sequential art. Just as Impressionism is too big a topic to explore thoroughly in a 10-page paper, so reality is too vast to record fully in a 3-minute video. The following questions can help you define an artwork's conceptual frame:

- *What to see?* Start with an interesting and easily accessible site. Explore several buildings on campus, then select one and begin your research. Find out the building's history, look for distinctive architectural details, and find out what happens each day in the building.

- *When to see it?* Each time of day is distinctive, both visually and emotionally. How does the building look at sunset or at midnight? Select the moments in time that are charged with meaning, then watch closely.

- *And then what happens?* To answer this question, you must become a storyteller.

Developing a Story

In 1908, the White Star Line began construction of three identical Atlantic ocean liners. The company launched the *Olympic* in 1910 and the *Titanic* in 1911. It never completed the *Gigantic*. The *Titanic* struck an iceberg during her maiden voyage and sank on April 15, 1912. She had lifeboat capacity for 1,178 people; there were 2,220 on board. The *Californian*, less than 10 miles away, did not respond to her distress signals. The *Carpathia*, 58 miles away, sped to the scene. Arriving four hours later, *Carpathia* rescued 711 people from the freezing lifeboats. The *Olympic*, *Titanic's* sister ship, provided reliable service until she was scrapped in 1937.

These are the basic facts. No narrative, however, is limited to facts. Even a newspaper reporter must make choices about organizing facts and determining the story's most important aspects. Fiction offers even more options. Using a familiar journalistic device, let's list a few basic questions:

- *Whose story is it?* That of ship designer Thomas Andrews, who perished? Of J. Bruce Ismay, director of the White Star Line, who survived? Of the captain of the *Carpathia*, who became a hero? Of the captain of the *Californian*, who was reviled?

- *When should the story begin and end?* We know that the sailors spotted the iceberg at 11:40 P.M. and that the collision occurred soon after. A storyteller, however, can start at any point in time. How does the story change when we begin with initial planning of the "unsinkable" ship? What happens when we start the story just as a survivor regains consciousness after her rescue?

- *Where does the story occur?* Each cabin, deck, and lifeboat contains its own specific characters and its own particular story.

- *Why did the tragedy occur?* Was the captain pressured to complete the crossing in record time, causing him to increase the ship's speed, despite the danger? Was the ship poorly constructed?

- *What is the story really about?* Courage? Arrogance? Injustice? Sixty-two percent of the first-class passengers survived, while only 25 percent of the third-class passengers survived. Whereas the sinking itself is the most obvious event, this tragedy contains many stories.

Knowing where to start the story is essential. If the storyteller shows the ship's planning and construction in detail, the most dramatic events (the sinking itself, the rescue, and the inquiry into the cause) may lose their impact.

Emotional Boundaries

In theater and performance art, communication often depends on a connection between the imaginary world on stage and the tangible world of the audience. Wole Soyinka demonstrated this beautifully in *Death and the King's Horseman*, performed by Syracuse Stage in 1999. The play explores a range of cultural conflicts between Africa's native Yoruba population and a group of British colonizers. The king has died, and the king's horseman, a powerful leader in his own right (14.8), must commit suicide so that he can guide the king in the world beyond life. The British government's attempts to stop this ritual are disruptive and tragic.

To feel the event's full impact, the audience must emotionally connect to the Yoruba world, which revolves around a village market. As we enter the theater, a dramatically lit stage piled with fruit, colorful baskets, and bolts of fabric invites us into this world.

One by one, seven female actors enter, assume the poses of various vendors, then freeze. The play begins with the sound of drumming coming from behind the audience. As the women become animated and the market comes to life (14.9), we are enveloped in the Yoruba world. Additional actors sing and dance down the aisles, finally joining the company on stage.

Establishing an emotional connection between the image and the audience is even more important in filmmaking. When we see a play, the entire stage is visible and each audience member views the scene a bit differently. In a film, a flickering beam of light creates the image rather than a live actor. The director defines the film frame. By using a close-up, the director can place the actor directly in front of us. A distance shot pushes the actor away, reducing the emotional connection.

Style

In a sense, an artwork's style provides another boundary. We can define **style** as the artwork's distinctive character or look. It can provide the overall ambience and indicate the historical or cultural setting. Three cinematic interpretations of William Shakespeare's *Romeo and Juliet* provide a striking example of the importance of style. Franco Zeffirelli's *Romeo and Juliet* (14.10) is closest to the written play in style and interpretation. There is some editing of the original text, but the lines spoken were

14.8 Scene from *Death and the King's Horseman*, **1999.** Performed by Syracuse Stage.

14.9 Scene from *Death and the King's Horseman*, **1999.** Performed by Syracuse Stage.

written by Shakespeare. Furthermore, the beautiful settings, opulent costumes, and graceful dancing that fill the screen are based on historical models.

West Side Story (14.11) offers a very different interpretation of the Romeo and Juliet story. Set in New York City in the 1950s, this film uses warfare between rival gangs to create the tragedy, rather than the familiar conflict between the Capulets and the Montagues. While the story is based on Shakespeare's play, the dialogue, setting, and specific actions are modern. Even the characters have new names, as Romeo becomes Tony, the leader of the Polish Jets, and Juliet becomes Maria, affiliated with the Puerto Rican Sharks.

We can find an unusual combination of these two sensibilities in *William Shakespeare's Romeo and Juliet* (14.12). Now set in contemporary California as a struggle between the skinhead Montagues and the leather-clad Capulets, the film begins with a prologue delivered from a television screen by a newswoman. The actors often deliver Shakespeare's words as a scream, and director Baz Luhrmann transforms familiar characters in amazing ways. For example, when we first meet Mercutio, he is wearing high heels, a silver-sequined miniskirt with a halter top, and a white wig. Luhrmann has retained Shakespeare's words, but has shifted the setting, characters, and action to create a bizarre contemporary variation on a sixteenth-century play.

14.10 Franco Zeffirelli, *Romeo and Juliet*, 1968. Romeo and Juliet.

14.11 Robert Wise and Jerome Robbins, *West Side Story*, 1961. Tony and Maria.

14.12 Baz Luhrmann, *William Shakespeare's Romeo and Juliet*, 1996.

key questions

BOUNDARIES

- How many ways can you "frame" your story?

- Of these options, which set of boundaries will provide the best balance between focus and richness? Too tight a boundary may result in a constricted story, while too loose a boundary may result in chaos.

- How important is an emotional connection to your audience? How can you create such a connection?

- How many stylistic variations are possible within the framework that you have set?

- Of these variations, which style will result in the strongest story?

CAUSALITY

Every story is constructed using a chain of events. In traditional narrative, the first event causes the second, which results in the third, and so on until the conclusion is reached. We call this chain of events **causality**. As in a crossword puzzle, the storyteller presents us with a series of clues, which we construct into meaning.

When the relationship between cause and effect is clear, the puzzle is easy to solve. When there is an extended delay between cause and effect, or when relationships among events seem arbitrary or irrational, the solution becomes much more elusive.

Un Chien Andalou (An Andalusian Dog), by Salvador Dalí and Luis Buñuel, presents such a puzzle. A quarrel between two lovers unfolds through a bizarre sequence of illogical events. As the film opens, a man smoking a cigarette calmly sharpens a straight razor. A sliver of cloud passes across the full moon. The man grasps a woman's face (14.13) and slits her left eye with the razor. He then bicycles down the street wearing a nun's uniform. The uninjured woman welcomes him to her apartment. Ants crawl out from a hole in his hand. A severed hand appears on the street below. A crowd gathers. A policeman gives the severed hand to a woman, who places it in a box. The crowd disperses. The woman (still in the street) is then hit by a car.

As the film continues, the man harnesses himself to a piano filled with slaughtered mules, shoots a double image of himself, and strolls along a beach with the woman, collecting and then discarding debris. While these two characters dominate the story, the film as a whole is mysterious and irrational.

In contrast, a series of very clear cause-and-effect relationships fuels the lovers' quarrel in James Cameron's *Titanic*. The film begins with a prologue showing a contemporary expedition to salvage a precious diamond from the sunken wreck. Rose, an elderly woman who survived the disaster, then describes the voyage she remembers.

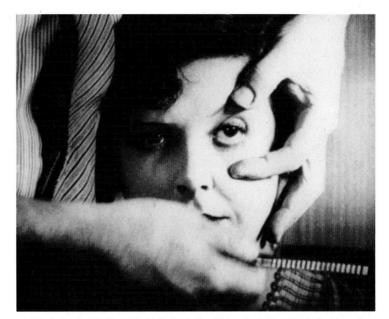

14.13 Salvador Dalí and Luis Buñuel, *Un Chien Andalou*, 1929. Staging of woman's eye being slit.

Through her memories, we meet the primary characters. Young Rose is a pampered society woman betrothed to the rich and arrogant Cal. Jack is an independent but impoverished artist who has won his passage back to America in a poker game.

Conflicts between Cal and Rose are apparent from the start. Rose is intelligent and strong-willed, with a love of art and ideas. Cal is arrogant and domineering; he demands obedience. Rose feels trapped, and, in despair, she climbs over a railing on the ship and prepares to jump (14.14). Jack saves her. The resulting romance develops through a sequence of cause-and-effect events and reaches a climax with a battle between Cal and the two lovers

14.14 James Cameron, *Titanic*, 1997. Young Rose preparing to jump.

14.15 James Cameron, *Titanic*, 1997. Elderly Rose at ship's railing.

on the sinking ship. Rose survives, and in a classic **denouement**, or summation, the film ends as the elderly Rose climbs the railing of the salvage vessel and flings the diamond into the sea (14.15). Beautifully filmed and carefully edited, the three-hour film easily sustains our interest. In this case, the traditional narrative structure served the director's purpose. There is no ambiguity: the director clearly shows all of the characters' actions and emotions.

Each film has its own purpose and its own power. *Un Chien Andalou* is suggestive, rather than descriptive; mystery is an essential part of its meaning. *Titanic* gains meaning from the escalating conflict between Cal and Rose. In each case, the director made the right choice for the film content.

> ## ▶ key questions
>
> ### CASUALITY
>
> - How rational is the chain of events in your story?
>
> - When do you require rationality, and when is an irrational structure the right choice?
>
> - What starts the chain of events? How does the chain of events end?
>
> - How do the beginning and the ending contribute to the overall meaning of your story?

CHARACTER-DRIVEN NARRATIVE

We strongly identify with the trials and tribulations of others. As a result, many of the most durable and popular narratives are **character-driven**. We learn about each primary character's aspirations and fears, explore their motivations, and cheer them on as they confront increasingly difficult challenges.

A League of Their Own (directed by Penny Marshall) is a wonderful example. It follows two sisters from rural Oregon who join the first professional women's baseball league in 1943. Older sister Dottie is an outstanding catcher and hitter, and even initially manages the team. Younger sister Kit pitches—and seeks desperately to match Dottie's accomplishments. Although there are numerous subplots, interpersonal dynamics between the sisters drive the action and the emotion of this film.

The Opening Sequence

Because most narratives are so dependent on the interplay between cause and effect, the opening sequence often presents the major characters in the film. The opening sequence in *A League of Their Own* introduces us to the sisters, and dramatically establishes their volatile relationship. As Kit prepares to bat, Dottie hurries forward with advice (14.16). She tells Kit to use a lighter bat, to aim for a weak spot in the outfield defense, and most importantly, to avoid swinging at high pitches. Kit rejects this advice, swings at high pitches, and strikes out. Dottie then strides up to the plate and hits a home run. Already frustrated by her failure, Kit is infuriated when one of the fans compares her poor performance to Dottie's success.

Increasing Conflict

As the story unfolds, we learn more about Kit's desire for success and her frustration that her brilliant sister overshadows her. When manager Jimmy Dugan replaces Kit with another pitcher in a crucial play-off game, she blames the decision on Dottie rather than accepting her own poor

14.16 Penny Marshall, *A League of Their Own*, 1992. Written by Lowell Ganz and Babaloo Mandel. Kit rejects Dottie's advice.

14.17 Penny Marshall, *A League of Their Own*, 1992. Written by Lowell Ganz and Babaloo Mandel. Replacing Kit in play-off game.

14.18 Penny Marshall, *A League of Their Own*, 1992. Written by Lowell Ganz and Babaloo Mandel. Triumphant Kit with championship team.

performance as the cause (14.17). The resulting argument results in the manager trading Kit to pitch on another team. This sets up a final showdown between the sisters.

The Crucible of Character

Director Marshall fully reveals each woman's essential character in this final showdown. The two teams are now in the final inning of the league's championship series. Dottie has played brilliantly—catching impossible fly balls and driving a crucial hit at opposing pitcher Kit's head. Never a strong batter, Kit walks apprehensively to the plate. Knowing Kit's weakness, Dottie advises the pitcher to throw fast, high pitches. Predictably, Kit misses the first two pitches. She then slams the final pitch into the outfield, and takes off running, barreling past first plate, then second, and then third.

As the defending catcher, Dottie is the only obstacle to Kit's triumphant run. She catches the ball just as Kit drives in for the home plate, slamming into her. As both sisters smash into the dirt, Dottie drops the ball, giving Kit and the opposing team the win. Since Dottie held onto the ball in a similar situation earlier in the film, it appears that Kit really has bested her sister at last. For the first time, the crowd chants Kit's name rather than Dottie's, and the exuberant teammates triumphantly carry the younger sister off the field (14.18).

The Closing Sequence

In a character-driven narrative, a quiet final scene often re-establishes equilibrium between characters or presents the calm after an emotional storm. In *A League of Our Own*, Dottie and Kit meet again

14.19 Penny Marshall, *A League of Their Own*, 1992. Written by Lowell Ganz and Babaloo Mandel. Dottie hugs Kit after the game.

after the game. As the heroine of the game, Kit is signing autographs. As a member of the losing team, Dottie quietly picks up a souvenir from a vendor. They then discuss their plans. Dottie and her husband are retuning to Oregon to start a family. Kit plans to remain in the Midwest so that she can play baseball again the next year. Dottie reminds Kit that she loves her, and Kit realizes that Dottie has only sought success, not dominance

key questions

CHARACTER-DRIVEN NARRATIVE

- Whose story is it? A 7-year-old girl's? A 17-year-old boy's? A priest's? A thief's?

- What is the point of view? Does the main character tell his or her own story (first-person narrative), or does someone else tell the story? How does this affect meaning?

- What are the strengths and weaknesses of each character?

- What conflicts occur? What causes these conflicts?

- How do the characters deal with conflict?

- How is the central conflict finally resolved?

over her younger sister (14.19). The conflict that drove the entire film has finally been resolved.

NARRATIVE COMPRESSION

Duration, framing, editing, and narration become especially charged with meaning in a television commercial design. Lasting only 15 seconds, the ad must immediately command attention, make a favorable impression, and influence consumer behavior. Whether you are selling soap or discouraging smoking, your approach must be clear, concise, and compelling.

Ads must appeal to the emotions as well as the intellect. The **hard-sell** approach in figure 14.20 relies on rational argument and clearly presents one major point. The narrative is linear, and the message is explicit: drinking and driving can kill a friendship. Words underscore the ideas that the ad communicates visually.

Soft-sell ads focus on emotion. While the message is still sharply focused, the designer may seek a sensory response rather than a rational response. For example, a recent FedEx ad begins with images of singing frogs, dancing bears, and friendly rabbits. A cartoon version of a FedEx truck arrives, and the driver is welcomed into the forest. The magical elements such as fairy dust, sprites, and singing animals then begin to disappear and a fuel-efficient Fed Ex airplane appears. The narrator notes that even without the animated animals, Fed Ex's emphasis on sustainable solutions is still pretty magical. Rather than giving us a lot of dry facts and figures, this ad encourages us to think favorably about the company.

Feeling good is not enough—the viewer must feel good about the specific product that is for sale. A National Park Service ad is a great example (14.21). Beautiful shots of rivers, mountains, and seashores are combined with quotes about nature. As we near the end of the ad, the message becomes more explicit: "To truly explore America,

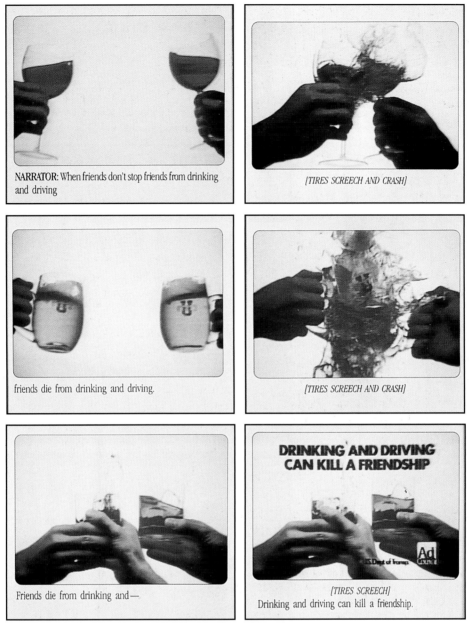

NARRATOR: When friends don't stop friends from drinking and driving

[TIRES SCREECH AND CRASH]

friends die from drinking and driving.

[TIRES SCREECH AND CRASH]

Friends die from drinking and—

DRINKING AND DRIVING
CAN KILL A FRIENDSHIP

[TIRES SCREECH]
Drinking and driving can kill a friendship.

14.20 Agency: Leber Katz Partners, New York. Production: Phil Marco Productions, New York. Editing Company: Cinemetric, New York. Music Production: Roy Eaton Productions, New York. Details: TV, 30 seconds, color. First appearance: December 12, 1983. Advertiser's Supervisor: Eleanor Hanley. Account Supervisor: Susan Wershba. Creative Director: Jack Silverman. Copywriter: Lou Linder. Art Director: Len Fink. Agency Producer: Herb Miller. Producer: Catherine Bromley. Director/Cameraman/Lighting Director: Phil Marco. Editor: Larry Plastrik. Music Director: Roy Eaton. Music Composers: Roy Eaton/Joe Hudson. Performers: Jon Carthay, Laurence White, Bobby Hudson. Voice: Doug Jeffers.

visit its national parks." We are drawn in using a soft-sell approach, which is followed by an explicit message. Because clues rather than literal content trigger a viewer's response, designers using the soft-sell approach pay particular attention to details, such as the sound track and lighting.

All ads rely on a clear message, strong imagery, and effective communication. Six common advertising strategies follow.

1. **Rational**. A rational ad provides the viewer with specific information. When the message is compelling in itself or the product is

truly unique, a straightforward demonstration can be effective. In *Book Burning Party Campaign* (14.22, page 323), the Leo Burnett agency combined rationality and irrationality in an unusual way. To remain open, an award-winning community library requested a modest tax increase. A well-funded anti-tax group opposed this, and the library seemed doomed. Library supporters then launched a *book burning* campaign, using television ads, websites, and lawn signs. Why not celebrate the loss of the library? Infuriated community members fought back. They then learned that the agency designed the campaign to raise awareness of the library's importance. Rationally, the community concluded that the library was worth saving and voted overwhelmingly in favor of the tax increase.

2. **Emotional**. When the product is not unique or the message lacks urgency, an emotional approach may be more effective. For example, to a dog owner, all dog food is pretty much alike. Neither the product nor the message is compelling in itself. When the dog food becomes a manifestation of love for the dog, however, the appeal is heightened. As a result, many dog food ads suggest that owners who really love their dogs will that buy the advertised brand.

The *Paralympics* ad in figure 14.23 (page 323) uses emotion in a different way. An athletic man sprints around a darkened track. He begins to pass wheelchairs, and we then realize that one of his legs is a prosthetic. He sprints through emergency room doctors and equipment, then past a horrific car wreck and emergency personnel.

14.21 Dave Hartvigsen, Scott Temme, Finley Holiday Films, National Parks Promotion Council, *Explore America*, 2011.

As he continues to power down the track, the word "unstoppable" appears, followed by the Paralympics symbol. Despite the injuries that caused him to lose his leg, this athlete continues his run—both on the track and through his life.

3. **Serious**. Public service announcements dealing with AIDS, drunk driving, or drug abuse are rarely funny. However, the ad will succeed only if people view it. Horrific images of starving children or tortured prisoners may so repel viewers that the message is lost. Finding the right balance between serious content and engaging

14.22 Leo Burnett/Arc Agency, *Book Burning Party Campaign to save Troy, Michigan Public Library*, 2011.

14.23 Peter Ignazi/Carlos Moreno, BBDO Toronto, Canadian Paralympic Committee, *Running (Unstoppable)*, 2012.

imagery is crucial. The *911 Thanks* ad (14.24), sponsored by State Farm Insurance and directed by Spike Lee is a great example. As the ad begins, Lee talks about his experiences on the day the World Trade Center fell. Firefighters who responded to the attack then describe comrades lost in the line of duty. This grim story then begins to shift, as children talk about their experiences growing up in New York. A children's choir sings about the still-magical city. This combination of stories honors the victims of the attack, while simultaneously celebrating New York City.

4. **Humorous**. Since designers create ads to encourage a change in behavior, remembering it is important. We must retain the advertising message that we receive while watching the nightly news when we buy a tube of toothpaste two days later. To be effective, however, a humorous ad must truly be funny, without insulting the viewer or demeaning the product. A Nike ad that featured an 80-year-old runner is a perfect example. The man ran 17 miles every morning in chilly San Francisco. Asked how he kept his teeth from chattering, he replied, "I leave them in my locker!" The ad used false teeth to emphasize his age, while footage of his vigorous running emphasized the importance of exercise.

5. **Realistic**. Communication requires connection. For a commercial to succeed, the viewer must feel connected to the ideas and images presented. For example, few adults will pay attention to an ad for the latest hip-hop band, while few teenagers will pay attention to an ad for life insurance. In either case, there is no connection between the audience and the message. Similarly,

when we like a character in an ad, we are more likely to listen to his or her argument.

A common form of realism is **testimonial**. In a testimonial, a trustworthy character (often a celebrity) addresses us directly. A 1998 Aleve commercial is a good example. An ordinary-looking middle-aged man wearing blue jeans tells us that two Aleve pills do the same job as a fistful of pills from a competing company.

14.24 **DDB Chicago,** *911 Thanks*, **2011.** Commissioned by State Farm Insurance, directed by Spike Lee.

When he ends the ad by saying simply "It works for me," we assume that it will also work for us.

6. **Exaggerated**. Exaggeration can be a great strategy when the product is commonplace or the message is uninteresting. Exaggeration tends to be memorable. Even if the event shown is ludicrous, the ad can be effective if the basic message is believable. An ad to promote mass transit in Boston combined a series of close-ups of snails with a voice-over by a traffic reporter. He described terrible expressway delays. Viewers knew that the snails were not literally stuck in traffic: they represented drivers who were moving "at a snail's pace." The metaphor was unexpected and funny. As a result, the "boring" mass transit ad became memorable.

▶ key questions

NARRATIVE COMPRESSION

- Which is more appropriate for your concept: a "hard-sell" or a "soft-sell" approach? How might you visualize each option?

- To what extent does your story need to be factual? What facts are most meaningful?

- Can exaggeration or metaphor strengthen the communication?

NONNARRATIVE

Titanic is a familiar type of popular film. It tells a fictional story, based on a series of actions and reactions. The opening and closing sequences provide an effective framework for the story of Rose, Jack, and Cal. The characters are believable, and the plot is plausible.

Many forms of sequential art, however, are nonnarrative in structure. For example, an ad for an expensive car may simply show its elegant contours and gleaming chrome. There is no story: viewers simply see a series of beautiful close-ups. Evocative artworks of this kind often require more audience participation and encourage an open-ended response.

Three common approaches to nonnarrative are the categorical approach, the rhetorical approach, and the abstract approach. A **categorical** approach is based on the exploration of a single concept, action, or emotion. *Giving Fear a Proper Name,* a visual book by Susan Kae Grant, uses text from a diary to explore fear. Contained within a clear Plexiglas box, the book itself is like a fetish. Hand-made paper and inserted objects cause the book to open on its own, and the tiny toy revolver that dangles from a bookmark string simultaneously suggests self-protection and self-annihilation.

This catalog of terror begins with kainophobia, the fear of change (14.25). From the diary, we learn that Grant has moved to Detroit, a profoundly foreign environment for her. On the first page of a double-page spread, she writes of "moving forward looking backward . . . I can never say good-bye." On the facing page we can see her profile, facing left, with straight pins piercing her face and an accompanying tiny compass and a plastic groom, suggesting a wedding cake. Topophobia, the fear of place, comes next. Grant now writes that she "stares in disbelief out smashed vacant beauties / violet oppressive depression surrounds me / people are angry, filled with hate." Her face in the photograph has now become a target. Eremophobia, the fear of solitude, follows. We see a close-up of her ear, pierced by pins, while a plastic toy phone dangles like an earring. The book continues, with pages devoted to various fears such as the fear of sleep, fear of being alone, and fear of being observed. In each case, increasingly painful words accompany a photographic self-portrait of some kind. The book ends with the fear of infinity. Now in profile facing right, Grant is accompanied by a pair of dice and a map of Texas, which will become

14.25 Susan Kae Grant, *Kainophobia, Fear of Change*, from *Giving Fear a Proper Name: Detroit*, The Black Rose Press, 1982–85. Edition of 15, printed letter press with silver prints. Mixed mediums, handmade paper, simulated bulletproof case, 5 × 5 in. (12.7 × 12.7 cm).

her new home. Using fear as a category, and then relentlessly exploring different types of fear, Grant transformed her personal experience into powerful communication.

In a **rhetorical** approach, sequential images are used to present an argument. One example is *Powers of Ten*, by Charles and Ray Eames (14.26). This 9½-minute film provides an elegant exploration of "the relative size of things in the universe." The central image is framed by a dark border, which includes information on each shot's spatial position on the right and its numerical equivalent on the left. Beginning with a shot of a man asleep in a park, the camera gradually moves out to the

farthest reaches of the known universe. Physicist Philip Morrison provides the narration, describing the meaning of the image at each step.

The process is then reversed, and the speed is greatly accelerated. Returning to the sleeping man, the camera now moves through his skin, into his blood, down to a cell, and finally into an atom in the man's right hand. The beautiful images entice us, while the mathematical narration teaches us. Moving from astrophysics to nuclear physics, this film presents an analysis of the distance between the largest and smallest known spaces.

Words for the World, by Ed Hutchins, presents a social argument using equally simple means.

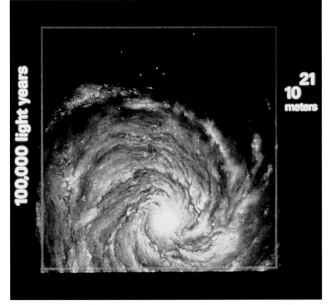

14.26 Charles and Ray Eames, *Powers of Ten*, 1977. Film frames.

By filling a small metal pencil box with 16 special pencils, he makes a plea for tolerance and peace. Hutchins prints a map of the world on the top of the box. He prints various texts on the pencils, in languages ranging from Arabic to Zulu, each accompanied by an English translation. The phrases are simple: "It doesn't hurt to listen." "The time is always right for justice." "We all live under the same sky." The message, however, is compelling. What words will we write with these pencils? What words can we say to each other? Hutchins is promoting a change in behavior rather than knowledge of the cosmos.

Finally, sequential art may be purely **abstract**. In a well-designed book or film, changes in color, shape, texture, and movement can provide all the required information for a compelling piece. *Blacktop,* another experimental film by Charles and Ray Eames, provides one example. An outdoor basketball court has been washed. As the residue is rinsed away, the film records the movement of soap bubbles and water over the asphalt surface. The delicate harpsichord music in the sound track suggests that this act of washing the asphalt is as elegant as a classical ballet. And in the hands of these inventive filmmakers, it is.

▶ key questions

NONNARRATIVE

- Create rough storyboards exploring categorical, rhetorical, and abstract approaches. Which of these nonnarrative strategies is best suited to the idea that you want to express?

- What is the glue that holds your nonnarrative together: an alphabet (as in *Giving Fear a Proper Name*), mathematics (as in *Powers of Ten*), or some other unifying force?

- When using an abstract approach, what aspect(s) of your subject will you emphasize?

summary

- Storytelling is one of the most ancient and effective forms of communication. Stories can increase self-awareness, provide inspiration, supply information, and encourage understanding.

- We can use multiple-image structures to express complex ideas using narrative and nonnarrative approaches.

- The group, series, and sequence are the multiple-image structures most commonly used by printmakers, photographers, and book artists.

- Filmmakers and playwrights use the beat, scene, and act to create screenplays.

- By establishing effective boundaries, we can develop more effective stories. Common questions include the following: Whose story is it? When should the story begin and end? Where does the story occur? Why did it happen? What is the underlying theme or message in the story?

- A change in style can substantially affect communication.

- We can communicate ideas and emotions through a straightforward series of causes and effects or through a series of seemingly unrelated images.

- The opening and closing, personal perspective, and characters that a filmmaker or playwright uses can make or break a story.

- Television advertisements can present complete ideas in 15 seconds. Hard-sell, soft-sell, rational, emotional, serious, humorous, realistic, and exaggerated approaches are the most common strategies.

- Categorical, rhetorical, and abstract are common nonnarrative approaches.

key terms

abstract
acts
beat
categorical
causality
character-driven
denouement
emotional (advertising)

exaggerated (advertising)
group
hard-sell (advertising)
humorous (advertising)
myth
rational (advertising)
realistic (advertising)
rhetorical

scenes
screenplay
sequence
series
serious (advertising)
soft-sell (advertising)
style
testimonial (advertising)

studio projects

To apply the concepts from this chapter in the studio, check out the Projects page in the Online Learning Center at www.mhhe.com/LTI5e. The following is a sample of the chapter-related assignments in step-by-step detail.

Casuality and Duration. An introduction to narrative.

Countdown. Exploring ways to compress, expand, and accelerate time.

Before and After. Understanding narrative implications of objects and interiors.

House of Cards. Exploring nonlinear narrative.

Profile:
Michael Remson,
Librettist and Composer
Story and Song

A dual Irish-American citizen, Michael Remson is primarily known as a composer of vocal, choral, and operatic works. He was featured in New York City Opera's Showcasing American Composers series and served as Composer-in-Residence with the Ulster Orchestra in Belfast. Our conversation focuses on Dr. Remson's opera dealing with the life and death of Mary Surratt, the first woman executed by the federal government in United States history.

MS: How did you become a composer?

MR: I grew up in a house filled with music. My father sang in the chorus of the Metropolitan Opera in New York City and I began singing and acting at a young age. At the age of 20, I co-formed a new-wave band and began writing songs. This led me to formal studies at NYU with composer Judy Klein, primarily in the area of electronic music. I then combined my electronic interests with my love of storytelling and soon found myself writing operas.

MS: What is a libretto?

MR: Literally, *libretto* is Italian for "little book." It's the term that describes the story, scene-by-scene breakdown, stage directions and, ultimately, the words that are sung. It's like writing a play that's meant to be sung instead of spoken. Generally, the composer hires or collaborates with a librettist, rather than writing it himself.

MS: What is the advantage of writing both the libretto and the music yourself?

MR: For me, it lets both the libretto and the music evolve more organically. As an aria or scene evolves, my dramatic instincts tell me whether I need more or less text or more or less music. I can then make the additions or sacrifices I feel are best. I'm also a big proponent of American English as a beautiful language for singing. Writing the libretto myself lets me work with the tone, sound, and color of language in tandem with those same aspects of the music.

MS: Tell me about your opera, *Mary Surratt*.

MR: Mary Surratt was condemned as a conspirator in the plot to kill Abraham Lincoln. Her son, John, was almost certainly involved but historians continue to debate Mary's guilt or innocence. Initially, I left it up to the audience to decide. But I realized that a historically accurate approach weakened the drama. In the next draft, I made a dramatic decision that Mary would be innocent. The compelling question, and therefore the crux of the drama, would become Why was she executed?

MS: How does it begin?

MR: The assassination of Lincoln is the dramatic impulse, the event that sets in motion all of the actions and emotions that follow. So, as soon as the audience is seated and the lights are down, a gunshot sounds. A spotlight focuses on a box above the stage and we see Lincoln dying. The baritone who plays John Wilkes Booth struggles with a guard and leaps to the stage. He shouts "Sic semper tyrannis!" (Latin for "Thus always to the tyrants") and runs off.

After that, the stage fills with eyewitnesses to the assassination, milling about in a fog, despondent and confused. Using actual quotes from people in Ford's Theatre, I am hoping to convey the shock and despair that gripped the nation. So, in effect the theatrical audience becomes the audience in Ford's Theatre on the night of April 14, 1865. Lastly, we see Mary at the gallows, declaring her innocence.

Mary Surratt's story is then allowed to unfold—some through flashbacks and some in real time.

Remember, the question isn't whether she is guilty or innocent but the conditions that would allow her to go to the gallows if she was, in fact, innocent. Mary was pious, retiring, and very devoted to her family; Booth was a nationally renowned actor, vehement in his devotion to the Confederacy and a very charismatic man. In the opera, Mary's actions are motivated by her misguided attempts to protect her son from Booth—regardless of the cost to herself.

MS: Why did you start off with the assassination?

MR: Think of a snowball rolling down a hill. It starts off as a small fistful of snow, but as it rolls along, it gets bigger and bigger. As a librettist, I must set the snowball in motion. And I must keep it in motion and on track; slowing down the action too much or letting the plot become cluttered reduces its dramatic impact. It must be inevitable and unstoppable. Lincoln's death is that snowball. My goal is to have the audience completely caught up in the drama as soon as that first scene is over.

MS: Do you have a technique for working out the pacing and chronology?

MR: I spent at least 18 months working out the chronology and structure. For this particular opera, I needed to keep all of the historical and dramatic events clear in my mind, so I wrote each detail on an index card, then pinned it to a large bulletin board. For example, one card said, "Mary delivers the shooting irons"; another said, "Booth kills Lincoln." By moving these cards around on the wall, I could envision various ways to tell the story and ultimately settle on a chronology that I felt was dramatically compelling.

This technique also helped me see actions I wanted to emphasize and actions or characters I felt I could omit or combine. I try to see everything as a thread. Dates and events are meaningless in the abstract. Drama occurs when the threads come together, like weaving a cloth. Now that I'm working on the music, I can fine-tune the pacing and dramatic impulses that hold the entire opera together.

MS: Your mentors are particularly renowned. Carlisle Floyd is often referred to as "the dean of American opera," and Edward Albee has had a stellar career as a playwright. What were the most valuable things you learned from them?

MR: Mr. Floyd helped hone my dramatic instincts and insisted that I take responsibility for every single word and musical note. Mr. Albee helped me focus on creating individual voices for each character and on the overall narrative. He helped me look at the forest rather than the trees.

MS: I have only listened to opera on the radio. What are the advantages of live opera?

MR: Opera is more than just music; it's about words, drama, sets, lighting, costumes, and acting on stage. When it's done well, there is nothing more thrilling than sitting in an opera house and being absorbed in that world. Listening to an opera on the radio is like going to a movie with your eyes shut!

MS: Any final bits of advice for my students?

MR: Realize that you can't base a career on talent alone. You must be punctual, prepared, easy to work with, and an asset to the group. In other words, be as good a businessperson as you are an artist. In the arts, people who don't meet deadlines don't get work!

Soprano Kelli Estes performing in the Lone Star Lyric Theatre Festival's production of Michael Remson's *Sorry, Wrong Number*, based on the play by Lucille Fletcher.

Interdisciplinary Arts

In this final chapter, we explore three forms of interdisciplinary art. In **interdisciplinary art**, two or more disciplines fuse to create a hybrid art form. The first section focuses on visual books, which combine words and images in a variety of structures. The next section is devoted to installation art, which presents an ensemble of images and objects within a three-dimensional environment. We will end the chapter with a discussion of **performance art**.

EXPLORING THE VISUAL BOOK

What is a visual book? A **visual book** is an experimental structure that conveys ideas, actions, and emotions using multiple images in an integrated and interdependent format. Every image is connected in some way to every other image. In a sense, there are no single pages in a visual book. It is the combination of the multiple pages that creates the complete artwork.

Any material may be used for pages, from the bags of tea that Nancy Callahan used for her *Daybook* (15.1) to the sheets of lead Anselm Kiefer used for *Breaking of the Vessels* (15.2). Pages may be of any size or shape, from the 3-inch triangles that Daniel Kelm and Tim Ely used in *Rubeus* (15.3) to room-sized screens. The subject matter can be profoundly philosophical, fiercely political, or painfully personal. For example, Susan Kae Grant created a catalog of terror in *Giving Fear a Proper Name* (see figure 14.25, page 326). The artist can generate images using photography, printmaking, drawing, or other techniques.

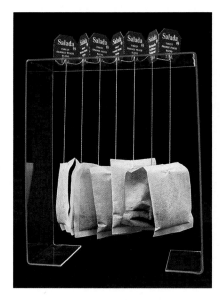

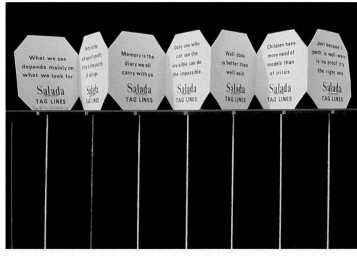

15.1 Nancy Callahan, *Daybook*, 1988. Artist's book, screen printing, and hand-fabricated tea bags, 16 × 12 × 6 in. (40.6 × 30.5 × 15.3 cm).

15.2 Anselm Kiefer, *Breaking of the Vessels*, **1990.** Lead, iron, glass, copper wire, charcoal, and aquatec, 12 ft 5 in. × 11 ft 3 in. × 4 ft 9 in. (378.5 × 343 × 144.8 cm).

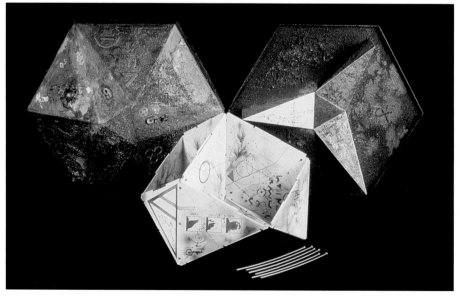

15.3 Daniel E. Kelm and Timothy C. Ely, *Rubeus*, **1990.** Book: Flexahexahedron (six cyclically linked tetrahedra with a circular axis of rotation), Arches paper, museum board, stainless steel wire, aluminum tubing, brass beads, cotton-covered polyester thread, with drawings using airbrush acrylics and ink, 5 × 10½ × 10½ in. (12.7 × 26.7 × 26.7 cm). Box: High faceted structure with hexagonal base and felt pad; paper consolidated paperboard and medium-density fiberboard, finished with polymer medium, copper leaf, plastic, metal bits, and sand from sacred sites, 6.25 in. (15.9 cm) high, 13 × 13 in. (33 × 33 cm) base.

15.4 Mary Stewart, a page in *Labyrinth*, **front and back view, 1999.** Intaglio, 13 × 18 × 39 in. (33 × 45.7 × 99 cm).

15.5 Keith Smith. Bound-edged codex structure.

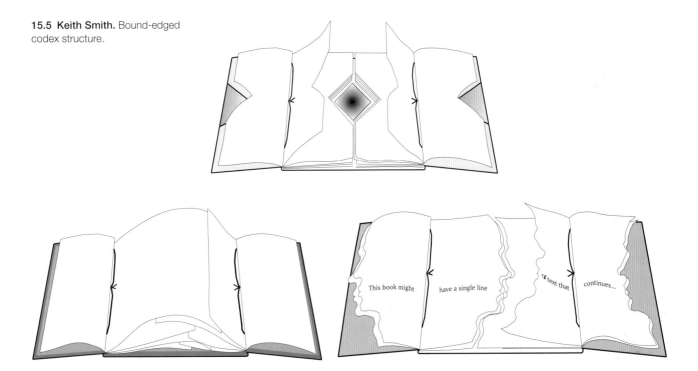

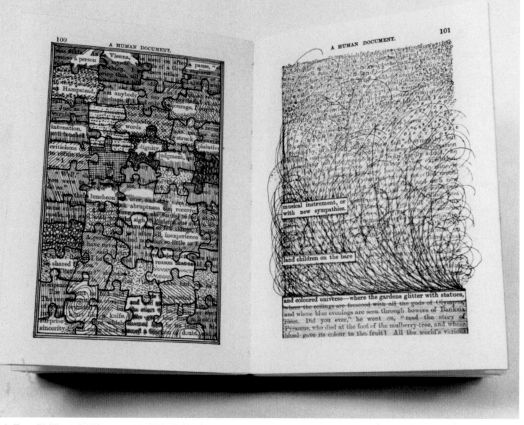

15.6 Tom Phillips, *A Humument*, 1980. From *The Cutting Edge of Reading: Artists' Books*, R. R. Hubert and J. D. Hubert. Granary Books, New York, 1999.

Visual books combine two-dimensional composition and three-dimensional structure. For example, I composed each page in my own *Labyrinth* (15.4) individually, then slotted them together to create a complex three-dimensional object. Even when a more traditional bound-edged **codex** structure is used (as in figure 15.5), variations in the page length and shape can substantially affect meaning.

Visual books may be entirely visual, as with Emily Frenkel's *Labyrinth Book* (15.9, page 336), or primarily verbal, as with Tom Phillips' *A Humument* (15.6), or it may mix visual and verbal information. An artist can also design visual books to self-destruct. Keith Smith used traditional chemical photography in designing *Book 50* (15.7). By leaving out the "fix" stage, he created a book that will turn black as the viewer turns each page. As a result, the viewer can see the images only once!

Generally seen by one person at a time, a visual book can create a direct connection between the audience and the artist. This contact is especially important with pop-up books, which come to life when we turn the pages and pull the tabs.

BOOK NUMBER 50
(Turning the page creates and destroys the image.)
Autumnal Equinox 1974

Construct a Western Codex book consisting of images on thirty transparencies. Process the film-positives by developing, short stop but no fix. Wash, dry and under proper safelight, hand bind as a leather case bound book. Place completed book in light-tight box.

Present the boxed book to the viewer. Upon opening the box and viewing, the entire book will not fog at once. Opening to the first page, the viewer will glimpse the image as it quickly blackens. The black will protect the remainder of the book from light. Upon turning each page, the viewer will momentarily see the image as it sacrifices itself to protect the remaining pages.

KE◉TH

15.7 Keith Smith, *Book 50*, 1974. A conceptual book.

Selecting a Text

Generative Potential

A short and engaging text can act as a springboard for the book artist. Such words provide a beginning point for expanded creativity. By contrast, a long-winded text often becomes a trap. The words take over, leaving little room for visual invention. More than verbal polish, a text must provide an opening for further development.

The labyrinth book project that I assign to my students provides such generative potential, both visually and conceptually. The students begin by developing a labyrinthine drawing of a complex building (15.8). Because this drawing will act as a stage set for the narrative, I encourage them to expressively explore balance, lighting, and the illusion of space.

After a critique of the initial work, students expand their ideas and refine their images, finally creating two rough drawings, one on the front and one on the back of a 22 × 30 in. sheet of sturdy paper. They then cut this sheet apart to create four 7½ × 22 in. strips, which they finally fold and sew to create sixteen 7½ × 11 in. front and back pages.

The final book is developed from this raw material. We consider dictionary definitions:

> **lab-y-rinth:** 1: a structure full of intricate passageways that make it difficult to find the way from the interior to the entrance or from the entrance to the center (for example, the labyrinth constructed by Daedalus for Minos, king of Crete, in which the Minotaur was confined); 2: a maze in a park or garden formed by paths separated by high, thick hedges; 3: something bewilderingly involved or tortuous in structure: a complex that baffles exploration; 4: a situation from which it is difficult to extricate oneself; 5: the internal ear, or its bony or membranous part; 6: a body structure made up of a maze of cavities and channels; 7: intricate, sometimes symbolic pattern, spec. such a pattern inlaid in the pavement of a medieval church; 8: in metallurgy, series of troughs in a stamping mill through which water passes for washing pulverized ore.[1]

We read the story of Theseus, the Greek hero who conquered the half-man, half-bull Minotaur, and meet the princess Ariadne, who provided

15.8 Emily Frenkel, *Labyrinth Drawing*, 1999. Pen and ink, 18 × 24 in. (45.6 × 61 cm).

him with a ball of golden thread that helped him to escape the maze. We investigate labyrinths as described by archaeologists, physiologists, and psychologists.

This assignment consistently results in an astonishing array of inventive books. Some students introduce characters into the setting, creating stories. Others use the illusion of space to move the viewer through mysterious corridors and down steep staircases. Emily Frenkel created a world of enchantment using light and pattern (15.9). All are valid solutions to the problem. Because the word *labyrinth* is so open to interpretation, the assignment has great generative potential.

Divisions and Connections

A text that easily breaks apart can suggest connections or divisions between book pages. An alphabet provides the page divisions in Edward Gorey's *The Gashlycrumb Tinies or, After the Outing* (15.10A and B). A rhythmic and rhyming text describing assorted accidents and childhood fatalities accompanies each letter, beginning with "A is for Amy who fell down the stairs, B is for Basil assaulted by bears, C is for Clara who wasted away, D is for Desmond thrown out of a sleigh," and so forth.

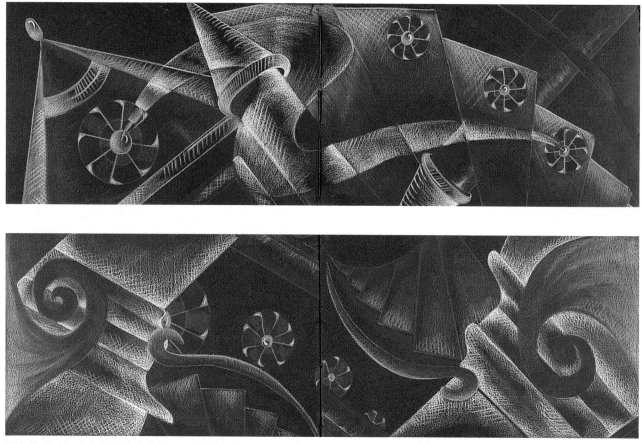

15.9 Emily Frenkel, *Labyrinth Book*, two double-page spreads, 1999. Colored pencil on black paper, 7½ × 22 in. (19 × 55.9 cm).

The alphabet provides a sense of anticipation as we wonder what wild expression of humor we will encounter on the next page, while the singsong rhythm and clever rhymes help unify the pages.

Similarly, a traditional song provides the structure for *The 12 Days of Christmas*, by Robert Sabuda. This song has become a holiday cliché,

and a conventional drawing of the familiar partridge in a pear tree would have been hopelessly predictable. Sabuda overcame the cliché by combining a lively imagination with elegant and elaborate pop-ups. The "six geese-a-laying" sit atop a slice of gooseberry pie, while the "seven swans-a-swimming" fill a crystal ball. For "eleven ladies dancing," nine ballerinas dance atop a music

15.10A Edward Gorey, *A Is for Amy Who Fell Down the Stairs*, 1963. Illustration from *The Gashlycrumb Tinies or, After the Outing*.

15.10B Edward Gorey, *B Is for Basil Assaulted by Bears*, 1963. Illustration from The *Gashlycrumb Tinies or, After the Outing*.

box, and Sabuda used a mirror to multiply some of the figures. And the "nine drummers drumming" (15.11) are mice, with their tails tapping out a lively beat! Imagination conquers cliché every time.

Music

Each language has a distinctive aural quality, or music, as well as a distinctive grammatical structure. English, which is dominated by words derived from Latin and the Germanic languages, provides at least two ways to say almost anything. For example, a Viking warrior is *strong* (a word derived from the Anglo-Saxon word for strength), while a Roman warrior is *vigorous* (a word derived from the Latin word for strength). Spanish provides great grammatical clarity and has similar word endings that encourage rhyme, while Chinese is literally musical—a change in the tone of voice changes word meaning.

Each text also has music. When words are poorly chosen, the text is discordant and painful to read. When we use words thoughtfully, however, both the meaning and the music improve. *Kubla Khan,* by Coleridge, uses wonderfully musical language:

In Xanadu did Kubla Khan
A stately pleasure dome decree:
Where Alph, the sacred river, ran
Through caverns measureless to man
Down to a sunless sea.[2]

You simply must read this aloud. A combination of rhyme, repetition, and alliteration makes the words sing.

Rachel Carson's *Under the Sea Wind* provides many examples of musical prose:

By September the eels of the sound country had begun to drop downstream to the sea. The eels came down from the hills and the upland grasslands. They came from cypress swamps where black-watered rivers had their beginnings; they moved across the tidal plain that dropped in six giant steps to the sea. In the river estuaries and in the sound they joined their mates-to-be. Soon, in silvery wedding dress, they would follow the ebbing tides to the sea, to find—and lose—themselves in the black abysses of mid-ocean.[3]

As with an alphabetic or a traditional song, the music of the text may suggest page divisions while simultaneously providing conceptual unity to the book as a whole.

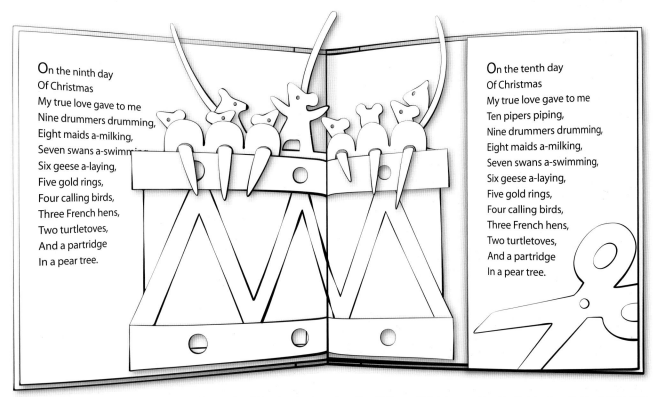

15.11 Robert Sabuda, "Nine Drummers Drumming." line drawing based on *The 12 Days of Christmas, a Pop-Up Celebration*. Simon & Schuster.

Writing a Text

At some point, most book artists and illustrators decide to generate their own texts. The ideas and emotions that they want to express are not available in a traditional text, and copyright laws may limit the use of a contemporary text.

Taking a creative-writing course is a good place to start. As with art courses, a well-designed writing course can provide a solid base of information and encourage the beginner to try various approaches. Try writing a page or two in response to any of these assignments:

- *Memory amplifier.* Describe an object, a sensation, or a setting that summarizes or epitomizes an event, a feeling, or an idea from your life. Looking at family photographs, childhood toys, or everyday objects is a good place to start.

- *Moment of truth.* Describe an event that clarified or transformed your life.

- *Homeworld.* Describe the physical or psychological place that is your home. Is it a particular house? A forest? Some form of social media?

- *Build a memory bank.* Triggering questions can help you start. Just fill in the blanks: (a) "The first time I ever____"; (b) "The best day of my life was____"; (c) list memorable events, such as trips or concerts; (d) list companions in triumph and adversity; (e) consider the greatest gift that you ever received or ever gave.

- *Concept generator.* Research a single word, using a thesaurus, a dictionary, an encyclopedia, or the Internet. Collect all the resulting meanings into a book.

Selecting or writing an appropriate text can increase a book's impact. The best texts reflect our personal interests (or obsessions!) and also are meaningful to an audience. Ask yourself the following questions as you assess the potential of several texts:

- *What is the conceptual, psychological, or political power of the text?* Does it embody ideas and emotions that you find personally compelling?

- *Does the text include any verbal patterns that can help unify the book?* You can use rhythm, repetition, and rhyme to create a stronger connection among the pages.

- *How resonant are the words?* Do they gain or lose strength when you read them repeatedly?

- *How accessible is the text?* Does the language make sense to the intended audience? How can you draw readers into the story that you want to tell or attract them with the images that you want to show?

- *How long is the text?* Generally, texts of 40 or fewer words are the easiest to use effectively. Extended texts can get long-winded and crowd out the images.

You can use any source, from graffiti to Shakespeare. Many visual books derive their power from an unexpected selection of words.

Text and Type Style

After you choose a text, book construction can begin. Each page that you design raises many questions. Let's concentrate on three major questions, using an 11 × 17 in. double-page spread. Ask yourself the following questions:

- *What type style and type size are most appropriate to the ideas you want to express?*

Each type style has a significant effect on communication. Let's experiment with a simple phrase: "Footsteps echoed emptiness."

A type style called *Impact* has an industrial look. Perhaps it is the echo of boots descending a factory staircase that we hear (15.12).

Garamond type, especially when italicized, is flowing and graceful. The footsteps that we now hear may be those of a child descending a staircase in a Victorian house on Christmas Eve (15.13).

Madrone type paints a much grimmer picture. A gang war has concluded, and the survivors are slowly leaving the deserted parking lot where it occurred (15.14).

FOOTSTEPS ECHOED EMPTINESS

15.12 Text using Impact type style.

footsteps echoed emptiness

15.13 Text using Garamond type style.

FOOTSTEPS ECHOED EMPTINESS

15.14 Text using Madrone type style.

- *Can more than one type style be used effectively?*

Artists and designers use multiple type styles to communicate the distinctive voices of multiple speakers or to convey multiple perspectives on the same event. *Sticky Buns: An Overnight Roll* uses this approach (15.15). A team of 12 artists developed this book during a workshop organized by the Paper and Book Intensive, a national book-arts group. The collaborators provided an actual recipe for cinnamon buns near the top of each page, while a **gloss**, or commentary on the text, was written in italic along the bottom. Words carefully selected from the recipe are thereby reinterpreted, suggesting a romantic afternoon in the kitchen as the emotions (as well as the dough) begin to rise.

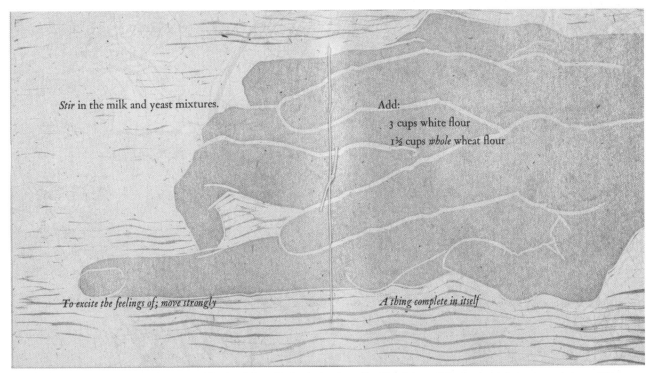

Stir in the milk and yeast mixtures.

Add:
3 cups white flour
1½ cups *whole* wheat flour

To excite the feelings of; move strongly

A thing complete in itself

15.15 *Sticky Buns: An Overnight Roll*, **1996.** A collaborative book developed by 12 artists participating in a letterpress workshop at the Paper and Book Intensive.

- *How should we position the words on the page?*

In figure 15.16 (page 341), an oversized "echoed" suggests that we are straining to hear a mysterious visitor's footsteps. Figure 15.17 further emphasizes the mysterious implications. Now, the footsteps seem to echo endlessly. With the addition of two more pages, figure 15.18 communicates the loneliness of the journey.

Combining Word and Image

Things get even more interesting when we combine words and images. The organization in figure 15.19 suggests the woman's memory of a past event. The same phrase describes a walk into the future in figure 15.20. Finally, the combination of words and images in figure 15.21 puts us back into a labyrinth.

Advantages of Visual Books

Through a combination of words and images, visual books can convey complex ideas and emotions to a broad audience. In some books, the words provide direct, explicit communication, while the images are more mysterious. In other books, the words are evocative, while the images are explicit and direct. In either case, we can create layers of meaning through a contrast between the visual and the verbal. Instead of overexplaining an image, we can use words to suggest alternative ideas and implications. For artists and designers with big ideas, this interplay between words and images can greatly expand communication.

▶ ## key questions

THE VISUAL BOOK

- What thoughts and emotions do you most want to express in your visual book?

- What thoughts and emotions are best expressed in words? Through images?

- What balance between words and images is most effective?

- Will a change in tempo increase impact? Try adding some blank pages to slow down the tempo or putting multiple frames on a single page to speed up the tempo.

INSTALLATION ART

An **installation** is an ensemble of images and objects that are presented within a three-dimensional environment. Because we occupy the actual time and space of the artwork, we become physically engaged in an installation. This can heighten the aesthetic experience.

Uses of Space and Time

Some installations are primarily spatial. For example, many installations by Robert Irwin emphasize direct experience within a constructed space. By devising a series of entrances, exits, and environments, Irwin creates a framework that each visitor activates. His *Part II: Excursus* (figure 9.56, page 206) was installed at the Dia Center in New York in 1998. This structure consisted of nine cubic rooms defined by delicate cloth walls. Two vertical fluorescent lights illuminated each cube, creating subtle changes in color from room to room.

Entering the installation was both inviting and disorienting. Multiple layers of cloth and the variations in light made the most distant rooms appear to dissolve. The vertical fluorescent lights, which always remained visible, read first as individual, then as mirror images, creating a hallucinatory experience similar to that in a carnival fun house. The visitors created all of the activity within the space themselves as they entered and explored the installation like ghostly silhouettes.

By contrast, *Floodsong,* by Mary Lucier, was primarily temporal. She installed six video monitors in a narrow room at the Museum of Modern Art in New York. Each showed an interview with a survivor of the 1995 Grand Forks, North Dakota, flood. A young girl, an old woman, an old man, a minister, and a farmer told the story of the terrifying event. In the enclosed space, the individual voices were indistinct. They echoed and merged, creating a litany of fortitude and grief, resilience and fear. In sharp contrast to the straightforward interviews, an enormous projection on the gallery's back wall took the audience through wrecked houses and piles of debris.

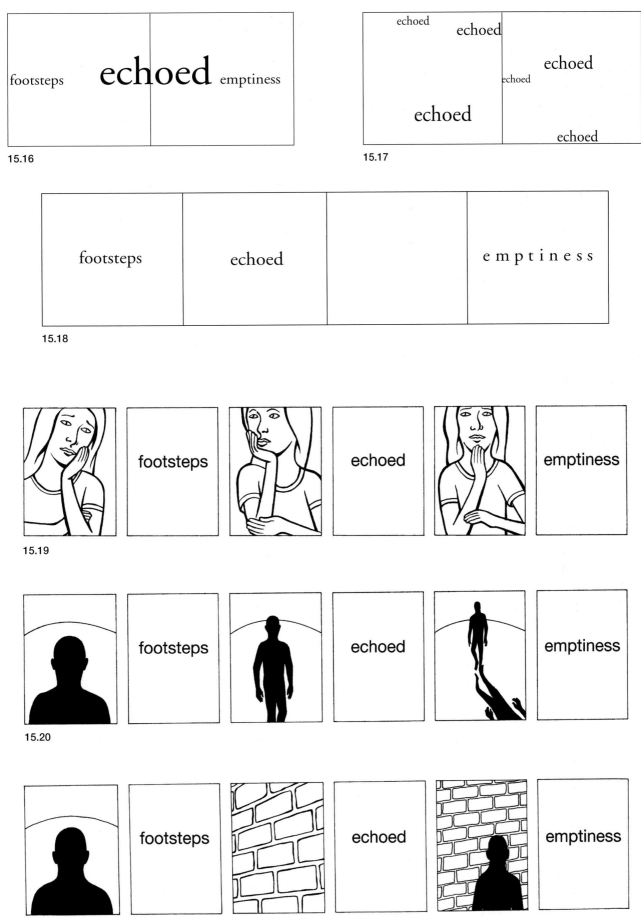

15.16

15.17

15.18

15.19

15.20

15.21

15.22 Bill Viola, *Hall of Whispers*, 1995. Video/sound installation.

Bill Viola's *Hall of Whispers* (15.22) was both temporal and spatial. In his catalogue for a retrospective exhibition of Viola's work, David Ross wrote:

> Viewers enter a long, narrow, dark room, and must pass between ten video projections arranged in two rows along the side walls, five on either side of the room. The projections are life-sized black and white images of people's heads facing the viewer, with their eyes closed and their mouths tightly bound and gagged. They are straining to speak, but their muffled voices are incomprehensible, and mingle in the space in a low, indecipherable jumble of sound.[4]

This installation, while similar to *Floodsong* in layout, created an entry into a nightmare. Lucier's installation evoked a range of emotions: fear, pity, and respect. Viola's *Hall of Whispers* was claustrophobic and terrifying.

The Importance of Context

Each gallery has its own distinctive characteristics, so the installation may change in size and shape each time it is shown. Echoes may be amplified in one space and muted in another. More importantly, each site adds its own *meaning* to the artwork. Each imparts its own emotional and spatial charge.

When the artist uses the context fully, a powerful connection can be made between art and life. For example, our associations with bathrooms, snakes, and hieroglyphics inform our understanding of Sandy Skoglund's *Walking on Eggshells* (15.23). For most of us, there is no place more private than a bathroom and there are few animals more frightening than snakes. This combination alone is sure to create tension. The addition of a floor covered with delicate eggshells, nude women, and playful rabbits expands the expressive range further. Even the wall tiles are deliberate. Dominated by hieroglyphics from the Egyptian Book of the Dead and other ancient images, they add to the sense of mystery. The women in this space seem like goddesses from antiquity, and the bathroom becomes loaded with conflicting emotions.

Artists may also use a site to expand their audience. In *Storefront Stories* (15.24), Nancy Callahan

15.23 Sandy Skoglund, *Walking on Eggshells*, 1997. Cibachrome print, 47 × 60 in. (119 × 152 cm). © 1997 Sandy Skoglund.

and Diane Gallo transformed empty shop windows in several small towns into a series of vignettes based on childhood memories. When shown in Cherry Valley, New York, the artists changed a single window every day over a six-week period. Callahan and Gallo combined everyday objects, such as chairs, items of clothing, and household equipment with written stories about growing up in the small town. Personal experience became public communication through the use of a non-traditional exhibition space.

Through *Truisms* (15.25, page 344), Jenny Holzer brought public art to an urban audience for a more political purpose. Printing various proverbs on posters, flyers, T-shirts, hats, and finally electronic signs, Holzer used mass-marketing techniques to convey messages such as "Abuse of power comes as no surprise" and "Raise boys and girls the same way." Shown next to the flashing neon signs in New York City's busy Times Square, Holzer's seemingly banal messages took on new importance and reached many viewers unfamiliar with contemporary art.

15.24 Diane Gallo and Nancy Callahan, *Storefront Stories*, 1999. Mixed-medium installation, 6 × 6 × 6 ft (1.83 × 1.83 × 1.83 m).

15.25 Jenny Holzer, *Truisms, 1977–79: Abuse of Power Comes as No Surprise*, 1982. Times Square, New York. Spectacolor Board No. 1.

Advantages of Installation Art

For the artist seeking new and expanded means of expression, installation art offers several advantages:

- *A fresh perspective on a familiar setting or situation.* The site itself is an essential component of the piece. We must see familiar settings afresh. Any aspect of reality can become a staging area for art. The installation may shift, invert, or overturn our expectations.

- *A large scale.* Most installations are made in a scale that invites physical entry. This eliminates distance between viewer and image: viewers become part of the artwork. The principles of time, space, and gravity that rule our everyday life can heighten the emotional impact or create a sense of disorientation.

- *A tranformative experience.* When we enter a space or interact with other audience members, we have a direct and memorable experience.

key questions

INSTALLATIONS

- What ideas do you most want to express? What emotions do you most want to evoke?

- What is the advantage of a confined space as opposed to an expansive space?

- How much lighting do you need and what is the most appropriate light source?

- What sounds will you provide? What sounds can the audience generate?

- How can you invite viewers into your artwork? What will they discover? What might they know on leaving that they didn't know on entering?

- Will interaction among viewers or between the viewers and the artwork expand meaning or heighten emotion?

PERFORMANCE ART

Mixing dance, theater, music, and art with politics, philosophy, and other disciplines, performance art pushes the possibilities of interdisciplinary work even further. Like any other art form, performance art is designed to communicate ideas and express emotions. Unlike traditional art forms, performance art is immediate and direct. Rather than paint an image on a canvas, the performers generally present images directly—on a stage, in a gallery, or outdoors. Performance art replaces the wood, bronze, or marble of traditional figurative sculpture with the performer's own flesh and blood. For example, in *Indigo Blue* (15.26), Ann Hamilton placed 18,000 pieces of used "blue-collar" work clothes, a seated "attendant," and a desk covered with history books in a large room. An army of volunteers meticulously folded and stacked the laundered clothes. Quietly seated at the desk, the attendant erased the historical texts from back to front, using a pink pearl eraser and moisture from her own saliva. In this artwork, the worn items of clothing became mute witnesses to the decline of the American labor movement.

15.26 Ann Hamilton performing *Indigo Blue*, 1991/2007. Cotton clothing, wood and steel platform, wood table and stool, book, eraser. Dimensions variable.

Historical Background

The roots of contemporary performance art may actually extend back in time to the Futurists, a group of Italian poets, musicians, and artists most active from 1911 to 1915. Determined to develop a new approach to art, they created revolutionary paintings and sculptures, wrote inflammatory manifestos, and staged theatrical performances that were both frenetic and shocking. In word and deed, the Futurists rebelled against good taste, traditional subject matter, compositional rules, and established institutions.

Performance art has become especially prominent in the past 30 years. Historians often trace the current surge in interest to the Happenings developed by Allan Kaprow and others in the 1950s and 1960s. In a **Happening**, the artist determined the time, place, materials, and general theme for the event. When they arrived, audience members created the artwork through their actions. Unrehearsed, these events often were chaotic as well as exhilarating.

Characteristics of Performance Art

To some extent, contemporary performance art shares many of the basic characteristics of Futurism. Four qualities are especially notable.

Ephemeral

Just as a concert ceases to exist as soon as the last note fades, so performance art is inherently ephemeral. The performance may persist in each audience member's memory, but the full force of the event disappears as soon as the audience leaves the site. Even when an artist plans a new production, new actors in new settings tend to change the artwork's meaning.

15.27 **Karole Armitage, *Predator's Ball*, 1996.** Brooklyn Academy of Music. Sets by David Salle, animation videos by Erica Beckman, costumes by Hugo Boss, Pila Limosner, and Debra Moises Co.

Collaborative

Working collaboratively, artists can expand their ideas and explore new modes of expression. Despite their interest in live art, few visual artists have extensive training in dance and theater. It may be physically impossible for them to perform a movement themselves. And, just as an amateur's drawing is very different from a professional's drawing, so amateur dance tends to look—amateurish. By working together, artists, actors, musicians, and dancers can combine forces to create powerful artworks.

Furthermore, a collaboration tends to extend each participant's ideas. Despite their similarities, art, theater, music, and dance are also distinctively different. Each has a long and complex history, an extensive theoretical background, and particular aesthetic values. By sharing information and discussing alternative approaches, each participant has an opportunity to rethink his or her own creative process.

Performance artists have combined many disciplines successfully. In *Predator's Ball* (15.27), Karole Armitage combined her choreography with sets by painter David Salle and videos by Erica Beckman. This tale about Wall Street junk bond dealer Michael Milken is both stark in its staging and frenzied in its energy. In *Available Light* (15.28),

choreographer Lucinda Childs sought a pulse in the spaces designed by architect Frank Gehry and the music composed by John Adams.

15.28 **Lucinda Childs, image from *Available Light*, 1983.** Performed at the Brooklyn Academy of Music.

Blurred Boundaries

During a performance, separations between art and life often dissolve. For some artists, performance art is a way to work outside of the rarefied world of the art museum or the competitive world of the commercial gallery. Viewing art as a creative process and a life-affirming philosophy rather than as a product, performance artists seek new venues and new audiences. Separations between high art and mass culture may become blurred. Graffiti, popular music, or television advertisements may provide more inspiration than a masterpiece in a museum. In describing his approach to a Happening, Allan Kaprow said that "the line between art and life should be kept as fluid and perhaps as indistinct as possible."

The Artist and the Audience

When we remove barriers between art and life, separations between artist and audience also become blurred. Indeed, many artists deliberately involve the audience in the work. In *Performance/Audience/Mirror,* Dan Graham confronted his audience directly, describing their appearance and commenting on their participation during the performance. And, with *Pull,* Mona Hatoum created a humorous interaction between audience and artist. Hatoum invited viewers to pull on an actual braid of hair, then watch the artist's apparent reaction on the video monitor. No longer an observer, each audience member had to physically engage with the artwork in order to view the video.

ADVANTAGES OF INTERDISCIPLINARY ART

Visual books, installations, and performance art all require interdisciplinary integration. These connections offer new opportunities for creative thinking and complex communication. Ideas and emotions outside the mainstream can become accessible to both artists and audiences. Furthermore, because each of these new mediums requires a substantial amount of audience participation, they redefine relationships between artist and audience. An active audience can contribute more to the experience than a passive audience. With performance art, boundaries dissolve not only between art and theater, but also between art and life.

▶ key questions

PERFORMANCE ART

- When working collaboratively, what can you offer your partner and what can your partner offer you?

- What similarities and differences are there in your creative processes? What is the best way to handle differences of opinion?

- How many performers are needed?

- What is the relationship between the performer(s) and the set? Should all the performers appear live, or can some appear via projections?

- In what context will your performance appear? A subway station is a very different venue than a gallery and may add meaning to the artwork.

- How can sound and light heighten emotion or expand meaning?

- How much change must occur during the performance? Is repetition a virtue?

- How can you heighten or reduce intensity?

- What is the most powerful beginning you can devise?

- What is the most memorable ending you can devise?

- Who is the intended audience, and what role can the audience play?

summary

- A visual book is an experimental structure that conveys ideas, actions, and emotions in an integrated and interdependent format. Each page is connected in some way to the preceding page and to the following page.

- Visual books combine two-dimensional composition with three-dimensional structure and may use time and narrative very deliberately. They may be entirely visual, may be entirely verbal, or may mix words and images.

- In selecting a text, consider its potential to generate ideas, how you will divide the text and distribute it over multiple pages, the rhythm and music of the words, and the significance of the ideas.

- Every type style has its own distinctive quality, which can add or detract from the book's meaning.

- The combination of words and images in a visual book can encourage the development of complex ideas using layers of meaning.

- An installation is an ensemble of images and objects that an artist presents within a three-dimensional environment. When the viewer enters an installation, he or she is physically surrounded and aesthetically engaged.

- An installation may be primarily spatial, may be primarily temporal, or may use both space and time equally. The context in which an installation occurs can add to, subtract from, or expand its meaning.

- Installation art offers a fresh perspective on a familiar setting or situation. The artist usually creates the piece in large scale, and it requires some viewer involvement.

- Performance art is live art designed by artists. Combining aspects of theater, music, art, and dance, it offers both the artist and the audience a laboratory for aesthetic experimentation.

- Many performance artists use time very deliberately, expand their ideas through collaboration, and seek to blur the boundaries between art and life.

- Each of the interdisciplinary arts that we described in this chapter requires substantial audience participation. As a result, contemporary artists are constantly redefining relationships between the artist and the audience.

key terms

codex	installation	visual book
gloss	interdisciplinary art	
Happening	performance art	

studio projects

To apply the concepts from this chapter in the studio, check out the Projects page in the Online Learning Center at www.mhhe.com/LTI5e. The following is a sample of the chapter-related assignments in step-by-step detail.

Labyrinth Collage and Book. Integrating multiple materials, methods, and structures to communicate a complex idea.

Visual Organization

Arnheim, Rudolph. *Power of the Center.* Berkeley: University of California Press, 1999.

Berger, Arthur Asa. *Seeing Is Believing: An Introduction to Visual Communication,* 3rd ed. New York: McGraw-Hill, 2007.

Berger, John. *Ways of Seeing.* London: British Broadcasting Corporation, 1987.

Dondis, Donis. *A Primer of Visual Literacy.* Cambridge, MA: MIT Press, 1973.

Two-Dimensional Design

Lupton, Ellen, and Jennifer Cole Phillips. *Graphic Design: The New Basics.* Princeton, NJ: Princeton Architectural Press, 2008.

Myers, Jack Fredrick. *The Language of Visual Art: Perception as a Basis for Design.* Orlando, FL: Holt, Rinehart and Winston, 1989.

Ocvirk, Otto G., Robert E. Stinson, Philip R. Wigg, Robert O. Bone, and David L. Cayton. *Art Fundamentals: Theory and Practice,* 11th ed. New York: McGraw-Hill, 2009.

Wong, Wucius. *Principles of Form and Design.* New York: John Wiley and Sons, 1993.

Color Theory

Albers, Josef. *Interaction of Color.* New Haven, CT: Yale University Press, 1963.

Gerritsen, Frans. *Theory and Practice of Color.* New York: Van Nostrand Reinhold, 1975.

Hornung, David. *Color: A Workshop Approach.* New York: McGraw-Hill, 2005.

Itten, Johannes. *The Art of Color.* New York: Van Nostrand Reinhold, 1974.

Koenig, Becky. *Color Workbook.* Upper Saddle River, NJ: Pearson Education, 2010.

Kuppers, Harald. *Color: Origin, Systems, Uses.* New York: Van Nostrand Reinhold, 1972.

Munsell, Albert H. *A Grammar of Color: A Basic Treatise on the Color System of Albert H. Munsell.* New York: Van Nostrand Reinhold, 1969.

Norman, Richard B. *Electronic Color.* New York: Van Nostrand Reinhold, 1990.

Wong, Wucius. *Principles of Color Design.* New York: John Wiley and Sons, 1997.

Creativity

Bohm, David. *On Creativity.* New York: Routledge, 2000.

Briggs, John. *Fire in the Crucible: Understanding the Process of Creative Genius.* Grand Rapids: Phanes Press, 2000.

Csikszentmihalyi, Mihaly. *Creativity: Flow and the Psychology of Discovery and Invention.* New York: HarperCollins, 1996.

Dewey, John. *Art as Experience.* New York: Capricorn Books, 1958.

Gardner, Howard. *Art, Mind and Brain: A Cognitive Approach to Creativity.* New York: Basic Books, 1982.

Gardner, Howard. *Creating Minds: An Anatomy of Creativity Seen Through the Lives of Freud, Einstein, Picasso, Stravinsky, Eliot, Graham, and Gandhi.* New York: Basic Books, 1993.

Gardner, Howard. *Frames of Mind: The Theory of Multiple Intelligences.* New York: Basic Books, 1985.

Lamott, Anne. *Bird by Bird: Some Instructions on Writing and Life.* New York: Anchor Books, 1998.

Le Boeuf, Michael. *Imagineering.* New York: McGraw-Hill, 1980.

Prince, George. "Creativity and Learning as Skills, Not Talents," *The Philips Exeter Bulletin,* 1980.

Root-Bernstein, Robert and Michele. *Sparks of Genius: The Thirteen Thinking Tools of the World's Most Creative People,* New York: Houghton Mifflin Harcourt, 2013.

Shekerjian, Denise. *Uncommon Genius: How Great Ideas Are Born.* New York: Penguin Books, 1991.

Tharp, Twyla. *The Creative Habit: Learn It and Use It for Life.* New York: Simon and Schuster, 2006.

Wallace, Doris B., and Howard E. Gruber, eds. *Creative People at Work.* New York: Oxford University Press, 1989.

Concept Development

Adams, James L. *Conceptual Blockbusting.* Reading, MA: Addison-Wesley, 1986.

de Bono, Edward. *Lateral Thinking.* London: Ward Educational Limited, 1970.

Grear, Malcolm. *Inside/Outside: From the Basics to the Practice of Design.* New York: Van Nostrand Reinhold, 1993.

Johnson, Mary Frisbee. *Visual Workouts: A Collection of Art-Making Problems.* Englewood Cliffs, NJ: Prentice Hall, 1983.

Kelley, Tom. *The Art of Innovation: Lessons in Creativity from America's Leading Design Firm.* New York: Doubleday, 2001.

Lakoff, George, and Mark Johnson. *Metaphors We Live By.* Chicago: University of Chicago Press, 1981.

Shahn, Ben. *The Shape of Content.* Cambridge, MA: Harvard University Press, 1957.

Von Oech, Roger. *A Kick in the Seat of the Pants.* New York: Harper and Row, 1963.

Von Oech, Roger. *A Whack on the Side of the Head.* New York: Harper and Row, 1986.

Wilde, Judith and Richard. *Visual Literacy: A Conceptual Approach to Graphic Problem Solving.* New York: Watson-Guptil, 2000.

bibliography

Critical Thinking

Barrett, Terry. *Interpreting Art.* New York: McGraw-Hill, 2003.

Tucker, Amy. *Visual Literacy: Writing About Art.* New York: McGraw-Hill, 2002.

Three-Dimensional Design

Andrews, Oliver. *Living Materials: A Sculptor's Handbook.* Berkeley: University of California Press, 1988.

Bachelard, Gaston. *The Poetics of Space,* trans. Maria Jolas. Boston: Beacon Press, 1969.

Beardsley, John. *Earthworks and Beyond: Contemporary Art in the Landscape.* New York: Abbeville Press, 1998.

Ching, Frank. *Architecture: Form, Space, and Order,* 2nd ed. New York: Van Nostrand Reinhold, 1996.

de Oliveira, Nicolas, Nicola Oxley, and Michael Petry. *Installation Art.* Washington, DC: Smithsonian Institution Press, 1994.

Dormer, Peter, and Ralph Turner. *The New Jewelry: Trends and Traditions.* London: Thames and Hudson, 1985.

Frantz, Suzanne. *Contemporary Glass: A World Survey from the Corning Museum of Glass.* New York: Harry N. Abrams, 1989.

Koplos, Janet. *Contemporary Japanese Sculpture.* New York: Abbeville Press, 1991.

Lane, Peter. *Ceramic Form: Design and Decoration,* rev. ed. New York: Rizzoli, 1998.

Lewin, Susan Grant. *One of a Kind: American Art Jewelry Today.* New York: Harry N. Abrams, 1994.

Lidstone, John. *Building with Wire.* New York: Van Nostrand Reinhold, 1972.

Luecking, Stephen. *Principles of Three Dimensional Design.* Upper Saddle River, NJ: Pearson Education, 2002.

Lynn, Martha Dreyer. *Clay Today: Contemporary Ceramicists and Their Work.* Los Angeles: Los Angeles County Museum of Art; and San Francisco: Chronicle Books, 1990.

Manzini, Ezio. *The Material of Invention: Materials and Design.* Cambridge, MA: MIT Press, 1989.

Miller, Bonnie J. *Out of the Fire: Contemporary Glass Artists and Their Work.* San Francisco: Chronicle Books, 1991.

Nunley, John W., and Cara McCarty. *Masks: Faces of Culture.* New York: Harry N. Abrams in association with the Saint Louis Art Museum, 1999.

Penny, Nicholas. *The Materials of Sculpture.* New Haven, CT: Yale University Press, 1993.

Selz, Peter Howard. *Barbara Chase-Riboud, Sculptor.* New York: Harry N. Abrams, 1999.

Wallschlaeger, Charles, and Cynthia Busic-Snyder. *Basic Visual Concepts and Principles for Artists, Architects and Designers.* New York: McGraw-Hill, 1992.

Williams, Arthur. *Sculpture: Technique, Form, Content.* Worcester, MA: Davis, 1993.

Wyatt, Gary. *Spirit Faces: Contemporary Native American Masks from the Northwest.* San Francisco: Chronicle Books, 1994.

Time Design

Baldwin, Huntley. *How to Create Effective TV Commercials,* 2nd ed. Lincolnwood, IL: NTC Business Books, 1989.

Bordwell, David, and Kristin Thompson. *Film Art: An Introduction,* 8th ed. New York: McGraw-Hill, 2008.

Eisner, Will. *Comics and Sequential Art.* Tamarac, FL: Poorhouse Press, 1985.

Goldberg, Roselee. *Performance: Live Art Since 1960.* New York: Harry N. Abrams, 1998.

Johnson, Lincoln F. *Film: Space, Time, Light and Sound.* Orlando, FL: Holt, Rinehart and Winston, 1974.

Katz, Stephen D. *Film Directing, Shot by Shot: Visualizing from Concept to Screen.* Studio City, CA: Michael Wiese Productions, 1991.

McCloud, Scott. *Understanding Comics.* New York: Harper-Perennial, 1994.

McKee, Robert. *Story: Substance, Structure, Style and the Principles of Screen Writing.* New York: HarperCollins, 1997.

Riordan, Steve, ed. *Clio Awards: A Tribute to 30 Years of Advertising Excellence, 1960–1989.* Glen Cove, NY: PBC International, 1989.

Ross, David. *Bill Viola.* New York: Whitney Museum of American Art, 1998.

Vogler, Christopher. *The Writer's Journey: Mythic Structure for Storytellers and Screenwriters.* Studio City, CA: Michael Wiese Productions, 1991.

Zettl, Herbert. *Sight, Sound, Motion: Applied Media Aesthetics,* 4th ed. Belmont, CA: Wadsworth, 2004.

Book Arts

Drucker, Johanna. *The Century of Artists' Books.* New York: Granary Books, 1995.

Gordon, Stephen F. *Making Picture-Books: A Method of Learning Graphic Sequence.* New York: Van Nostrand Reinhold, 1970.

La Plantz, Shereen. *Cover to Cover.* Asheville, NC: Lark Books, 1995.

Lyons, Joan. *Artists' Books: A Critical Anthology and Sourcebook.* Rochester, NY: Visual Studies Workshop Press, 1985.

Smith, Keith A. *Structure of the Visual Book.* Fairport, NY: The Sigma Foundation, 1992.

Smith, Keith A. *Text in the Book Format.* Fairport, NY: The Sigma Foundation, 1991.

bibliography

Chapter Two Works Cited

1. Johannes Itten, *The Art of Color* (New York: Van Nostrand Reinhold, 1974), p. 16.

2. Alexander Theroux, *The Primary Colors: Three Essays* (New York: Henry Holt and Company, 1994), p. 6.

Chapter Five Works Cited

1. Keith A. Smith, *Structure of the Visual Book* (Fairport, NY: The Sigma Foundation, 1991), pp. 17–18.

Chapter Six Works Cited

1. Mihaly Csikszentmihalyi, *Creativity: Flow and the Psychology of Discovery and Invention* (New York: HarperCollins, 1996), pp. 55–76.

2. George Prince, "Creativity and Learning as Skills, Not Talents," *The Philips Exeter Bulletin*, June–October, 1980.

3. Anne Lamott, *Bird by Bird: Some Instructions on Writing and Life* (New York: Anchor Books, 1998), pp. 18–19.

Chapter Nine Works Cited

1. John Beardsley, *Earthworks and Beyond: Contemporary Art in the Landscape* (New York: Abbeville Press, 1998), p. 31.

2. Jonathan Fineberg, *Art Since 1940: Strategies of Being* (Englewood Cliffs, NJ: Prentice Hall, 1995), p. 383.

3. Alexander Theroux, *The Primary Colors: Three Essays* (New York: Henry Holt and Company, 1994), p. 86.

4. Theroux, p. 6.

5. Theroux, p. 6.

Chapter Thirteen Works Cited

1. David Bordwell and Kristin Thompson, *Film Art: An Introduction*, 5th ed. (New York: McGraw-Hill, 1997), pp. 277–78.

2. Scott McCloud, *Understanding Comics* (New York: HarperPerennial, 1994), pp. 70–74.

3. Richard Kostelanetz, *Aaron Copland: A Reader: Selected Writings, 1923–1972* (New York: Routledge, 2003), p. 107.

4. Keith A. Smith, *Structure of the Visual Book* (Fairport, NY: The Sigma Foundation, 1991), pp. 102–4.

Chapter Fourteen Works Cited

1. Keith A. Smith, *Structure of the Visual Book* (Fairport, NY: The Sigma Foundation, 1991), p. 106.

2. Robert McKee, *Story: Substance, Structure, Style and the Principles of Screen Writing* (New York: HarperCollins, 1997), pp. 37–41.

Chapter Fifteen Works Cited

1. Jean L. McKechnie, *Webster's New Universal Unabridged Dictionary* (New York: Simon and Schuster, 1983), p. 1011.

2. Maynard Mack, *World Masterpieces* (New York: W. W. Norton and Company, 1965), p. 478.

3. Rachel Carson, *Under the Sea Wind* (New York: Viking Penguin, 1996), p. 23.

4. Bill Viola, *A Twenty-Five-Year Survey* (New York: Whitney Museum of American Art; Paris: Flammarion, 1997).

notes

Glossary by

Mary Stewart and Peter Forbes

abstract artwork; abstract form 1. an artwork or form derived from visual reality that has been distilled or transformed, reducing its resemblance to the original source. 2. a multiple image structure, such as a film, in which the parts are related to each other through repetition and visual characteristics such as shape, color, scale, or direction of movement.

abstract shape a shape that is derived from a visual source, but is so transformed that it bears little visual resemblance to that source.

accent a specific shape, volume, color, musical note, etc., that has been emphasized. Using an accent, a designer can bring attention to part of a composition and increase rhythmic variation within a pattern.

achromatic a color (such as black and white) that has no hue.

act a major division in a film or theatrical event. Acts are generally constructed from a group of sequences that increase in intensity.

action-to-action transition in comic books, the juxtaposition of two or more panels showing a sequence of actions.

actual lines lines that are physically present in a design.

actual time the duration of an actual temporal event. For example, it takes less than a minute for the bowling ball to roll down the ramps in Jean Tinguely's *Chaos 1.*

additive color color created by combining projected beams of chromatic light. The additive color primaries are red, green, and blue, and the secondaries are cyan, magenta, and yellow.

additive sculpture a physical object constructed from separate parts that have been connected using glues, joints, stitching, welds, and so on.

aesthetics the study of human responses to art and beauty.

afterimage in color theory, a ghostly image that continues to linger after the actual image has been removed.

ambient light the quality of light within an entire space or setting. For example, when we enter an open courtyard on a sunny summer afternoon, we are surrounded by warm ambient sunlight. Everything we see is colorful and bright.

amplified perspective the exaggerated use of linear perspective to achieve a dramatic and engaging presentation of the subject. Amplified perspective is often created using an unusual viewing position, such as a bird's-eye view, accelerated convergence, or some form of distortion.

analogous a color scheme based on hues that are adjacent on a color wheel, such as red, red-orange, and orange.

analogy a similarity or connection between things that are apparently separate and dissimilar. For example, when a teacher describes wet plaster as having the "consistency of cream," he or she is using an analogy.

anesthetic a chemical or action used to induce insensitivity or unconsciousness.

anomaly an obvious break from the norm in a design.

appropriation a postmodern practice in which one artist reproduces an image created by another and claims it as his or her own.

approximate symmetry a form of balance that occurs when roughly similar imagery appears on either side of a central axis.

armature an internal structure created to strengthen and support a three-dimensional object.

array a collection of points.

assemblage an additive method in which the artist or designer constructs the artwork using objects and images that were originally created for another purpose. Essentially, assemblage can be defined as three-dimensional collage.

asymmetrical balance equilibrium among visual elements that do not mirror each other on either side of an axis.

atmospheric perspective a visual phenomenon in which the atmospheric density progressively increases, hazing over the perceived world as one looks into its depth. Overall definition lessens, details fade, contrasts become muted, and, in a landscape, a blue mist descends.

attached shadow a shadow that directly defines a form.

balance the equal distribution of weight or force among visual units.

beat 1. a unit of musical rhythm that creates the pulse of a sound. 2. in acting, the most basic element in a story. A beat is an exchange of behavior, based on action and reaction.

bend one of the five major forces affecting structural strength.

brainstorming any of a number of problem-solving techniques that are designed to expand ideas and encourage creativity. List making, mapping, associative thinking, and metaphorical thinking are common strategies used.

calligraphic line derived from the Greek words for beautiful and writing, a flowing and expressive line that is as personal as handwriting. Calligraphic lines generally vary in thickness and velocity.

cast shadow a dark shape that results from placement of an opaque object in the path of a light source.

categorical (form) in film, a multiple image structure that is based on categories, or subsets of a topic. For example, a film on predators might begin with a discussion of wolves, then move on to lions, and conclude with a discussion of hawks.

causality the interrelation of cause and effect, based on the premise that nothing occurs without cause. Narrative film is based on causality: because the starting pistol was shot, the footrace began.

cause-and-effect critique (or formal analysis) a critique in which the viewer seeks to determine the cause for each visual or emotional effect in a design. For example, the dynamism in a design may be caused by the diagonal lines and asymmetrical balance used.

centricity as identified by Rudolph Arnheim, a compressive compositional force.

character-driven narratives where something about the character's essential self, aesthetics, or feelings leads to a particular action or event.

chiaroscuro (from Italian meaning "light-dark") The gradual transition of values to create the illusion of light and shadow on a three-dimensional form.

chroma the purity, intensity, or saturation of a color.

chromatic gray a gray made from a mixture of various hues, rather than a simple blend of black and white.

chronology the order in which events occur.

cliché an overused expression or a predictable visual treatment of an idea.

close-up in film, a type of framing in which the scale of the object shown is relatively large, as in a close-up of an actor's face.

closure the mind's inclination to connect fragmentary information to produce a completed form. Closure is an essential aspect of Gestalt psychology.

codex traditional bound-edged format used for modern books, with separate pages normally bound together and given a cover.

collage an image constructed from visual or verbal fragments initially designed for another purpose.

color harmony use of compatible colors to help unify a composition.

color interaction the way colors within a composition influence one another.

color key a color that dominates an image and heightens its psychological and compositional impact.

color overtone a secondary hue "bias" in a primary color. For example, alizarin crimson is a red with violet overtones, while scarlet is a red with orange overtones.

color theory the art and science of color interaction and effects.

complementary (colors) hues that oppose one another on a color wheel. When paired in a composition, complementary colors create contrast; when mixed, complementary colors produce a wide range of browns.

composite a new material created when two or more materials of differing strengths are fused together. Examples include Fiberglas and foamcore.

compression the forcing or crushing of material into a smaller, denser condition and its visual dynamics and implied psychological effects.

cone of vision in perspective drawing, a hypothetical cone of perception originating at the eye of the artist and expanding outward to include whatever he or she wishes to record in an illusionistic image, such as

a perspective drawing. The cone's maximum scoping angle is 45–60 degrees; anything outside the cone of vision is subject to distortion.

containment a unifying force created by the outer edge of a composition or by a boundary within a composition.

content the emotional and/or intellectual meaning or message of an artwork.

context in art, the set of circumstances or facts that surround when a work of art was made, where, how, and for what purpose.

continuity degree of connection or flow among compositional parts.

contour line a line that describes the edges of a form and suggests three-dimensional volume.

contrast the degree of difference between compositional parts or between one image and another. Contrast is created when two or more forces operate in opposition.

contrasting colors colors that are substantially different in hue, value, intensity, or temperature.

convergent thinking a problem-solving strategy in which a predetermined goal is pursued in a linear progression using a highly focused problem-solving process. Six steps are commonly used: 1. define the problem, 2. do research, 3. determine your objective, 4. devise a strategy, 5. execute the strategy, 6. evaluate the results.

critique any means by which the strengths and weaknesses of designs are analyzed.

cross-contours multiple lines running over the surface of an object horizontally and/or vertically that describe its surface configuration topographically, as in mapping. This process is much like wire-framing in three-dimensional computer modeling. Cross-contours can also be used in drawing to suggest three-dimensional form through tonal variation.

crosscutting in film, an abrupt alternation between two or more lines of action.

cross-hatching a technique used in drawing and printmaking to shade an object using two or more networks of parallel lines. Darker values are created as the number of networks increases.

curvilinear shape a shape whose contour is dominated by curves and flowing lines.

cut in film, the immediate change from one shot or frame to another.

D

definition 1. the degree to which a shape is distinguished from both the ground area and from other shapes within the design. 2. the degree of resolution or focus of an entire image. Sharply defined shapes tend to advance, while blurred shapes tend to recede.

denouement the outcome, solution, or point of clarification in a story.

descriptive critique a critique in which the viewer carefully describes what he or she sees when observing a design.

diegetic describes the world created in a film or video.

directed light localized and focused light, such as a spotlight on a singer.

direction actual or implied movement of an element within a design.

disharmony a combination of colors that clash with one another and appear to be jumping out of the picture.

displacement a forming method in which a solid material is physically forced into a new configuration. The stamping process used to mint coins is an example of displacement.

dissolve a transition between two shots during which the first image gradually disappears while the second image gradually appears.

divergent thinking an open-ended problem-solving strategy. Starting with a broad theme, the artist or designer expands ideas in all directions.

dominant describes the principle of composition in which certain elements assume greater importance than others. Also see **emphasis.**

duration 1. the length of time required for the completion of an event, as in the running time of a film, video, or performance. 2. the running time of events depicted in the story (plot duration). 3. the overall span of time the story encompasses (story duration).

dynamic forms forms that imply change.

dynamic space compositional organization that emphasizes movement or the illusion of movement.

E

earth colors colors made primarily from pigments in soil, including raw sienna, burnt sienna, raw and burnt umber, and yellow ochre.

earthwork commonly, an artwork that has been created through the transformation of a natural site into an aesthetic statement.

eccentricity as identified by Rudolph Arnheim, an expansive compositional force.

economy distillation of a design down to the essentials in order to increase impact.

editing in film, selecting and sequencing the details of an event to create a cohesive whole.

elements (of design) basic building blocks from which designs are made. For example, the essential elements of two-dimensional design are line, shape, texture, color, and value.

emotional in advertising, use of emotion to sell a service, product, or idea. This strategy is often used when a product is neither unique nor demonstrably better than a competing product.

emphasis special attention given to some aspect of a composition to increase its prominence.

engraving a printmaking process in which lines are carved into a metal plate or wooden board, then filled with ink and printed.

environmental work (or environment) an artwork that must be entered physically. Installations (which are usually presented indoors) and earthworks (which are usually presented outdoors) are two major types of environmental works.

ephemera materials that decay rapidly.

exaggerated in advertising, pushing an idea to an extreme to make a point.

exoskeleton an external support structure.

eye level (or horizon line) in linear perspective, the eye level is determined by the physical position of the artist. Sitting on the floor creates a low eye level, while standing at an easel creates a higher eye level. All vanishing points in one- and two-point perspective are positioned on the eye level.

F

fade a gradual transition used in film and video. 1. In a fade-in, a dark screen gradually brightens as a shot appears. 2. In a fade-out, the shot gradually darkens as the screen goes black.

fidelity the degree of connection between a sound and its source. For example, when we hear the sound of a helicopter and see a helicopter on the screen, the sound matches with the image, creating tight fidelity.

figure/ground reversal an arrangement in which positive and negative shapes alternately command attention.

flashbacks in film, alternations in chronology in which events that occur later in a story are shown first.

flying buttress a type of exoskeleton commonly used by medieval architects in designing cathedrals.

focal point primary point of interest in a composition. A focal point is often used to emphasize an area of particular importance or to provide a strong sense of compositional direction.

form 1. the physical manifestation of an idea, as opposed to the content, which refers to the idea itself. 2. the organization or arrangement of visual elements to create a unified design. 3. a three-dimensional composition or unit within a three-dimensional composition. For example, a sphere, a cube, and a pyramid are all three-dimensional forms.

formal analysis a type of critique in which compositional causes are connected to compositional effects.

fractured space discontinuous space that is created when multiple viewpoints are combined within a single image.

frame a single static image in film or video.

freestanding work an artwork that is self-supporting and is designed to be viewed from all sides.

function the purpose of a design or the objective that motivates the designer. For an industrial designer, the primary purpose of a design is often utilitarian. For example, he or she may be required to design a more fuel-efficient automobile. For a sculptor, the primary purpose of a design is aesthetic: he or she seeks to

glossary

create an artwork that engages the viewer emotionally and intellectually.

fusion the combination of shapes or volumes along a common edge.

geometric forms three-dimensional forms derived from or suggestive of geometry. Examples include cubes, spheres, tetrahedrons, etc.

geometric shapes shapes derived from or suggestive of geometry. Geometric shapes are characterized by crisp, precise edges and mathematically consistent curves.

Gestalt psychology a theory of visual perception that emphasizes the importance of holistic composition. According to this theory, grouping, containment, repetition, proximity, continuity, and closure are essential aspects of visual unity.

gesture drawing a vigorous drawing that captures the action, structure, and overall orientation of an object, rather than describing specific details. Often used as a basis for figure drawing.

gloss 1. in writing, words of explanation or translation inserted into a text. 2. a secondary text within a manuscript that provides comments on the main text.

gradation any gradual transition from one color to another or from one shape or volume to another. In drawing, shading created through the gradation of grays can be used to suggest three-dimensional form.

graphic relationship the juxtaposition of two or more separate images that are compositionally similar. For example, if a basketball is shown in the first panel, an aerial view of the round free-throw zone is shown in the second, and the hoop of the basket itself is shown in the third, a graphic relationship based on circles has been created.

grid a visual or physical structure created from intersecting parallel lines.

grisaille a gray underpainting, often used by Renaissance artists, to increase the illusion of space.

group in sequential structure, a collection of images that are related by subject matter, composition, or source. For example the trombone, trumpet, and tuba are all members of the group known as the brass section in an orchestra.

grouping visual organization based on similarity in location, orientation, shape, color, and so on.

handheld a small-scale object that can be held in your hands.

Happening an assemblage of improvised, spontaneous events performed by artist and audience alike, based on a general theme. There is no rehearsal, and any location, from a parking lot to a factory interior, can be used. The Happening is most commonly associated with Alan Kaprow and is a precursor to performance art.

hard-sell an advertising approach in which a major point is presented in a clear, direct manner. The narrative is usually linear, and the message is usually explicit.

harmony a pleasing or soothing relationship among colors, shapes, or other design elements.

hatching a technique used in drawing and printmaking to create a range of gray tones using multiple parallel lines.

high definition sharply focused visual information that is easily readable. High definition creates strong contrast between shapes and tends to increase the clarity and immediacy of communication.

hue the name of a color (such as red or yellow) that distinguishes it from others and assigns it a position in the visual spectrum.

human scale a design that is roughly our size.

humorous advertising use of humor to sell a service, product, or idea. By entertaining the viewer, the designer can make the message more memorable.

hybridity the creation of artworks using disparate media to create a unified conceptual statement.

iconography the study of symbolic visual systems.

imbalance the absence of balance.

implied line 1. a line that is suggested by the positions of shapes or objects within a design. 2. a line that is suggested by movement or by a gesture rather than being physically drawn or constructed.

implied time the suggested location or duration of an event.

installation an artwork or a design that presents an ensemble of images and objects within a three-dimensional environment.

intensity 1. the purity, saturation, or chroma of a color. For example, fire engine red is a high-intensity color, while brick red is a low-intensity color. 2. in time design, the power, concentration, and energy with which an action is performed or the quality of observation of an event.

interdisciplinary art the combination of two or more different disciplines to create a hybrid art form.

invented texture a form of visual texture that has been created without reference to perceptual reality.

kinesthetics the science of movement.

kinetic forms forms that actually move.

L

lap dissolve in film, a dissolve in which two shots are temporarily superimposed.

layered space compositional space that has been deliberately separated into foreground, middle ground, and background.

layering a postmodern practice in which an accumulation of multiple (and often contradictory) visual layers is used to create a single artwork.

line 1. a point in motion. 2. a series of adjacent points. 3. a connection between points. 4. an implied connection between points. Line is one of the basic elements of design.

linear perspective a mathematical system for projecting the apparent dimensions of a three-dimensional object onto a flat surface. Developed by artists during the Renaissance, linear perspective is one strategy for creating the illusion of space.

long shot in film, a type of framing in which the scale of the subject shown is relatively small, as with an image of a human figure within a landscape.

loudness the amplitude of a sound wave; the volume of a sound.

low-definition describes blurred or ambiguous visual information. Low-definition shapes can increase the complexity of the design and encourage multiple interpretations.

M

maquette a well-developed three-dimensional sketch, comparable to a two-dimensional thumbnail sketch.

mass a solid three-dimensional form.

matrix a three-dimensional grid.

mechanical forms gears, belts, hoses, and other forms suggestive of machinery.

medium shot a type of framing in which the scale of the subject shown is of moderate size, as in a view of an actor from the waist up.

metaphor a figure of speech in which one thing is directly linked to another, dissimilar thing. Through this connection, the original word is given the qualities of the linked word. For example, when we say "She's a diamond in the rough," we attribute to a woman the qualities of an unpolished gem.

metaphorical thinking the use of metaphors or analogies to create visual or verbal bridges.

meter the basic pattern of sound and silence in music or positive and negative in design.

model in three-dimensional design, a technical experiment or a small-scale version of a larger design.

modeling the process of manipulating a pliable material (such as clay) to create a three-dimensional object.

modernism a collection of artistic styles, most prominent from around 1860 to 1960, that emphasized the importance of form, introduced new materials and production methods, and sought to express universal truths.

monochromatic a color scheme based on variations in a single hue. For example, a light pastel blue, a medium navy blue, and a dark blue-black may be used in a room interior.

montage time-based structure constructed from multiple and often seemingly unrelated sources; a temporal collage.

monumental scale of objects that are much larger than humans.

movement in design, the use of deliberate visual pathways to help direct the viewer's attention to areas of particular interest.

myth a traditional story collectively composed by many members of a society. The creation of the world, sources of evil, the power of knowledge, and even the nature of reality may be explained through these grand expressions of the imagination.

N

negative shape (or ground) 1. a clearly defined area around a positive shape or form. 2. a shape created through the absence of an object rather than through the presence of an object.

negative space space surrounding a positive form or shape.

nonobjective artworks artworks that have no reference to perceptual reality.

nonobjective shapes shapes created without reference to specific visual subject matter.

non-sequitur transition the juxtaposition of multiple frames or shots that have no obvious conceptual relationship.

O

objective criticism the assessment of strengths and weakness in a design based solely on the visual information presented.

one-point perspective a form of linear perspective in which the lines receding into space converge at a single vanishing point of the eye level or horizon line.

opponent theory an explanation for the electric glow that occurs when two complementary colors are placed side by side.

organic forms forms that are derived from nature.

organic shapes shapes that visually suggest nature or natural forces. Also known as **biomorphic shapes.**

organizational lines lines used to create the loose linear "skeleton" on which a composition can be built. Also known as **structural lines.**

orientation the horizontal, vertical, or diagonal position of a composition or design element.

orthographic projection a drawing system widely used by artists and designers to delineate the top, bottom, and four side views of a three-dimensional object. Unlike perspective drawing, which is designed to create the illusion of space, an orthographic projection is constructed using parallel lines that accurately delineate six surfaces of an object.

overlap placement of one shape in front of another to create the illusion of space.

P

pace the rate of change in a temporal event.

pattern a design created through systematic repetition. Many patterns are based on a module, or a repeated visual unit.

pedestal a vertical support for a sculptural object.

performance art a live presentation, often including the artist and usually combining elements from a variety of art forms, such as film, video, theater, and dance.

physical texture actual variation in a surface.

picture plane in linear perspective, the flat surface on which a three-dimensional image is mentally projected.

pitch in music, the relative highness or lowness of a sound. Pitch is determined by wave frequency, as compression and expansion occur within the sound wave.

plane a three-dimensional form that has length and width but minimal thickness.

plinth a horizontal support for a sculptural object.

plot duration the running time of the events depicted in a story.

point a basic mark, such as a dot, a pixel, or a brushstroke. A point is used to create a dialog with the surrounding space.

polyhedra (or polyhedrons) multifaceted volumes.

positive forms areas of physical substance in a three-dimensional design.

positive shape (or figure) the principal or foreground shape in a design and the dominant shape or figure in a figure-ground relationship.

postmodernism a collection of artistic styles that arose in the 1970s as a reaction to modernism. Notable characteristics include conceptual emphasis, social commentary, irreverence, and skepticism about universal truths.

primary colors colors from which virtually all other colors can be mixed. The additive (or light) color primaries are red, green, and blue. The subtractive (or pigment) color primaries are yellow, magenta red, and cyan blue.

process colors in four-color process printing, the subtractive primary colors: yellow, magenta, and cyan, plus black.

proportion the relative size of visual elements within an image.

prototype a well-developed model, as with the fully functional prototype cars developed by automobile companies.

proximity the distance between visual or structural elements or between an object and the audience.

pure form a circle, sphere, triangle, cube, or other form created without reference to specific subject matter.

R

radial symmetry a form of balance that is created when shapes or volumes are mirrored both vertically and horizontally, with the center of the composition acting as a focal point.

rational a type of advertising in which logic and comparisons of quality are used to sell a service, product, or idea. A rational approach is most effective when the message is compelling in itself or the product is unique.

realistic in advertising, use of a familiar setting or situation to involve the viewer and relate a product, service, or idea to use in everyday life.

recontextualization a postmodern practice in which the meaning of an image or object is changed by the context in which it is placed.

rectilinear shapes shapes composed from straight lines and angular corners.

reflective light that is bounced off a reflective surface back into space.

refracted light that has been bent as it passes through a prism.

relief sculpture in which forms project out from a flat surface. The degree of projection ranges from low to high relief.

repetition the use of the same visual element or effect a number of times in the same composition.

representational artworks commonly, the lifelike depiction of persons or objects.

representational shapes shapes derived from specific subject matter and strongly based on visual observation.

rhetorical a type of sequential organization in which the parts are used to create and support an argument. Often used in documentary films.

rhythm 1. presentation of multiple units in a deliberate pattern. 2. in filmmaking, the perceived rate and regularity of sounds, shots, and movement within the shots. Rhythm is determined by the beat (pulse), accent (stress), and tempo (pace).

rhythmic relationship the juxtaposition of multiple visual elements or images to create a deliberate pulse or beat.

S

saturation the purity, chroma, or intensity of a color.

scale a size relationship between two separate objects, such as the relationship between the size of the Statue of Liberty and a human visitor to the monument.

scene in film, continuous action in continuous time and continuous space.

scene-to-scene transition in comic books, the juxtaposition of two or more frames showing different scenes or settings.

scope conceptually, the extent of our perception or the range of ideas our minds can grasp. Temporally, scope refers to the range of action within a given moment.

screenplay the written blueprint for a film, commonly constructed from multiple acts.

secondary colors hues mixed from adjacent primaries. In paint, the secondary colors are violet, green, and orange.

sequence 1. in filmmaking, a collection of related shots and scenes that comprise a major section of action or narration. 2. in narrative structure, any collection of images that have been organized by *cause and effect*. In a simple sequence, action number two is caused by action number one. In a complex sequence, there may be a considerable delay between the cause and the effect.

series in sequential structure, a collection of images that are linked simply, like cars in a train.

serious advertising that treats a topic in a somber or solemn manner. Often used for public service announcements, such as drunk driving commercials.

setting the physical and temporal location of a story, the props and costumes used in a story, and the use of sound.

shade a hue that has been mixed with black.

shape a flat, enclosed area created when a line connects to enclose an area, an area is surrounded by other shapes, or an area is filled with color or texture.

shear a force that creates a lateral break in a material.

shot in film, a continuous group of frames.

side light a light positioned to the side of a person or an object. Can be used to dramatically increase the sense of dimensionality.

sight line 1. a viewing line that is established by the arrangement of objects within one's field of vision. 2. a straight line of unimpeded vision.

simile a figure of speech in which one thing is linked to another, dissimilar thing using the word *like* or *as*. Through this connection, the original word is given the qualities of the linked word. For example, when we say "He's as strong as an ox," we attribute to a man the strength of an animal.

simultaneous contrast the optical alteration of a color by a surrounding color.

site-specific an artwork specifically designed for and installed in a particular place.

skeleton (or endoskeleton) a structure that provides internal support.

soft-sell an advertising approach that uses emotion, rather than reason, to sell a service, product, or idea. The narrative is often nonlinear, and ideas or actions may be implied.

solidification a forming method in which a liquid material is poured into a mold or extruded through a pipe, then allowed to harden.

space the area within or around an area of substance. The artist/designer defines and activates space when constructing a three-dimensional object.

spatial context the space in which a sound is generated. A sound that is played outdoors behaves differently from a sound that is played in a small room.

spatial relationship the juxtaposition of two or more images that are spatially different, such as a close-up, a medium shot, and a long shot.

split complementary a complementary color plus the two colors on either side of its complement on the color wheel.

static forms forms that appear to be stable and unmoving.

stereotype a fixed generalization based on a preconception.

stippling a technique for producing an image from multiple dots.

story duration the overall length of a story.

style the recurring characteristics that distinguish one historical period or particular artist's group from another.

subject the person, object, event, or idea on which an artwork is based.

subjective criticism the assessment of strengths and weaknesses in a design based on nonobjective criteria, such as the narrative implications of an idea, the cultural ramifications of an action, or the personal meaning of an image.

subject-to-subject transition in comic books, the juxtaposition of two or more frames showing different subject matter.

subordinate of secondary importance. See **emphasis.**

subtractive color hue created when light is selectively reflected off a colored surface.

subtractive sculpture a forming method in which materials are removed from a larger mass. Carving, drilling, cutting, and turning on a lathe are all subtractive processes.

symbolic color a color that has been assigned a particular meaning by the members of a society. For example, in the United States, the white color of a wedding gown symbolizes purity, while in Borneo white symbolizes death.

symmetrical balance a form of balance that is created when shapes are mirrored on either side of a central axis, as in a composition that is vertically divided down the center.

take in film or video, one version of an event.

temperature the physical and psychological heat suggested by a color's hue.

tempo the pace at which change occurs. A fast tempo is generally used in action films, while a slow tempo is usually used in a dramatic film.

temporal relationship how the shots in a film are related in time.

tension the extension of an object through stretching or bending.

tertiary color a hue that is mixed from a primary color and an adjacent secondary color.

testimonial in advertising, use of a trustworthy character or celebrity to provide endorsement for a product, service, or idea.

texture the visual or tactile quality of a form. Texture can be created visually using multiple marks, physically through surface variation, or through the inherent property of a specific material, such as sand as opposed to smooth porcelain.

three-point perspective a form of linear perspective in which the lines receding into space converge at two vanishing points of the eye level (one to the left of the object being drawn and one to the right of the object being drawn) plus a third vanishing point above or below the eye level. Used when the picture plane must be tilted to encompass an object placed above or below the eye level.

three-quarter work a physical object that is designed to be viewed from the front and sides only.

timbre the unique sound quality of each instrument. For example, a note of the same volume and pitch is quite different when it is generated by a flute rather than a violin.

tint a hue that has been mixed with white.

tone a hue that has been mixed with black and white.

torque the distortion of an object through a twisting movement. Also known as **torsion.**

translucent a surface that partially permits the passage of light.

transparent a surface that permits the passage of light, such as clear plastic or glass.

triadic describes a color scheme based on three colors that are equidistant on a color wheel.

tromp l'oeil a flat illusion that is so convincing that the viewer believes the image is real. A French term meaning "to fool the eye."

two-point perspective a form of linear perspective in which the lines receding into space converge at two vanishing points of the eye level (or horizon line), one to the left of the object being drawn and one to the right of the object being drawn.

U

unity compositional similarity, oneness, togetherness, or cohesion.

V

value the relative lightness or darkness of a surface.

value contrast the degree to which values in a composition differ from one another.

value distribution the proportion and arrangement of lights and darks in a composition. Also known as **value pattern.**

value scale a range of grays that are presented in a consistent sequence, creating a gradual transition from white to black.

vanishing point in linear perspective, the point or points on the eye level at which parallel lines appear to converge.

variety the differences that give a design visual and conceptual interest, notably, use of contrast, emphasis, differences in size, and so forth.

viewing time the time an audience devotes to watching or exploring an artwork.

visual book an experimental structure that conveys ideas, actions, and emotions using multiple images in an integrated and interdependent format. Also known as an **artist's book.**

visual texture texture created using multiple marks or through a descriptive simulation of physical texture.

visual weight 1. the inclination of shapes to float or sink compositionally. 2. the relative importance of a visual element within a design.

volume 1. an empty three-dimensional form. 2. in two-dimensional design, a three-dimensional form that has been represented using the illusion of space. 3. in time design, the loudness of a sound.

volume summary a drawing that communicates visual information reductively, using basic volumes such as spheres, cubes, and cylinders to indicate the major components of a figure or object.

volumetric three-dimensional in nature.

W

wipe in film, a transition in which the first shot seems to be pushed off the screen by the second. Wipes were used extensively in *Star Wars.*

Part One

Page 2: © Lilian Garcia-Roig. Private collection courtesy of Valley House Gallery & Sculpture Garden, Dallas.

Chapter One

Page 4 (left): © Andrew Beard, Think Point Design, www .thinkpointdesign.co.uk;

4 (right): Courtesy of Pentagram Design;

5 (top left): Courtesy of Pentagram Design;

5 (top right): © Charis Tsevis;

5 (bottom): South Australian Museum. © 2014 Artists Rights Society (ARS), New York/VISCOPY, Australia;

6 (top right): © Kevin Haran;

7 (top left): AP/Wide World Photos/© Disney Enterprises, Inc.;

7 (top right): © Michael Mazur, Canto XI (Overview of Hell), from the portfolio Dante's Inferno, 1999. Courtesy of Michael Mazur Estate and Mary Ryan Gallery;

7 (bottom left): Iris & B. Gerald Cantor Center for Visual Arts at Stanford University. Gift of Dr. and Mrs. Louis J. Rattner;

7 (bottom right): © Rico Lebrun. Collection of David Lebrun, Courtesy of Koplin Gallery, Los Angeles;

8 (top): © The Trustees of The British Museum/Art Resource, NY;

8 (bottom left): The Nelson-Atkins Museum of Art, Kansas City, Missouri. Gift of Mrs. George H. Bunting, Jr., 73-27. Photograph by Mel McLean;

8 (bottom right): © Gu Gan. Courtesy of Hai Gallery, London;

9 (top left): © Alfred Leslie;

9 (bottom right): © Minor White, San Francisco, 1949. The Minor White Archive, Princeton University Art Museum, bequest of Minor White (MWA 49-78.1). © Trustees of Princeton University;

10 (top): Vatican Museums, Vatican State. Scala/Art Resource, NY;

10 (bottom): Gift of Victor S. Riesenfeld. The Museum of Modern Art, New York. Digital Image © The Museum of Modern Art/Licensed by SCALA/Art Resource, NY. © 2014 Artists Rights Society (ARS), New York;

11 (top): © David Mach;

11 (bottom): Photograph by Michèle Bellot. © RMN-Grand Palais/Art Resource, NY;

12: © Sara Mast;

13 (top left): PATH Station Maps, Louis Nelson Associates Inc, NY. Artist: Jennifer Stoller, Louis Nelson. © Louis Nelson Associates for the Port Authority of New York & New Jersey;

13 (top right): © Joel Peter Johnson;

13 (bottom): Courtesy of Pentagram Design;

14 (bottom): Schomburg Center for Research in Black Culture, The New York Public Library. Schomburg Center/Art Resource, NY;

15 (top left): Gift of Edsel B. Ford, Photograph © 2001 The Detroit Institute of Arts/The Bridgeman Art Library. © 2014 Banco de México Diego Rivera Frida Kahlo Museums Trust, Mexico, D.F./Artists Rights Society (ARS), New York;

15 (right): Galleria Moderna Venice, Italy. Cameraphoto Arte, Venice/Art Resource, NY;

15 (center): Courtesy of Cecilia Sorochin, Sorodesign, www.SoroDesign.com;

16 (bottom): © The Murray-Holman Family Trust. Courtesy of Pace. Philadelphia Museum of Art: Purchased with the Edward and Althea Budd Fund, the Adele Haas Turner and Beatrice Pastorius Turner Memorial Fund;

17 (top left): The Department of Theater Arts, California State University, Los Angeles, Courtesy of David McNutt, 1985;

17 (top right): M.C. Escher, *Metamorphosis II* © 2014 The M. C. Escher Company-Holland. All rights reserved. www.mcescher.com;

17 (bottom left): © 2014 Sam Francis Foundation, California/Artists Rights Society (ARS), NY;

18: The Stapleton Collection/The Bridgeman Art Library;

19 (top): Art © Robert Rauschenberg. Licensed by VAGA, New York, NY;

19 (bottom left): San Francisco Museum of Modern Art, Gift of the Women's Board, © Helen Frankenthaler. © 2014 Artists Rights Society (ARS), New York. Photograph by Geoffrey Clements/Corbis;

19 (bottom right): Courtesy of the author;

20 (top): The Museum of Modern Art, New York. Blanchette Rockefeller Fund. Digital Image © The Museum of Modern Art/Licensed by Scala/Art Resource, NY. Art © Romare Bearden Foundation/ Licensed by VAGA, New York, NY;

21: Collection of David Geffen, Los Angeles. Art © Jasper Johns/Licensed by VAGA, New York, NY;

22 (top): © 2014 Conner Family Trust, San Francisco/ Artists Rights Society (ARS), New York;

22 (bottom): © The Trustees of the British Museum/Art Resource, NY;

23 (top): © Brad Holland, Drawing: Literary Beast;

24 (left): © Douglas Smith, 2005. Courtesy of Richard Solomon Agency;

Chapter Two

Page 38: Courtesy of Neenah Papers and Partners Design. Color Attributes courtesy of Dewey Color System®, deweycolorsystem.com;

39: © Audrey Flack. Courtesy of Louis K. Meisel Gallery, NY;

41 (top left): © Audrey Flack. Courtesy of Louis K. Meisel Gallery, NY;

42 (top): © Pat Steir. Courtesy of Cheim & Read, NY;

42 (bottom left): © Munsell Color;

43 (bottom left): © Audrey Flack. Courtesy of Louis K. Meisel Gallery, NY;

43 (bottom right): Art © Kenneth Noland/Licensed by VAGA, New York, NY;

44: © Heritage Images/Corbis;

45 (top right): Louvre, Paris, France/Giraudon/The Bridgeman Art Library;

45 (bottom right): © David Hockney/Gemini G.E.L.;

46 (top left): Smithsonian American Art Museum, Washington, DC/Art Resource, NY;

46 (top right): © 2014 Succession H. Matisse/Artists Rights Society (ARS), New York;

47 (top): © Cat Crotchett. Photograph by Mary Whalen;

47 (bottom): © Samantha Fields. Courtesy of Western Project;

48 (bottom left): © Mark Tansey. Courtesy of Gagosian Gallery;

48 (bottom right): "Chromatics," 1970. Gerald Gulotta, Jack Prince, Arzberg, Porzellanfabrik. Block China Company, American, founded 1963. Porcelain, printed. Dallas Museum of Art, gift of Gerald Gulotta;

49 (right): © Estate of Francis Bacon. All rights reserved. ARS, New York/DACS, London, 2014;

49 (bottom): © Chris Kienke;

50: © 2014 Georgia O'Keeffe Museum/Artists Rights Society (ARS), New York. Alfred Stieglitz Collection, Bequest of Georgia O'Keeffe. Image courtesy of the Board of Trustees, National Gallery of Art, Washington;

51 (center): Courtesy of TYS Creative;

51 (bottom): Alfredo Dagli Orti/The Art Archive at Art Resource, NY;

52 (top): South Australian Museum. © 2014 Artists Rights Society (ARS), New York/VISCOPY, Australia;

52 (bottom left): © Estate of Francis Bacon. All rights reserved. ARS, New York/DACS, London, 2014. Tate, London/Art Resource, NY;

52 (bottom right): Courtesy of Steve Quinn;

53: © Guerrilla Girls. Courtesy www.guerrillagirls.com;

54 (top): Art © Wolf Kahn/Licensed by VAGA, New York, NY;

54 (bottom left): University Art Museum, University of California, Berkeley, Gift of the artist. © 2014 Renate, Hans & Maria Hofmann Trust/Artists Rights Society (ARS), New York;

54 (bottom right): © 2014 Succession H. Matisse/Artists Rights Society (ARS), New York. Astor, Lenox and Tilden Foundation, Spencer Collection, The New York Public Library/Art Resource, NY;

55: © Nancy Crow, Photograph by J. Kevin Fitzsimons;

56 (top left): PATH Station Maps, Louis Nelson Associates Inc., NY. Artist: Jennifer Stoller, Louis Nelson. © Louis Nelson Associates for the Port Authority of New York & New Jersey;

56 (top right): Courtesy of Mark Schwartz and Greg Oznowich, Nesnadny + Schwartz, Cleveland, OH;

56 (bottom): © Vernon Fisher. Collection of Michael Krichman;

57 (top): Andrew Wyeth, *Wind From the Sea*, 1947. © Andrew Wyeth, National Gallery of Art, Gift of Charles H. Morgan, 2009.13.1;

57 (bottom): © The Estate of Richard Diebenkorn. The Nelson-Atkins Museum of Art, Kansas City, Missouri. Gift of the Friends of Art, F63-15. Photograph by E. G. Schempf;

58 (top): © 1980 Sandy Skoglund;

58 (bottom left): © Joe Spadaford;

58 (bottom right): Gift of the P.D. McMillan Land Company, The Minneapolis Institute of Arts/The Bridgeman Art Library;

59 (top): © Chaz Maviyane-Davies;

59 (bottom): © Hiroshi Senju. Courtesy of Sundaram Tagore Gallery. Photograph by Nacasa & Partners Inc.;

60 (top left): © Museum of Northern Arizona Photo Archives, Negative number 83C.45, Catalogue number E561;

60 (center): Museo del Prado, Madrid. Bridgeman-Giraudon/Art Resource, NY;

60 (bottom right): © 2014 Artists Rights Society (ARS), New York/VG Bild-Kunst. Bonn. Staatliche Kunstsammlungen der DDR. Kupferstichkabinett Dresden.

61: © 2014 Artists Rights Society (ARS), New York/ VG Bild-Kunst. Bonn. Gift of Robert and Chris Petteys. Image courtesy of the Board of Trustees, National Gallery of Art, Washington. 1956.1;

63–64: © Suzanne Stryk.

Chapter Three

Page 66 (top left): © Mark Riedy. Courtesy of Scott Hull Associates;

66 (bottom): Viga Celmins, Untitled (Ocean), 1969. Philadelphia Museum of Art: Purchased with a grant from the National Endowment for the Arts and Matching Funds;

67 (left): © 2014 Artists Rights Society (ARS), New York/ VG Bild-Kunst. Bonn. Staaliche Museen zu Berlin. Photo: Jorg Anders, Preussiher Kulturbesitz, Nationalgalerie/ NG57/61;

68 (top): © The British Library Board;

69 (top left): © Larry Moore, Winterpark FL;

69 (top right): Interaction The Solomon R. Guggenheim Foundation/Art Resource, NY. © 2014 Artists Rights Society (ARS), New York/ADAGP, Paris;

69 (center right): © Aaron Macsai;

70 (bottom left): Vatican Museums. Photo: A. Bracchetti-P. Zigrossi. Scala/Art Resource, NY;

70 (bottom right): Toledo Museum of Art, Toledo, OH. Purchased with funds from the Libbey Endowment, gift of Edward Drummond Libbey (1972.4). © 2014 Frank Stella/Artists Rights Society (ARS), New York;

71 (top): Musée du Louvre, Paris. © Réunion des Musées Nationaux/Art Resource, NY;

71 (bottom): © Devorah Sperber. Photograph by Aaron Deetz;

72 (top left): © Morla Design, Inc., San Francisco;

72 (top right): Syracuse University Library, Department of Special Collections, Syracuse, NY;

73: © Dorothy LeBoeuf. Photograph by Bruce Decker;

74 (left): © Berenice Abbott/Getty Images;

74 (bottom right): © Kathryn Frund. Courtesy of Chase Young Gallery, Boston, MA;

75 (top): © Ansel Adams Publishing Rights Trust/Corbis;

76 (top): Pushp Deep Pandey/2kPhotography/Getty Images;

76 (bottom): © Richard Estes. Courtesy of Marlborough Gallery, New York;

77 (top right): © 2014 Judy Chicago/Artists Rights Society (ARS), New York. San Francisco Museum of Modern Art, Gift of Tracy O'Kates;

77 (bottom right): The Ella Gallup Sumner and Mary Catlin Sumner Collection Fund. Wadsworth Atheneum, Museum of Art, Hartford, CT. Wadsworth Atheneum, Museum of Art/Art Resource, NY;

79 (top left): © Richard Diebenkorn Foundation. San Francisco Museum of Modern Art, Gift of Friends of Gerald Nordland;

79 (top right): Interaction/Motion: A poster for the 2006 "Exposed" lecture series sponsored by the Graphic Design Department, The University of the Arts, Philadelphia. Concept and Design: Hans-Ulrich Allemann, Principal. Allemann Almquist & Jones, Design/Strategic Communications, Philadelphia;

79 (bottom): © 2014 Banco de México Diego Rivera Frida Kahlo Mueums Trust, Mexico, D.F./Artists Rights Society (ARS), New York;

80: © Eric Fischl. Courtesy of Mary Boone Gallery, NY;

81 (bottom left): Courtesy of Pentagram;

81 (bottom right): Courtesy New Museum, New York. Photograph by Benoit Pailley;

82 (top): Claes Oldenburg and Coosje van Bruggen. Donald J. Hall Sculpture Park at The Nelson-Atkins Museum of Art, Kansas City, Missouri. Purchase: acquired through the generosity of the Sosland Family, F94-1/3-4. Photograph by Louis Meluso;

82 (bottom): © Ken Stout. Photograph by Don House;

83 (top): Gift of Seymour H. Knox, 1967. Albright-Knox Art Gallery, New York/Art Resource, NY;

83 (bottom left): Courtesy of the author;

83 (bottom right): Design by Niklaus Troxler;

84 (top): © 2014 Artists Rights Society (ARS), New York/ADAGP, Paris/Succession Marcel Duchamp. Philadelphia Museum of Art/The Bridgeman Art Library;

84 (bottom): Publisher: Art Center: College of Design, Pasadena, CA. Emphasis by isolation. Courtesy of Pentagram, NY;

85 (top left): CB2/ZOB/WENN.com/Newscom;

85 (top right): © 2014 Sam Francis Foundation, California/Artists Rights Society (ARS), NY;

85 (bottom): © Jacey, Debut Art Ltd;

86 (bottom): © Robert Crawford;

87 (top): Ella Gallup Sumner and Mary Catlin Sumner Collection, Wadsworth Atheneum, Museum of Art, Hartford, CT/Art Resource, NY;

87 (bottom): Courtesy of Photofest.

Chapter Four

Page 89: Erich Lessing/Art Resource, NY;

90: Stanza della Segnatura, Vatican Palace, Vatican State/Scala/Art Resource, NY;

91 (center right): Public Domain;

91 (bottom): © Frank Lloyd Wright Collection. Avery Architectural and Fine Arts Library, Columbia University;

93 (top): Museo del Prado, Madrid. Bridgeman-Giraudon/Art Resource, NY;

93 (bottom): The Metropolitan Museum of Art, Rogers Fund, 1907 (07.123). © The Metropolitan Museum of Art/Art Resource, NY;

94 (left): Kimbell Art Museum, Fort Worth, Texas/Art Resource, NY;

94 (right): Art Gallery and Museum, Kelvingrove, Glasgow, Scotland/© Culture and Sport Glasgow (Museums)/The Bridgeman Art Library;

95 (top): © David Hockney. Photograph by Steve Oliver;

95 (bottom): Courtesy of Photofest;

96 (left): © Robert Stackhouse. From the Collection of the John and Maxine Belger Family Foundation;

96 (right): © Ann Strassman;

97: © Mark Messersmith;

98 (top): Museo Nazionale Romano delle Terme, Rome, Italy. Scala/Art Resource, NY;

98 (bottom): © Robert Longo. Courtesy of Metro Pictures. Albright-Knox Art Gallery/Art Resource, NY;

99 (top): © Henri Cartier-Bresson/Magnum Photos;

99 (bottom): "Under the Rug" from THE MYSTERIES OF HARRIS BURDICK by Chris van Allsburg. © 1984 by Chris van Allsburg. Reprinted by permission of Houghton Mifflin Company. All rights reserved;

100 (top): NYPL/Getty Images;

100 (bottom): The Cleveland Museum of Art. Bequest of Leonard C. Hanna, Jr., 1946.83;

101: Paul Jenkins (Writer) and Jae Lee (Artist), *Inhumans*: "First Contact," Volume 2, Issue 5, March 1999. © 2014 Marvel Comics, Inc. Used with permission;

102: George A. Hearn Fund, 1956. © The Metropolitan Museum of Art, New York. Art Resource, NY/DC Moore Gallery.

Part Two

Page 105: © Roger Shimomura. Private Collection.

Chapter Five

Page 107 (left): Gift of Gary Laredo. Cooper-Hewitt National Design Museum, Smithsonian Institution/Art Resource, NY;

107 (right): The Museum of Modern Art, New York. Gift of Edgar Kaufman, Jr. Digital Image © The Museum of Modern Art/Licensed by Scala/Art Resource, NY;

108 (bottom left): The Museum of Modern Art, New York. Gift of Herman Miller Furniture Company. Digital Image © The Museum of Modern Art/Licensed by Scala/Art Resource, NY. © 2007 Eames Office/www.eamesoffice.com;

108 (bottom right): Courtesy of Knoll, Inc.;

109 (center): © Ray Rogers;

109 (bottom): Collection of The Corning Museum of Glass, Corning, NY, Anonymous gift (86.4.180);

110 (top): © Dr. Richard Hunt, www.richardhunt.com;

110 (bottom): © The Trustees of the British Museum/Art Resource, NY;

115: © Keith Smith, www.keithsmithbooks.com;

117: © Peter Forbes;

118: © Jim Elniski;

120–122: Courtesy of Steve Quinn.

Chapter Six

Page 124: Brand X Pictures/Getty Images RF;

128: M.C. Escher, *Metamorphosis II*. © 2014 The M. C. Escher Company-Holland. All rights reserved. www.mcescher.com;

129 (top): Courtesy of the author;

129 (bottom): © Lynda Lowe and Georgian Nehl, www.lyndalowe.com;

130 (top left): Honolulu Academy of Arts, gift of James Michener, 1991 (21.971). Photograph © Honolulu Academy of Arts;

130 (top right): Honolulu Academy of Arts, gift of James Michener, 1991 (13,695). Photograph © Honolulu Academy of Arts;

130 (center): Honolulu Academy of Arts, gift of James Michener, 1991 (21,968). Photograph © Honolulu Academy of Arts;

130 (left): © Eddie Chiu, United Curve Design, LLC;

130 (right): © Sergio Silva;

131 (top): © Matthew Ritchie. Courtesy of Andrea Rosen Gallery, New York. Photograph by Oren Slor;

131 (bottom): © Matthew Ritchie and Aranda/Lasch. Courtesy of Andrea Rosen Gallery, New York. Photograph by Massimo Venchierutti/Cameraphoto Arte Venezia;

132: Courtesy of Rusty Smith, University School of Architecture;

134: © Michelle Litvin/Redux Pictures;

135: © 2008 Frances Whitehead;

136: © Jim Elniski.

Chapter Seven

Page 138: © Mary Lucier. Courtesy of Lennon, Weinberg, Inc., New York. Photograph by Charlie Samuels;

140: Erich Lessing/Art Resource, NY;

143 (top): Stanza della Segnatura, Vatican Palace, Vatican State. Scala/Art Resource, NY;

143 (bottom left): Cally Iden. Courtesy of the author;

143 (bottom right): Tricia Tripp. Courtesy of the author;

147 (bottom): Claes Oldenburg and Coosje van Bruggen. Donald J. Hall Sculpture Park at The Nelson-Atkins Museum of Art, Kansas City, Missouri. Purchase: acquired through the generosity of the Sosland Family, F94-1/3-4. Photograph by Louis Meluso;

149: © Spongelab Video Game, www.spongelab.com;

150–151: © Jason Chin;

153–155: © Kendall Buster.

Chapter Eight

Page 156: National Palace Museum, Taipei, Taiwan/Werner Forman Archive/The Bridgeman Art Library;

157 (top): © William Kentridge. Courtesy of Marian Goodman Gallery, NY;

157 (bottom): © Deborah Haylor McDowell;

158 (left): Courtesy of Milton Glaser Studio;

158 (right): The Menil Collection, Houston; © 2014 C. Herscovici, London/Artists Rights Society (ARS), New York;

159 (top right): Courtesy of Photofest;

159 (top left): Los Angeles Ballet, Serenade; Balanchine® is a Trademark of The George Balanchine Trust; Photo: Reed Huytchinson; Graphic Design: Catherine Kanner. Permission granted for LA Ballet;

159 (bottom): Michael A. Mello, Dead Wrong: A Death Row Lawyer Speaks Out Against Capital Punishment. © 1997. Cover design and illustration by Mark Maccaulay. Reprinted by permission of The University of Wisconsin Press;

160 (top): © Markus Schaller, Berlin;

161 (top): © Roger Shimomura. Private Collection;

162 (top): California Department of Health;

162 (bottom): © Shi Jinsong. Courtesy of Chambers Fine Art;

163 (top): SEER Training Modules, National Cancer Institute, Conducting Respiratory Passages, 2013. http://training.seer.cancer.gov;

163 (bottom left): © Kim Martens;

163 (bottom right): © dieKleinert/Alamy;

164 (left): Art © Robert Rauschenberg/Licensed by VAGA, New York, NY;

164 (right): © Kiki Smith. Courtesy of Pace, New York. Photograph by Ellen Page Wilson;

165 (top): The Solomon R. Guggenheim Museum, New York. Gift, Solomon R. Guggenheim, Founding Collection. 41.283. © 2014 Artists Rights Society (ARS), New York/ADAGP, Paris;

165 (bottom left): Photograph © Ansel Adams Publishing Rights Trust/Corbis;

165 (bottom right): © Robert Moskowitz;

193 (bottom): © Maya Lin Studio, Inc. Courtesy of Pace, New York. Photograph by G. R. Christmas;

194 (top): © Kendall Buster;

194 (bottom left): © Xiao Min. Courtesy of 1918 ArtSPACE;

194 (bottom right): © Manuel Villa, www.manuelvillaarq .com;

195 (top): © 2014 Ettore Sottsass, Los Angeles County Musem of Art Associates/LACMA. Licensed by Art Resource, NY. © 2014 Artists Rights Society (ARS), New York/ADAGP, Paris;

195 (bottom): © 2014 The Henry Moore Foundation Archive/Artists Rights Society (ARS), New York;

196 (top left): Superstock;

196 (top right): © Tom Friedman. Courtesy of the artist;

196 (bottom): © Ledelle Moe;

197: © Alice Aycock, Collection of the University of Illinois at Urbana-Champaign;

198 (top left): Art © Estate of David Smith/Licensed by VAGA, New York, NY. Solomon R. Guggenheim Museum, by exchange, 1967. 67.1862. Photograph by David Heald. © The Guggenheim Foundation, New York;

198 (top right): Gianni Dagli Orti/The Art Archive at Art Resource, NY;

198 (bottom right): Karen Karnes, Vessel, 1987. Stoneware glaze, 16 1/2 × 10 1/2 inches. Los Angeles County Museum of Art, Gift of Howard and Gwen Laurie Smits. Photograph © 2008 Museum Associates/LACMA. Art Resource, NY;

199 (top): © 2014 Richard Serra/Artists Rights Society (ARS), New York;

199 (bottom): © Walter De Maria. © Dia Art Foundation. Photograph by John Cliett;

200: © Jose Fuste Raga/Corbis;

201: © Lucas Samaras. Gift of Seymour H. Knox, Jr., 1966. Albright-Knox Art Gallery, Buffalo, NY/Art Resource, NY;

202: © Donna Dennis, The Margulies Collection at the Warehouse. Photograph by Peter Aaron;

203 (top): © Walter Oltmann. Courtesy of Goodman Gallery, South Africa. Private collection, USA;

203 (bottom): Museum of Indian Arts and Culture/ Laboratory of Anthropology, Museum of New Mexico, Santa Fe;

204 (top left): Department of Archaeology and Anthropology, University of Ibadan/The Bridgeman Art Library, NY. Photograph by Heini Schneebeli;

204 (top right): © Francesco Mai;

205 (top left): Scala/Art Resource, NY;

205 (top right): © Stan Rickel;

205 (bottom): © Ruth Asawa. Photograph by Laurence Cuneo;

206 (top): © 2014 Robert Irwin/Artists Rights Society (ARS), NY. Courtesy of Dia Art Foundation. Photograph by Thibault Jeanson;

206 (center): Designers: Bill Cannan, Tony Ortiz, H. Kurt Heinz. Design Firm: Bill Cannan & Co. Client/Mfr. NASA Public Affairs;

206 (bottom): © Stephen Knapp. Photograph by Satoshi Yamamoto;

207 (top): © Krzysztof Wodiczko. Courtesy of Galerie Lelong, New York;

207 (bottom): © Bill Viola. Courtesy of James Cohan Gallery. Edition 1: Collection of Marion Stroud Swingle. Edition 2: Collection of the Artist. Photograph by Roman Mensing;

208 (center): Courtesy of Fisher-Price;

208 (bottom): Courtesy of Toshiyuki Kita/IDK Design Laboratory, LTD, Japan;

209 (top left): © Do Ho Suh, courtesy of Lehmann Maupin Gallery, New York;

209 (top right): © Keith Edmier, courtesy of Sadie Coles HQ, London;

209 (bottom): © Michael Graves & Associates, photo by William Taylor;

210 (top): © Kurt Perschke;

210 (bottom): Whitney Museum of American Art, New York; Purchase, with funds from the Louis and Bessie Adler Foundation, Inc., Seymour M. Klein, President, the Gilman Foundation, Inc., the Howard and Jean Lipman Foundation, Inc. and the National Endowment for the Arts 79.4a-f. © The George and Helen Segal Foundation/ Licensed by VAGA, New York, NY;

211 (top): DeAgostini/SuperStock;

211 (bottom): © Ned Kahn;

212 (top): Claes Oldenburg and Coosje van Bruggen. Donald J. Hall Sculpture Park at The Nelson-Atkins Museum of Art, Kansas City, Missouri. Purchase: acquired through the generosity of the Sosland Family, F94-1/3-4. Photograph by Louis Meluso;

212 (bottom): © Kim Karpeles/Alamy;

214: © Stephen Knapp;

215–216: © Marilyn da Silva.

Chapter Ten

Page 217 (left): Courtesy of Humanscale, NY;

217 (right): © Martin Puryear. Solomon R. Guggenheim Museum, Purchased with funds contributed by the Louis and Bessie Adler Foundation, Inc., Seymour M. Klein,

President, 1985. 85.3276. Photograph by David Heald. © The Guggenheim Foundation, New York;

218: © Juan Munoz. Courtesy of Marian Goodman Gallery, NY;

219 (top): © Roni Horn. Courtesy of Hauser & Wirth;

219 (bottom): © 2014 Estate of Louise Nevelson/ Artists Rights Society (ARS), New York. Giraudon/Art Resource, NY;

220 (top right): © Aaron Macsai;

220 (center): © Zac Freeman. Courtesy of J. Johnson Gallery;

221 (top left): © Timothy Hursley. Holocaust Memorial Museum, Washington, DC;

221 (top right): © Alice Aycock, 1994. Collection, University of Illinois at Urbana, Champaign. Photo courtesy of the artist;

221 (bottom): Courtesy of Fowler Museum of Cultural History, UCLA. Photograph by Don Cole;

222 (top): © The Estate of Eva Hesse. Detroit Institute of Arts, Founders Society Purchase, Friends of Modern Art Fund, and Miscellaneous Gifts Fund, 1979. Courtesy Hauser & Wirth, Zurich, London/The Bridgeman Art Library;

222 (bottom): © Sarah Sze. Collection Nancy and Stanley Singer. Courtesy of the artist and Tanya Bonakdar Gallery, New York;

223 (top): © Leonardo Drew. Courtesy of Mary Boone Gallery, NY;

223 (bottom): Superstock;

224 (left): © David Becker/Reuters/Corbis;

224 (center right): Courtesy of the Library, American Museum of Natural History, New York. AMNH Trans. #2104(2);

225: © Theodore Gall;

226 (left): Scala/Art Resource, NY;

226 (right): Santa Maria degli Angeli, Rome, Italy/Mauro Magliani/Superstock;

227 (top): © Chuichi Fujii, courtesy of Kurkje Gallery, Chrong Ku, Seoul, Korea;

227 (bottom): © Todd Slaughter;

228 (center right): Designers: James E. Grove, John Cook, Jim Holtorf, Fernando Pardo, Mike Boltich. Design Firm: Designworks/USA. Client/Mfr: Corona Clipper Co;

228 (bottom right): © Vector Stock RF;

229 (bottom): Fratelli Alinari/Superstock;

230 (top): Digital Image © The Museum of Modern Art/ Licensed by Scala/Art Resource, NY. © 2014 Successioin Giacometti/Artists Rights Society (ARS), NY. Licensed by VAGA, New York, NY;

230 (bottom): © Destinations/Corbis;

231 (top): © Liza Lou. Courtesy of the artist;

231 (bottom): © Mary Ann Scherr. Courtesy of the National Ornamental Metal Museum, Memphis, TN.;

232 (top): © 2014 Artists Rights Society (ARS), New York/ ADAGP, Paris. Photo © CNAP Command Publique, Ministére de la Culture, Paris;

232 (bottom): CB2/ZOB/WENN.com/Newscom;

233 (bottom): © Tanija & Graham Carr;

234 (left): Musée d'Orsay, Paris. Réunion des Musées Nationaux/Art Resource, NY;

234 (right): © Steve Woodward. Collection Walker Art Center, Minneapolis. Acquired with Lannan Foundation support in conjunction with the exhibition Sculpture Inside Outside, 1991;

235 (top): © Magdalena Abakanowicz. Courtesy of Marlborough Gallery, New York. The Nelson-Atkins Museum of Art, Kansas City, Missouri. Gift of the Hall Family Foundation, F99-33/1 A-DD. Photograph by Jamison Miller;

235 (bottom): Siegfried Layda/Getty Images.

Chapter Eleven

Page 238: Courtesy of Gehry Partners LLP. The Solomon R. Guggenheim Foundation, Bilbao. FMGB Guggenheim Bilbao Museo, 2001. All rights reserved;

239 (bottom): © Shoji Decor;

240: Thorncrown Chapel. Photograph by Whit Slemmons;

241 (top): © Robert Fried/Alamy;

241 (bottom): Courtesy Agnes Gund Collection. © 2014 The Joseph and Robert Cornell Memorial Foundation/ Licensed by VAGA, New York, NY;

242 (top): © 1988 by Larry Fuente. Gift of the James Renwick Alliance and Museum purchase through the Smithsonian Collections Acquisition Program. Smithsonian American Art Museum, Washington, DC/ Art Resource, NY;

242 (center): Courtesy of Clark & Delvecchio. Photograph by Pierre Longtin;

244 (bottom left): © Katherine Wetzel and Elizabeth King;

242 (bottom right): © Darryl Leniuk/Getty Images;

244 (top): © Mary Miss, Wright State University, Dayton, OH;

244 (bottom right): © John Okulick. Collection Marjorie & Arnold Platzker;

245 (top): © Kunstindustrimuseet I Oslo (Museum of Decorative Arts & Design) Norway;

246 (top): The Cleveland Museum of Art, Leonard C. Hanna Jr. Fund, 2002.29. Art © Louise Bourgeois/Licensed by VAGA, New York, NY;

246 (bottom): © Virgil Ortiz, Private Collection, Robert and Cyndy Gallegos;

247: © Mariko Kusumoto. Courtesy of Mobilia Gallery, Cambridge, MA;

248 (top): © Crystal Kwan;

248 (bottom): © Patrick Dougherty. Photograph by Tadahisa Sakurai;

249 (top): © Eric Hilton with the assistance of Ladislav Havlik, Lubomir Richter, Peter Schelling, and Roger Selander (engraving) and Mark Witter (cutting). United States, Corning, NY, Steuben Glass, 1980. Cast lead glass, ground, polished, sandblasted, cut, engraved, assembled, H. 9.9 cm, W. 49.e cm. (86.4.180) Anonymous gift, Collection of The Corning Museum of Glass, Corning, NY;

249 (bottom left): © Gene Koss. Courtesy of Arthur Roger Gallery;

249 (bottom right): © Nick Cave, courtesy of Jack Shainman Gallery, New York. Photograph by James Prinz;

250 (top): Photograph © the IFF, Institute For Figuring, www.theiff.org;

250 (bottom): © Cathy Strokowsky. Courtesy Galerie Elena Lee, Montreal;

251: © Ron Mueck;

252: © Ernest Daetwyler;

253: © Tara Donovan. Courtesy of Pace, New York. Photograph by Raymond Meier;

254: © Rick Paul;

255: © Michele Oka Doner, Collection of the Art Institute of Chicago. Courtesy of Marlborough Gallery;

256 (top): © Art © Deborah Butterfield/Licensed by VAGA, New York, NY;

256 (bottom): Los Angeles County Museum of Art, Gift of Howard and Gwen Laurie Smits. Photograph © 2006 Museum Associates/LACMA. Art Resource, NY;

258–259: © David R. MacDonald.

Chapter Twelve

Page 260 (left): © moodboard/Corbis;

260 (right): © Tadashi Kawamata. Courtesy the artist & kamel mennour, Paris. Photograph by Shigeo Anzai;

261: © Mierle Laderman Ukeles. Courtesy of Ronald Feldman Fine Arts, New York;

262 (top): © Araldo de Luca/Corbis;

262 (bottom left): © Sandra Enterline. Collection Oakland Museum of Art;

262 (bottom right): © Myra Mimlitsch-Gray;

263 (left): Collection: Rothko Chapel, Houston, dedicated to Reverend Martin Luther King, Jr. © 2014 The Barnett Newman Foundation, New York/Artists Rights Society (ARS), New York;

263 (right): Courtesy of P.P.O.W., NY;

264 (top): © James Lee Byars, University of California, Berkeley Art Museum. Photograph by Ben Blackwell;

264 (bottom): © Yong Soon Min;

265 (top): © Maya Lin. Courtesy of Pace, New York. Photograph by Henry Arnold;

265 (bottom): © Susan Trangmar;

266 (left): © 2006 Olafur Eliasson. Installation at The Center for Curatorial Studios (CCS Bard), New York. The Center for Curatorial Studies and The Luma Foundation;

266 (right): © Barbara Chase-Riboud. On loan to The Philadelphia Museum of Art, Philadelphia, PA;

267 (top): © RMN-Grand Palais/Art Resource, NY;

267 (bottom left): © Scala/Art Resource, NY;

267 (bottom right): The Museum of Modern Art, New York. Acquired through the Lillie P. Bliss Bequest. Digital Image © The Museum of Modern Art/Licensed by Scala/Art Resource, NY;

268: © Steve Raymer/National Geographic Stock;

269 (top left): Denver Art Museum Collection: Gift of Ginny Williams, 1997.205. Photograph courtesy of the Joseph Helman Gallery, NY;

269 (top right): © Antony Gormley. Courtesy Jay Jopling Gallery/White Cube, London;

269 (bottom): © 2014 Fairweather & Fairweather LTD/Artists Rights Society (ARS), New York. Courtesy of Pace. Photograph by Ellen Page Wilson;

270 (top right): © Courtesy of The North Face, San Leandro, CA;

270 (bottom left): © Cornelia Parker. Courtesy of SITE Santa Fe, 1999;

270 (bottom right): © Maren Hassinger. Photograph by Adam Avila;

271 (top): © Reuters/Corbis;

271 (bottom): © 2014 Artists Rights Society (ARS), New York/VG Bild-Kunst, Bonn. Courtesy of Jack Shainman Gallery, NY;

272 (top): © Todd Slaughter;

272 (bottom): © 2014 Hans Haacke/Artists Rights Society (ARS), New York/VG Bild-Kunst. Bonn;

273 (top): Photograph by Lonnie Graham, courtesy of The Fabric Workshop and Museum;

273 (bottom): © 1996 Lorna Jordan;

274 (top): Courtesy of Samuel Merrin, The Merrin Gallery, Inc. Photograph by Stefan Hagen;

274 (bottom): Gift of Margaret Fisher in memory of her parents, Mr. and Mrs. Walter L. Fisher, 1957.165, The Art Institute of Chicago. © The Art Institute of Chicago;

275: The Museum of Modern Art, New York. The Sidney and Harriet Janis Collection. Digital Image © The Museum of Modern Art/Licensed by Scala/Art Resource, NY. © Succession Marcel Duchamp/ADAGP, Paris/Artists Rights Society (ARS), New York 2014;

276 (top): © Andrew Parker/Alamy;

276 (bottom left): © Glen Onwin. Photograph by Jerry Harman-Jones;

276 (bottom right): Courtesy of Adjaye Associates. Photograph by Andrea Pozza, 2008;

277: © Karin Giusti;

278 (left): © PhenomenArts, Inc. Christopher Janney, Artistic Director;

278 (right): © Leo Villareal. Courtesy of Sandra Gering Inc.;

279 (top): © Christian Marclay. Courtesy of Paula Cooper Gallery, New York. Photograph by Will Lytch;

279 (bottom left): © Shelagh Wakely;

279 (bottom right): © Darroch Donald/Alamy;

280 (left): © Kiki Smith. Courtesy of Pace, New York. Photography by Ellen Page Wilson;

280 (right): Allen Memorial Art Museum, Oberlin College, OH. Fund for Contemporary Art and gift of the artist and the Fischbach Gallery, 1970. The Estate of Eva Hesse, Hauser & Wirth, Zurich, London.

Part Four

Page 282: © 2014 Eames Office/www.eamesoffice.com.

Chapter Thirteen

Page 284: © Apple Inc. Use with permission. All rights reserved. Apple® and the Apple logo are registered trademark of Apple Inc.;

285 (top): Musée du Louvre, Paris. © Réunion des Musées Nationaux/Art Resource, NY;

285 (center): © Sam Shere/Getty Images;

285 (bottom): © Christian Marclay. Courtesy of Paula Cooper Gallery, New York;

288: Courtesy of Photofest;

291: Courtesy of Photofest;

292: Captain America, *Silver Surfer, Infinity Gauntlet* #4, Cover Date: October 1991. Writer: Jim Starlin. Penciler: Ron Lim. Inker: Josef Rubinstein. Characters Featured: Captain America, Thanos, Adam Warlock, and Silver Surfer. © 2010 Marvel Characters, Inc. Used with permission;

293 (left): © 2014 Marina Abramovic. Courtesy of Sean Kelly Gallery/Artists Rights Society (ARS), New York;

293 (right): © Mary Lucier. Courtesy of Lennon, Weinberg, Inc., New York. Photograph by Charlie Samuels;

294: Courtesy of Photofest;

295 (top): Paul Jenkins (Writer) and Jae Lee (Artist), *Inhumans: "First Contact,"* Volume 2, Issue 5, March 1999. © 2014 Marvel Comics, Inc. Used with permission;

295 (bottom): Erich Lessing/Art Resource, NY;

296: © Tatana Kellner, courtesy of the Syracuse University Library, Department of Special Collections;

300: Courtesy of Photofest;

303–306: Courtesy of Photofest.

Chapter Fourteen

Page 309: Musée du Louvre, Paris. © Réunion des Musees Nationaux/Art Resource, NY;

310: © Jerome Witkin, Courtesy of Jack Rutberg Fine Arts, Inc.;

311 (top right): © Bart Forbes, 2005. From Frogfolio 10, Dellas Graphics, Syracuse, NY;

311 (bottom left): © 2014 Charles Santore and Cidermill Press;

311 (bottom right): © Murray Tinkelman, from Frogfolio 10, Dellas Graphics, Syracuse, NY;

312: © Duane Michals. Courtesy of Pace/MacGill Gallery;

315: Courtesy of the Syracuse Stage;

316: Courtesy of Photofest;

317 (top): © 2014 Salvador Dali, Gala-Salvador Dali Foundation/Artists Rights Society (ARS), New York;

317 (bottom): Courtesy of Photofest;

318–320: Courtesy of Photofest;

321: Courtesy of the Ad Council, National Highway Traffic Administration, U.S. Department of Transportation;

322: © Finley Holiday Films;

323 (top): Courtesy of Leo Burnett Agency;

323 (bottom): Client: Canadian Paralympic Committee. Agency: BBDO Toronto. Creative Directors: Peter Ignazi/Carlos Moreno. Copywriters: Michael Clowater/Craig

McIntosh. Art Director: Linda Carte. Producer: Terry Kavanagh. Account Team: Lori Davison/Rebecca Flaman Production Company: Sons & Daughters. Director: Mark Zibert. Cinematographer: Chris Mably. Editor: Mark Paiva. Posterboy Transfer: AlterEgo. Visual Effects: Crush Inc. Audio: RMW. Music Hero Athlete: Alister McQueen;

324: Courtesy of State Farm Insurance, DDB Chicago;

324 (top): © Allstar Picture Library/Alamy;

324 (center): Courtesy of Anthony Anthony Cavalieri, Staten Island Rescue 5;

324 (bottom): © Ocean/Corbis RF;

326: © Susan Kae Grant, Black Rose Productions;

327: © 2014 Eames Office/www.eamesoffice.com;

329: Courtesy of Michael Remson. Photograph by Mark Rubin;

330: Courtesy of Michael Remson. Photograph by Buck Ross. Used by permission.

Chapter Fifteen

Page 331: © Nancy Callahan;

332 (top): Anselm Kiefer, Breaking of the Vessels, 1990. Lead, iron, glass, copper wire, charcoal, Aquatec. 12′ 5″ × 27′ 5 1/2″ × 17″. Saint Louis Art Museum, Funds given by Mr. and Mrs. George Schlapp, Mrs. Francis A. Mesker, the Henry L. and Natalie Edison Freund Charitable Trust, The Arthur and Helen Baer Charitable Foundation, Sam and Marilyn Fox, Mrs. Eleanor J. Moore, Mr. and Mrs. John Wooten Moore, Donna and William Nussbaum, Mr. and Mrs. James E. Schneithorst, Jain and Richard Shaikewitz, Mark Twain Bancshares, Inc., Mr. and Mrs. Gary Wolff, Mr. and Mrs. Lester P. Ackerman Jr., the Honorable & Mrs. Thomas F. Eagleton, Alison and John Ferring, Mrs. Gail K. Fischmann, Mr. and Mrs. Solon Gershman, Dr. and Mrs. Gary Hansen, Mr. and Mrs. Kenneth S. Kranzberg, Mr. and Mrs. Gyo Obata, Jane and Warren Shapleigh, Lee and Barbara Wagman, Anabeth Calkins and John Weil, Museum Shop Fund, the Contemporary Art Society, and Museum Purchase;

Dr. and Mrs. Harold J. Joseph, estate of Alice P. Francis, Fine Arts Associates, J. Lionberger Davis, Mr. and Mrs. Samuel B. Edison, Mr. and Mrs. Morton D. May, estate of Louise H. Franciscus, an anonymous donor, Miss Ella M. Boedeker, by exchange;

332 (bottom): Courtesy of Daniel E. Kelm and Timothy C. Ely;

333 (top): Courtesy of the author;

333 (bottom): © Keith Smith, www.keithsmithbooks.com;

334 (top): © 2014 Artists Rights Society (ARS), New York/DACS, London;

334 (bottom): © Keith Smith, www.keithsmithbooks.com;

335: © Emily Frenkel. Courtesy of the author;

336 (top): © Emily Frenkel. Courtesy of the author;

336 (bottom): Illustration from The Gashlycrumb Tinies or, After the Outing. © 1963 and renewed 1991 by Edward Gorey, reproduced by permission of Harcourt, Inc;

339: Courtesy of author;

342: © Bill Viola. Courtesy of James Cohan Gallery. Collection: Edition 1: Museo Nacional Centro de Arte Reina Sofia, Madrid. Edition 2, Los Angeles County Museum of Art, Modern and Contemporary Art Council Fund. Photograph by Roman Mensing;

343 (top): © 1997 Sandy Skoglund;

343 (bottom): © Nancy Callahan and Diane Gallo;

344: © 2014 Jenny Holzer, member Artists Rights Society (ARS), New York;

345: © Ann Hamilton;

346 (bottom): © Lucinda Childs;

346 (top): Courtesy of Armitage Gone! Dance, New York. Karole Armitage, Predator's Ball, 1996. Brooklyn Academy of Music. Sets by David Salle, table design by Jeff Koons, animation videos by Erica Beckman, costumes by Hugo Boss, Pila Limosner, and Debra Moises, Co.

Index

index

Index

index

Index

index

index